The
Book of
Runic
Astrology

The
Book of
Runic
Astrology

Unlock the
Ancient Power of
Your Cosmic Birth Runes

RICHARD
LISTER

HAY HOUSE

Carlsbad, California • New York City
London • Sydney • New Delhi

Published in the United Kingdom by:
Hay House UK Ltd, The Sixth Floor, Watson House
54 Baker Street, London W1U 7BU
Tel: +44 (0)20 3927 7290; Fax: +44 (0)20 3927 7291
www.hayhouse.co.uk

Published in the United States of America by:
Hay House Inc., PO Box 5100, Carlsbad, CA 92018-5100
Tel: (1) 760 431 7695 or (800) 654 5126
Fax: (1) 760 431 6948 or (800) 650 5115; www.hayhouse.com

Published in Australia by:
Hay House Australia Ltd, 18/36 Ralph St, Alexandria NSW 2015
Tel: (61) 2 9669 4299; Fax: (61) 2 9669 4144; www.hayhouse.com.au

Published in India by:
Hay House Publishers India, Muskaan Complex,
Plot No.3, B-2, Vasant Kunj, New Delhi 110 070
Tel: (91) 11 4176 1620; Fax: (91) 11 4176 1630; www.hayhouse.co.in

A catalogue record for this book is available from the British Library.

Tradepaper ISBN: 978-1-78817-945-4
E-book ISBN: 978-1-78817-947-8
Audiobook ISBN: 978-1-78817-946-1

Interior illustrations: all runic/astrological symbols © Richard Lister; all other images shutterstock.com

This product uses papers sourced from responsibly managed forests. For more information, see www.hayhouse.co.uk

MIX
Paper | Supporting
responsible forestry
FSC® C018072

For Lisa.
Without you, this would not work.

Contents

Introduction

As I write this, I'm sitting in an ancient fortified Angevin farmhouse, deep in Aquitaine, southwest France. I'm surrounded by lush green fields and the days are short. The dogs are full of leftovers and the cats are warming themselves by the fire. Sheep are grazing outside the windows and geese are honking at anything they don't like. And from what I can tell, they don't like a lot of things. Like wind, other geese, a fence, the house, me.

My soul takes me back over generations long dead. Past the occupation, the trenches, past the Terror and the time of the aristos. Back along the lines of the English kings, who flow back to the Norman dukes, to the jarls of the north, back to the frozen fjords of Norway, Sweden, Denmark and the Faroes.

The ancient walls that surround me, built by people to keep the descendants of those ancient Norwegian tribes out, are warmed by a fire burning wood that was growing before the United States was even a 'thing'.

I feel the well of the past, the flow of the energy, the frequency of life pulsing and changing with each generation. From republic to kingdom to dukedom to burg people, living, loving, trading and dying in these walls and this land.

The constants over all this time have been the pinpricks of light – the stars. And the star pathways illuminating the worlds below them, affecting those living their lives there in subtle but distinct ways.

Rogue stars predicted massive change – the Norman invasion of England was preceded by Halley's comet, for example. Energy changed with equinoxes and solstices. We who walk this world *feel* the effects of these cosmic frequency changes. And we've built entire systems as ways of interpreting and understanding these energies, systems that have been refined, used and adapted (and sometimes abused) over millennia. From Atlantis to Mesopotamia and Babylon, through ancient Greece to Los Angeles and Paris, the most dominant of those systems has been and continues to be astrology, a system of understanding ourselves based on star and planetary movements that has influenced and directed the ideas, decisions and beliefs of so many that have gone before.

Now, what if... what if other cultures had other ideas of what those energies meant? What if there was another way to interpret those star pathways? A way of myth and song, of victory and defeat, of life and death, a way that worked with the magic, mystery and medicine of the ancients and was really relevant for now?

What if you held that way in your hands?

Are you willing to explore ancient star paths to help navigate your future?

Then let us begin.

First, I'd like you to know me, my bias, what has led me here and why you would benefit from putting your trust and energy into me and all that I choose to share.

I'm a man, born and raised in Kent in England. I'm 6 feet 7 inches and big, I have a beard and I've spent a lot of the last 20 years dressed as a Viking (historical re-enactment has been my 'thing'). 'Vikingness', Nordic energetics and the northern wisdom tradition literally run through my blood and bones. My ancestry goes back to the Normans, and further back still to the Norwegian Vikings of Rollo the Walker.

While drinking my way through university, I discovered 'heathen paganism' and it felt good. I got to hang out in nature and talk with like-minded people, and this led me to the runes.

There was one focal event, and I shared this in my book *Runes Made Easy*, but it's important that I share it here too, in devotion and deep respect.

I was at a pagan camp in a field in the middle of an ancient forest. Most people had gone to sleep and the diehards were the only ones left around the fire.

This next bit is going to sound weird, but it's true.

I had a vision. A full-blown deity-standing-in-the-fire vision, telling me to go and learn about the northern traditions, to do better so I could serve better. I can't remember the exact words, but this was the gist. The deity had one eye and a spear. I was shaken to the core. Literally. From what I've been told, I stood there for half an hour staring at the fire, then silently turned around and went to my tent.

And because it's not an everyday occurrence to see who I now know was Odin, Nordic king of the gods, in the flames of a campfire, I went on to learn about the northern traditions in order to serve better.

Over the next decade and a half, I used the runes as I worked in a hospital Accident and Emergency Department, trained as a nurse and yoga teacher, learned Ayurveda, massage and NLP, and undertook psychological, psychotherapeutic and trauma training. I used the teachings and magic of the runes to co-create and construct my life and my reality. Marriage, moving house, changing careers – runes have been cast for guidance for them all, and I've allowed myself to be guided by them. They support me in trusting myself and trusting my personal power, and this is why I am passionate about sharing them as a supportive tool for others, because what I've learned is that so many of us have been stripped of our power, or given it away, either consciously or unconsciously. And yet we *all* have access to power, because it resides within, and we all knew how to wield power hundreds of years ago – the power to look into the mists of the future, the power to heal ourselves, the power to seek the correct help and guidance and make the right decisions.

This was why I wrote *Runes Made Easy*.

Except... there was more.

So much more.

The gods have spoken again, aware that we need the tools of the ancients so we can navigate our way through the choppy seas of the times we're currently in and co-create a better future.

The *Wyrd* has called me. The *Wyrd* is the place where all things are possible and all potential resides. As I explained in *Runes Made Easy*, it could be pictured as a shirt made up of millions of threads, each subtly influenced by those around it. Imagine what happens if you have a loose thread and you pull that thread – the threads around it become tight or loose, pucker up or flail away. This is what the *Wyrd* looks like. Every time we make a decision, that decision influences the threads around us.

In turn, the *Wyrd* can influence us – call us, as I was called. The celestial energies of the universe were seeking to be expressed. They showed up in how I worked and how I played – much to the annoyance of those around me, I'm sure!

Through this process, the thing that has become clear to me is that the language I previously used was that of a teacher, but I'm not a teacher, I'm a way-shower, a guide, a mentor. I'm not interested in teaching, I'm interested in showing the way we move and navigate through the universe. I'm here now, ready to show you how to navigate your way through life using runic astrology. Runic astrology takes the Vikings' runes, stories and myths and shows how they are expressed in the night sky, forming a cosmic map, a star path for us to follow.

Much of what we know about the ancient Nordic people has been lost, and what little remains has been through 1,000 years of propaganda, reinterpretation and nationalization. This leaves a void that has to be filled with knowledge and wisdom that come directly from the goddesses, gods, *Jotun* (giants) and *Svartalf* (dark elves or dwarves) of the Nordic pantheon, through trance, magic and dream.

This guide energy, mentor energy, is here for you in book form. To bring it to you, I've meditated for freaking ages. I've performed Viking rituals. I've gone under the cloak in power points across northern Europe to dream, travel and journey.

When a deer walks through woods or a person walks across grass, a pathway is formed. Broken branches, depressed grass, residual scent and sound all show where they have walked. And runic energies leave an imprint on the vibration of the universe as they move through it. They leave their marks, just as you can tell where your lover has slept on your pillow by their scent. And, like the deer and the lover, each rune has its own energetic imprint.

Out there in the cosmo-verse, I found the energetic trail of the runes. This trail has revealed how they resonate with the gigantic energetic powers of our solar system. How they interact and influence us on both an individual and a societal level. And how the censured and burned civilizations of old interpreted this energy.

You and I, using the tools, wisdom and power within this book, will be able to track the energetic influences of the runes across the cosmos – the Runic Star Paths.

Let me show you the way as you set off into the inky blackness of the sky. Let me point out to you the energy and passion available to you, the energetic vibrations that make the journey an experience of pleasure and bliss. Let me help you navigate these wild times in which we live. Let me show you the stars to navigate by.

Follow me, if you will, down the misty paths of the *Wyrd* to bring the energy and frequency you desire into your life. I will guide you through the rudiments of runic astrology, so that you can explore your own Runic Star Path. I'll share how to discover its main energetic resonances – your Sunna rune (Sun sign), Manni rune (Moon sign) and Jord (pronounced Yord) rune (rising sign) – and how to work with these resonances, and those of the gods in the skies, to co-create your life in the world.

Because we are part of the world, the universe, we are co-creators. And we co-create in relation to our experience of the world, the vibrational energy of the universe and how it affects us.

So, get ready to experience the energy and might of the ancient runes and walk your own Runic Star Path.

Astrology provides insights into your own energetic vibration – the way you do the things you do and why, and how you relate to others and interact with the world. It's also a way to forecast the future.

So what I'm calling for, what the northern tradition gods are calling for, is for you to immerse yourself in runic astrology, in all the Nordic myth and legend and the getting drunk in the mead hall that sits alongside the myth and legend, and, let's face it, the doom and tragedy of the Graeco-Roman stories. (Jeez, did those Greeks *love* a tragedy!)

Alongside is important. This is *not* a replacement for classic astrology, far from it. No one, least of all me, is saying, 'This way is right and that way is wrong.' Nope, this is purely an invitation, from me and the gods, to explore your terrain using your Runic Star Path.

I've been exploring mine for a number of years now, and I know runic astrology works. If you've had a Runic Star Path reading with me, you will know it works. But it's no good just a few of us knowing it. Of course, I'm always happy to offer Runic Star Path readings to those who ask, but I want runic astrology to be accessible and useful for *everyone* who hears the call of the ancients in the northern tradition.

So, are you ready now?

Then we shall begin.

OPENING RITUAL

Back in the ancient wooded fjords and burgs of the north, ritual and ceremony drove life, helping the people to build energetic resonance with the gods and the cosmos. These rituals were called *Blöts* (pronounced *bloats*, like '*boat*').

To activate your own connection with the powers of the universe, your Runic Star Path and the runes, I invite you perform your own *Blöt*.

Formerly, a *Blöt* was performed with a drink of mead or ale. In modern times, any drink of your choice will work. (In my experience, Thor likes chocolate milk.)

I carry out my *Blöt*s around a fire. If you don't have space for a fire, a candle works fine. You'll also need a journal or notebook and a pen.

+ Light your candle and pour two drinks – one for yourself and one for the gods.

+ Take at least nine big slow breaths, counting in for seven and out for 11.

+ Feel your toes. Wiggle them.

+ Feel your legs. Bend and straighten them.

+ Feel your hips. Wiggle your butt.

+ Touch your belly, chest and arms with your hands.

+ Roll your neck this way and that way.

+ Wiggle your jaw and your tongue.

+ Rub your eyes.

+ Sip your drink.

+ In your journal, write down what comes to you when you hear the term 'Runic Star Paths'. What does that energy feel like to you?

- What colour is it?

- What texture is it?

- Does it have movement?

- Is it warm or cool?

- Is it hard or soft?

- Do any words, phrases or ideas come through?

- Make a note of anything and everything that you experience as a response. Even if it doesn't make any sense. Especially if it doesn't make any sense.

- Now sit in the energetics of your connection with the Runic Star Path concept. Give yourself a few minutes to see if anything else comes through.

- Then offer thanks to the gods and to the energetics of your own Runic Star Path. You can do this out loud with your voice or quietly in your mind. Both work.

- Stamp your feet. Clap your hands. Shout so loudly that the cat jumps.

- As your candle burns down, you can enjoy your drink. Or give it and the gods' one to a plant – something that will get nourishment from it.

Chapter 1

What Is Runic Astrology?

In the far frozen north, on the harsh, sparse soil of the frozen fjords, power was etched into stone. This power was gifted from the gods and goddesses to the people to help them communicate, cast spells, divine the future and memorialize their lives.

It came in the form of runes.

RUNES

Runes are lines carved on rock, bone, metal or wood to convey meaning and energy. These ancient sigils – mystic symbols – are found carved onto primal rocks all over Scandinavia, and they extended their reach down to the Mediterranean, to France, Britain, and even, according to some, Canada.

The earliest runes, the Elder Furtharc, were used 1,700 years ago and were a series of 24 of these symbols, associated with sounds, like our alphabet. They were primarily an alphabet and were used to record the deeds of the brave and the noble, or document who owned a sword or a piece of land. They gave names, deeds and dates. There is even a runic calendar on a piece of bone marking 28 days – the length of an average menstrual cycle and/ or moon cycle.

The shapes and symbols of the runes started off relatively basic, expressing concepts drawn from their users' surroundings: beasts that stalked the lonely woodlands, thorns that ripped flesh, trees that grew. Community, family, seasons and elements were all held within the runes.

As time rolled on, the runes evolved. Different parts of Europe had slightly different versions, which grew through the people interacting with nature, the gods and the cosmic energies. In Scandinavia, the Elder Furtharc became the Younger Furtharc, which has more abstract ideas and fewer runes. The Saxons, Angles, Jutes and Northumbrians living in Britain had their own songs of the runes, and Northumbria even had extra runes. Denmark and the people around the Balkans had their own take on the runes too.

As the people who used the runes evolved, the magic of the runes followed suit. Different languages brought the need to make the runes fit the sounds the people were hearing and speaking.

Then, as Christianity spread, the ways of worship changed, the ways of making letters changed, and the mighty runestones began to grow moss.

Empires rose and fell, wars raged across the lands, and the energy of the runes lay dormant for hundreds of years, aside from in some isolated areas.

Now, as people are beginning once again to put effort and energy into working with the runes, their power is reawakening. Their energy is beginning to flow through a world that has moved on 800 years.

In that world, where so many of us are feeling stripped of or disconnected from our power, the runes allow us to reclaim it – to regain the power to look into the mists of the future, to support and heal ourselves, and to move in the right direction. They aren't fortune-tellers, but they are way-showers.

If you're new to the runes, I've made an easy-to-follow table that includes each rune and a brief interpretation:

Rune	Rune name	Pronunciation	Association
ᚠ	Fehu	Fee-huo	Wealth, abundance, reputation
ᚢ	Uruz	Urr-uhzz	Strength, power, stubbornness
ᚦ	Thurizaz	Thur-ee-sarz	Focus, cutting, sharpness
ᚨ	Ansuz	Ahn-sooz	Communication, magic, words, leadership
ᚱ	Raido	Ray-do	Adventure, curiosity, mobility
ᚲ	Kenaz	Ken-az	Self-belief, self-discovery, light in the darkness
ᚷ	Gebo	Gee-boh	Gifts, respect, mutual support
ᚹ	Wunjo	Wun-yo	Bliss, contentment, working towards those goals
ᚺ	Hagalaz	Ha-ga-laz	Change, renewal, surprise
ᚾ	Nauthiz	Naou-th-iz	Need, requirements, basics
ᛁ	Isaz	Eees-az	Glamour, distraction, smoothness

Rune	Rune name	Pronunciation	Association
ᛃ	Jera	Yer-ra	Harvest, fruitfulness, hard work
ᛇ	Eihwaz	Yeehu-waz	Travelling through dimensions, changing states, holding energy
ᛈ	Peroth	Per-oth	Luck, sex, chance
ᛉ	Algiz	Al-geez	Boundaries, defence, standards
ᛋ	Sowolio	Sow-ol-io	Guidance, pathways, direction
ᛏ	Tiwaz	Tee-waz or Tay-waz	Honour, leadership, doing the right thing
ᛒ	Berkanan	Ber-karn-an	Regrowth, resilience, renewal
ᛖ	Ehwaz	Eh-waz	Trust, swiftness, friends
ᛗ	Mannaz	Man-ahz	Human spirit, human awesomeness, human resourcefulness
ᛚ	Laguz	Lah-gooz	Healing, water, washing away

Rune	Rune name	Pronunciation	Association
◇	Ingwaz	Ing-waz	Potential, heroic action, self-development
⟑	Othala	Oth-al-la	Home, castle, family
⋈	Dagaz	Dah-ghaz	Change, transition, new beginnings, the end of the old

Table 1: The Runes

HELLO, RUNES!

I'm so happy to share my interpretation of the runes and runic astrology, but it's really important that you build your own relationship with them and let them become alive and personal to you. Why not do the following:

- Draw each one in your journal.

- Add one or two words to each description. What energies do you feel are attracted to those runes?

This is an invitation,
from me and the gods, to
explore your terrain using
your Runic Star Path.

Now that you know a little bit about the runes, we're going to explore how you can work with them each day to tune in to their magic, wisdom and guidance.

Runes are *meant* to be used. You can throw them on ceramics, paint them on things, draw them on your palm, and do some really good social media posts with them, if that's your thing. You can create magic spells by writing them on pieces of wood or bone or horn.

Rune Magic

Rune magic is a powerful way to really work with the forces of the universe to co-create the results that we want. This is where we *really* come into our power as rune workers. But how does it happen?

Well, runes are like magnets, or fuzzy felt. (Remember that? Just me... oh....) The point is, they stick to things. Magnets stick to ferrous metals, like steel and iron, so they are always drawn to those metals. Fuzzy felt sticks to other fuzzy felt. Lego pieces stick to other Lego pieces, and to feet at 3 a.m., if you're super tired and forgot to clear up after the kids. Ouch.

Each rune sticks to the energies that resonate, vibrate or pulse with its frequency. And how does that work?

Well, each rune is magical, but in the Nordic animist tradition *everything* holds magic, from the keyboard on your computer to the car I drive, to the tree in the field, the grass, the dirt, you, the cat, your clothes, and so on. Everything has magic, has energy, has spirit. Everything is a being. The way we treat other beings directly affects how they respond to us.

So, there's a connection between you and me and that thing. That rock? Connected to you. Did you plant that flower? Its energy is wrapped around yours. Do you have a dog? Guess whose energy is infused with yours?

All the energies in the universe are entangled. All have been spun into existence. Interacting with any of them, any thread, will have consequences. Grumpy today? The rock you kicked exposed a snail and caused it to get eaten by a crow, which caused the crow to be full of food, so it didn't eat the worm, and that allowed a baby sparrow to feed. All linked by energy weaving. In modern science, we call this 'the quantum field' or 'quantum entanglement'. In the ancient north, it was called the *Wyrd*. The idea has been around a while. Yogis knew everything was linked via energy, vibration, frequency, as did the Christian Church, the Islamic imams, the Druids and witches, and the *Völva* or *Spel-mann*, the magicians from the north. Essentially, this is how runic energy interacts with the universe – through quantum entanglement.

This is how rune magic works too, by attracting the energetic frequencies that will manifest your intent. When you or I make magic with the runes, we draw and magnetize threads of the *Wyrd* to us for a desired outcome.

Like the bind rune I wear on my necklace, for example. This is for protection and bliss. When I burned the rune into the bog oak, I called in certain energetics and frequencies to create the bind in the *Wyrd*. If I now want this rune to do other things, it won't work well. This is because it was constructed and created and infused and woven, in co-creation with the *Wyrd*, with a very clear intent.

So, rune magic requires both the power of intention and the activation of intention in time and space. Remember, though, that *everything* has spirit, and some things will resist being magic-ed. Others however, are more easily magnetized, like money for example.

Your adventure with the runes will also be helped by a basic understanding of the magical concepts within the Nordic energetic cosmos.

MAGICAL CONCEPTS OF THE NORTHERN TRADITION

The Wyrd

Fate, destiny, doom. Woven by the Norns, the three goddesses at the root of the world tree, the *Wyrd* is not as prescribed as Graeco-Roman fate, it's more of a guideline that we can influence, especially *with* the runes.

The *Wyrd* is always consensual. I'm not saying that bad stuff doesn't happen – the *Wyrd* can grab you so that you find yourself in a learning experience that you'd never have expected – but we do get to influence what happens.

Say you're getting on a bus. First of all, you choose to get on the bus that is going to where you want to go. Then you get to choose where you sit. If you choose to sit next to a weird guy with one eye and two ravens, you may have a different experience than if you choose to sit next to a body-builder with ginger hair. You also have to choose to get on the bus going the best way for you. Not going all over town and spending six hours in the back of beyond. Unless that's what you want. You do you boo.

Hamingja (Hai-ming-ya)

Luck or fortune. In the northern tradition, this can be recharged by being awesome. It's also more of a community gathered and gained energy than an individual one. When you're an effective part of your community and your community supports you, your luck increases. Do good, get good. There is more on this later.

Yggdrasil (Yig-dra-sil)

The cosmos is connected by a tree, the world tree, a giant ash called Yggdrasil. At its foot, the Norns weave the *Wyrd*.

Norns

I mentioned these earlier, and they are quite the crux of belief and magic in the northern tradition. The Norns are three goddesses – Urðr (Fate), Verðandi (Now) and Skuld (What Will Happen) – who sit at the foot of the world tree and spin the very fabric of the universe into reality. Just knowing they are around, weaving the threads of universal energy into the complex quilt that is life, the universe and everything, is important.

Völva and Spel-Mann (Vohl-va and Spell-man)

These were the magic users, the wise people, those who accessed the deep and connective energies back in the ancient north. A *Völva*, witch, tended to be female, a *Spel-Mann* male. *Ergi* (*Err-ghe*) were those between genders, those in modern language we'd call 'trans' or 'non-binary'. The ancient Nordic people realized the *Ergi* could connect with different energies in the universe.

Asir

These are the gods and goddesses of the northern pantheon, who normally live in Asgard, a beautiful world of green valleys and towering walls at the top of the world tree, and are quite interested in people.

Vanir

Another tribe of gods, but more interested in farming and fertility than in people.

Jotun (Yo-tun)

Primitive tribal gods of the elemental and primal energies, often called giants. The Saxons called them *Etin*. These gods are interested in the energies that existed before humankind started farming. They don't really care about humans, and unless they respect you, they can be downright hostile.

Now, with the ideas, concepts and myths built into runic astrology starting to resonate in your energy, your aura, let us begin to journey into the cosmos of the runes.

ASTROLOGY

Astrology is looking for patterns in the stars and planets. It's mythology in the skies, stories and magic told through astral movements. It's a cosmic guidance system from ancient Greece, Babylon, Persia and Mesopotamia that has evolved over thousands of years, drawing on people's experience of life and making correspondences with how events and people show up in the world.

Over the generations, through different cultures and epochs, different pantheons of deities and different rulers and ideologies, it has been refined and defined, and now we find ourselves with a very well-honed system for interpreting the cosmic influences on our experience of the world. From weekly magazines with 'star signs' on the back pages, to daily papers with 'horoscopes', to broadsheets with full-page astrology segments, there's a lot of astrological guidance out there. Hundreds of books are written every year to teach us astrology, and tens of thousands of people provide astrological readings and other services around the globe. What we have now is massive collective power to understand the subtle influences of the cosmos on our experience.

How I see astrology is like this. We have the sun that provides life to our little blue ball in the darkness. The sun transmits energy, and that energy isn't consistently the same – there are different sunspots, solar flares, vibrations, and resonances at work. So from day to day, minute to minute, we get hit by a unique combination of solar rays. Those rays make our food grow, and we eat the food, so we get to consume and experience the energy of the sun in many different ways.

Another science thing is that *everything* has a gravitational pull. Something big like a planet or star has a bigger pull than something little like a kitten, me, or a moon.

But, and this is important, even those little gravitational pulls change how energy moves. So, the energy hitting us from the sun goes through the filter of the gravitational energy of the other planets and asteroids in the solar system, and –

this is the fun bit – it is also impacted by the constellations that form our astrological zodiac.

The Zodiac

The zodiac is a band of sky with 12 different constellations in it, all named after Greek myth, and all with dates assigned to them, which are static from year to year:

Aries	♈	21 March – 19 April
Taurus	♉	20 April – 20 May
Gemini	♊	21 May – 20 June
Cancer	♋	21 June – 22 July
Leo	♌	23 July – 22 August
Virgo	♍	23 August – 22 September
Libra	♎	23 September – 22 October
Scorpio	♏	23 October – 21 November
Sagittarius	♐	22 November – 21 December
Capricorn	♑	22 December – 19 January
Aquarius	♒	20 January – 18 February
Pisces	♓	19 February – 20 March

Table 2: The Zodiac

These have an energetic cycle, starting in Aries and finishing in Pisces, and getting 'wiser' and more developed as it progresses. Think of Aries energy as 16-year-old you and Pisces energy as 65-year-old you.

Everyone, according to this system, has a zodiac sign, according to their date of birth. I'm a Libra and my wife is a Scorpio, as is King Charles III. My editor is a Taurus.

I'm not going to explain astrology in full, as there are many different versions and ways of understanding it. I'm guessing that as you're here you might know a little about it already, and I'll share the parts that you'll need in order to activate your Runic Star Path. I do think that knowing what energies affected you as the first solar and cosmic rays hit your infant skin is important, as those codes went deep into your body, mind and aura. These are what we'll access when working with your Runic Star Path.

To be honest, though, classical astrology is a discipline that I've often found hard to grasp, even though I've a good knowledge of classical myth, and it wasn't until I met my wife that I was able to understand it more fully.

Lisa, my radiant wife, delves into the feminine stories of the stars and planets. She comes from a line of women who are what's called in the Traveller tradition *Sky Readers*, which means they care little for the 'mathematics' of astrology and instead feel the energetics of the stars and planets through their body. It was the realisation of 'Wait, there's more than one way to do this?' that made it easier for me to start exploring astrology on my own terms.

Naturally enough, I asked the gods of the northern tradition for their support.

'What is the navigation tool we need for now? Is it astrology? Is there a way we can work with the runes *and* astrology to navigate these current times and co-create our future?'

Their response? Well, it's what you have here in your hands. It's been collaborative and channelled with the gods. It's runic astrology.

RUNIC ASTROLOGY

Runic astrology is a guide to the cosmos through the lens of the northern tradition. It fits completely into the mechanics of classical astrology, but the zodiac of the runes adds different stories, myths and vibrations to the astrology we've known before. The heroic nature of northern spirituality brings a unique cosmological view of the universe.

What is important to note is that runic astrology could not exist in its current form without classical astrology and astronomy. Thousands of years of study of the celestial energies and planetary bodies have led us to where we are now, and there is zero point in reinventing the wheel and making things complex, so the maths and science have been carried over. Runic astrology is simply another way of looking at the energies that spin from the galactic centre. It's applying the myths, mysteries and majesty of the ancient Nordic tribes to the dots of light in the sky above that influence our lives, and using them, *collaborating* with them, to navigate and co-create our lives.

Much as CT scans see bones and soft tissue one way and MRI scans see them another, and our eyes see them another, and ultrasound yet another, classical astrology and runic astrology see the same world though different lenses. Quite literally, the iron-grey mountains, cloud-covered sky and inky black sea of the north are far from the burning sky and azure sea of the Mediterranean. The context and references are different.

Runic astrology can actually be considered to give a more detailed view, because it has twice as many data points. So we can get a little more precise about the energies that are affecting and influencing us.

Also, classical astrology is a system that is often prescriptive and can sometimes use fear-based language, along the lines of 'If you don't do this, that will happen.' What runic astrology tries to do is reframe this into a more open system that is designed to help you grow, develop and become more powerful in yourself.

What's important to remember is that different lenses provide different views and insights. More insights provide more wisdom, and more wisdom leads to better decisions.

I love looking at the world through many different lenses.

I want to help you to see life slightly differently too, and the lens of runic astrology is one that allows you to conjure up and feel empowered to work with the cosmic vibrations of the universe to navigate your Runic Star Path through life.

So, where to begin?

Let's Start at the Beginning...

Back in the day, we didn't mark calendar years, but we knew that spring followed winter, summer followed spring, autumn followed summer and winter followed autumn. That was as accurate as life got, time-wise. Farmers knew when to sow and they knew when to reap.

As culture developed, we added more structure to our experience of the year.

The earliest calendar in the north was carved on a bone comb. I mentioned it earlier. It marked a 28-day cycle. This calendar grew into a formalized way of counting moons, 13 a year.

When kings, armies and taxes came, more formulation was required. There were many different calendars in the ancient world. The old Roman calendar had 304 days divided into 10 months, starting with March, with the remaining days unaccounted for in the winter. Then January and February were brought into the count, and later still some ego got involved, and Julius Caesar and Augustus added their names to the calendar and made further revisions.

Time moved on and the runic calendar was devised, starting when the days were at their longest, with the most light in the sky.

And then came 1582, and the Julian calendar was reorganized by Pope Gregory to form the Gregorian calendar. The ins and outs of this aren't that important, but from a runic astrology perspective, one date moved. At first, midsummer was around 10 July, but when Pope Gregory moved stuff around, actual midsummer fell on 21 June. This moved the start month of the runic calendar.

While there can be some variance in dates, I've formalized the runic calendar to start on 21 June, which is usually the summer solstice.

And now we know where to begin, let's look ahead. What are we going to explore on our journey through runic astrology?

✦ The birth chart or natal chart – this shows the cosmic pattern at the time of our birth (though a birth chart can be drawn up for other things, too, such as nation states) and how this influences us.

✦ Nornir runes – how to access our luck and superpowers.

✦ The runic elements and how the runes form relationships. And how we can use this to work out who to date/work with/choose a puppy with.

✦ The planets as gods – their energies and interests. How they interact with us and their influence.

✦ Wandering gods – what it means when the gods get bored of their throne and 'go retrograde' or wander around.

✦ The world tree – how it throws shade (not like that) and how that energy influences our energy.

✦ And, most importantly, the runic zodiac. This is a huge one, so we will concentrate on the Sunna (Sun), Manni (Moon) and Jord (Earth/rising) runes, the three main energies in runic astrology, and their importance for our Runic Star Path.

So, let's step onto that path. What are Runic Star Paths and where do they lead?

Chapter 2

Runic Star Paths

Runic Star Paths are the routes of the stars and planets that move around the cosmos. Remember the ancients did *not* see a difference between the dot in the sky that is the planet Jupiter and the dot that is the Andromeda galaxy. They saw stars. Therefore, Runic Star Paths. 'Runic' because in runic astrology, the celestial bodies are symbolized by runes.

These paths can be plotted on a map, showing the energies, cosmic vibrations and frequencies that interact with us. Your own Runic Star Path explores the movements of the cosmos in relation to your own lived experience and supports you in feeling into those energetics, navigating them and co-creating with them.

LENSES OF MAGICAL ENERGY

You remember that planets have a gravitational pull? Well, one of the things this does is to distort how energy moves through it. Have you ever watched someone in a swimming pool? They look weird, as if their body is tiny and their head is normal size. The gravitational pull of the planets does this to the cosmic energies.

Another way of looking at this is as a lens. I've got some blue light blocking glasses that I put on at night to stop my brain being fried. The lenses of these glasses stop blue light from hitting my brain. And light is a form of energy. So, what happens when energy flows past a planet is that certain frequencies, certain vibrations, get distorted or blocked.

Each planet has a lens effect of its own, blocking energies it doesn't like and allowing and even amplifying energies it does. So, when we look through the lens of a planet's influence, we see the world how that celestial energy sees it. The frequencies of these energies are translated by our brain.

Now, I'm going to go off on a bit of a tangent right now. It's worth it. Back in the 1500s, when Europeans were sailing all over the world to trade, the Indigenous peoples of many other lands found this to be a completely new experience.

The European sailors couldn't understand why the Indigenous peoples didn't respond to the arrival of their big ships, but when they put the tenders out, the natives sent dug-out canoes.

The new experience was the thing. We tell stories to help ourselves cope with the unknown. What if there were no stories about sailing ships in your culture's history? Would you have the mental ability to see them? Or would your brain simply shut off and say, 'Nope, not dealing'?

We know that the brain says 'no' in these circumstances.

Runic astrology provides the cognitive constructs for our brain to understand the unseen, or to be more accurate the previously unseen, energies of the cosmos. As you learn how the vibrations that come from the stars and planets work together, you'll see where the runes show up with this energy.

The runes are our MRI scanner for cosmic energies, allowing us to grasp the messages, stories and insights that come from the stars.

Because everything on this planet is made from and fuelled by star energy, everything has a runic resonance. So, the paths of the stars influence how grass grows, how cows moo and how llamas... do whatever llamas do. What do llamas do? (Spit, I believe....)

What I'd like you to be able to do, to feel into, when you finish this book is to find your birth runes and those of your friends and family. And cat, dog, goldfish, etc. Then, when you know what influences are in your life, you can navigate your way forward. You can identify a good day for, say, finding love. Or telling a story.

EVOLVING MYTHS

Aettir (Et-tear), families and communities, were big parts of the ancient Nordic mindset, with huge amounts of interdependence between people. This interdependence, and the need to tell stories about everything (our Nordic ancestors loved a story), brings the concept of *Aettir* into the runic universe. The runes themselves are broken up into three families of eight runes.

The runic *Aettir* tell the story of life from the basics of survival to the growth of a person and a species. This isn't a story like that of the Tarot, which has a very clear and well-defined narrative, it's much more about the evolution of concepts:

+ The first *Aett* represents the individual, starting with resources (Fehu) and ending with joy (Wunjo).

+ The second *Aett* is how the individual is tested, weathers the storm and can grow and develop, starting with change (Hagalaz) and ending with the sun (Sowolio).

+ The third and final *Aett* tells the story of how the individual becomes part of society, starting with duty and honour (Tiwaz) and ending with initiation and passing through the doorway to the beyond (Dagaz).

*Runic astrology provides
the cognitive constructs
for our brain to
understand the unseen
energies of the cosmos.*

In runic astrology, the runes progress from a land of peace, with Fehu and Uruz, slowly building more strife and learning as they move through the runic cosmo-verse until, by Wunjo, it's all nice, with gifts, adventures and bliss. Then the tone changes to one of strife, with hail, hunger and fire, then mellows with lessons learned, luck, edges and pathways, before moving into honour, resilience, companionship and family.

So the runes tell a very basic story of initiation, of becoming a meaningful part of the community through the trials of life and becoming more powerful, before transitioning at the end back to the beginning.

The energies follow the seasons through the runic calendar of the year, with Hagalaz, Nauthiz and Isaz, hail, lack and ice, coming in the darkest parts of the year, when life is hardest. When it's coldest, when resources are low, luck plays a part, with Peroth, as do strong boundaries, with Algiz. Then life gets easier if you trust yourself and the process as the seasons change and the year moves on.

The runes are a map to victory throughout the year. If you follow it, you'll have victory in your life.

Chapter 3

The Birth Chart

The birth chart, or natal chart, of classical astrology, the Runic Star Path of runic astrology, is one of our pivotal tools. It tells us where the planets, asteroids and constellations were when we popped out of our momma – the energetic reverberation that flowed through us at the moment of our birth. It reveals the pattern and path laid out for us by the Norns.

THE NORNS

The Norns, as you now know, are three powerful goddesses whose role is to create the fates of all things. They spin the threads of fate on a celestial spinning wheel, using the very stuff of the universe to create the stories and complex experiences of life.

✦ Urðr (Fate) takes the stuff of the universe, the atoms, energy and vibration of creation, and feeds it to her sister Verðandi (Now).

✦ Verðandi (The Happening) takes it and spins it into threads, creating what we can become.

✦ Skuld (What Will Happen) takes the strands and uses them to create the infinitely complex paths of vibration and frequency that all life follows.

So, these goddesses create patterns, the web, that we live our life on, in and through.

ENERGETICS

But, and this is an important but, we – you and I, the cat, the planet, the gods and goddesses, the spider plant – get to choose how we interact with that energy. We aren't pawns in some giant game of chess. We are autonomous and get to choose to pick up the threads of life or not. Sometimes that choice is hard, but we do get it.

And, though we are really quite small on the scale of the universe, we have big potential. Kind of like a toddler on a long-distance flight, we are small but the impact we can have is huge. We can influence the universe around us. And in turn be influenced (unlike the in-flight toddler).

How does it work? We have a massively complex body full of nerves and neurons, cells, bones and all the squishy bits in the middle, a body that acts as an antenna for the cosmic frequencies that can affect us. Like tuning a radio, we can pick up different cosmic energies if we act in different ways. We become *magnetic* to them, and *this* is where the power lies....

When we are born, the Norns give us an energetic resonance, a frequency that pulls certain energy to us. This energy is a double-edged sword that can limit as well as enliven. Because life isn't that simple. But by mapping the energies of the cosmos at that moment, we can see how our cells and neurons were influenced by the world outside the protective film of the womb, and so understand our inherent strengths and weaknesses.

This is looking at cosmic energy from an epigenetics standpoint – modification of gene expression. According to epigenetics, certain genes in our DNA are turned on or off in response to environmental factors. It's been suggested that trauma can trigger or repress genes, even intergenerationally. So it's not much of a jump to consider that the cosmic rays that we experience every day can turn on and turn off DNA codes in our body when we are born. This is what our birth chart shows: the energies that affect our DNA when we are born.

By knowing which energies were present, we can understand our personality traits, propensity to environmental factors, strengths, weaknesses and preferences.

So the birth chart is like a guidebook to the energetic body. Much like a mechanic will have a service manual for your car, your birth chart is the service manual for your life.

LOOKING AT YOUR BIRTH CHART

The birth chart is the basic chart that most, if not all, astrology software on the internet or in app form will give you. You don't need to pay for it. Literally search on the internet for 'birth chart' or 'natal chart' and you should have lots of free options.

Sooo... If you've not already done that, go do it.

Some things you need to make sure your chart has are the degrees which each of the planets, signs and asteroids are in.

Access your birth chart and print it out. Fold it in half and stick it in the cover of your journal, or in this book. Having it on paper means you can access it wherever and draw all over it.

The energies that arrive
in our bodies and in our
souls at the moment of
our birth are mapped in
our Runic Star Paths.

CONNECTING WITH YOUR BIRTH CHART

Open up your chart. If you're using a digital chart, bring it up on your phone or tablet.

I put music on for this and you may like to do the same. I choose Wardruna (current favourite, 'Lyfjaberg').

Now, with the intent of connecting with, activating and receiving from your chart, place your hand on the chart.

Place your other hand on the centre of your chest, over your sternum and heart. Feel your breath lift that hand.

Breathe for a couple of minutes, connecting to the energies that are flowing to you from the cosmos, through your Runic Star Path, your birth chart.

When you feel you have finished, thank the energies and grab some chocolate or some other treat.

Stamp your feet, eat the chocolate and get ready for the energy to come. What sort of energy? Well, cosmic energy can feel like a sugar rush. Depending on how much chocolate you've just snaffled.

Now you have connected with the energies of the cosmos that the Norns have woven into your soul's energetic tapestry. The runes that are woven into this tapestry are known as your *glóa stigr* (*Glow-a St-eye-g*) or Glowing Path Makers.

Sounds good, right? *Glowing Path Makers*. Let's look at three of the most influential.

Chapter 4

The Sunna, Manni and Jord Runes

We're going to start simple here, by looking at the main energetic influences on your DNA, namely the goddess Sunna (the Sun), the god Manni (the Moon), and the goddess Jord (the Earth/your rising sign), and I'm going to tell you how to work out what yours are.

So, let's get looking through the pile of papers that your birth chart is in, so you've got it to hand. If you're super organized, unlike me, you may even have folded it up and used it as a bookmark. Get it out, as we are going to be using it in a minute.

SUNNA (THE SUN)

Let's start with the biggest energy pull in the solar system: the sun, Sunna. (The sun is feminine in the Nordic pantheon, as it brings life to the frozen north, whereas in Mediterranean or African paganism the sun tends to be male, as there it can burn or kill.) She puts out loads of energy too, so you get a double whammy. This is why the Sunna rune, or Sun sign, is so important.

Sunna likes to put people on the right path, show the way and help things happen. She provides energy, guidance and light.

What kind of guidance does Sunna give you? What sort of energy does she attract?

I'm going to assume that you've got your birth chart. Look for the circle with a dot in the middle.

Make a note of the zodiac sign it is in – this is your Sun sign – and the degree. For example, Sun is at 24° of Libra.

We'll look at how to translate this into a rune in a moment.

MANNI (THE MOON)

Then find the sign with the symbol of a crescent moon and again note down the degree.

My Moon is at 22° of Virgo.

Your Wyrd is woven by the
Norns – the threads held
in your Runic Star Path.

JORD (EARTH/RISING)

Now look at what would be about 9 o'clock if your chart were a clock. There you'll see a line, like a horizon. Again, note down the sign this is in. This is your rising sign, the sign rising up above the horizon when you were born. Again, note down the sign and the degree.

My rising sign is 14° of Libra.

SIGNS AND RUNES

So, you've got three data points. I know you love data points. And you know what I keep saying about data points? The more you have, the more accurate you can be.

Your Sunna Rune

To find your Sunna rune, the simplest way is to check the following table. You'll see that while each zodiac sign has about 30 days assigned to it, in runic astrology each rune has about 15 days. This makes the energy association of runic astrology that much more accurate than classical astrology.

Birth rune	Date start (at midday)	Date end (at midday)
Fehu	21 June	7 July
Uruz	7 July	23 July
Thurizaz	23 July	7 August
Ansuz	7 August	23 August
Raido	23 August	8 September
Kenaz	8 September	23 September
Gebo	23 September	8 October
Wunjo	8 October	23 October
Hagalaz	23 October	7 November
Nauthiz	7 November	22 November
Isaz	22 November	7 December
Jera	7 December	22 December
Eihwaz	22 December	6 January
Peroth	6 January	20 January
Algiz	20 January	4 February
Sowolio	4 February	19 February
Tiwaz	19 February	5 March
Berkanan	5 March	20 March
Ehwaz	20 March	4 April
Mannaz	4 April	19 April
Laguz	19 April	5 May

Birth rune	Date start (at midday)	Date end (at midday)
Ingwaz	5 May	20 May
Othala	20 May	5 June
Dagaz	5 June	21 June

Table 3: Birth Rune Dates

Your Manni and Jord Runes

Still got your Post-its with the degrees on? Awesome. Check out the table below and you'll find your Manni rune and Jord rune (and your Sunna rune again, if you wish).

Fehu	0 – 15 degrees Cancer
Uruz	16 – 30 degrees Cancer
Thurizaz	0 – 15 degrees Leo
Ansuz	16 – 30 degrees Leo
Raido	0 – 15 degrees Virgo
Kenaz	16 – 30 degrees Virgo
Gebo	0 – 15 degrees Libra
Wunjo	16 – 30 degrees Libra
Hagalaz	0 – 15 degrees Scorpio
Nauthiz	16 – 30 degrees Scorpio
Isaz	0 – 15 degrees Sagittarius
Jera	16 – 30 degrees Sagittarius

Eihwaz	0 – 15 degrees Capricorn
Peroth	16 – 30 degrees Capricorn
Algiz	0 – 15 degrees Aquarius
Sowolio	16 – 30 degrees Aquarius
Tiwaz	0 – 15 degrees Pisces
Berkanan	16 – 30 degrees Pisces
Ehwaz	0 – 15 degrees Aries
Mannaz	16 – 30 degrees Aries
Laguz	0 – 15 degrees Taurus
Ingwaz	16 – 30 degrees Taurus
Othala	0 – 15 degrees Gemini
Dagaz	16 – 30 degrees Gemini

Table 4: Degrees of the Runes in the Zodiac

If your degree is 15 point something, read it as 16.

Boom! You have your Runic Star Path. Thank you. Book over. Or this chapter at least.

Ready for the next bit? Want to know what it all means?

Chapter 5

Finding Your Runic Resonance

Now you know your three main runic energies, you can begin to understand your Runic Star Path. Prepare to see the magic that is happening around you – the energy that is being magnetized into your life, ready for you to work with.

And get your Post-its and highlighter ready, for this is one of the reference bits of the book. Don't get overwhelmed, just look up the wisdom that's applicable to you.

SUNNA RUNE – YOUR SOUL PURPOSE

Sunna is a pathway and direction energy, and a Sunna rune is a rune that illuminates your guiding path. Like a spiritual streetlamp!

Your Sunna rune shows your soul purpose and I advise you to use it as a guide for decision-making. If you act with its energy in mind, you won't go far wrong.

Let's look at how your Sunna rune energy guides you through life.

Fehu

With Fehu as your Sunna rune, your guiding light leads you to bring abundance and fertility to yourself and those around you. Fehu is the rune of Frey, the fertility god, and provided you live your life in ways that increase wealth, abundance and fertility, you will have no problem feeling fulfilled.

Your soul will also be happy when you are building up your reputation. The more people have your name on their lips (either your real name or an assumed name, as long as it's yours), the greater the flow of energy into your life. Resources will flow to you, and in turn those resources will bring growth to your reputation and standing in your community.

When you use your ability to manifest resources, abundance, fertility and/or reputation, you'll find that those around you will quite literally vibrate with your excess. You ensure that those who work for you or with you have what they need, and they in turn ensure that you have what you need.

Uruz

Your Sunna rune is attracted to the raw, wild power of Uruz, the aurochs, which can be expressed either physically or energetically, or indeed both. A wild man o' the mountains-type approach, or being in wild places, or both, will fill you with power.

Be warned, though, that constraints that don't meet with your ethics mean nothing to you, so you are likely to quickly trample over them or ignore them entirely, and others may not feel the same way. To avoid conflict, learn the skills that will help you live by *your* rules without antagonizing others.

You are driven by the power to be wild and untamed in thought, word and deed, so putting yourself in places where your wildness will serve you will lead to victory and contentment. Power, stubbornness and strength will see you through, but you choose when to apply them. Remember, 'to a hammer, everything looks like a nail'. But when necessary, go forth and bash things out of your way!

Thurizaz

Thurizaz is a rune of focus and direct action. This energy is that of a magnifying glass held under the midday sun, or the prick of a thorn, or the focus of a laser pointer. This is where you can find your power and pathway.

When you act, choose to focus on one thing and put your not inconsiderable power into it. This way, your energy isn't being bled away into areas where it's under-utilized. For you, success, victory and contentment come from not deviating from your focus.

You don't want to be having to change direction a long way down the path, so stop every now and then to check the lie of the land. In fact, short sharp bursts of action are probably your friends – going forward with power and grace, but stopping before you get exhausted and blunt.

Your wit, humour and world-view may well be sharp and cutting, like the claw of a cat, or a thorn in a bush. But they're always to the point!

Ansuz

Ansuz is the rune of the voice, words and leadership, and as such is the rune of Odin (Mercury). The Runic Star Path it sets out is one of communication, leadership and inspiration. With Ansuz as your Sunna rune, you'll find this energy flowing to you.

Look to where your voice can get you into – and out of – situations that you are required to be in. Remember words are magic, yours especially. Words are power, and using the right words will ease your path through life.

With power flowing in the direction of leadership and creativity, look to where you can be in charge, be seen or otherwise be important thanks to your creativity and voice. This is where huge power lies for you.

When life gets hard, remember that your path is smoothed with words and magic. Use your voice, use your magic. Your biggest allies will come if you form your words in ways they can grasp and resonate with.

Raido

Wanderlust – this is the radiant energy that flows through your Sunna rune. Setting out on an adventure is powerful magic for you. Be it for healing or joy, or both!

Being constantly curious and ready to find out what's on the other side of the mountain is the way that you'll find bliss and contentment in life. Do you always want to travel? Or do you want to find out how this molecule bonds with that one? Or do you want to explore how to create amazing art to inspire others? Whatever your preferred form of exploration, you have the power and the drive to see what's 'over there'.

Don't be afraid to bring others along for the journey, as your innate adventurous spirit will enthuse them. If they do have a tantrum at any time, they can just sit on a bench while you go and look at that amazing thing over there.

Trust your adventurous spirit. It will never lead you wrong.

Kenaz

 With Kenaz flowing through Sunna's energy, you are doubly blessed with light energy to use as you see fit. Are you a 'lightworker', by any chance?

Finding what is hidden in the darkness may be a superpower of yours. Hidden things probably drive you potty. Kenaz wants to shine light everywhere, and it's this energy that will propel you forward. Forward with insatiable curiosity....

This runic resonance is your pathway to victory and heroic achievements. Consider where you can bring enlightenment to situations. Where you can chase away ignorance and darkness from yourself and from others. Where you can shed light on the hidden or disguised things that others ignore. This is your power. Don't be afraid to use it.

You may find that people are drawn to you when the unknown or confusing arise. This is also part of your heroic path, as you are a beacon of light and safety in the darkness.

Gebo

Gebo and Sunna are a combination that enhances your innate talents. Your ability to bring life, light and love to the environment around you is of huge importance and can have far-reaching effects.

This runic energy calls you to strive for self-expression in any way that feels good to you. Clothes, jobs, pastimes, lovers – anything that helps you express your energy will help you fulfil your soul purpose.

The celestial combination of Gebo and Sunna also indicates a personality that is driven to seek out the messages, gifts and secrets of the esoteric. Delving into the *Wyrd* and wonderful ways of the cosmos will bring you victory and fulfilment.

This curiosity, this drive to seek out obscure facts and remarkable things, will in turn set your innate talents pulsing for more – more exploration, more adventures, more looking, feeling and being awesome.

To utilize this energy in your cells and molecules, ensure that you are feeling and looking as you would like. This will allow your power to radiate out fully.

Wunjo

As the nights get longer and the animals and resources are brought in, your Wunjo energy shines through. Your ability, both energetically and practically, to make sure that everyone's needs are met will stand you in good stead in the communities in which you find yourself.

Your frequency drives you to seek contentment and do the work to get it. This makes you the ideal person to have around when things get stressful or unsettled. Finding, or building, bridges between people and making sure needs are met are your superpowers. So, you may be drawn to caring roles, or leadership ones. Wunjo isn't all fluffy blanket hugs, it's also the discipline that ensures that wood is chopped and water carried. And everything else is done to make sure that needs are met.

Your energy is very communal. This shows itself in how you lead and how you follow. And you want to be *comfortable*. If the basic tasks aren't done properly, it will probably drive you mad.

Hagalaz

At first glance, a soul purpose of 'Crush everything and everyone around me' may not be the most inspiring destiny. Or, with a Hagalaz Sunna rune, maybe it is.

This is taking Hagalaz at a very, very surface level, however. On a deeper one, Hagalaz is the ability to take what has gone before and use its death as fuel. Where others despair, you see opportunity. You see a situation, let it be resolved and then empower yourself through the learnings, adventures and experiences you receive as a result.

So, trust yourself in challenging situations, as your instincts will aid you in fuelling yourself and becoming even more powerful than you can possibly imagine.

Also, look to the experiences in life that fill you up, that make your heart sing and your soul yearn. These experiences, too, will fuel you and your exploration of life. And with Hagalaz energy, *you* happen to situations. Not the other way around.

Nauthiz

Your Sunna energy shines through the lens of Nauthiz, the rune of need. At first glance, this is a rune of suffering and pain. But while that energy is there, this rune brings a resolute power. It's not all doom and gloom, trust me.

The guiding light of Sunna shining through the energy of need brings you the tendency to be guided by your will. Your focus and your devotion to your ideas bring you the ability to create and be artistic.

Truth, honesty, loyalty and independence are guiding factors in your life, and your optimism is rooted in them. If someone hides the truth or tries to be dishonest, it is likely to cause you confusion and pain. They may well become dead to you.

Acting in ways that build loyalty and trust in yourself and others will always help you create and achieve your goals and bring you victory.

Isaz

Isaz is a twofold rune, with both glamour and distraction in place. Like a woolly mammoth in a glacier. And, like a glacier, Isaz moves slowly but inevitably.

With Isaz as your Sunna rune, look to find your life purpose in the unstoppable movement towards a goal. Or the distraction and glamour of glittering ice sculptures. You get to choose, as you are epic. Choose to crush everything in front of you with your unstoppable will. Or, if the mood takes you, dazzle all around you with glamour and misdirection like a hall of mirrors.

This dual path can lead you to acquire an interesting skill-set of being steady and reliable and getting everything done, while appearing bright and shiny and too good to be true.

Remember, though, that ice doesn't like heat, and pressure makes heat. Keep yourself cool and don't let others take advantage of your work ethic. Just let them be distracted by the shiny things, while you get stuff done. Remember, you cannot be stopped.

Jera

Your soul purpose is wrapped around the rune of Jera, the rune of harvest and rewards. Everyone likes rewards, so why is this special for you?

Well, Jera energy hinges on the work being done to get the best harvest. Your ability to make sure that the right things are done at the right time for the required result is a manifestation of this energy.

You, awesome one, are able to bring the energy of manifestation into the real world with more ease than others. Your manifestation ability is that of the farmer growing a crop. They know exactly what they will get if they follow their plan. This is how your energy flows – it's methodical, organized and focused. It will make sure all the steps are completed, even though you may not think about this consciously, or even realize it.

If your harvest hasn't yet come, check out where you have given up power to others and taken your energy away from your process.

Eihwaz

Your soul purpose is very wrapped up in your ability to manage. Manage energy, not pushing papers in an office kind of manage. Well... maybe, if that's your jam. But mainly managing energy so it flows consistently for all those you care about. Even if that's just you and the cat.

Essentially, Eihwaz is the rune of energy control. So, storing and using energy is part of your soul purpose, be it practically with electrics or fire, or in more esoteric ways like energy healing or things of an oracular nature. Or in interactions with people, getting the best from a team, or friend, or situation.

You get to choose the energy you store. Storing negative energy would be an 'interesting' experience, kind of like putting rotten leftovers in the fridge, whereas storing positive energy will provide a very different experience. This ability to store energy makes it easy for you to be included in parties, rituals or other energetic experiences, as you bring the magic naturally.

Peroth

Peroth is a two-dimensional rune, the first dimension being luck. In the time of the Vikings, luck was called *Hamingja*. It was earned by hard work. The more you contributed to the collective, the luckier you would be. This was true for everyone. You, though, with a Peroth Sunna rune, have this on steroids. Luck may well find its way into your life, maybe not on a lottery-win level, but on an everyday level. The universe has your back. Follow the unexpected, as this has great potential for you.

The other aspect of Peroth is sex, so follow your sexual energy too, as this will lead to passion and imagination not just between the sheets, but in every corner of your life.

Sexual energy is also the energy of potential and joy – the potential of conception, the joy of that act, the potential creative energy contained within.

Combined, these two energies bring a powerful vibration to your life, one that will drive you to be inventive and resilient. And lucky.

Algiz

With Algiz as your Sunna rune, you will have strong and powerful boundaries and standards, as Algiz brings you a strong sense of edges, and when to cross them and when to hold them.

When you choose to let boundaries be crossed, either by you or by others, you are empowered. This is Algiz energy. When they are crossed inadvertently, through your apathy or inattention, your energy is sapped. When you let people walk over you or take advantage, because of social conditioning or a need to be a 'good' person, your energy will be depleted, leaving you to get sick.

When you choose to be strong in your standards and boundaries, however, Algiz will bring you safety and power. And in turn your Algiz energy will spread to your kith and kin. Their boundaries will be stronger because of you. This is how you manifest your heroic destiny.

Sowolio

With Sowolio, rune of the sun, navigation and guidance, as your Sunna rune, your Runic Star Path is that of the way-shower. When you stand up, people follow. You have the ability to lead by inspiration or, like the sun in the desert, to burn up those around you. Your call.

You can also choose to quietly motivate and encourage as a teacher or mentor, or to stand at the front of the line as you stride forth into the uncharted jungle. Any way you choose to motivate, lead or show the way will work.

Being a way-shower can lead you into coaching, therapy, leadership and ownership. A manager you are not – petty BS isn't going to cut it with you – you are about getting on the right path and following it. And not just your own right path, but the path that is right for those you are leading. Showing people the way is your heroic purpose.

Tiwaz

Your guiding light is that of action, decisive action, with a heavy slab of honour on top. This may not win you friends, but people will speak of you with respect and, when you are expressing your true self, awe.

This energy is, however, one of self-sacrifice, and if you aren't a paragon to those around you, it will manifest in ways that are detrimental to your evolution. It may even lead to you acting out of someone else's view of what you 'should' be rather than your own vision of yourself. This will hurt, in many and varied ways. Tyr is the god who sacrificed his hand to keep the world safe from Fenrir the wolf. Don't put your hand near wolves. Just saying.

Instead, be active and proud of who you are. Then you'll have lesser folks falling at your feet. People who lead from the front and aren't afraid of hard decisions are few and far between. Stick to your values and you'll be inspirational.

Berkanan

Berkanan is the glow that brings life to the ravaged, and your soul purpose is tied to this frequency of recovery and restoration.

In the frozen mountains of Scandinavia, the first tree to regrow after a fire is the birch. And the bear lives in a cave beneath the snow during the winter. The birch and the bear are representations of the energy that you bring to yourself and those around you.

The ability to help remove toxicity and promote life is your path of heroism. So, removing confusion, helping investments grow and bringing life to abandoned projects is where your energy will flow well.

When you trust your ability to weather the storm by either getting yourself some bear time and keeping yourself warm and cosy or simply recovering faster than anyone else, you harness the recovery frequency of your Sunna rune and can use this to bring restoration to yourself and those around you and enjoy power and success.

Ehwaz

Ehwaz holds both the energy of companionship and of the horse, and with it as a Sunna rune, your soul mission or heroic self is tied into the energy of companionship and swiftness.

You have the power to be swift – in thought, feeling, body, or some other way – so use it. Leap the chasm. Trust yourself and your tribe. Make a decision and act.

You may be conditioned by life and society, but your ability to think and act in one breath is magic. You are moving while others are dithering, debating and procrastinating. They're still sitting on the sofa when you've done the thing and are enjoying the rewards. Or are off to the next thing. You can happily move from situation to situation, building relationships and having adventures.

You're also able to inspire others and to benefit from their support. Lean into your companions. Not just friends, but companions, for this is the path that leads to victory for you.

Mannaz

Mannaz is the rune of spirit and humanity. This is the energy that will drive a momma to push, or a soldier to risk death to save their buddy. It flows like fire through your veins. Your human spirit, your magic, can influence the world around you. Think Harry Potter. You can be magic like a wizard, or magic like Louise Hay.

Mannaz manifests through your every action. If you choose, you can be a manifesting genius, or an inventive creator, or a compassionate healer. You can channel your spirit through anything you focus on. Even bingeing a boxset. You choose where your spirit flows. It's never wasted, but is it more fun for you to use it in a specific way? Again, you choose. When the chips are down, you have the power.

Mannaz is the human rune, and you, awesome one, bring the power of humanity for all to see, hear and feel.

Laguz

Laguz is the water rune, and water is life, and this energy is what drives your heroic Runic Star Path. One of the magical powers of water is that it is the universal solvent, and everything will eventually dissolve as a result of its movement and power. Laguz brings that energy to you – the gentle power to process away, almost imperceptibly, the injury, the hurt, the toxic, from yourself and/or those you choose to grace with your power. It brings the ability to heal, to wash away sickness.

It also brings life in the form of water itself, and fishing. So, your soul purpose is tied to being able to remove the unwanted, unneeded or blocking, and to the ocean, the massive energy sink that can both hold energy and transmute it into something good.

When life gets difficult, remember that water wears through the most resilient of materials. Use your flowing nature to push through and open the cracks in any situation.

Ingwaz

Ingwaz is the rune of the archetypical hero, the hero's journey and the inner potential we all hold. All we can be, could be, would want to be is held here.

Activating both your own potential and the potential of those around you is what resonates most powerfully with your life path. You can either choose the 'Light the blue touchpaper and walk away' model of activation or the Hagrid/Obi Wan/Aragorn model of guidance.

In life, love and work, look to where you can either activate yourself or, if you choose, those around you. That is, activate into epic awesomeness. No story ever started with 'I was drinking tea quietly at home.' Well, maybe *The Hobbit* came close.

But forget the tea, activate the potential. That is where your power lies. *Potential* is your watchword. Every action you take can expand your experience of the world, so choose to actively participate in life. Choose the adventure.

Othala

With your Sunna energy glowing with Othala vibrations, your life path and focus are linked to family, home and security. Now, it's important to remember that there are many ways that family can manifest. You choose yours. But whatever you choose, look to where you can create the security and harmony that you require in life. This kind of thing may well come easy to you. In fact, building harmony and community may be super easy for you in other situations and settings too, such as work, or teams, or hobbies. It's your solar superpower.

The Othala frequency is also linked to genetics. The rune itself looks a little bit like a primitive DNA helix. So, look to where you can interact with genetics, personal legacies and building heritage and traditions both for yourself and those you love, perhaps by involving yourself in scientific research, families or other groups of people. This is definitely another superpower of yours.

Dagaz

Dagaz energy is one that could be seen as 'hard' or painful, but it's simply part of life. All things change. Time and entropy affect us all. What Dagaz brings through its vibrational magnetism is the cyclic nature of life, the energy of transition, of changing states.

Dagaz itself sits at the end of the runic Furtharc, but it is also at the beginning, as the flow of energy moves forward to Fehu again. With Dagaz as your Sunna rune, use its energies to ease the transition between ending the old and beginning the new. Perhaps you're a great entrepreneur, starting up new businesses, or you have the ability to help people move from addiction to sobriety. Manifesting and actioning change is where your power lies.

Change isn't always pleasant, of course, but remember it is inevitable. You may even find that you ride the cycle of change as a unicycle. While others run in fear.

MANNI RUNE – YOUR EMOTIONAL PURPOSE

The energy of your Manni rune illuminates the emotional path that will help you find peace and contentment in your life. I call this your emotional purpose.

Let's look at how your Manni rune energy shows your emotional purpose.

Fehu

Fehu is the rune of abundance and reputation, and Manni's influence here brings that vibration to your emotional field. Trust your reputation to stand you in good stead when you interact with people. You have the energetic vibration to bring out the best in them and bring an abundance of good fortune and wealth to both your and their emotional experience.

This is definitely an energy of 'Feel it to make it.' Feel the sensations you wish to create and your energy field will bring that energy to you, possibly in the form of money or resources. Or cows. But there are only so many cows most people can cope with. So make sure you are clear on your goals. And your time-scales. As grain takes months to grow, so do dollar bills.

Your energy is one of slow and steady increments. Lots of awesome little interactions will bring you the best results.

Uruz

With the rune of the giant aurochs as your emotional guide, your passions have huge power. Own it. It took a whole tribe to hunt the aurochs, and some of them would not go home. This is how powerful your emotions are. Enjoy your tantrums – I'm guessing no one else does!

Use this unassailable emotional power to fuel your endeavours in life, whatever they may be. Once your passion is engaged, the Uruz energy will trample everything in its way to satiate it.

Uruz energy can be solitary and moody, enjoying its own company. So, take time alone, or you may trample those around you. By accident, of course. It's entirely their own fault.

Above all, remember your emotions and passions are powerful and strong. You're probably the only one who can tame them. So, perhaps, be careful where you point them. Rule them, or let them rule you. Either way, it's going to be an adventure!

Thurizaz

Thurizaz is an energy of penetration and focus, and neither are Manni's strong suit. Manni loves to stop and stare, but with your laser focus, you can bore past all the distractions straight to the heart of the matter. Your emotional superpower is tied in with being able to feel right into the heart of a situation.

Use this how you will, but you may well find it useful working with people who are hiding things or selling things. Hidden agendas may be an open book to you. Got oracle cards or a rune set? I'd suggest that you modify the messages that come through to you, or they will be a little too cutting to the receiver.

Your cutting words or tongue may well be a tool for righteous rage. Or, after a tequila or two, something you have to apologize for. Find a balance that works for you. And remember, whatever you're told or shown, you know what is hidden beneath. As you can get there straight away.

Ansuz

The energy of Ansuz flowing through Manni the moon is that of the voice, communication and magic. Your voice is your power. Use it however you choose – singing, speaking, whispering or chanting, to name but a few of the ways. Harness the passion within you to amplify your song, your sound, your tone, your frequency. This will build your magical resonance and power.

Your emotions drive this connection to magic and mystery, so ensure that they are fuelling your experience of the world. Passion is a good one to use to direct your power, but so are anger and love, though they are not nearly as consistent. But any emotion married to your voice will lead you to victory and contentment.

Let your voice, your song, your ability to communicate, sing to you, in whatever form you choose to express it. There's power and magic there for you.

Raido

With Raido as your Manni rune, your emotions have the power and the energy to 'go there'. Your inquisitive and adventurous nature is what drives your passion, and there is nothing your emotional power cannot shed light on, no feeling you are unprepared for. Wherever you go and however you get there, you will be able to bring the light of passion, joy and courage with you. And if by chance those feelings aren't there? Well, move on, there's bound to be something fun over there, right?

To do so, you must be resourced, nourished and supported. So, make sure you fill your life with adventure, but remember to nap and explore in dream time too. Manni loves dream time, and this energy is yours too. Filling your life with passion via adventures will allow you to bring a flame of guidance, positivity and growth to even the darkest of situations.

You have this innate power – use it.

Kenaz

Emotional insight and pulse are your guides with Kenaz in your Manni energy. Using your insight and power to 'go there' is a resource that others won't value until they are in need of it. This sucks. But what it does mean is that you have this 'see in the dark' vibe with emotions. Perhaps you resonate with the word 'empath' – or 'badass'. Whatever label you choose to take, or none at all, you're highly sensitive. Be ready with your emotional vibe to provide insights into situations where there is darkness or hidden intent.

Others may get frustrated by your ability to see through their dark night of the soul. But you are a beacon of guidance and emotional light when others are in darkness. Trust your ability to dispel shadows, as this is the way for you to squash fear and shine a light on the path that leads to victory.

Gebo

Emotional connection is your gift to those around you. You're the shoulder to cry on, the friend to rage with, the ally in a fight. If emotions are going there, your energy can add to them. If you choose. Just remember that when you're emotionally invested in something, it's everything to you.

If you're able to be aware of your emotions, you'll be able to gift that understanding to others, be it compassionately, emphatically or intellectually. This will build an emotional relationship that allows you to help those without the emotional gifts you have to share. Your ability to bring the gift of your emotions to any situation is profound. If the party is thumping and *you* are thumping, then *everyone* is having a good time. The reverse is also true.

Use your power wisely, as the gift of your emotional balance, passion and energy can knock those who are less connected off their feet!

Wunjo

Manni is the most easily distracted of gods, pulling the moon around the heavens. Wunjo is the energy of contentment and feeling good. Together, they bring comfort and safety to your emotions. Trust your 'Spidey sense', as this is Wunjo guiding you down paths that lead to being chilled out and calm.

Trust is part of that path. When you trust someone, you get to connect with them on a deep level. In any event, you can tap into others' energies and desires and read what they are feeling. This may not be conscious on your part. And when that energy disrupts your state of calm, there may be explosions.

Wherever you are, make sure that you aim for calmness and contentment. When you do so, you'll be magnetic and potent. When you're out of that alignment, those who knocked you out of it had better run for cover.

Hagalaz

Emotional fall-out is an energy that fills your world when Manni energy attracts Hagalaz vibes. With Hagalaz as your Manni rune, look to the relationships, emotional stimulation and experiences you have in your life, and then you'll be able to take yourself back to the emotional footprint in your soul and fill yourself with power, even though at times you may feel a long way from that.

How do you do it? Whatever situations arise, you're able to use your Hagalaz energy to find the frequency, the learning, that is needed. Especially if the situation is highly emotionally charged. This usually won't apply in the middle of the situation, though, as you'll probably want to bring down hellfire on the entire area instead. Afterwards is when you can apply your power and gain results. Your Hagalaz energy will help you survey what has gone on and make something good from it.

Nauthiz

The energy of Nauthiz and Manni brings several needs to your world. Emotions and actions may need to be simultaneous. Feeling may flow naturally into action, like a hunter of old sighting their prey and raising their bow, or you pressing that app automatically when you open your phone. You have the ability to read situations and respond to them in ways that others may find abrupt or hasty, but you're able to make the intuitive leaps that are needed.

71

Using your ability to disregard all but the most necessary tasks will bring you success, but also annoy people. You know what is needed, and their thoughts on the matter aren't that relevant. This energy will serve you well in fast-moving environments or situations that require lots of fast adaption. You know where energy needs to flow to get the job done.

Trust your ability to get things done in specific or unconventional ways, as your energy will have spotted something your brain has not.

Isaz

Isaz and Manni bring the ability for you to be super single-minded and focused, with your emotions flowing along one set path, much like a glacier pushing all before it. How you use this focus and directness is up to you, but when you choose to release your emotions, you can move mountains.

Of course, this is super useful when it comes to doing one job or task and not so useful when jumping from task to task.

Also, be aware that Isaz is the rune of ice, and with it as your Manni rune, you may find it all too easy to freeze people out, or indeed freeze them in, especially if you feel they are treating you badly or not behaving the way you expect them to. When you are angry, you can crush people with your stare.

Your cutting wit and temper may also be too sharp sometimes. Remember revenge is deffo not a dish served warm, right?

Jera

Jera is a rune of cycles and harvests, and when it is your Manni rune, your emotional power is fuelled by the seasons around you, the growth, the warm soil and wet earth, the sun, sky and river.

Peaking and dipping as nature's power ebbs and flows is how you express yourself in the world, maybe even feeling the pull of Manni too. Your emotions will flow in cycles – maybe lunar, maybe solar, maybe seasonal.

Becoming aware of your cyclic emotional flow and patterns will bring you increased power and mastery over yourself. Check in with your mind and body as to how you are feeling. Magic flows where your emotions pulse. The cycles of sowing, growing, harvest and rest will dictate where your emotional powers manifest. Pay attention, as this is where your superpowers sit.

Check your personal cycles, daily cycles and monthly cycles. Discover when your emotional power is at its greatest to get the harvest you want.

Eihwaz

With Eihwaz as your Manni rune, emotional power is part of your Runic Star Path. The ability to store and hold the emotive energy of any situation and take it to another time and place is not to be sniffed at.

Emotional stability is something you can choose to cultivate in yourself. And you can bring that energy to those around you just by your presence.

There is another aspect of Eihwaz that can be useful too, that of astral travelling or otherwise connecting with the ethereal realms of the universe. The combination of Manni and Eihwaz will help you, should you choose to build a connection to those around you just by your presence. This is especially useful when tensions or other emotions are high. Moving energy and breaking states and patterns may well be a superpower that you can harness in your life. Or even bringing emotive energy into art and creativity. Look to the emotional energy you can move around.

Peroth

Luck and passion are energies that Peroth brings to your Runic Star Path. With Manni guiding your emotional energy through the lens of Peroth, you have great potential to excel.

You will benefit from trusting your intuition, your emotions and that little twinge in your gut. Spend some time learning how your intuition manifests, as when you are connected to this aspect of yourself, your energy can begin to flow towards the goals you have in life with renewed vigour.

Trust your emotions in all situations, as creativity, luck and fortune will come to you through them. They may not be feelings that others can relate to, but that's not important. With Peroth as your Manni rune, they are definitely powerful for you, so take note of them, trust them and above all act on them. When you act on them, they will bring you opportunity, creativity and luck.

Algiz

Algiz is the rune of edges, barriers and crossing those barriers. What does this mean when it's your Manni rune? You've heard the saying 'How you let people treat you trains them how to treat you'? Well, now you have. Algiz as your Manni rune wants you to have standards for your emotional connections and relationships. It wants you to set boundaries.

Have those standards, set those boundaries. If a person isn't respectful, then they don't deserve your energy or attention. It's as simple as that.

Another expression of your emotional energetic power is to explore the feelings and emotions that are fringe, on the edge, and to challenge accepted wisdom. Go beyond it. Where are the edges that you require for your emotional power to flourish?

With your connection to the other side of the line being so potent, you may also find that stepping over the edge of 'normal' human experience is super easy for you. And why not?

Sowolio

When Sowolio is your Manni rune, your emotions are your guide on your Runic Star Path. When a question comes up in life, don't ask your brain, as your brain will give you some well-reasoned answer, ask your heart, as your heart will guide you better than anything else. This is the magic of Sowolio and Manni.

So, trust your emotions, your feelings and sensations, as you will tend to make the right choices if you go with them. If you go with cold, hard logic, well, yes, it may be 'right', but where's the fun? If you follow your emotions, Sowolio will take you into the adventures that your heart and soul crave.

Bear in mind that with this as your Manni rune, others may find that your ability to read and understand their emotions borders on the supernatural. That is because you are! Use your supernatural emotional knowledge with skill and discernment to grasp victory in life.

Tiwaz

Tiwaz is the rune of action, beliefs and values. Not what you associate with the Moon? Think again. Tiwaz as a Manni rune is passionate and direct, the essence of the warrior poet. Who better to sing epic verse in the mead hall and inspire feats of bravery and honour?

Your focused and honourable approach may not win you friends, but people will speak of you with respect, even awe.

Being a paragon to those around you won't be a conscious choice, but if not realized, this energy will manifest in ways that are detrimental to your evolution, possibly including following someone else's ideals rather than your own. This will hurt, in many and varied ways.

Instead, double down on your passions and your artistic self. Take action in ways that make you feel good. Be proud of yourself. People who lead from the front and are not afraid of hard decisions are few and far between. And you can do this with a song on your lips.

Berkanan

With Berkanan as your Manni rune, you are gifted with the emotional energy of renewal and regeneration. This will offer you solace when things get hard and an extra boost when things are good.

Use this energy to ensure that the storms of life pass you by, as far as possible. Like the bear in winter, you know when to back off and rest if your energy is low. You know how to recover. The birch is the first tree to reappear when the forest has burned down, the first to grow in damaged soil, the first pulse of life in a scorched land. Could finding the wins in situations that seem bleak be one of your skills?

Your energy of birch and bear will serve you when life gets hard, or hectic, or overwhelming. You will instinctively know when to retreat to a 'cave', and when you emerge, your energy will pulse into the world with unparalleled vigour. You have the power to regrow and regenerate after every setback or storm.

Ehwaz

Manni's energy at the time of your birth brings the vibration of Ehwaz, the horse. A horse runs in a herd, and as a human, being part of a team will help you go faster for longer. When you're working and collaborating and moving with others, you're doing what the cosmos breathed into you when you took your first breath.

So, for the best results, utilize the Ehwaz energy of working with a herd of like-minded people. A tribe or team will allow you to more easily access the cosmic frequency that is your

Manni rune. Use the support of others to bolster your mind and body, and support them in turn. It's a two-way street.

Together, a herd survives, and when surrounded by like-minded people, you triumph over everything. Destiny will slide right into your world when you are with your tribe. To achieve fulfilment, don't be an island.

Mannaz

When the soft light of Manni is combined with the rune Mannaz, it brings you energy and power. Emotional energy is Manni's jam. And Mannaz, the human spirit rune, brings that energy in spades.

Manni's influence on your Mannaz vibration brings a powerful connection to the human magic of existence, along with the ability to feel, to have empathy and to take action. A good phrase for this energy is: 'Feel it, do it.'

For you, action is an extension of your felt experience. Perhaps others have called you impulsive? Well, so was Joan of Arc. Mannaz energy is that of the human spirit and the human ability to adapt, overcome and push forward. This vibration fuels your emotional purpose, so you can adapt your emotional energy to fit the situation or environment you find yourself in. It may take some practice, but once you allow that energy to flow, you'll find it's your superpower.

Laguz

Manni's energy at the time of your birth brings the vibration of the rune Laguz, the lake or water. I'm not going to lie, Manni and Laguz bring all the emotions, but also all the healing. You may find your world has a strong emotional undercurrent, with energies flowing to and from your heart.

Because of the watery energy flowing around you, radiance is your key. You will glimmer like light in water, physically and/or energetically. This makes you very attractive to people who need your brand of awesome.

So, Manni and Laguz energy attracts love and devotion, but it's healing and soothing too. The healing can manifest in all kinds of ways. You may be a gifted healer, and if you want to dive into this, look first to water-based or flowing modalities.

In general, think dance, flow and creative processes. All life comes from the ocean and nothing exists without water. Allow life to flow around you and in turn flow around life to find your emotional path.

Ingwaz

Ingwaz is the stereotypical hero, in your case tempered with the softness and liquid-like nature of Manni. Use this heroic energy to flow with the influences around you and adapt to them. Redirect, don't confront. Respond, don't react. The combination of Ingwaz and Manni make for a Muhammad Ali-type energy. 'Float like a butterfly, sting like a bee.' Twenty-one punches dodged has nothing on you.

If someone does sling muck at you or tries to get into an argument with you, when you're channelling this combination of Manni and Ingwaz power, you have already risen above it and left them in your dust. Their wasted energy will only serve to highlight your power.

When you lead, others will follow – not through 'death and glory' energy, but 'Let's get this job done and then the first beer is on me.' Whatever you wish to achieve in life, let your inspirational superpowers flow, as they will lead you to victory.

Othala

When emotional power is vibrating through the rune of Othala in your birth chart, your emotional energy is strengthened and empowered by experiencing life in a place where you feel secure. Othala brings the vibration of security and community, and this energy resonates most strongly when you work with people you value and are in turn valued by.

Enhance your emotional stability and strength by leaning back into the energies of your family and friends. You can even make yourself a nexus of those energies, the point through which all interaction and stimulation flow in a group of people. This will reward you by making your energy a safe space for you to interact with others in.

With this safe energy, others will unconsciously be drawn to you, as you provide the stability and security they crave. And so you in turn can build a supportive community around yourself and enjoy the feeling of security.

Dagaz

Dagaz is the initiator, and when this is your Manni rune, you can use your connection with your emotions and those around you to aid in the initiation of change. Yours. Theirs. Anyone's. You can use your words and/or magic to powerful effect by helping others change their opinions, feelings and entrenched ideas.

This magic is best used softly, just as the day dawns and sets with gentle poise and power. Hard edges of change can disrupt others' energy pathways.

Don't be too hard on yourself, either. I know it's your default. Dagaz sees all the options, but you only need to take one, not and *never* all of them. When you make a decision, stick to it and let your energy flow that way. Ride the wave, no matter how many shiny things present themselves to distract you. Don't get thrown by ideas of what could be. Stay the course and you will find fulfilment.

Know yourself better
through the astrological
and cosmological vibration
of your Runic Star Path.

JORD RUNE – YOUR PRACTICAL PURPOSE

Your Jord rune is a practical Runic Star Path for you to follow. I call this energy your practical purpose. It leans into the practical aspects of your life, those areas where you can make sure things work how you want them to work.

Let's look at how your Jord rune reveals ways to go about it.

Fehu

Fehu, the energy of abundance. When this is your Jord rune, this is an abundance of whatever you choose – smiles, euros, gold, food, babies.... You're supremely placed to use both the Momma Goddess energy of the Earth and the warm glow of Sunna to ensure there is plenty for all your kin. Creating abundance in all its forms will be a practical and focused life path for you to follow.

What do you get when the sun shines on the fertile Earth? Harvest. You bring that energy to projects and endeavours. Your ability to make even the most barren space produce the resources needed is your superpower. Just let it happen. If you try too hard... well, you know what they say about perfect ponytails. Simply trust your superpower to bring projects, courses or whatever it is you are working on to fruition.

Uruz

With Uruz as your Jord rune, the momma energy of Jord is giving you the power of Uruz – the power, the strength, the ability to withstand all that is thrown at you.

Uruz is strength – gym strength as well as strength of will. Being able to bring your strength, however it manifests, to a situation is how you achieve victory. When you let your powers flow, nothing and no one can stand in your way. Don't play polite with this energy, or it will wander off into the mists, leaving you with a tame milk cow, rather than a primal ox with horns that can destroy a village. Own your ability to be strong and resilient. People might as well get used to the fact that you can crush them energetically with your will.

Being super strong can exhaust you, of course. So make sure you take time to be alone to recharge your batteries.

Thurizaz

With Thurizaz as your Jord rune, your practical purpose is, simply put, to get straight to the point. You want more?

The point of the thorn is your watchword here. Make things as simple as possible, as uncomplicated as possible and as direct as possible. If you remove complexity and confusion from your world, your life will be better for it. As will the lives of those around you. Looking for the direct path or direction is going to make you feel and act with more power and verve. Keeping it simple and straightforward will make your life and plans much more enjoyable and efficient. Efficient is good, right?

While working on a project, make sure that there is a clear focus and intent. Without that, you are likely to feel lost and undervalued. The same goes for doing magical things – make sure that you are focused. If not, your powerful gaze will lose its energy trying to do everything.

Ansuz

Ansuz is the energy of speech and inspiration – god voice energy. In Old English the Ansuz rune was Os, meaning 'god'. With this as your Jord rune, your practical purpose will be tied up neatly with your ability to communicate clearly and get your point across.

Ansuz energy will also allow you to find inspiration in the most mundane things. And to inspire even the gloomiest energies – and people.

Your own inspiration will come from things that are tied with your passions and focus and, as this is your Earth rune, perhaps from the rise and fall of the oceans, from the mountains and the woodlands. So you can bring your innate ability to be inspired and communicate to your everyday experience of life, wherever you happen to be.

In fact, your greatest ally is your ability to talk yourself into and out of any situation, inspiring emotions in others as you go.

Raido

With Raido, the rune of adventure and exploration, as your Jord rune, your practical purpose is tied with adventure. Do you find it hard to stay in one place for long? Why are you even there anyway, when there's something on the other side of the hill — and wait, is that another hill?

Given the chance, your basic energy will happily flow into an adventure, any adventure, be it exploring the unknown or making mundane tasks for your team exciting. The military life may call you. So will any challenge. For you, seeing new places may make any challenge worthwhile.

Picture the van-life experience, or overlanding, or even the long highway to somewhere, anywhere. Doesn't that make you feel good? When you experience life as an adventure, you release all the power within you.

So, always choose adventure. That way you'll never be bored and your passions will flow with purpose and power.

Kenaz

Kenaz is the rune of light, the torch in the darkness, the flame chasing away the fear. As Jord, the mother goddess, is rooting this power into you, whatever you do, do it with the intent of bringing light and knowledge to the world.

In Old English, the *cunninga* was the cunning woman, the witch. The cunning helm became the crown of the cunning man, the king. Kenaz is the root energy of both these archetypes. So, use your connection to yourself and your connection to the world to bring knowledge and light to all those you want to illuminate. Remember, part of the wisdom of shining the light is choosing where you point it. It can be laser focused or shining over everyone like the sun. You choose.

Whatever you choose, you have the power to chase darkness away, or let it in and direct it as you wish. That's your choice too.

Gebo

Practically, with Gebo as your guide, you have the gift of the gift, the ability to make sure that your needs are met by making sure that others' needs are met. The Runic Star Path that Gebo leads you down is one of feeling into where you can meet others' needs and where they can meet yours. Not a tit-for-tat kind of energy, more that how you choose to gift your energy, whether that be in the form of money, work, listening or something else, will determine the energetic response.

Keep in mind that gifting makes a twist in the *Wyrd*, the web of fate, and by giving your energy, you link yourself with that of the receiver. Your personal vibration will bring the receiver slightly more into alignment with your energy. So, part of your practical purpose is levelling up people with your innate power.

Wunjo

Wunjo is the essence of contentment, of bliss. You know that feeling of yumminess when everything is as it should be, you are warm and cosy and the drink is just right, and no one will bother you? That is Wunjo.

With Wunjo as your Jord rune, you're working towards that energy, working to make yourself content. Bringing that energy to those around you is your superpower. You can put people at ease in any situation and utilize this skill any way you want, be it talking someone round or calming someone down. Whatever you choose to do, your ability to make people feel loved and content will flow easily from you.

Wunjo energy also recharges you when you are depleted. You draw your power from being warm and fuzzy and from making sure the resources are in place to be warm and fuzzy in the future. This practical element of Wunjo is great when it comes to making your way in the world.

Hagalaz

When Jord brings the Runic Star Path of Hagalaz to you, look to what your passion pulls you to do, as your practical purpose is really tied with your passion. With Hagalaz energy, you may well find yourself in a role that sorts out problems. Just remember that a scorched earth approach is not the way forward for all the problems in the world!

Remember that hail hurts when it falls, and when your power to change things really starts flowing, then those in the way may get crushed. It may well be their own fault, but....

The ability to thrive and excel when everything around you is changing and growing is part of your path. Perhaps high-stress environments are your jam? Emergency workers or recovery teams? Or planning for rebuilding after everything has changed.

This innate urge to let things go and restart after learning the lessons will serve you well in life. Just don't set fire to everything, okay?

Nauthiz

Nauthiz is the rune of need, of the pulse to survive. When it is your Jord rune, this energy flows through you and helps you connect to those around you. This is where your practical purpose and skills will reside.

Jord, the Earth, wants you to be aware of what needs to be done, felt and spoken. Meeting this need will give you purpose and drive.

This isn't to say that you are a saviour to others, or a slave to their needs, though at times the needs of others may supersede your own, or indeed yours may supersede theirs. This is an important distinction to make, because if you're tapped out, you'll burn out. Make sure the needs you attempt to meet are ones that fill you up, not tear you down. This is a vital lesson for you, and the earlier you learn it, the better. But by giving your energy to the needs you wish to meet, you will find infinite power and fulfilment.

Isaz

Isaz as your Jord rune gives you the potential for endless patience and huge power – the power to grind down even the most stubborn of wills. Ever been called stubborn yourself? Well, this is where that comes from. You're as stubborn as an ice floe.

Looking to where you're doing you is the way forward. Take note of this, as it will be somewhere you could excel in the world. And remember that distracting others with your wit, glamour and beauty while getting the job done is deffo a superpower. Yours.

Practically, look to where you can maximize this ability to skate over obstacles or distract naysayers while getting your needs met in the most potent way possible – the way that works best for you. While you're doing this, don't worry about being abrasive. The results will speak for themselves. Glacial valleys are the most fertile in the world.

Jera

 Your practical purpose is wrapped around the rune of Jera, the rune of harvest and rewards. Everyone likes getting rewards. Why is this special for you?

Well, the energy of Jera hinges on doing the work to get the best harvest. You give nothing, you get nothing, right? Making sure that the right things are done at the right time to get the required result is a manifestation of Jera energy. And speaking of manifesting, you are an expert manifester.

How do you do it? You manifest though the energetic lens of making sure everything is in place to bring about the manifestation. Others may miss steps, but you'll make sure they're all completed, even though you may not consciously think about it.

Natural cycles are your friend here. Doing winter work at the height of summer won't produce the best results. Trust your nature to guide you as to when to plant and when to enjoy the harvest.

Eihwaz

Eihwaz as a Jord rune brings the power to store and control energy, and this is part of your practical purpose and power in life. Be it practically with electrics or fire, or in more esoteric ways like energy healing or things of an oracular nature, this is an area in which you will excel.

The path of practical energy storage is one of choosing to be where the energy you want exists, be it in the form of people, animals or work. Choose the environments where you can fill up on the energy you need. Then you can take that energy to other places, people and environments.

Environments are important to you. Focus on the feeling of any environment that you find yourself in. That way you can choose whether to pick up the energies or not.

Talismans or crystals may aid you in this. But you're the one with the power.

Peroth

Jord loves things to be practical and applicable and grounded in the Earth. The creativity energy that Peroth brings is very Jord, a very practical pathway. Working in a creative environment would be inspiring for you and a powerful way of expressing yourself and fulfilling your practical purpose.

The luck of Peroth is a different feeling. It flows. But trust your instincts and that little feeling. Because it's the energy of the universe giving you a little hint.

The luck you act on may not be 'good' luck. It may not feel good at the time, or indeed for 20 years. In itself, luck isn't good or bad, it's just the energy of the fates. The magic for you is working where you can improve the situations you find yourself in by acting on your luck. Your Runic Star Path is one where you can create opportunities for yourself. So, trust yourself. Trust your luck. For opportunities can lead to victory.

Algiz

Algiz brings a complex energy to your Runic Star Path. (I'm sure you enjoyed reading that.) It adds edges to your experience and the ability to adapt and overcome, Bear Grylls style, but hopefully without drinking urine.

Your ability to walk the edges of life, to see where one thing starts and another ends, is a power that is both useful and a pain. Unless you're careful, you can fall into the unknown. This is okay, though, as you can adapt to new situations and extend your edges to cope with new experiences.

You can use your ability to find edges and build barriers when working with others too. Especially those who need, or try to leach, your capable energy.

Don't be afraid to adapt your thinking to new situations, as your Jord energy really wants you to flow into victory through expanding experiences. This may be by working in fields where the ability to adapt while maintaining strong boundaries is required. Like the emergency services or crisis management.

Sowolio

When your practical purpose is linked with Sowolio, the rune of the sun, navigation and guidance are the energies you have to work with. Even if you don't wish it, people will be energetically drawn to follow your guidance, your example, your path.

Feel into the ways you can use this to achieve your goals in life. Practically, you'll probably find that situations where people are being foolish, or inefficient with energy, especially yours, will cause you to lose your cool. A cool that is probably a little too close to being lost in any event.

More positively, you are a leader, an inspirer, a thought leader. Let your art, creativity and passion lead you into a happy and creative life. One that sees your light showing the way. This urge to lead, to inspire, will serve you. Just be aware that leading from the front, while being your jam, may open you up to attack, perhaps from behind. Keep your cool, okay?

Tiwaz

Tiwaz as your Jord rune brings a powerful energy of action based on values and beliefs. It brings that 'Less talking, more doing' feeling to life. Your energy wants to be doing things, either with your mind or with your body. Choosing to act will always have a favourable feeling for you. And constant meetings? They'll probably have you climbing the walls!

Look to ways you can choose action over inaction. Perhaps you're a great innovator, or inventor, or entrepreneur. Or your world is improved in some way through the energy of being first. However you choose to express this aspect of yourself, know that your creativity and passion will become clearer and more focused as you take action.

Even if you're plagued by anxiety or doubt, know that moving towards a goal that is in alignment with your values and beliefs will always make life better for you.

Berkanan

When your Jord rune is Berkanan, the energies of the birch and the bear are coming to you through the Earth Mother. Jord is grounded, relaxed, and can take all that we throw at her and still love us. Berkanan has the power to withstand the storm, the fire and the winter, not through toughing it out, but through getting underground and staying there. What does this mean in practical terms?

Your practical purpose is to make sure you and those you care about aren't at risk when disaster strikes. Not through hiding, but by being resourced – energetically, emotionally, physically and practically. The bear has energy stores in its fat. The birch has sweet sap and fertile seeds, as well as the ability to turn toxicity into nourishment thanks to the mycelium that live on its roots.

Trust your ability to weather the firestorm by getting out of the way, and then, when it's over, to heal and transform the energy around you.

Ehwaz

Jord, the Earth, is grounded and relaxed, and Ehwaz, horse energy, excels at working with others. So, when Ehwaz is your Jord rune and the proverbial hits the fan, which it inevitably will, you know you've got this.

What you bring to the table is the reassurance of being firmly grounded in the real. Your companionship and kindness are super comforting to those around you and, like a horse, you will run long and hard, and always with purpose. For example, a drive for driving's sake is not for you, but hitting that store in the next city or perhaps going to see some awesome trees will make it worthwhile.

In fact, you have the ability to make even the most mystical feel practical. This may aggravate more esoteric people. But don't worry. The woollier-thinking people you love will get where they are going. And because of you they'll have fuel in the car, a bug-out bag in the boot and probably snacks in the glove box too.

Mannaz

Your practical purpose is what grounds you in the world, and in your case it is linked with Mannaz, the rune of the human spirit. So, should you wish, you can move your spirit in practical ways – ways that open up energetic pathways to help yourself and others through the power that you bring.

This is likely to be structured power. Mannaz loves structure. Take care not to get stuck in rigid ways of thinking, though. Structure is great, but flowing around, through and in it is where your real power can be found.

You have the ability to manifest physical rewards for yourself if you choose to make it so, but don't let that be the main focus of your energy.

People will be drawn to you for your ability to be practical and stable. Let them come, as you will grow because of it. And so will they.

Laguz

With Laguz as your Jord rune, the Great Momma is calling you, telling you that you have depths to explore, power to draw on when needed, and energy and mystery to bring to the lives of those around you.

When all around you are depleted, lost or out of their depth, you have the energetic vibration to find connection, grounding and a way forward in even the most unpredictable of circumstances.

Bringing healing, or life itself, is also one of your practical gifts. The healing doesn't have to be in the form of bandages or herbs. The mere vibration of your presence can help others to shift their perspective, change their behaviour and heal their wounds, washing away all the negative and leaving just clarity behind.

Trust your depths, even if you don't actually know how deep you go, and know that anyone making waves for you will reap the tsunami.

Ingwaz

Jord is the Great Momma of Midgard and you are the hero, Ingwaz. When you're seen for the amazingness that you are, when people are awed by your sheer brilliance, you're expressing what the cosmos breathed into you when you took your first breath.

Ingwaz is the stereotypical hero, and your hero archetype is rooted firmly in the rock and earth of the Great Momma, so you can literally crush your naysayers in order to be seen in your radiant glory.

Your ability to stand out from the crowd will fuel your sense of correctness, your passions and your sense of self. Don't be afraid to take the path that makes others question you and to carry on regardless. That's what heroes do.

When you do the things that make you happy, people will look at you in awe and speak of you in hushed tones. Your ability to be seen and to see the hero's path before you is what makes you the powerful human that you are.

Othala

The Great Momma Jord is super practical and likes to get stuff done. She brings you Othala energy to get that stuff done so that those around you are supported and safe. That will bring you support and stability too.

With this vibration comes freedom, which stimulates your creativity. When you're with people you trust and in a place where you feel secure, you'll find it easy to create, work or otherwise be awesome. Working from home may be the best thing that has ever happened to you.

Making sure all around you are feeling free and uninhibited will help you really get your life mission going. Because as their energy rises, yours reaches new heights. However, free and uninhibited people can be really annoying, especially when living and working together. So make sure there are some boundaries in place.

Make your home your super-comfortable fortress and lean into your community too, and you will be both powerful and productive.

Dagaz

 Dagaz is the rune of initiation, and with this as your Jord rune, your practical purpose is to initiate yourself and those who are drawn to you.

Initiation doesn't have to be walking for 40 days across a desert or hanging from a tree. It can be the soft questioning of long-held beliefs, the permission slip to be different. Your heroic purpose is to softly – or harshly, as you decide – initiate yourself and others into new paradigms of life and experience.

Dagaz energy will help you change minds, opinions and beliefs to aid the expansion of your family and the collective. This is a superpower that you can use however you like in your world.

Utilizing this skill will help you in work, life and love, as people will be attracted to you when they need to be initiated. The skill here lies in keeping yourself fulfilled and happy and not being constantly surrounded by people sucking your energy to 'up-level' themselves. Strong boundaries will bring you joy.

Chapter 6

Exploring Runic Resonance

The Norns provide us with energy and direction as we emerge into the world. They put things on our path that we can act on to create the world we desire. Some things are hard to get, but others are as easy as breathing. This is how we know we are on a path that will fulfil us. If we are constantly struggling, then we aren't picking up what the universe is putting down.

Or, and here's the kicker, we've not told the Norns what we want in a language that they can understand.

SPEAKING TO THE NORNS

Our Runic Star Path is the language of the Norns. It's how they speak to us and through us, and how we can speak to them. And the language of the universe is the language of cause and effect. When we do something, something else happens in response.

Knowing this gives us real power. You know when you order a burger from that place down the road, you get a good burger, but the pizza isn't so good and you don't like it. So you don't order it. That way, you get the good burger, right?

It's the same with the universe and the Norns. You speak to them in a way they understand and you don't ask for what you don't want and you do ask for what you do want. Otherwise you'll just get the default energies that are simply lying around. Like the rubbish pizza.

This is where we can delve into your Runic Star Path. The runic energies there are a key, a lexicon, a Rosetta stone to your soul. To what you really want.

So, more lists, but this time lists of associations, with the aim of providing more information on the energies of the runes so you can deepen your connection to them and experiment with expressing your wishes and bringing the energies you want into your life.

These associations are:

+ Dates: The dates the rune energy appears in the calendar.

+ Degrees: The degrees of the rune on the birth chart.

✦ Totems: Animism energies that are like the runic energy.

✦ Colours: Colours that resonate with the rune.

✦ Crystals: Crystals that work well with the rune.

✦ Connection frequency: The brainwave frequency of the rune.

✦ Transmission frequency: The musical frequency of the rune.

✦ Element: The element associated with the rune.

✦ Ruler: The god/goddess/planet that has influence over the rune (more on this in Chapter 9).

✦ Keywords: Words to help you connect to the rune.

You can get as creative with these as you wish, perhaps making altarpieces, or jewellery, or soundscapes for each rune. If you want to connect to Fehu, perhaps with a crystal, then iron pyrite is a great way to do so. Or how about charging water to bring Fehu energy into your cup of tea in the morning? You can play it the G# note with the intention of bringing Fehu energy into the water. And then place the teapot on a Fehu rune.

Perhaps colours are your bag? They aren't mine – I'm colour-blind. But I can say that writing Fehu on a gold card will bring that energy in. And you can charge it in your sleep using the brainwave pattern at 10 Hz (Alpha).

To build an altar to a rune you can also use totems of the gods who have influence over that rune. Freya, for instance, again for Fehu.

Really allow yourself to get to know each rune, remembering that these are my interpretations, and as you start to work and weave with them, you may create and sense your own, and that's totally okay too. I want you to work, and play, with the tools that work best for you. I've got a friend who is a world-class cellist, and he connects to the runes through music.

And, as we love to see how we can make connections with others, there is a runic compatibility element here too. This is great for exploring your relationships with others. I've provided Sunna rune interactions here, but this isn't the be-all and end-all of relationship building, so look more deeply into how the energies work together. A Fehu Sunna energy person will probably get on well with a Manni Eihwaz person, as the controlled emotions in Manni help direct the raw power in Fehu. So they won't end up spending all the resources on kittens.

The resonance of the
runes flows from the
world tree at the galactic
centre. This is the source
of runic frequencies.

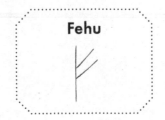

Fehu

- ✦ Dates: 21 June–7 July (from midday to midday)

- ✦ Degrees: 0–15 degrees Cancer

- ✦ Totems: Cow, grain

- ✦ Colours: Gold

- ✦ Crystals: Iron pyrite

- ✦ Connection frequency: 10 Hz (Alpha)

- ✦ Transmission frequency: 210.42 Hz (G#)

- ✦ Element: Fire

- ✦ Ruler: Freya (Venus)

- ✦ Keywords: Wealth, abundance, reputation

Runic compatibility

✓ Fehu works well with Wunjo and Berkanan. Relationships between them will be abundant and creative. Fehu brings abundance to Wunjo's comfort, and warmth to Berkanan's cave.

✗ Fehu does not work well with Eihwaz, as one grows and the other controls.

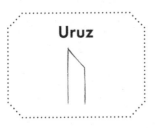

Uruz

✦ Dates: 7–23 July (from midday to midday)

✦ Degrees: 16–30 degrees Cancer

✦ Totems: Ox

✦ Colours: Dirt brown, red ochre

✦ Crystals: Iron

✦ Connection frequency: 10 Hz (Alpha)

✦ Transmission frequency: 126.22 Hz (B)

✦ Element: Earth

✦ Ruler: Sunna (the Sun)

✦ Keywords: Strength, power, stubbornness

Runic compatibility

✓ Uruz gets on best with Hagalaz and Ehwaz. The power and endurance of Uruz bring the stability Hagalaz lacks, and Ehwaz and Uruz rock each other's worlds through the power Uruz brings to the valued companionship.

✗ Uruz isn't a fan of Peroth — this less grounded rune jars Uruz's solidity.

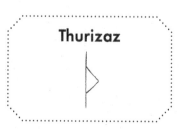

Thurizaz

✦ Dates: 23 July–7 August (from midday to midday)

✦ Degrees: 0–15 degrees Leo

✦ Totems: Thorn, spear

✦ Colours: Mahogany

✦ Crystals: Garnet

✦ Connection frequency: 10 Hz (Alpha)

✦ Transmission frequency: 126.22 Hz (B)

✦ Element: Water

✦ Ruler: Thor (Jupiter)

✦ Keywords: Focus, cutting, sharpness

Runic compatibility

✓ Thurizaz is a supporter rune, providing focus and movement to others. Its direction and focus lift Nauthiz up, and Nauthiz, by its very nature, is magnetic to Thurizaz. Mannaz and Thurizaz also get on, through the energizing nature of Thurizaz and Mannaz's power of sub-state energy. They do awesome things together.

✗ Thurizaz and Algiz don't get on, as Thurizaz is movement and energy, whereas Algiz is static and likes an edge, a boundary. The still and contemplative Algiz gets wound up by Thurizaz's penetrating nature.

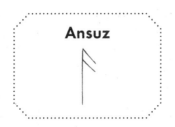

Ansuz

✦ Dates: 7–23 August (from midday to midday)

✦ Degrees: 16–30 degrees Leo

✦ Totems: The mouth, words

✦ Colours: Sky blue

✦ Crystals: Aquamarine

✦ Connection frequency: 10 Hz (Alpha)

✦ Transmission frequency: 141.27 Hz (C#)

✦ Element: Air

✦ Ruler: Odin (Mercury)

✦ Keywords: Communication, words, leadership

Runic compatibility

✓ Ansuz is a powerful rune, as it's Odin's favourite. It gets on well with Isaz and Laguz. Isaz is a good match for Ansuz, as each rune loves to tie the other in playful knots of language, light and confusion. Laguz and Ansuz are also a good match, as the words of magic spoken through Ansuz can be used by Laguz to power its healing.

✗ Ansuz does not get on well with Sowolio, as Ansuz is in charge and knows the way, and Sowolio knows that it is right. Who will lead and who will follow?

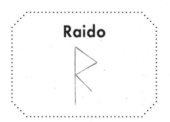

Raido

✦ Dates: 23 August–8 September (from midday to midday)

✦ Degrees: 0–15 degrees Virgo

+ Totems: Hills, the explorer

+ Colours: Grass green

+ Crystals: Moonstone

+ Connection frequency: 10 Hz (Alpha)

+ Transmission frequency: 141.27 Hz (C#)

+ Element: Fire

+ Ruler: Odin (Mercury)

+ Keywords: Adventure, curiosity, mobility

Runic compatibility

✓ Raido works well with Jera and Ingwaz. Relationships here will bring adventure and new discoveries. Raido helps Jera not to be rooted in one place and helps Ingwaz to develop in other directions.

✗ Raido does not work well with Tiwaz, as one wants to walk the path of responsibility, while the other wants to play on the other side of the hill.

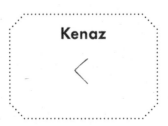

Kenaz

+ Dates: 8–23 September (from midday to midday)

+ Degrees: 16–30 degrees Virgo

+ Totems: Torch, fire

+ Colours: Fire yellow

+ Crystals: Ruby

+ Connection frequency: 9 Hz (Alpha)

+ Transmission frequency: 221.23 Hz (G#)

+ Element: Earth

+ Ruler: Freya (Venus)

+ Keywords: Self-belief, self-discovery, light in the darkness

Runic compatibility

✓ Kenaz brings light and inspiration to Eihwaz, allowing it to grow. Kenaz also brings power and hope to Othala, allowing it to step beyond what is known.

✗ Kenaz does not get on with Berkanan, as Berkanan likes to be hidden, while Kenaz likes to be seen!

Gebo

- Dates: 23 September–8 October (from midday to midday)

- Degrees: 0–15 degrees Libra

- Totems: Gifts, presents, respect

- Colours: Soft blue, off-white

- Crystals: Star ruby

- Connection frequency: 9 Hz (Alpha)

- Transmission frequency: 221.23 Hz (G#)

- Element: Water

- Ruler: Freya (Venus)

- Keywords: Gifts, respect, mutual support

Runic compatibility

✓ Gebo's energy of exchanging gifts to build respect is drawn to Peroth and Dagaz. Peroth's sexy, lucky nature is a natural companion to Gebo, as respect is important with sex and love, and especially with building *Hamingja*. Dagaz and Gebo also get on well, as the changing energies Dagaz brings suit Gebo's flow into new situations and connections.

× Gebo and Ehwaz are troublesome for each other, as the implicit trust Ehwaz brings is more intimate than the demonstrated respect of Gebo. They are not incompatible, but approach the same thing from different directions. And they don't pay attention to each other.

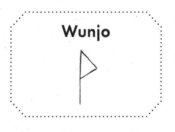

Wunjo

+ Dates: 8–23 October (from midday to midday)

+ Degrees: 16–30 degrees Libra

+ Totems: Fluffy blankets, full wood store

+ Colours: Baby blue

+ Crystals: Golden beryl

+ Connection frequency: 3 Hz (Delta)

+ Transmission frequency: 140.25 Hz (C#)

+ Element: Air

+ Ruler: Myrmir (Pluto)

✦ Keywords: Bliss, contentment, working towards those goals

Runic compatibility

✓ Wunjo is a fairly easy-going energy, once it has sat down on the sofa. Algiz and Fehu are good matches for it – Algiz, as Wunjo likes a blanket fort and Algiz likes making the fort, and Fehu, as it brings abundance for Wunjo to consume, wrapped in a burrito. Fehu likes providing.

✗ Wunjo doesn't get on too well with Mannaz. There are elements of Mannaz in Wunjo, namely getting the snug built, but that's it. Mannaz likes to rush and create and manifest and do human stuff. Wunjo is fine with that, 'Just don't do it near me, I'm chilling out.'

Hagalaz

✦ Dates: 23 October–7 November (from midday to midday)

✦ Degrees: 0–15 degrees Scorpio

✦ Totems: Hail

✦ Colours: Bruise black/blue

+ Crystals: Mookaite

+ Connection frequency: 3 Hz (Delta)

+ Transmission frequency: 140.25 Hz (C#)

+ Element: Fire

+ Ruler: Myrmir (Pluto)

+ Keywords: Change, renewal, surprise

Runic compatibility

✓ While not working well with anyone, Hagalaz tolerates Sowolio and Uruz more than most. Their relationship will be one of change and evolution, whether they like it or not. The combination of Sowolio and Hagalaz brings a potent energy of walking a path to new horizons while the path is collapsing. And Uruz brings strength and endurance, which Hagalaz doesn't have a lot of.

✗ Hagalaz is quite antagonistic in general, but with Laguz the energy is more akin to a pyroclastic burst. Think Eyjafjallajökull (Ey-a-fee-alla-yock-ul) eruption.

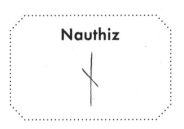

Nauthiz

+ Dates: 7–22 November (from midday to midday)

+ Degrees: 16–30 degrees Scorpio

+ Totems: The heart

+ Colours: Black

+ Crystals: Obsidian

+ Connection frequency: 7 Hz (Alpha)

+ Transmission frequency: 183.53 Hz (F#)

+ Element: Earth

+ Ruler: Thor (Jupiter)

+ Keywords: Need, requirements, basics

Runic compatibility

✓ Nauthiz is a very clingy energy that grasps and holds, but it works well with several runes. The direction and focus of Tiwaz bring it into alignment, and Thurizaz helps Nauthiz focus on what it needs. Both Tiwaz and Thurizaz like to look after others, and Nauthiz needs this.

× Nauthiz and Ingwaz don't work well together, though, as Ingwaz wants to grow and expand, while Nauthiz wants to stay put.

Isaz

+ Dates: 22 November–7 December (from midday to midday)

+ Degrees: 0–15 degrees Sagittarius

+ Totems: Ice

+ Colours: Iceberg blue, crystal clear

+ Crystals: Clear quartz

+ Connection frequency: 7 Hz (Alpha)

+ Transmission frequency: 183.53 Hz (F#)

+ Element: Water

+ Ruler: Thor (Jupiter)

+ Keywords: Glamour, distraction, smoothness

Runic compatibility

✓ Isaz gets on well with Berkanan and Ansuz. With the power of Isaz, Berkanan is able to endure and recover much more quickly, and Ansuz loves the glamour and sparkle Isaz brings, while Isaz loves Ansuz's wordplay.

✗ Isaz and Othala don't get on. Othala wants to build warmth and family connectivity, while Isaz is cold and frozen. Independent even, though more through circumstances than choice. Still, quite the opposite end of the energetic spectrum.

Jera

+ Dates: 7–22 December (from midday to midday)

+ Degrees: 16–30 degrees Sagittarius

+ Totems: The year, harvest

+ Colours: Deep forest green

+ Crystals: Citrine

+ Connection frequency: 6 Hz (Theta)

+ Transmission frequency: 147.85 Hz (D)

✦ Element: Air

✦ Ruler: Loki (Saturn)

✦ Keywords: Harvest, fruitfulness, hard work

Runic compatibility

✓ Jera's powerful harvest energy gels well with Ehwaz and Raido. Jera loves to make sure things happen at the right time, and Ehwaz will move heaven and Earth to make them happen. Raido and Jera work well, as Jera likes to be able to expand its energies to bring more harvest, and Raido likes to see what is on the other side of the hill.

✗ Jera and Dagaz don't get on. Jera likes things to happen on schedule, whereas Dagaz likes things to happen, full stop. With no regard to Jera's plans or timetable.

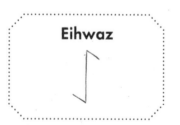

Eihwaz

✦ Dates: 22 December–6 January (from midday to midday)

✦ Degrees: 16–30 degrees Capricorn

✦ Totems: Yew tree

✦ Colours: Berry red

✦ Crystals: Selenite

✦ Connection frequency: 6 Hz (Theta)

✦ Transmission frequency: 147.85 Hz (D)

✦ Element: Fire

✦ Ruler: Loki (Saturn)

✦ Keywords: Travelling through dimensions, changing states, holding energy

Runic compatibility

✓ Eihwaz's stabilizing energy works well with Mannaz and Kenaz. Mannaz is a Water rune (for the elements, see Chapter 8), and the combination of Fire and Water is often poor, but Eihwaz is designed to weather the Water, and adds heat to the human spirit, while bringing longevity to the exploration of Kenaz.

✗ Eihwaz doesn't work well with Fehu – while one grows, the other controls.

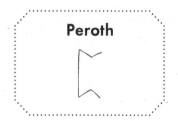

Peroth

+ Dates: 6–20 January (from midday to midday)

+ Degrees: 16–30 degrees Capricorn

+ Totems: Dice cup, womb

+ Colours: Lip pink

+ Crystals: Carnelian

+ Connection frequency: 6 Hz (Theta)

+ Transmission frequency: 147.85 Hz (D)

+ Element: Earth

+ Ruler: Loki (Saturn)

+ Keywords: Luck, sex, chance

Runic compatibility

✓ Laguz and Peroth are a good match, as are Peroth and Gebo. Laguz helps Peroth feel nurtured. Gebo helps Peroth keep its self-respect while being itself.

✗ Peroth and Uruz don't work too well, as Uruz is solid, whereas Peroth is anything but. Rock vs sand.

Algiz

✦ Dates: 20 January–4 February (from midday to midday)

✦ Degrees: 1–15 degrees Aquarius

✦ Totems: Elk antlers, shield wall

✦ Colours: Antler brown

✦ Crystals: Kyanite

✦ Connection frequency: 6 Hz (Theta)

✦ Transmission frequency: 147.85 Hz (D)

✦ Element: Water

✦ Ruler: Loki (Saturn)

✦ Keywords: Boundaries, defence, standards

Runic compatibility

✓ Algiz gets on well with Ingwaz and Wunjo. Ingwaz wants to grow everywhere and Algiz wants to make sure there are some edges and focus, so both are contained and grow with some semblance of order. Wunjo and Algiz work well together too, as Wunjo likes to be cosy in one place and Algiz likes to be able to keep things safe.

× Algiz does not get on so well with Thurizaz, as they tend to work at cross purposes. Thurizaz moves around a lot, whereas Algiz likes to be still and have boundaries.

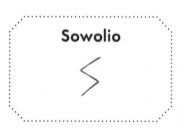

Sowolio

+ Dates: 4–19 February (from midday to midday)

+ Degrees: 16–30 degrees Aquarius

+ Totems: The sun

+ Colours: Bright yellow

+ Crystals: Crystal calcite

+ Connection frequencies: 4 Hz (Theta)

+ Transmission frequencies: 211.44 Hz (G#)

+ Element: Air

+ Ruler: Sunna (the Sun)

+ Keywords: Guidance, pathways, direction

Runic compatibility

✓ Sowolio works well with Hagalaz and Othala. Its energy of guidance is actually compatible with Hagalaz, as a path will be clear once Hagalaz has flattened everything. Its clear direction is also useful to Othala, as Othala likes to know what's going on.

✗ Sowolio and Ansuz are not the best suited of energies, as Ansuz likes to develop new ideas by leaving the path and Sowolio *is* the path.

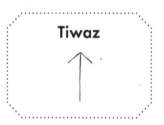

Tiwaz

✦ Dates: 19 February–5 March (from midday to midday)

✦ Degrees: 0–15 degrees Pisces

✦ Totems: Spear, sword, one arm

✦ Colours: Violet

✦ Crystals: Amber

✦ Connection frequency: 4 Hz (Theta)

✦ Transmission frequency: 211.44 Hz (G#)

+ Element: Fire

+ Ruler: Tyr (Mars)

+ Keywords: Honour, leadership, doing the right thing

Runic compatibility

✓ Tiwaz's honour and action energy work well in pacifying Nauthiz and empowering Dagaz. Nauthiz needs direction to satiate its need and hunger, and with the values of Tiwaz, Dagaz flows more confidently into a new state.

✗ Tiwaz does not work well with Raido, as Tiwaz wants to walk the path of responsibility, while Raido wants to play on the other side of the hill.

Berkanan

+ Dates: 5–20 March (from midday to midday)

+ Degrees: 16–30 degrees Pisces

+ Totems: Bear, birch tree

+ Colours: Earth brown

+ Crystals: Epidote

+ Connection frequency: 8 Hz (Alpha)

+ Transmission frequency: 144.72 Hz (D)

+ Element: Earth

+ Ruler: Njord (Neptune)

+ Keywords: Regrowth, resilience, renewal

Runic compatibility

✓ With the energies of Fehu, Berkanan's resilient energy comes to the fore with grace and power. And with the energy of Isaz, Berkanan is able to endure and recover much more quickly than on its own.

✗ Berkanan and Kenaz are not so compatible, as Berkanan wants to leave the cave and Kenaz wants to go deeper into it.

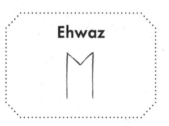

Ehwaz

+ Dates: 20 March–4 April (from midday to midday)

+ Degrees: 0–15 degrees Aries

+ Totems: Horse
+ Colours: Chestnut
+ Crystals: Peridot
+ Connection frequency: 4 Hz (Theta)
+ Transmission frequency: 211.44 Hz (G#)
+ Element: Water
+ Ruler: Tyr (Mars)
+ Keywords: Trust, swiftness, friends

Runic compatibility

✓ Ehwaz, the horse rune, likes to run with a herd of like-minded people. Jera and Uruz have a great relationship with it, as Jera loves to make sure things happen as they are meant to, and Ehwaz moves heaven and Earth to make them happen, while Uruz's slow, stomping moodiness is lifted by Ehwaz's excitement. Much like Eeyore and Tigger.

✗ Ehwaz does not get on well with Gebo. Ehwaz trusts implicitly and Gebo's need to demonstrate trust grates on its sensibilities.

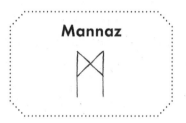

Mannaz

+ Dates: 4–19 April (from midday to midday)

+ Degrees: 16–30 degrees Aries

+ Totems: The human

+ Colours: Blood red

+ Crystals: Carnelian

+ Connection frequency: 9 Hz (Alpha)

+ Transmission frequency: 211.44 Hz (G#)

+ Element: Air

+ Ruler: Freya (Venus)

+ Keywords: Human spirit, human awesomeness, human resourcefulness

Runic compatibility

✓ Mannaz and Eihwaz get on well, as do Mannaz and Thurizaz. Eihwaz brings heat and contained power to the human spirit. Thurizaz brings focus and action.

× Mannaz and Wunjo are not the most compatible of energies. There are parts of Mannaz in Wunjo, mainly doing the work to chill out, but that's it. Mannaz likes to rush and create and manifest and do human stuff, and Wunjo is fine with that, 'Just don't do it near me, I'm chilling out.'

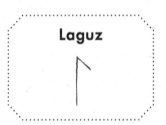

Laguz

✦ Dates: 19 April–20 May (from midday to midday)

✦ Degrees: 0–15 degrees Taurus

✦ Totems: Sea, lake, river

✦ Colours: Aqua blue

✦ Crystals: Clear quartz

✦ Connection frequency: 9 Hz (Alpha)

✦ Transmission frequency: 211.44 Hz (G#)

✦ Element: Fire

✦ Ruler: Freya (Venus)

✦ Keywords: Healing, water, washing away

Runic compatibility

✓ Laguz's healing warmth brings compassion to Ansuz and flows in and around Peroth to allow its unpredictable nature to feel nurtured.

✗ Although fairly easy-going, Laguz does not get on with Hagalaz. Combined, think Vesuvius eruption.

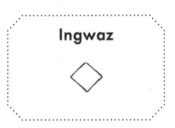

Ingwaz

✦ Dates: 5–20 May (from midday to midday)

✦ Degrees: 16–30 degrees Taurus

✦ Totems: Heroes, seed

✦ Colours: Purple

✦ Crystals: Amethyst

✦ Connection frequency: 10 Hz (Alpha)

✦ Transmission frequency: 141.27 Hz (C#)

✦ Element: Earth

✦ Ruler: Odin (Mercury)

✦ Keywords: Potential, heroic action, self-development

Runic compatibility

✓ Ingwaz works well with Raido, generating adventure-based development, and Algiz, because Algiz sets some necessary limits to Ingwaz's massive expansion.

✗ Ingwaz and Nauthiz will mire themselves in confusion, trying to grow one minute and hunkering down the next.

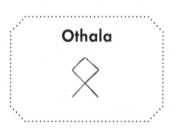

Othala

✦ Dates: 20 May–5 June (from midday to midday)

✦ Degrees: 0–15 degrees Gemini

✦ Totems: Matriarch, home

✦ Colours: Slate grey

✦ Crystals: Carnelian

✦ Connection frequency: 10 Hz (Alpha)

✦ Transmission frequency: 141.27 Hz (C#)

✦ Element: Earth

✦ Ruler: Odin (Mercury)

✦ Keywords: Home, castle, family

Runic compatibility

✓ Othala may feel like an Earth rune, but the watery emotions of kith and kin flow all around it like blood. It works well with Kenaz, as there will be no secrets between these two. Sowolio also gets on well with Othala. The guiding and nurturing energy of this bond makes for a strong, supportive relationship.

✗ Othala and Isaz don't gel well as Isaz is super cold, whereas Othala is like a warm cup of tea. Othala wants things to be nurturing and cosy, while Isaz likes pointed lessons and glamorous misdirection.

Dagaz

✦ Dates: 5–21 June (from midday to midday)

✦ Degrees: 16–30 degrees Gemini

✦ Totems: The day, transitions

✦ Colours: Sunset orange

✦ Crystals: Moss agate

✦ Connection frequency: 10 Hz (Alpha)

✦ Transmission frequency: 141.27 Hz (C#)

✦ Element: Air

✦ Ruler: Sunna (the Sun)

✦ Keywords: Change, transition, new beginnings, the ending of the old

Runic compatibility

✓ Tiwaz and Gebo are good companions for Dagaz. Tiwaz brings direction, honour and values to Dagaz's evolution. Gebo gives it respect and recognition as it changes state.

✗ Dagaz does not get on well with Jera. Jera likes to have measured, ordered change, while Dagaz likes all the change NOW.

Chapter 7

Nornir Runes

This is secret and hidden lore. Or was, but now I'm telling you about it. Why not? You'd like to know how to use runic energy to get lucky, wouldn't you? And the Norns like to help you connect with your destiny, your *Orlog*. So they put energies your way to help you – Nornir runes.

Nornir runes are an energy that is unique to runic astrology. They are a hidden pathway to luck. Luck in the northern tradition is super important. As anyone who took to the iron-grey seas before the compass was invented knew, luck is life. In the frozen darkness of the ancient north, it was a powerful tool. When a cut could easily lead to sepsis and women had children young to ensure they survived childbirth, luck meant the continuation of life. When foamy-necked ships slipped into the whale road, luck would carry them home. When screaming berserkers fought each other at the behest of their king, luck would lead to victory.

Napoleon, the guy who conquered most of Europe in the early 19th century, said he'd rather have a lucky soldier than a good one.

Your Nornir rune shows how your luck manifests and how you can build it and use it most effectively. Your Nornir rune is the energy that first touched you when you emerged from your momma, right down to the very second. The Norns chose this energy to help you achieve greatness.

HOW TO FIND YOUR NORNIR RUNE

- Open up your birth chart.

- On the left of the circle, at 9 o'clock, is your rising sign, your Jord rune.

- Go to the other side of the chart, the other end of that horizon line, at 3 o'clock, and find the astrological sign and the degrees. It'll be something like 7 degrees of Aries.

- Use the 'Degrees of the Runes in the Zodiac' table (pages 42–43) to find your Nornir rune.

*Nornir runes are a path
to accessing your innate
luck and expanding your
capacity for more.*

HOW YOU GET LUCKY

What does this mean for you? Read on for how to take advantage of situations that you are presented with by using the runic energy the Norns have gifted to you.

Fehu

Fehu is the rune of abundance and resources. The three goddesses who spin energy into creation have spun abundance into yours. This energy is pulsing around you, ready for you to access it.

To do so, try spotting recurring patterns in your life, patterns that maybe you don't have the ability to access readily. You do have the ability to access abundance and resources by seeing these patterns and stepping into the whirl of cosmic energy that comes with them. This may be something of a stretch at first, but once you recognize the patterns and learn where the activation points are, you will be able to access all the abundance you want.

Uruz

The energy the Norns brought to your birth is that of strength and power – the strength of mental fortitude and physical power. Your gift from the Norns is to be able to bring unmatched power and strength into any situation you wish. Consciously, with grace.

In situations where nothing else is working, your strength of will, of body, mind and/or spirit will come to the fore and literally push everything else out of the way. Like the mighty aurochs, you are unassailable, immune to attack, damage or attrition. Use your strength to achieve the victory that you wish to achieve, whatever that may be, as you have the strength to make it work for you.

Thurizaz

The energy the Norns brought to your birth is that of focus and power. Thurizaz is the rune of the thunderer Thor, and when you need it, you have the power to bring yourself to a point of focus like a laser or a thorn to get what you want done. Moving towards a goal – a very specific goal – will bring you energetic fulfilment, mentally, physically and/or spiritually.

This frequency manifests in your world when you have a goal or task to work on, and will help you overcome seemingly impossible odds. Tap into it with clear goal-setting. Ignore the distractions and you will succeed, if not with grace, with a primal scream of awesome.

Ansuz

When you popped into this world, the Norns gave you the power of the voice, of communication and of the spoken word. You'll probably find that luck and fortune follow you when you trust your words and your voice. Are you expert at talking yourself into and out of situations? Does your work involve speaking? Or do you find joy in words, language and song? However you use them, words will lead you to unexpected success.

Trust your ability to talk yourself into and out of situations and use words to achieve your goals, whatever these may be. Draw on the power of communication to build your luck and enhance your experience of the world.

Raido

The moment you came into the world, the Norns blessed you with the energy of Raido, the rune of the journey, the adventure. This is where you will find luck and fortune. I'd suggest that the most awesome experiences are going to come your way when you are exploring, travelling, doing something new.

In fact, whatever you are doing, make sure there is an adventure there for you. Do you yearn to find out what happens if you press that button? That's the spirit of adventure pulsing into your life. Channel it in ways that make you feel awesome. Maybe you shouldn't press the button if there's something even better to do. Is another adventure calling you?

Kenaz

The Norns blessed you with the energy and spirit of Kenaz. Kenaz is the light in the darkness, so when everything is bleak and people are feeling down, you have the power to bring hope and light to the situation – empowering hope based on epic insight. It's built into your DNA.

Shining a light on darkness, of whatever form, may not be an obvious path to luck, but it's yours. It makes you especially powerful when working with others, as you can see the truth of a situation regardless of the confusion and darkness around you and illuminate the way forward. Which has to be good, right? Trust your ability to see things for what they really are.

Gebo

At the moment of your birth the Norns spun a web into your Runic Star Path, a web of Gebo energy, the energy of respectful giving to build relationships, alliances and co-operation.

You may well find that when the chips are down, your Nornic Runic Star Path will light up, allowing you to bring people together with respect and grace. It's in hard or stressful times that these strengths will really come to the fore, which may not sound particularly lucky, but it is in these situations where you have the power to resolve matters and achieve the victory you require. So, have confidence and draw on these diplomatic skills whenever the opportunity arises.

Wunjo

The Norns have given you the Runic Star Path of Wunjo as your helper in life, giving you the power to bring relaxation and bliss to the universe. Especially the part that you're in.

As you move through the world, you can access luck by simply allowing your Wunjo Runic Star Path to take you to the places where there are rewards for hard work. Yes, hard work, but then, for every hour you work or toil, Wunjo and the Norns will conspire to reward you with comfort and bliss. You can relax, much like a cat. In fact, 'feline' may well be how people describe you – self-assured, purring, enjoying life. How lucky is that?

Hagalaz

The Norns have decided that Hagalaz is your helper in life. They have given you the ability to take all the learning, all the gold, from a difficult situation, then burn the situation to the ground and rebuild with what you've chosen to salvage. This sounds quite drastic, but it's not. Everything in life is constantly evolving, and you're just better at it than most people.

So, lean into your ability to let entropy take its course and a bad or stale situation fall apart, then pick up the pieces. You can make your fortune from creating something new from what seems like desolation. You can even cause the desolation, if you wish.

Nauthiz

Nauthiz is need, and on the face of it need is not a pleasant sensation, it's the gasp for breath when you've been underwater too long, or the longing for a hug. Yet the Norns have spun your Runic Star Path to bring this energy to you as an asset.

In this context, Nauthiz is the ability to sense lack or need in the cosmos, including your own unconscious needs and those of others. This brings the ability to innovate, adapt and even utilize the spaces others may shy away from to ensure your needs and those of others are met. Being able to discern need is truly a gift. Use it to advantage.

Isaz

The moment you chose to pop into the world, the Norns wove the energy of Isaz into your Runic Star Path. This energy of ice, glitter and glamour is where your luck resides. When you trust what may seem ethereal or otherworldly to those around you, you may gain an unexpected victory.

The misdirection, the sleight of hand (and of mind), the 'rise above it all and skate on' energy that you have in your aura will serve you well. Your luck and fortune will grow when you lean into the confusing ways in which the world can be seen. It may be a hall of mirrors, but you will always see the truth, while others get confused.

Jera

The Norns have spun the energy of Jera into your Runic Star Path. Jera brings the harvest, and with your luck, you will get the harvest – in whatever way that energy chooses to show up.

Jera's energy will constantly attract rewards for hard work – a pay rise for showing up, a bonus for success, a client rebooking because of your good work.

The harvest can also come in the form of an internal harvest, anything from fertility to creativity. Trust your creative instincts to bring whatever project you are working on to fruition. This energy can be used communally as well. When others do what you tell them, they will reap a small portion of your harvest.

Eihwaz

Eihwaz is the yew tree – completely toxic apart from the flesh of the fruit, but able to hold a fire that will smoulder for days. So, the Norns have given you the ability to be well resourced, tough and able to withstand even the most intense heat.

You do this through filtering and controlling the energy that flows through and around you. You get to choose what energy you pick up and what you drop. If it works for you and feels good, then it's your friend. Store it until you're ready to use it. That way you have the power that is needed when it is needed. Especially useful in a crunch.

Peroth

There are two aspects to Peroth: luck and chilling with friends. The translation that I prefer is slightly more carnal. After all, what do a bunch of young men want to do after drinking and fighting all day? You get the idea, right?

When Peroth is gifted by the Norns, whenever you need to be lucky, you will be, especially if you include a sexual component, along the lines of: 'If I get this job done, I'm taking my partner out for dinner.' Luck is your friend, but don't rely on it so much that you don't do the work necessary to make things happen. When you need it, though, it will show up for you.

Algiz

The moment you popped into this world, the Norns blessed your Runic Star Path with the energy of Algiz. This brings the power to transcend borders and edges, to walk the edge of your experience, the edge of your comfort zone. This boundary-setting, edge-walking way is your lucky path. It is by being clear about where you are that you will find power and luck in your world.

The fates also conspire to bring you luck and fortune when you are clear what your 'yes' is and what your 'no' is. Being in your body, certain of where you are in time and space, will bring the victory you crave. Just don't step mindlessly over the edge.

Sowolio

The Norns wove the energy of Sowolio into your Runic Star Path as you emerged into this world. So, when a question comes up in life, don't ask your brain, as that will just give you some well-reasoned answer. Ask your heart, as that will be a better guide than anything else. This is the magic of Sowolio.

So, you'll access your luck if you go with your gut feeling, your instinct. Then Sowolio will guide you to the right choice and to the adventures that your heart and soul crave. Others may find that your ability to read situations borders on the supernatural. For you, reading paths, people and environments simply leads to fortune.

Tiwaz

The energy of Tiwaz, the rune of honour and strong values, was woven into your Runic Star Path when you were born. This energy can be relied on when the going gets tough, and you can use it to build your luck and come through those times.

Roman philosopher and statesman Cicero said, '*Esse quam videri*' – always be true to yourself – and that is so true for you. Your body and spirit will always know the right course of action, so pay attention to them. When the chips are down or you are feeling unsure, trust how you feel. Your sense of honour and your values will always lead you to victory.

Berkanan

The Norns gave you the energy of Berkanan as you emerged into the world. This is the energy of birch and bear, renewal and regeneration. So, like the bear in winter, you know when to retreat and recover when your energy is low. But you're the first to reappear when the forest has burned down. The birch is the first tree to grow in scorched soil.

When life gets hard, or hectic, or overwhelming, draw on this resilient energy. Get in your cave and ride your luck while the storms of life pass you by. When they have passed, you can emerge and grow. You have the power to recover from every setback, storm or challenge.

Ehwaz

The moment you chose to pop into the world, the Norns wove the energy of Ehwaz into your Runic Star Path. Ehwaz is the companion and horse rune, so when you need luck, don't be afraid to make a friend, or to trust a friend. Or preferably several. Step into your power as a trust-builder and friend-maker. Trust others and be trustworthy yourself – dependability will draw more luck to you.

Also, use Ehwaz energy to move away from threats and hazards. A herd moves as one to find safety. You can too. It's a power move for you. You will build luck by reaching out to those you trust and moving when you need to.

Mannaz

The Norns wove the vibration of Mannaz into your Runic Star Path when you were born, and Mannaz is the energy of the human spirit, so this is where your luck and fortune lie. When life gets you down, it's time to lean into your human instincts, into the energy that has driven our species from the primordial swamp to the civilization of today.

This is a spirit of overcoming obstacles and claiming victory. In your DNA, you hold the victories of all your ancestors. When you need this vibration, it will be waiting for you. You're human, after all, aren't you? Call upon it and it will come through in every action you take.

Laguz

Laguz is the water rune, and this energy is the universal solvent – a solvent that can dissolve all toxicity and turn it, eventually, into goodness. Your Runic Star Path gives you the ability to remove the toxic energy around you to allow yourself, and others, to grow, and in your case, build your luck.

Just don't get carried away with washing the toxic away, or it will wash right back into you. Just as with dumping rubbish into the sea, if there's too much of it, it gets brought back to you on the tide. You can process it, but you may not enjoy that very much. Like having a great buffet followed by food poisoning. Unlucky.

Ingwaz

Ingwaz is the energy is of huge potential and heroic deeds. As the Norns have given it to you, draw on your potential to build your luck, especially when you need a little help in life.

Your heroic nature will come to the fore when you are under pressure. Heroism is feeling the fear and doing the thing anyway. You have this explosively epic nature. You can manifest it in dramatic Hollywood-style ways. And/or simply by growing and out-epic-ing and out-awesome-ing those who would drag you down. Know that you have the potential for heroic deeds and huge personal development built into your very energetic patterning. And you can use it however you want.

Othala

The energy that the Norns brought to your Runic Star Path at your birth is that of building community and being part of a collective. This is where your luck and fortune can be found.

Othala, the rune of the hearth and home, is the basis for this. When you are feeling secure in your home and it smells safe and feels safe, you can manifest awesome power. This applies to your community too. That community can be whatever and wherever is right for you – anything from a packed dance floor under the stars to a wooden table with a couple of friends. Just lean into it and know that the more you do, the more luck you will build.

Dagaz

The Norns have brought the energy of Dagaz to your Runic Star Path. So you can change your state – your emotions, energies, persona or physical expression – to meet the needs of a situation or access your luck. Your transformational ability will only get you so far, but your other energetic and personality traits will take you the rest of the way to victory, be that in the form of a kiss, a job, a win or a prize.

Use your shape-shifting ability to make sure that you are where you need to be and with the people you need to be with to get your needs met. And to serve your world how you want to serve.

Chapter 8

Elemental Giants

So, we've looked at the runes and their energies. Now let's look at the other energies that flow around the cosmos and into our lives.

Here we'll look at the elements and how they interact with one another. In the northern tradition, there are four connective elements within the *Wyrd*, which is itself the fifth, the energy that binds it all together and is called *aether* in yogic circles and 'spirit' or 'the field' in metaphysical ones, and 'the force' in certain copyrighted places. These elements are primal, and if we're talking primal in the northern tradition, we're talking *Jotun*, giants.

ELEMENTS AND RUNES

The four elements are Fire, Earth, Water and Air. Each rune resonates with one of them, as follows:

Fire	Earth	Water	Air
Fehu	Uruz	Thurizaz	Ansuz
Raido	Kenaz	Gebo	Wunjo
Hagalaz	Nauthiz	Isaz	Jera
Eihwaz	Peroth	Algiz	Sowolio
Tiwaz	Berkanan	Ehwaz	Mannaz
Laguz	Ingwaz	Othala	Dagaz

Table 5: Elements and Runes

Look, I know you're going to say, 'Laguz is the water rune!' This is true. But in this context its energy is the cleansing power of Fire, the heat that comes from a healing wound.

Elemental Compatibility

The elements support or suppress one another, and sometimes cancel one another out by changing states, for example Fire and Water make steam – Water and Air.

Here's the full list:

✦ Earth and Air cancel each other out.

✦ Earth and Water are a powerful combination, super grounded.

✦ Earth and Fire are neutral.

✦ Earth and Earth are super grounding.

+ Fire and Air expand each other. Not very grounded.

+ Fire and Water cancel each other out.

+ Fire and Fire can be a massive energy, or can consume each other.

+ Air and Water work well together, but have little substance.

+ Air and Air can go either way and are not even slightly grounded.

+ Water and Water is the massive neap tide or a tsunami or a calm mill pond.

This is a rule of thumb, and a very broad one at that, as Laguz is fiery Water, and Kenaz is earthy Fire, and Sowolio fiery Air. There is a lot of scope to play around with this, so get to know it and make it yours.

And remember, while the gods of Asgard, the ones we see in myth and story, are relatively benevolent towards humans, the *Jotun* don't give a rat's ass. They see us as a transient annoyance. Their energy is powerful but subtle. Not like the grandeur of Odin and his one eye, or Freya and her Valkyries, more like the break in the power supply when you are trying to save your work.

Let's look at each in turn.

FIRE

In the northern tradition, the *Jotun*, the giant, who is the King of Fire, is Surtur. He lives in Muspelheim, the land of fire. Unsurprisingly.

The runic element of Fire isn't necessarily like the raging wildfire or the log fire in the camp. It *is* those things, but it's also the wildfire in the woods, the lighting strike on the pine, the cooking fire in the hearth, and the volcano spewing liquid rock into the sky. And the hammer blow of the sun in the south.

Each of the Fire runes has a different type of Fire energy:

+ Fehu: the Fire of creation
+ Raido: the Fire of adventure
+ Hagalaz: wildFire
+ Eihwaz: stored Fire
+ Tiwaz: the Fire of obligation and honour
+ Laguz: the Fire of the healing wound, the sterilization heat. And the Fire of petrol burning on water. Search for a video of it – it's scary.

All these energies interact with one another relatively well. You could say, 'They get on like a house on fire.' Have you ever been in a house fire? There's a lot of running and screaming. And a lot of heat!

The raw elements of creation – Fire, Earth, Water and Air – come together to form potent energies of life, magic and experience.

EARTH

Earth energy in the north is that of rock and mountain, shore and forest, wood and peat.

Earth energy in the runes is the power of the ground beneath your feet, the rock of the mountain, the basic needs of life. If it were a chakra, it would be the root chakra. It is an energy of grounding and earthiness.

Angrboða, the Witch of the Iron Wood, is the mistress of the Earth runes.

The Earth runes are:

+ Uruz: the power and strength of the forest

+ Kenaz: the cave in the mountain

+ Nauthiz: the need and drive for life

+ Peroth: the base need for sex and luck

+ Berkanan: the energy of recovery and resilience

+ Ingwaz: the potential for growth

WATER

Water, as you might think, tends to be the antithesis of Fire, and vice versa. But in runes things aren't so straightforward. Water energies in runes are more about the movement of the energies that the runes embody and the powers that they bring from the source of life that is Water.

The Water runes, governed by Ran, the Goddess of Water, are:

✦ Thurizaz: the thunder and lightning rune

✦ Gebo: the respect rune

✦ Isaz: the ice rune

✦ Algiz: the edge rune

✦ Ehwaz: the companionship rune

✦ Othala: the hearth and home rune

AIR

The element of Air is ruled by Hræsvelgr (Hr-aes-vel-gr), a giant eagle who controls the winds that blow across the seas and mountains. His name could be translated as 'Ship-wrecker'. That gives you an idea of how he views the world.

Air is a very fast-moving element and easy to dismiss as ephemeral, but it is essential to life.

The Air runes are:

✦ Ansuz: the rune of the voice

✦ Wunjo: the rune of comfort and bliss

+ Jera: the rune of harvest

+ Sowolio: the pathway rune

+ Mannaz: the human rune

+ Dagaz: the rune of initiation and change

CONNECTIVITY

The elements are useful in looking at connectivity, either relationship-wise or in any other way, by looking at where complementary energies exist within your Runic Star Path.

Say you want to get to know someone and to know how best to do it. In classical astrology, you'd look at your birth chart to find out where your Mercury was and therefore what communication traits you had, and you'd find out where the other person's Mercury was too. Then you could see whether you were elementally compatible (see the list on page 156 for elemental compatibility). Air and Fire tend to get on well, for example – if you've ever blown on a campfire then you'll know that! Air and Earth may find it harder to ignite a spark.

In runic astrology, Mercury is Odin (more on the gods in the next chapter). So, you'd check out where he was and what sort of runic energy he was utilizing by looking at your birth chart and the 'Degrees of the Runes in the Zodiac' table (pages 42–43).

My Odin, for example, is utilizing Hagalaz energy. So my communication style is likely to be blunt and direct. And to be honest, I kind of think it is. My wife's Odin energy is using that of Nauthiz, meaning her communication is likely to be very direct and searching for meaning.

Elementally, this is Fire and Earth energy, so not too much of a problem, relationship-wise. In terms of runic energy, these runes are close together and are both in the second *Aett*, so are on the same part of the runic pathway.

The elements aren't the only energies affecting our Runic Star Path, however. Let's look at the gods and how they rule our lives – to a greater or lesser extent, of course!

Chapter 9

The Planets and Gods

Gods and goddesses are a big deal in the northern tradition. And their energies are not to be trifled with. Let's see how they affect us.

PLANETARY BODIES

Throughout time, the planets of the solar system have had names and stories associated with them, and by knowing those stories, we can see what sort of power flows around those planets. In the northern tradition, power was wielded by the gods. So, in runic astrology, the gods can represent the planets.

The gods, in planetary form, have energetic magnetism too, meaning that they are attractive to or rule (to use the astrological term) certain runes. Runic astrology hasn't gone through the mill of evolution that classical astrology has and is much less refined, so there's often a bit of an energetic tussle.

It's worth noting that in runic astrology the runes have different rulers than in 'normal' rune lore. If they work for you for all rune work, then that is right. If not, that is also right. This is your experience. Make it yours.

Also, when you've read about the gods, let them stir your soul. Get to know them. Do the rituals suggested here. Go on a voyage of discovery and find some more information about them. There are TV series, books, songs and stories out there. (I recommend the music of Wardruna.)

It's important to note that this form of discovery is an art, not a science. What you take from the stories, what you feel from the energies, is right for you. Take it all and make the meaning that feels right in your heart. Because this will be right for your work with runic astrology. The meanings you make through the experiences and events of your own life are more vital and alive than those of old, handed down through the ages.

So, let's dive into the energies, stories and resonances of the cosmos. What follows is a description of the major planetary bodies, the gods of runic astrology, and their energies and powers, which, by the way, can be illuminated by your interest. Just as when you touch your phone screen and it comes to life.

The gods, in planetary form,

have energetic magnetism.

Let them stir your soul.

Sunna (the Sun)

Sunna is the goddess of life and light. She flows around the world (or seems to), pulling her chariot with the burning disc on it. Her light brings life and warmth, showing the way and allowing all on Earth to see the world around them.

Sunna is, however, chased by a wolf, *Sköll*, Traitor. Sköll is a very lean and tired wolf, as he doesn't stop, because Sunna doesn't stop. And he is ultimately fated to be out of luck, as the giant wolf Fenrir is destined to get to the sun before him anyway!

Sometimes, just sometimes, Sunna takes a rest, and Sköll catches her, and the light of the chariot is dimmed as the wolf grows near. But then Sunna escapes and shines her light again.

She represents the self.

Keywords
Light, life, guidance, finding your way, purpose, the self.

Colours
Yellow, white.

Energies
The way forward, guidance, navigation.

Rulership

Sunna rules Uruz, Kenaz, Sowolio and Dagaz.

Totems

Sun wheel, chariot.

Lens through which this god sees the universe

Sunna is very interested in life paths, purpose and direction. She wants the best for you and will see everything in that light. Her lens is best described as that of a kindly teacher at school who believed in you, or a favourite song that goes straight to that hidden part of you. (Mine is Starship, 'We Built This City', fyi.)

RITUAL TO SUNNA

Sunna loves to be seen, worshipped and adored. And why not? A ritual to Sunna is to get up early and greet her. This is easier in winter. Getting that first light of dawn on your face, your skin, and into your energy fields is a powerful way of expressing your gratitude to this bountiful goddess.

Manni (the Moon)

In Nordic mythology, Manni is male. A super-fluid male. Think of the most fabulous human you can think of and turn their volume up to 12. This is Manni. He travels around the cosmos in his chariot, which glows a soft luminous white.

Manni is easily distracted, and will often stop and look at things or wander off. So the wolf that chases him isn't as lean and tired as Sköll. This wolf is called *Hati*, Hate. He spends a lot of time biting Manni and his chariot. That's why Manni has lots of bites taken out of him over the course of a month and eventually gets eaten.

Manni is intuitive and mystic and is super interested in emotions and relationships.

Keywords

Emotions, feelings, intuition, sensations, psychic abilities and energy.

Colours

Pale white, neon colours.

Energies

Emotions, sensations, feelings, the metaphysical.

Rulership

Manni isn't a ruler of runes, as he's too flighty. But he has an interest in them all.

Totems

Cycles, tides, love, lust.

Lens through which this god sees the universe

Manni is a dreamer, and sees things in that way. Much like the movie *Midnight in Paris*, he always imagines the best in things and will look for the magic in any situation. As he's a mystic, he will find the magic in any situation. His world is full of goblins, wizards and trolls. He probably listens to Bowie.

RITUAL TO MANNI

As Manni is the god of emotions, connections and dreams, to ritualize your connection with him, choose a night when he's full and the sky is clear. Extra points if it's a super moon.

Go out and put yourself under Manni's gaze. If you feel comfortable, do it nude. Clothes are okay too, of course, especially if you're in a built-up area!

Feel the energy flowing from this god onto your body, into your pineal gland and through your entire system. Then go and warm up!

Odin (Mercury)

Odin is the planet closest to the sun. He is the king of the gods, and he's a warrior, magic user and rune master. He's super interested in making sure everything works. Maybe not so much legally, but practically. He's also a master orator. His words motivate millions. He loves the communication, he loves the magic. So his lens is one of communication and magic – both integral parts of leadership.

Odin regularly wanders the worlds to check that everything is going on as it should. Back in the day, this was called a progress. But remember that when the king is on his progress, either others make the decisions or you have to go and find the king to get a decision.

Odin is also a way-walker; he walks the paths of the *Wyrd* to find out what is going on in the universe. And what will be going on in the cosmos.

He chooses the most valiant dead to go to the halls of Valhalla, where they drink and fight. This keeps Odin happy, as he needs to keep an army ready for Ragnarök, the end of the world. He is a great doomsday prepper.

Keywords

Communication, leadership, magic, kingly duties, details, harmony, management, strategy.

Colours

Grey, purple.

Energies

Communication, clarity, focus, victory.

Rulership

Odin rules Ansuz, Raido, Othala and Dagaz.

Totems

Spear, raven, wolf.

Lens through which this god sees the universe

Odin is primarily interested in communication, magic, power and victory. He sees the world as a motivational seminar. Tony Robbins it and you've got Odin's lens.

RITUAL TO ODIN

Odin is the god of leadership, among many other things. A powerful ritual to him is to use his most powerful of tools: the voice.

In the shower, or on your jog, on your commute or when you walk the dog, find the time and space to sing 'Odin!' in as many different ways as you can. You can use his other names, too, such as Mr Wednesday, Grimnir, Way-walker, Furious One, or any other of his names you think fit.

Freya (Venus)

Freya is the goddess of battle, fury, beauty, feminine magic, love and lust. She also likes cats. As a goddess of magic and battle, she has very few limits on her desire to express herself and is fond of using her wit, body and magic to get her needs met.

Freya is the mistress of the Valkyries, female figures who lead the souls of the valiant dead to Valhalla – after she gets first pick for her hall. Her hall is full of beauty, love and power. The warriors there are the ones Freya wants to spend time with. It's the noisy, uncouth ones, in her eyes, that go to Valhalla.

Freya has many handmaidens who perform duties for her, anything from healing to looking after unmarried girls and uninitiated children, to birthing babies, to casting spells, to crushing the skulls of her enemies and leading her forces in battle. These handmaidens can be seen as separate from the queen of the gods, or aspects of her, depending on how you view the world. I prefer the aspects version.

Keywords
Love, beauty, joy, lust, victory, fury, cats, feminine magic.

Colours
Golden yellow, deep reds and purples.

Energies
Sex, attraction, passion, relationships.

Rulership
Freya rules Fehu, Gebo, Wunjo, Mannaz and Othala.

Totems
Valkyries, cat.

Lens through which this god sees the universe
Freya loves passion and all things passionate, such as art, love, lust and creativity. She sees the world through the lens of a Baz Luhrmann movie, all art and creativity.

RITUAL TO FREYA

Freya loves the energy of passion in any way it manifests, so a ritual to honour her is one that utilizes your passion. You can be as adult as you want here. Put passion into whatever you want to do – painting, cooking, dancing, love-making, running, practising kung fu. Whatever it is, do it with passion for the goddess of passion, love, magic and violence.

Tyr (Mars)

Tyr is the god of war, action and honour in Asgard, the home of the Norse gods. He used to be the king of the gods, but Odin took over. Probably because Odin gets people to agree, whereas Tyr shouts orders. Tyr is action-oriented and likes to think and do in the same breath. He also has firm values. His honour is unshakeable.

There's a story here. When Fenrir the great wolf was born, he was too big, and kept getting bigger, until the gods decided to chain him up, as otherwise he'd have eaten the sun. I don't know why. Maybe because the sun looks like a tennis ball and dogs like chasing tennis balls? Anyway, they chained him up with the biggest chains they could find, and Fenrir broke them. Which was annoying.

So the gods got some magic chains made out of impossible things – the roots of a mountain, the spit of a bird, the sound of a cat's footfall, the beard of a woman, the nerves of a bear and the breath of a fish. How these were forged is another story. But the gossamer-thin golden thread that was produced was used to wrap up the wolf. Who, after breaking the biggest chain in the world, wasn't going to let the gods wrap thread around him, was he? So Tyr said he'd put his right arm in the wolf's mouth, and if Fenrir couldn't break the magic chain, he could bite off the arm.

Agreed? Right.

Annnnnddddd... *unk*.

The world-ending wolf was bound safely and Tyr's arm was bitten off. Because he had given his word to the wolf and he deemed the safety of the universe to be more important than his arm. The wolf wasn't best pleased. But that's another story.

Keywords
Action, focus, war, battle, decisions, honour, values, truth.

Colours
Reds.

Energies
Action, honour, truth.

Rulership

Tyr rules Tiwaz and Ehwaz.

Totems

Chains, antlers.

Lens through which this god sees the universe

When Tyr views the universe, he sees it through the lens of doing the right thing. His view is that of the stereotypical knight in shining armour, slaying the baddies, rescuing the maidens, being true to his word. Maybe a bit like an old Schwarzenegger or Stallone movie from the eighties or nineties.

RITUAL TO TYR

The best way to honour Tyr, beyond starting a war (I think we can all agree that's a bit extreme), is to do the thing. You know the thing. You've been putting it off for ages. Procrastinating, avoiding it. Act in line with your values and beliefs and do the thing you've been putting off. Call the person, or write the letter, go to the place, have the conversation, run the marathon, join the paintball club. Whatever it is, just take action and do the thing. And do it while being mindful of Tyr.

Thor (Jupiter)

Thor is Odin's son. He has various titles, Defender of Humanity being one. He's massively strong and wields his hammer, Mjölnir, to fight off the ice giants.

Thor is, like his planet, physically bigger than the other gods. He's physically too big to walk across the Bifrost sky bridge, as he falls through it, so he gets around in a chariot pulled by two goats.

We see the Bifrost bridge, by the way, when the rain and the sun come together, especially after particularly violent thunderstorms. We call it a rainbow.

Huge himself, Thor also has huge abilities to make things bigger. He once wrestled old age and almost drank the sea dry. And dressed as a blushing bride to get his hammer back when it was 'misplaced'. But that's another story.

Thor's main role is to keep everyone safe from the giants, the elemental beings who bring fire or frost to the worlds. This is shown in astronomy as Jupiter protecting the Earth by catching or redirecting incoming asteroids.

Keywords

Big, powerful, strength, protection, expansion.

Colours

Ginger.

Energies
Protection, growth, expansion.

Rulership
Thor rules Algiz, Thurizaz and Berkanan.

Totems
Hammer, lightning.

Lens through which this god sees the universe
Thor loves protection, and food. So, he sees the universe like a German Shepherd would. Can I bite it? Is it tasty? Is it a threat?

RITUAL TO THOR

Thor isn't very picky about his rituals. He's very direct and simple. To be honest, keeping his rituals simple is definitely the way forward.

Thor likes beer, mead and food, as well as thunderstorms, so a good connecting ritual to him is, if safe during a thunderstorm, take some food and drink out for him and leave it somewhere natural, or as natural as you can.

Say, 'Mighty Thor, please accept this offering.'

If you aren't keen on being out in a storm, do it just afterwards, or wait until the planetary energy of Thor is high in the sky and do the same.

NB. Don't get struck by lightning.

Loki (Saturn)

Loki gets a bad rap. He has been demonized by Christian monks, turned from an agent of change into a monster. In truth, he's simply a god who hates being bored. So he'll actively look for ways in which things can be changed, adapted or torn down to make way for something that works better.

In the legends, Loki is completely gender and species fluid, fathering Hela, the goddess of death, Jörmungandr, the world serpent, and Fenrir, the giant wolf, while also giving birth to Sleipnir, Odin's horse. He did this while distracting a giant from building a wall.

Loki only likes structures and systems that work. If they even slightly don't work, he will set fire to them to see what happens. Whatever happens, just knowing that what comes next will be different makes it better.

Keywords

Structure, efficiency, order, challenge, change, evolution, chaos, non-binary.

Colour

Crimson.

Energies

Evolution, change, transition.

Rulership

Loki rules Jera and Eihwaz.

Totems

Fire, iron.

Lens through which this god sees the universe

Loki is super interested in what works and what doesn't work. He wants things to work. Actually, he requires things to work. On the one hand, his view is that of the old mechanic who can fix any car with a lump hammer and a socket set; on the other, he is Elon Musk on Adderall after his third espresso. Either way, he looks at the universe to see where it needs improving. And how to bring about that improvement.

RITUAL TO LOKI

๏)⟨⟨◈⟩⟩⟨๏·⋄·◈··X·⟪◯⟫·X··◈·⋄·๏)⟨⟨◈⟩⟩⟨๏

Loki loves structures and systems to work. If they don't, he'll pull them down. So, a ritual to Loki is to challenge structures you feel aren't working. How? Political action, non-compliance, anything that challenges the norms of a structure that you don't agree with. You get to choose – choose the anarchy, or the structure you want to create, and do it for Loki.

These first six gods are quite interested in us as individuals. As we move out from the Earth, though, the gods get more existential in their interests and influence. They take a long time to orbit Sunna and their energy stays with each rune for a while.

So, moving on, let's have a look at these more detached energy influencers.

Urðr (Uranus)

Urðr is one of the Norns. She is the goddess of potential – she sees the potential in any situation. She loves to bring energy into being and allow her sisters to shape it. She will always act in what she sees as the best way, but she has very little compassion. Because she handles the energy of trillions, she doesn't really care about one individual, but if you make an interesting case, well... that's different.

Keywords

Fate, chance, potential, destiny, purpose.

Colours

Deep blues and purples.

Energies

Fate, potential, destiny, purpose.

Rulership

Urðr rules Peroth.

Totems

Womb, dice cup.

Lens through which this god sees the universe

Urðr has something of a soft-focus view of the universe, being drawn to energies that sparkle. Think of her gaze as that of a toddler in a toy shop. She will always be drawn to the next shiny thing, while spinning tens of trillions of threads into a complex tapestry of life. Her gaze is soft and all-seeing, but will only focus on something if it's interesting to her.

RITUAL TO URÐR

A ritual to honour Urðr is one that recognizes her weaving of the threads of fate into the *Wyrd*. This one requires some energy and focus from you: spin or weave or knit something.

Spin fleece into thread, weave thread into cloth, or knit yarn into cloth. Or, if that isn't for you, 'man knitting' paracord can work too. Choose bright, bold colours.

Njord (Neptune)

Njord is the Nordic god of the sea, of its unknown depths and hidden mysteries. He follows the tides of fate and mystery, discovering hidden treasure or resources, while with the other hand dragging you down into inky darkness. He's interested in what lies beneath, in dreams and altered states, and in hypnotic energy, mind control, glamour, magic and the depths of the soul.

Keywords

Dreams, depths, altered states, walking between worlds, between universes.

Colour

Deep sea greens and blues, and darkness as the absence of light.

Energies

Dreams, shamanic journeys, altered states.

Rulership

Njord rules Isaz and Laguz.

Totems

Boat, fishing net.

Lens through which this god sees the universe

Njord sees the universe as a dream, kind of like the movie *Moulin Rouge*, when everyone has drunk absinthe. The connections and correlations are weird, wonderful, and work. Njord loves the dreamy energy that comes from the imagination and depths of creativity. But you've got to get super Dali-like to get his attention.

RITUAL TO NJORD

Njord is the lord of the seas, rivers and lakes, and loves sparkling copper. So, making an offering of chocolate (biodegradable) 'copper' coins to waters is a powerful way of getting his blessing. Take the wrapping off first. The wilder the water, the more powerful the blessings. Be sensible, though – a Force 9 hurricane is not the place to seek blessings!

Myrmir (Pluto)

Myrmir is a *Jotun*, a giant. He lives in a deep, dark, icy pool. And he's a disembodied head. Which makes it hard to get out and about. Because of this, Myrmir keeps himself occupied by harvesting the universe's wisdom. Anything that could be even slightly useful finds its way into the vast memory of this bobbing head. Ever bobbed for apples? Myrmir is the apple.

Odin went to Myrmir to find the secrets of the runes. And that wisdom cost him an eye – an eye that now bobs next to Myrmir in his dark well.

Myrmir holds all the potential wisdom and power of the universe. But can't do anything about it. So he manipulates others to get his needs met.

Keywords

Wisdom, knowledge, power, learning, sarcasm, development, manipulation.

Colours

You know the colour of freshly hewn icebergs? That dark blue is Myrmir's colour.

Energies

Wisdom, power, manipulation.

Rulership

Myrmir longs for power, and his runes, Hagalaz and Nauthiz, help it flow his way.

Totems

Scrying mirror, well.

Lens through which this god sees the universe

Myrmir sees the universe as one of those sleazy pick-up artist seminars – it's all about having power over others and getting his needs met. This lens may not be a pleasant one, but it is effective.

RITUAL TO MYRMIR

Myrmir is notorious for asking for weird things in his rituals. Odin had to sacrifice an eye. *Do not cut out your eye.* Use a mirror for your ritual, or a scrying stone if you have one. Or you can use a well, or other pool of water.

Slow your breath and gaze at your reflection. Ask for Myrmir's blessing. He'll probably send you weird dreams if he does take an interest in you.

Mengloth (Chiron)

Mengloth is a *Jotun*, of the same clan as Myrmir but with very different interests. Her home is a mountain in the heart of the icy wastes. Within said mountain are many rooms, each with a special function.

These are not *Fifty Shades*-type rooms. They are healing rooms – saunas, apothecary shops, birthing chambers, rooms of dying, rooms of bone-setting, rooms of any other form of healing you can think of. And Mengloth's doors are open to all. She is a healer in the purest sense of the word. She has many acolytes who go out into the universe and heal. But she is the original and best.

Keywords
Healing in all its forms.

Colour
Infra-red.

Energies
Healing – spiritual healing, physical healing, mental healing, diagnostic healing.

Rulership
Mengloth does not rule any runes.

Totems

Geothermal pool, ice plunge pool.

Lens through which this god sees the universe

Mengloth is the ultimate healer. She looks at the universe with an eye to heal and help. She views everyone as a patient and will provide healing whenever she is asked.

RITUAL TO MENGLOTH

Mengloth loves healing. And she is super practical. So, a powerful ritual to her would be to do a first-aid course or community CPR course. Do this mindfully and she is likely to pay you some attention.

WORKING WITH THE GODS' ENERGY

Right, we've had a look at how the gods view the universe and what they are interested in. With that information, we can begin to work out how they will influence the energies flowing around them.

When cosmic energy flows past these cosmic entities, it gets manipulated by their gravitational pull. Just as light shines through raindrops and splits to form a rainbow, so energy flows around the planets and splits. This energy then lands on the Earth in frequencies and wavelengths that affect us in very subtle ways.

Looking at the energy distortion that comes through the lens of each planet, we can see where that affects the world, and the runes and us. The fact that the gods' energy impacts us at birth means that it influences our cells. And as such, how we develop. And not just us – everything.

Let's look at how we can use this.

This is how we can use runic astrology to connect to the deeper powers of the universe to see when and how to act to achieve our goals and find victory.

For example, my last book, *Runes Made Easy*, came out on 30 November 2021. The gods interested in books are Odin and Loki – Odin from the communication, magic and runes angle, and Loki in terms of structure and time-scale. Where were they in the cosmos at that time?

Odin brought his energy to my book launch in Algiz, and Loki brought Gebo energy. So I could see that the launch would be guarded and limited from a communications perspective, but the book's reputation would grow over time. Loki likes time. This has proven to be accurate. *Runes Made Easy* had a guarded launch, but has gained in energy as time has gone on.

Would you like to look at the cosmos and see how that might affect your own life?

CONSULTING THE GODS

Choose an upcoming event in your life – a new job maybe, or first date.

Plug that date into your astrology app and see where the planets will be then.

Go through and translate this information into the runic energies (see 'Degrees of the Runes in the Zodiac' table, pages 42–43). The fact you have to do it manually will build those Runic Star Path energies into you.

What type of energy do you need? Will you be having an interview or giving a presentation? If so, see what runic energy Odin holds on that date.

What about love? What's the best way to impress that special person? See where Freya is and if there are any gods bringing Peroth energy.

Being able to see where the energy you require is present in the cosmos is a powerful tool. And sometimes an energy is worth waiting for.

PLANNING AHEAD

You know what you'd like to do and the result you'd like to get. You've worked out what sort of energy would suit your needs. So all you need now is a little patience, because you might not need to do anything now, for the best may be yet to come.

You may, for example, just take a look at the cosmos and go, 'Ooh, in two years' time the beginning of June is going to be epic for moving house. And this December is going to be the best time for us to get married, as Freya will be in Othala.'

Patience and planning can bring a host of power and victory to your world. This is how the gods do things.

Chapter 10

Wandering Gods

In classical astrology there is a concept called retrograde. This is when a planet or astral body appears, from our perspective on Earth, to go backwards in the sky.

In runic astrology, what this does is move the energy of a god away from their domain. The gods can find that sitting on the throne all the time is tiring, so they get up sometimes and have a look around. Wander off. Leave their responsibilities behind. When Odin (Mercury) wanders, for example, communication gets squiffy. Professional word, squiffy.

There is another way of looking at a wandering god. The planets aren't physically going backwards, our view of them is. So this means that this time of wandering is a time of reassessing and revisiting the energies that come from that god. It's a time of reflection.

Let's look at the gods in turn and what their wandering means for us.

Sunna (the Sun)

Sunna does not wander. She is the heart of the solar system and all life flows from her and the other gods dance for her. She does sometimes get eclipsed, though. When she is, her energies of life and creation, path-setting and purpose, stop. Kind of like the reset button on the computer. When she comes back, though, there is fresh energy to utilize. The old can be dropped. You don't have to open the proverbial browser with all the tabs on it, just open a new window on life.

Manni (the Moon)

Manni does not wander but, like Sunna, he does get eclipsed, and he has a cycle of being full and then having chunks bitten out of him by the wolf Hati, who bites him to get him to keep moving, until he is finally eaten altogether and then has to regrow to become full again.

The fuller Manni is, the more influence he has. And when he is eclipsed, about once every 18 months, his energy is reversed. So check where his influence is when the eclipse is happening.

When the gods wander,
their attention drifts.
The energies they
rule can go awry.

Odin (Mercury)

Odin wanders around the skies regularly, and when he does, his interests get left on the table. So energies around communications lose any oversight and can go haywire.

This happens about three times a year for about a month.

Freya (Venus)

Freya is primarily interested in keeping house, raising children and being the queen of slaughter and magic. So when she wanders, you may find that passion, friendships, relationships and home life gets confusing, or that things you've previously ignored in those areas come and bite you on the bum.

What's different and interesting about Freya's wandering is that she doesn't *just* go backwards, she also goes behind the sun for a while and is no longer visible in the sky. She begins her cycle as the morning star for approximately seven months, disappears into the darkness for about 40 days and returns as the evening star for roughly seven months. (Lisa Lister talks more about this in her book *Self Source-ery*.)

In Norse mythology, the darkness is where the *Draegr*, the dwarves, live, in the caves below the mountains and volcanos. The *Draegr* are the best weapon smiths, armour smiths and craftspeople. If you want bling, go to them. They also host a mean party.

So, Freya goes into the darkness to have fun, get the best bling and reinvent herself. Whereas the other gods go exploring when they wander, Freya gets drunk, has fun, goes to the spa and goes shopping. She returns refreshed and renewed as a wild warrior.

Freya wanders every 18 months, for about 43 days.

Tyr (Mars)

When Tyr goes wandering, decisive action, honour, values and beliefs are left unattended, which may result in poor decisions and actions and a lot of blundering into situations without checking them out effectively. Be especially aware of energy around promises at this time. They can be misjudged easily.

Tyr goes wandering every 26 months. And this meander around the cosmos lasts eight to 10 weeks.

Thor (Jupiter)

When Thor gets bored and wanders off, because he is too big for the rainbow bridge, he falls through it, and his energy sinks deep, and growth, expansion and safety may feel less grounded and life feel a little more trying. Remember Thor is a first-line defence only, and he expects you to look after yourself for the most part. Imagine a guard dog full of sausages. He is there, but getting him to move is hard.

Thor wanders every year for about four months.

Loki (Saturn)

Loki likes to party like a college kid in Ibiza, and when he wanders, he doesn't so much drop his interests as slam-dunk them, and doesn't even bother with an out-of-office. If it won't keep going without him watching over it, why should he bother with it anyway? So, during this time structures and standards that you may hold dear may well show cracks. Pay attention to those cracks. As where they are is where you can grow.

Loki wanders for about four and a half months a year.

Urðr (Uranus)

When this Norn wanders, relying on your 'fates' to sort you out may not be the best idea. What you'd planned to do may well get a little confused. Urðr's energy is much more etheric than that of the previous gods, and much more subtle. But when she gets back, she'll definitely pick up the reins again.

Urðr spins off on adventures for about five months of the year.

Njord (Neptune)

Njord is even further away from Earth than Urðr, so his domain of altered states and untapped depths needs less control. When he gets bored and wanders off, though, you may find that connection to the unconscious is less stable, or indeed more solid, depending on your personal energy codes.

Njord wanders off every six months or so.

Myrmir (Pluto)

Let me start this with the fact that Myrmir doesn't give a toss. He lives in a well in the bottom of a cave and will quite happily ignore the universe to bask in his own awesomeness. He is a disembodied head, after all.

He can't wander, but he does sulk and spend time deliberately ignoring everything and everyone, and then his hold over the innate subtle powers of development, deep learning and hidden wisdom is less firm. And thus they are harder to find. Not that it's easy in the first place. But Myrmir kind of likes the idea that the search for self-knowledge should be a challenge.

Myrmir goes wandering for six months a year. Less wandering, more turning his face and bobbing away, content to keep his knowledge and wisdom to himself.

Mengloth (Chiron)

When the cosmic healer goes wandering, this is more like a doctor stuffing a sandwich at the nurses' station than a sabbatical. The other parts of the team are still functioning, but healing isn't quite as efficient during this time, because the expert is enjoying a cup of bad coffee and a slightly stale sandwich. Expect that your energetic healing experiences will require a little more effort. Perhaps more crystals and more sacred smoke.

Mengloth goes retrograde for about five months of the year.

Chapter 11
The World Tree

Yggdrasil, the world tree, or Milky Way as you may know it, stretches across the night sky, its branches reaching glimmering into the infinite darkness and casting energetic shadows that have a profound influence on those below.

From the runic to the cosmic, Yggdrasil is the source of the energies that flow into us. Over billions of miles, these energies flow towards us, to help us be as powerful as possible.

Within classical astrology there is the concept of houses – twelve 30-degree segments of the chart wheel that run counter-clockwise from the rising sign. Each house has a theme, which provides context for the signs and gods/planets within that house.

In runic astrology, the house system comes from Yggdrasil's branches, *Stamme*, stretching across the heavens and casting shade in which the gods and runes rest. This system came to me straight from the *Wyrd*.

Like the houses, the *Stamme* run anti-clockwise from your rising sign, your Jord rune, on your birth chart, changing every 30 degrees. In fact, they map onto the houses that a classical natal or other astrology chart would give you – you can find them both on the outer rim of the chart, numbered one to twelve – but the energies are different. What are they?

As well as an outline of each *Stamme*, I'll give you the runic energies that resonate with each one. These runes are more powerful when found in this *Stamme* on your Runic Star Path/birth chart.

Also listed is the god whose energy works well with that particular *Stamme*. Their energy is magnified when they are found there.

First *Stamme*: Mod (Moad)

 Mod is the branch of emotions and feelings. Its energy is that of the internal self. Emotions, feelings, self-belief, drive, values and beliefs all reside here.

Having a god in this *Stamme* means the energies of that god are swayed towards the internal emotions, feelings, ego and self.

✦ Runic energies: Ehwaz and Mannaz

✦ God energies: Tyr

From the runic to the cosmic, Yggdrasil, the world tree, is the source of the energies that flow into us.

Second *Stamme*: Litch (Leech)

 Litch is the branch of the physical – the body, the physical connection to the world. It's about the potential held within our cells and how we act in the world.

Having a god in this *Stamme* leads the energies of that god towards our physical experiences of life, from our body and health to how we interact with the physical world.

✦ Runic energies: Laguz and Ingwaz

✦ God energies: Freya

Third *Stamme*: Vili (Vi-li)

 Vili is the branch of the will – the inner energy, force and power that motivates us, pushes us through hard times and allows us to survive and excel. Odin has a brother named after this power.

Having a god here lends the resonance of that god to our will-power, our drive, business ventures, conquests and victories.

✦ Runic energies: Othala and Dagaz

✦ God energies: Odin

Fourth *Stamme*: Kinfylgja (Kin-feel-gh-yah)

 Kinfylgja is the branch of ancestry, the energy of our forebears – our ancestors of blood, bone and spirit:

✦ Ancestors of blood are those who have the same blood as us, or have taken us into their blood – usually immediate family and close friends.

✦ Ancestors of bone are those who are long dead, who are bones. For example, those who fell in the Great War, or took dangerous journeys across the seas to a new world and a new life. Those who fell stopping those invaders.

✦ Ancestors of spirit are those who inspire us with their deeds – artists, warriors, leaders, lovers, mothers. These spirits can have existed in the real world or be mythic energies. They are equally powerful.

So, this *Stamme* holds the magic of the spiritual wisdom that flows through our DNA, our blood, and the wisdom that sings in our soul from a story or movie.

Having a god in this *Stamme* brings that energy to our experience of family, ancestry, past lives, friendships and relationships. As well as sex, dating and pets.

✦ Runic energies: Fehu and Uruz

✦ God energies: Manni

Fifth *Stamme*: Æthem (Ahh-th-em)

 Æthem is the branch of magic and creativity. *Æthem* means 'power' or 'energy' in Old English. This energy is that of creation, inspiration and joy.

Magic lies in this *Stamme*, as do inspiration and personal power. Anything that stimulates, motivates or encourages our growth in the world resides here. A god, if present, brings their influence to that creative aspect of life.

✦ Runic energies: Thurizaz and Ansuz

✦ God energies: Sunna

Sixth *Stamme*: Litr (Leet-r)

Litr is the branch of health, of life energy. This energy is more than just good health, it's the ability to bring the experience of life to bear. To be resilient, supple and soft. To be adaptable, strong and powerful. Eastern traditions call this energy *kundalini*.

The energies affecting our health and experience of health in the world are held in this *Stamme*. While Litch controls the physical, Litr brings the energy of, well, energy to our experience. From an Eastern viewpoint, this is chakra energy, or *chi*, or *prana*. *Ond* in Nordic terms. Shamanic power and other energies like this live here, and any gods who are present influence how our energy flows.

✦ Runic energies: Raido and Kenaz

✦ God energies: Odin

Seventh *Stamme*: Gothi (Go-thee)

Gothi is the branch of connectiveness. A Gothi is a holy person, a higher self. Picture this energy as the roots of a tree, linked to all the relationships you have in your life – not just in terms of sex and intimacy, but work, life, dogs and that goose that cackles at you in the park.

This *Stamme* also brings the energy of our higher self, of how we connect to the spiritual powers of the universe, of the spiritual connections we build. Our spiritual life-partner energy lives here – this is where we can look to get insights into how to find our life partner.

✦ Runic energies: Gebo and Wunjo

✦ God energies: Freya

Eighth *Stamme*: Maegen (Maah-gen)

Maegen is the branch of the actions that elevate us in the world. Not external experiences, more personal evolution. This *Stamme* has great power to direct the course of our life. And to surprise us in ways we may not expect. The energies here show us how to mitigate those surprises.

The gods within this *Stamme* show us the path to self-development – where we can excel and what energies we'd benefit from cultivating to improve ourselves.

✦ Runic energies: Hagalaz and Nauthiz

✦ God energies: Myrmir

Ninth *Stamme*: Orlog (Or-lag-gh)

 Orlog is the branch of personal destiny. Not to be confused with the *Wyrd*. These energies are sisters, not the same. Orlog is our path through life. This energy helps us access spirituality and make a connection to the divine.

This life-path energy is influenced by the gods that reside in this *Stamme*. The experiences we encounter will be amplified if we look at them through the lenses of these gods.

✦ Runic energies: Isaz and Jera

✦ God energies: Thor

Tenth *Stamme*: Hamingja (Hai-ming-ya)

 Hamingja is the branch that holds the reputation and luck we experience in life. This *Stamme* helps us plot a course through life by showing us where we will excel and find our victory.

The gods that reside here will help us discover our path to luck, our *karma* if you will. Look to the little choices in life that can lead you down the path of victory and make them with these gods in mind.

✦ Runic energies: Eihwaz and Peroth

✦ God energies: Loki

Eleventh *Stamme*: Fylgja (Feel-gyah)

Fylgja is the branch of our connection to spirit, the divine and the gods. It shows us the practical and spiritual path to follow to make that connection. *Fylgja* is the Old Norse for 'spirit guides'.

This *Stamme* holds the energy of our spirit guides, angels, ancestors – any spirits that we can connect with in order to be in communion with the divine and other realms.

✦ Runic energies: Algiz and Sowolio

✦ God energies: Urðr

Twelfth *Stamme*: Ve (Vay)

Ve is the branch of the hidden or mystic parts of life – the occult, the forbidden, the hidden motivations, the fetishes, all that is unspoken and concealed. All of that is here, ready to be known. Psychic, prophetic and other forgotten abilities are here too.

This is the *Stamme* of the darkness in our soul, and the path through that darkness and fear. But we don't have to take it.

✦ Runic energies: Tiwaz and Berkanan

✦ God energies: Myrmir

CONNECTING WITH YOUR *STAMME*

The *Stamme* of your Runic Star Path show you how to navigate your life and deepen your experience of it.

- Right now, get your natal chart and check where the houses are (on the outside of the chart). Usefully, as mentioned earlier, *Stamme* and houses map onto each other, so now you know where your *Stamme* are too.

- Look at the chart and find your Sunna rune. See what *Stamme* your Sunna is in.

- What energies, frequencies and vibrations are coming from the world tree with your Sunna rune? Feel into that energy.

- When you feel called, feel into the other planets and build your understanding of your Runic Star Path.

Chapter 12

Connections

We've come a long way. We've reached so far. Now it's time to bring all this information together to see, and more importantly feel, how the energies of the runes and the gods interact to form Runic Star Paths.

In Norse mythology, cosmic interactions are likely to be expressed in the form of arguments, make-ups, break-ups, stupid pranks and consuming too much ale. Ours is a different world, with different stories, but still the interactions between cosmic bodies create energetic waves, connections and distortions that affect us in different ways. So let's have a look at these energy patterns.

What happens, for instance, when the gods form aspects to one another? First of all, I'm going to look at five of these aspects, the major ones.

THE MAJOR ASPECTS

As you know, runic astrology works alongside classical astrology. 'Aspects' is a term from classical astrology. It describes the patterns that are formed when gods/planets are in certain places around us, and the vibrations that follow on from energy being shaped by those patterns. They've been formalized in classical astrology, and they work. So I'm not going to mess with them.

What I'm going to do is use planet names to describe the celestial bodies being plotted here, but of course you can think of these energies in terms of Norse gods if you wish.

Let's look at the five major energetic interactions.

The Conjunction

This is when two planets are so close to each other they are in the same runic energy. For example, if Mars (Tyr) and Mercury (Odin) are both at 0 degrees of Libra, they will be 'conjunct in Kenaz'. Looking at a chart where planets are conjunct, you'll see two planetary symbols with the same zodiac symbol and the same or a very close number in brackets.

A conjunction means that the planets' energies are united. They are working together. Perhaps at a party, perhaps in battle, or perhaps just putting IKEA furniture together. Whatever it is, their energies are pulling in the same direction, working together for success. The closer they are in degrees, the more powerful their joint energy.

The Sextile

 This is when two planets are 60 degrees apart from each other. In this formation, their combined energy makes a triangle, which causes the energies to combine to work towards the same goal. This is more likely to be throwing a party than starting a war, as there will probably be drinks involved. But not too many – the sextile shows the *intelligent* use of the combined power.

The Square

Here, the two planets are 90 degrees apart. This formation sees them at opposite ends of an energy, creating tension. Think series finale of *Housewives of Asgard*. Or being drunk at 1 a.m. outside a sleazy pub and not talking properly. Heading to the kebab shop, but not really caring any more. Probably losing a shoe. 'And who's got my phone? Really? And why is there sick in my bag?'

With this energy, you'll get there. It probably won't be fun. But what good story ever started with 'We were drinking tea'? (Okay, as mentioned earlier, *The Hobbit* came close.)

The Trine

This is when the planets are 120 degrees apart and making a very strong triangle. Remember maths at school? Trigonometry? Remember triangles are the strongest shape for load-bearing? Planets in trine support each other.

This energy makes for super-strong alliances, so it's a beneficial frequency to use to get stuff done.

The Opposition

Here the planets are opposite each other. In opposition. They are 180 degrees apart on a chart. Think of this energy as two sides of a bargaining table, or a tug-of-war. Both sides are right, and they are both trying to win.

The real win here is to make sure you take a breath and try to see things from the other side, or it's going to get messy.

Fuzziness

Because we're humans, not computers, I always allow some 'calculation' error in looking at aspects, usually one to five degrees. This gives me chance to catch the fast-moving celestial bodies like Mercury, Venus, the Moon and the Sun.

You can be as draconian as you like with your readings, but remember the difference in a degree of movement for Mercury can be less than a day. So if you are doing a runic astrology reading in New York for someone in London, there may be different degrees in play because of time zones. Just something to bear in mind if you ever become a professional runic astrologer. Studying the Runic Star Paths of others, like the dog, your partner, your friends, or even paying clients, is a way of getting a deeper understanding of the runic influences on their lives, and so coming to understand the runic influences on us all.

THEN VS NOW

Or for you astro-geeks, natal chart transits

The gods/planets don't just make connections in the here and now, they also make connections with the then – the moment you were born, and the gods/planets of your natal chart. Your natal chart, you'll remember, is the term traditional astrology uses to refer to your birth chart, or in my terms, your Runic Star Path.

In traditional astrology, these connections are called transits, because the god/planet is transiting through the cosmos. I'm going to use that word too.

Transiting Gods

Throughout the myths and stories of the ancient north, the gods fall out, make friends, play pranks on one another and generally get on or don't get on. That's how gods work. And, as we've already seen, each god has interests and influences, and sometimes they align, others not so much.

The way to work out if the gods are friends at the moment is to look at where they are now. What patterns are they making?

As you now know, as a (very) broad rule of thumb, if two gods are conjunct, they're on the same page; if sextile, they're getting ready for a party; if trine, there's a strong supportive energy between them; if in opposition, it's time to grab your sword!

We can also look at the rulers of the runes and the mythology of the northern tradition to find out if the gods are getting on. Some gods have obvious alliances. Freya and Odin get on well, as they are married. Freya and Loki, however, tend to get annoyed with each other quite quickly, as Loki likes to play pranks and Freya likes slightly more adult humour.

Looking at what the gods are up to now can be compared to getting an overall weather forecast, but let's get personal. Comparing what's happening now to what was happening at the moment of your birth will show how your personal energies are being affected by the current now of the cosmos.

Can you see, and more importantly feel, how the energies of the runes and the gods interact to form your Runic Star Path?

For example, what is your Sunna rune? Let's use my wife's, Hagalaz. As I write this, Sunna has energy from Laguz. Going back to Chapter 6, where we looked at runic compatibility, we can see that Laguz and Hagalaz aren't the best of friends and they don't mix well. So there is potential for energies to combust here. As Sunna shows the way, and Hagalaz and Laguz are causing problems and explosions, there is the potential for Lisa's way ahead to be a bit 'choppy'. She'll need to take care not to be thrown off course.

Remember when I talked about lenses of energy? Well, think of your natal chart as a light source and the current transits as the lenses through which you see said light. Like looking at the sun through a stained-glass window in a church. You are the sun. Isn't that nice?

So, if, for example, you've got Freya in Fehu on your Runic Star Path and transiting Freya is in Gebo, then you've got to look at the abundance of passion and love through the gifts and respect of that passion.

We can also apply the above aspects to this interaction. To take another example, say Freya in Gebo is conjunct your natal Freya (there are some astro words for you), meaning that these energies are both present for you. That's just going to amp up that power, making the frequency of that energy even more potent for you.

On a practical note, when you look at current transits vs the positions of the planets/gods on a natal chart, the picture your app will usually give you is one that has your birth chart in the middle of some circles, like the hub of a wheel, and the current energies are on the outer ring. Your app may well do it differently. Have a play.

The important takeaway from looking at current transits vs your natal chart is that you can look at how the energies of a specific date affect your personal energy. Isn't that useful? Which brings us to our final chapter....

Chapter 13

Using Runic Resonance

Now we're going to get practical. Because I like things to be useful and I want you to be able to use what I share here in a really tangible way to understand yourself better, know why you do the things you do and work with the energetics of the cosmos to navigate the seas of the current times.

We've touched on this along the way, but now we're going to look more closely at how to use the powerful energies that you have come to know are part of your life. This is the point of runic astrology: to understand and utilize the patterns and processes of the universe to create the experience we crave and long for. To work with the energies that are happening anyway to find joy, love, success and victory.

This isn't to say that you are bound by the paths in the stars. Far from it. Runic astrology shows us the paths we *can* take.

It provides navigational aids to help us through the confusion – aids we can choose to access or not. Kind of like how bears can take advantage of the spawning time to go and eat salmon.

Be the bear, not the salmon.

UNDERSTANDING

Of course you've got to know where you are before you can go anywhere, or start to tweak the threads of the *Wyrd* to create what you'd like to see in your life.

Runic astrology can give us a greater understanding of where we are and how we are. From our birth chart, we can come to understand our strengths and weaknesses and the energies we have to work with, and how we can work with other people. For example, you might be wondering, 'If I go on a date with this person, will it work?' or 'My team-mate is this Sunna rune, will our energies work well together?'

To work out whether you are compatible with someone, look to where there are complementary energies in the runes in your charts. For instance, my wife and I have the same Mengloth energy, similar Odin energy and complementary Sunna energy.

What if you're working with someone and want to know about their ability to manage change? Where is their Loki energy?

What if you have your eye on them and are wondering about their style of love, romance and magic? Where is their Freya energy?

Say, for example, you're looking for love. Where can you find it? This is a common question.

To find out where love (or anything else) might be for you, you need to translate your thinking into the language of the Norns and the cosmos. Try it now.

WHAT IS LOVE IN RUNIC LANGUAGE?

First of all, ask yourself what love means to you. Is it honour perhaps? Adventure? Sex? Family?

Check the table of runes starting on page 4. See which runic associations marry with your ideas.

Now look to where those energies are on your Runic Star Path.

Remember to look for the gods too, and see where they are, which Stamme they are influencing.

Your next question may be: 'When am I going to find love?' Which brings us to...

DIVINATION AND TIMING

One of the things people are desperate for is insight and wisdom in regard to a situation, or how the future is going to pan out. We love to meaning-make, we rarely like to be surprised and we love to know *why*.

What does a toddler ask? 'Why? Why? Why?'

Astrology is able to provide a why. And a when. And a 'yes' or 'no'. From 'When will I find my one?' to 'Will I get promoted?' to 'Shall I write that book?' You know the questions that you'd like to ask the fates, right? Well, it's possible that *all* the answers are to be found in your natal chart.

What astrology is good at is spotting the energies that will be experienced through the frequencies of the waves that hit the Earth at any given time, depending on the planetary alignments. And what makes it accessible is that it's an art married with science, relying as much on creativity as on a calculator.

Astronomy is the science bit. Astronomy tells us where the planets and moons and asteroids will be. They follow predictable courses. People in dark rooms with big telescopes spend their whole careers looking at the night sky to discover new things and to study the paths that we *think* we know.

Astrology is the art of said science. The predictability of planetary movement means that we know that when the sun is in one place, and the moon in another, and the constellation of Libra is in another place, the energies that affect our world are the same, or roughly the same, as they were when this happened last year, or last decade, or last century, or last millennium.

The art of astrology helps us know that people with a Libra Sun sign have similar tendencies. Or that Leo people are gregarious. And we know that those specific energies will be present at certain times in the cyclical calendar of planetary alignments. This extends past people into events.

Look at big collective events such as the coronation of King Charles in the UK, or the timing of elections or invasions. The people who are making the decisions may well be basing them on the cosmic energies. We know the British royal family has used astrologers for centuries, and that titans of industry use astrology too, as do politicians and warlords. Why? Because it works.

Another example of this is the Super Bowl. The dates, start times and location of this great sporting event all change. Why? Why not have a national stadium or standard date? Or any other standardization? Because the cosmic energies hitting the stadium at the time influence results, sales and the collective ritual that is 100 million people focusing on one event. Powerful stuff.

Due to the predictable nature of the cosmos, we know where planets, moons and asteroids are going to be on any specific date. Using maths that is more complex than my brain can cope with (I checked), we can find out where the energy of the cosmos is flowing and when and how. For any date, past, present or future, anywhere in the world.

So, perhaps you want to write a book. You can look at when the planets will be most supportive to writing that book. Where are the planets now? Are they harmoniously aligned or not? What transits are affecting you personally? What will it be like next week?

I work this out by looking at an astrology chart that an app or program has given me. I know proper astrologers do this with a protractor and calculator. My friend David Wells is a master at this (give him a Google). I'm not, so I use tech. Modern Viking, me.

What date will the energies of the cosmos be good for my book to be well received? When should I send my proposal to the editor, knowing that there are cosmic energies that will help me get the result I need and want?

This is how we can divine with astrology: we look at known energy points, known book publishing success for example, and use that known space to find where and when the cosmological energies will be similar again.

Would you like to know how to find two or more energy points that you can use to work out how to get your needs met within the *Wyrd* of the cosmos?

*The pulse of cosmic runic
energy that touches
our planet has subtle
and profound effects.*

Using Your Runic Star Path for Divination

Each god has influence over at least two and often more runes (see Chapter 9). Freya, for example, has influence over Fehu, Gebo, Wunjo, Mannaz and Othala. This means that when any of those runes in your Runic Star Path are being influenced by Freya, by being in a positive aspect to her, you'll have a better chance of finding the love you want.

Now let's get epic. If you have any of those runes (Kenaz, Gebo, Wunjo, Mannaz, Laguz and Ingwaz) in your Runic Star Path, then Freya has influence over that aspect of your energetic being.

Look to where your Sunna rune ruler and Freya are in relationship. Perhaps your Sunna rune is Ansuz, you great speaker, you, and Odin and Freya are conjunct on the chart. This means that there is the potential for relationship or love energy to come through your language skills and Odin's leadership and Freya's passion.

With three points like this, you can have a very clear direction to go in. You know you must act with your voice, leadership and passion. So, take the first step. Speak to the person. Ask them out. Perhaps send them a text. With those three energetic influences to navigate by, you can find a clear Runic Star Path for your lovin'.

The same is true for all aspects of life – health, wealth, pets, book launches, starting a new job. Use the same process:

+ Find the energies you want.

+ Find the ruler of those energies.

+ Using your app, look to where those points come together in a beneficial relationship.

Want to get a promotion? Loki in Fehu may be good, but Loki in Fehu and Sunna in Hagalaz will shake stuff up when they are square, and that might be good for your prospects too.

Say you've met a hot human in a café. Knowing their Sunna rune will help you realize where their energetic influences are. Perhaps they are a Nauthiz Sunna, so Thor is their ruler. From that you know that when Thor is in your own energies, or your energies are being influenced by Thor, super-direct action to get the relationship moving will be effective. And as Nauthiz is their Sunna rune, well, they will appreciate direct action and communication.

Choosing the right energy for your decision, event, proposal, job interview or kiss is important. There's plenty of energy to choose for your event. Look at how the transits of a specific time affect you. Be specific. If you want healing energy, look to Mengloth, or planets in Laguz. If you want shamanic energy, look to Odin. He's useful for communication as well. And Mannaz has that vibe too, while Tyr has action and honour. So does Tiwaz, and Thurizaz has a similar action energy – a very direct one.

My wife and I got married on a day that suited our natal charts. I try as much as possible to get my books released on good energy days, and I launch products and courses on days that are filled with the energy I want them to be. I'm not saying that the cosmos does the work for me, far from it, but acting in alignment with its energetic flow does make life much easier.

I talked about consulting the gods earlier and it's useful to know how often they move through the runic zodiac, so you can plot where they'll be. See below:

God	Runic Zodiac Time
Sunna	About 15 days
Manni	About 1.25 days
Odin	About 7 days
Freya	About 14 –18 days
Tyr	About 25 days
Thor	About 180 –190 days
Loki	About 1.25 years
Urðr	About 3.5 years
Njord	About 7 years
Myrmir	About 7–15 years

Table 6: Gods/Planets in the Runic Zodiac

Finally, I want to make sure you realize this is more than just rune maths and planet maths. It's trusting your intuition, your insight and your heart. Trust your feelings as you build Runic Star Paths for yourself, your events or your clients. This is where power is to be found. Right there. In you. Your heart will lead you to victory.

Have fun using runic astrology for love, business, wealth, happiness, or whatever you choose.

Afterword

Once you've opened the door to the mystic, it does not close. And now you've activated power within yourself that the gods and goddesses cannot fail to notice. Even though you're probably not wearing copper armour and standing on a hilltop shouting, 'Hey, Odin!', you may well find that the powerful one-eyed one turns that baleful eye towards you. Or the queen of the heavens raises an eyebrow in your direction. Maybe if you're super unlucky (or privileged?), the bobbing head in the cave will bless you with a sneer.

Whatever energy casts its eye over you, by reading this book you've accessed a frequency of the *Wyrd*, the Norns have spun more power into your specific thread of destiny and you have gained the power to navigate and co-create your next steps in ways that you may not have even imagined before you started reading.

You want proof? You've just read it. I am not an astrologer, but I was and am keen to learn. I learned the lore and sang the songs. And the universe moved to make it so, from getting my very patient editor on side, to the CEO of the company signing off on it, to my wife patiently loving me, suggesting ideas and correcting my errors, again and again and again, to being here now, sharing this with you.

My life's *Wyrd* has changed since I started reading and interpreting Runic Star Paths. Yours will too if you choose to act on the frequencies that are drawn to you and through you.

You have already begun to learn the lore. You have begun to feel the energy of the songs. You are now walking your Runic Star Path – a path that has lain forgotten and decayed for far too long, a path that is now becoming activated by fresh new footprints, a path that you can walk along and leave your mark on in whatever way you choose.

Be ready to become more and more of yourself as you navigate these times.

You've chosen this. Embrace it.

I've mentioned before that gods will take an interest in you as you work with the runes. Let me finish this with a small story that illustrates this.

As I was finishing editing this book, I went to Normandy with my wife.

If you don't know Normandy, it was named after the settlers that came from Norway in the ninth century. They spent lots of time raiding and settling along the big French rivers, and left their marks all over Europe.

In Rouen, Hrolf the Walker was the first Norman count. Hrolf is a Norwegian name, and when Latinized by the Franks became Rollo. Rollo's home became Rouen.

We got to Rouen on Wednesday, Odin's day. And after a frustrating drive around the city trying to find our way to the hotel, we dumped the car and went exploring.

Rouen is a medieval city, with cobbled streets, ancient buildings and massive churches. It's also where Jeanne d'Arc was held before her execution. That's its own story, and not one for me to tell here.

If, like me, you are interested in how people's ideas of the divine evolve, then this may be of interest. When the pagan Northmen became Christian Normans, the Church turned Odin into St Cnut, and Thor into St Olaf. And surprisingly in this very Christian church in Rouen we found a shrine to St Olaf. I'd not seen one outside Scandinavia, though to be honest, I'd not looked too hard, so that was a surprise. He even had a Viking longship in his shrine. And a relic of the saint. The description was stamped in brass in a dark corner and I couldn't get at it to read it, but just the fact that it's there is quite cool. I lit a €2 candle to St Olaf and we made our way to the church of Jeanne d'Arc.

This is a church built in the 1970s on the site of her execution. It's meant to look like a wave. To me, it looks like a longhouse from Norway, but that's just how I look at things.

This flowing building has a massive burning sword sculpture in its grounds and is surrounded by medieval buildings, once wattle and daub, mud and straw, but I suspect now painted brick and plaster. People throng around the ancient marketplace, with street hawkers, police and beggars everywhere.

As we entered the church, down a surprisingly narrow concrete corridor, there was a beggar at the door. As with most of the beggars I'd met, I ignored him. As I'd previously learned, if not, you get swamped by people asking for money.

He greeted Lisa as she passed and gave me a derogatory snort. I glanced up, and saw a surprisingly strong and lean body clad in a worn leather jacket, faded jeans and worn army boots, and a ragged face, lined with the years, a salt-and-pepper beard and, what knocked me back, one eye, the other scarred over, as if from a blade or other wound.

I paused, but the push of tourists forced me through the doors and into the church.

To say I was a little shaken would be an understatement. I sat on the edge of a pew while Lisa explored. Looking back, I couldn't see where the beggar was standing.

As I sat looking at the altar, made in the image of flames, I realized that I hadn't honoured the, to me, quite blatant incarnation of the All-Father.

I went back out to find him, but he was nowhere to be seen. Instead, there were a lot of police, obviously doing a sweep of the 'undesirables' in the area. I wandered the area, poked my head in alleyways and watched as the police chased groups of people away from the tourist hotspot.

Then I saw him. I approached him and made my offering. He looked at me, nodded and disappeared into the crowd.

Feelings that I'd been pondering for a while came and went as I waited for Lisa to finish her investigations.

And that, dear friend, is how I met Odin in Rouen. And knew he was taking an interest in how I was moving through the world. So, dear walker of the Runic Star Path, be ready for when the gods take notice of you. Because they will.

CLOSING RITUAL

You'll need:

- a candle

- two drinking vessels

- a drink of some sort

- your journal

Ritual is the cornerstone of developing your connection to runic astrology. So, to close this book and to continue your journey into ancient runic knowledge, I invite you to honour the energy of the one-eyed god who brought the knowledge of the runes to humankind, or indeed to honour any goddess, god or energy that draws your vibration.

There are many ancient rituals that have been lost to the sands of time and others that don't fit with the ethics of the current time. One that has persisted and remains suitable is that of honouring others by sharing food and drink with them. So...

- Find yourself a still space. I know that may not be easy with life going on and children and partners demanding your time, but take a few quiet moments for yourself and the gods.

- In your quiet space, lay out your journal and two drinking vessels. I've a couple of Viking drinking horns, but then I'm a purist (or perhaps pedant). Wine glasses, tumblers or even sippy cups work.

- Pour yourself a generous measure of your favourite drink. I use mead (see, purist!), but wine, beer, juice and squash are all fine. And pour an equally generous measure into the other vessel.

- If you feel comfortable, then light a candle. Again, as I'm anal, I have beeswax ones. But tea lights work well, or even tallow if you're going for the full ancient experience!

- With your journal in front of you, take three deep breaths slowly in through your nose and out through your mouth, one for each of the Norns. As you exhale, let your shoulders relax and give your jaw a wiggle.

- Either out loud or internally, say:

  Norns, gods and goddesses of the cosmos, thank you for guiding me on this path. I offer you this drink to honour your wisdom.

- Sip, glug or otherwise consume your drink. And allow some time for any energetic shifts you may feel. They may be super subtle.

- When you have finished your drink, take the gods' drink and use it to water the plants or drink it yourself. Don't just pour it away, as there is energy in it.

- Tidy up and ready yourself. This is the end of this book and you have opened portals, pathways, to the Wyrd and the cosmos. Remember to journal what you feel, dream and experience. These feelings are uniquely yours and have power.

Go forth, create Runic Star Paths for yourself, your friends, your dog. Explore and create magic, mystery and power.

They are yours by right.

Own them.

Big love,

Rich xxx

*You've come searching
and have started on the
path. The goddesses and
gods have noticed. Their
gaze is upon you.*

Acknowledgements

I'd like to give deep love and appreciation to my radiant and powerful wife, Lisa, without whose insight and guidance I'd not be half the man I am today. And this book would not exist.

Thanks to Jon, Paul, Andy, Seb and Dylan and the Scouts at 1st Fareham for your tolerance of all the times I've missed sessions and your patience as I've brain-dumped on you during this process.

To Kay and Ron, Masie, Megs, Tilly, Buffy and Blaze, and the sheep, ducks, chickens, and goose (probs not the goose, you are a git), for providing a place to manifest ideas and create awesomeness in darkest Aquitaine.

To Kezia and the kitten, for your patience.

Credit: Lisa Lister

About the Author

Richard Lister is a trained nurse, intuitive body worker, life coach and spiritual guide. He works with clients globally, offering one-to-one sessions, workshops and online coaching, and specializes in embodiment, spiritual resilience and personal connection. Rich is made from the stuff of Vikings. His interest in all things Norse began at the age of four and he has been reading and working with the runes for 20 years.

 www.richardlister.com

 **@richlisteruk**

CONNECT WITH
HAY HOUSE
ONLINE

 hayhouse.co.uk   **f** @hayhouse

@hayhouseuk   **X** @hayhouseuk

@hayhouseuk   @hayhouseuk

Find out all about our latest books & card decks • Be the first
to know about exclusive discounts • Interact with our authors
in live broadcasts • Celebrate the cycle of the seasons with us
• Watch free videos from your favourite authors •
Connect with like-minded souls

'*The gateways to wisdom and knowledge
are always open.*'

Louise Hay

'Sami Moubayed has wr....... ......ead book. As a Syrian historian, Moubayed astutely explore..... ....ise of the Islamic State first by tracking the historical origins of its ideology. He then smoothly takes the reader to the vivid details of life on the ground to explain how ISIS grew and established its so-called state. It is a perfect way to elucidate this complex phenomenon.'

HASSAN HASSAN
author of *ISIS: Inside the Army of Terror*

'Sami Moubayed's new book on ISIS is a great read. It is the best introduction to ISIS so far. He neither loses the reader in a cascade of foreign names nor overwhelms them with detail. What Moubayed does do with consummate skill is provide essential background and history to understand why Syria fell apart and where ISIS came from. Sami is the premier Syrian historian of his generation writing in English. He comes from an illustrious Damascene Sunni family and continues to live much of the year in Damascus, which gives him a unique and valuable perspective on events unfolding in his region.'

JOSHUA LANDIS
Director of the Center for Middle East Studies at the
University of Oklahoma, author of *Syria Comment* and
past President of the Syrian Studies Association

UNDER THE BLACK FLAG

At the Frontier of the New Jihad

SAMI MOUBAYED

I.B. TAURIS
LONDON · NEW YORK

Published in 2015 by
I.B.Tauris & Co. Ltd
London · New York
www.ibtauris.com

ISBN: 978 1 78453 308 3
eISBN: 978 0 85772 921 7

A full CIP record for this book is available from the British Library
A full CIP record is available from the Library of Congress

Library of Congress Catalog Card Number: available

Inside-cover author photo by Nedal Al Abdullah

Text designed and typeset by Tetragon, London
Printed and bound in Sweden by ScandBook AB

To Sahban, who guided me
along a thorny path, from Shukri
al-Quwatli and Hashem al-Atasi
to Abu Bakr al-Baghdadi and
Abu Mohammad al-Golani.
It has been a sad journey.

Contents

Acknowledgements

THIS BOOK WAS WRITTEN DURING THE MOST DIFFICULT OF times. My country was at war, its social fabric shattered, its economy in ruins. Over 250,000 of my countrymen have died. Most were tragically killed in the ongoing violence, while others drowned in the waters of the Mediterranean. My friends, who had been a comfort to me – who had stood by me since I first began writing back in the 1990s – were all gone. Some had simply fled the carnage of Syria. Others were now investing time and money in careers in Europe and the Arab world. From the four corners of the globe, however, they all pitched in to help me complete this book, either by reading drafts, or by helping me with the original research. Abdulsalam Haykal, now based in Abu Dhabi, ranks high on the list. For nearly 20 years, he has given his time and offered priceless advice for every one of my books since our student days at the American University of Beirut. Even when physically absent, he has always been there – a hand to hold and a brother to lean on when times get rough. Mohammad al-Sawwah was my sounding board, spending endless hours at night in Damascus discussing Islam and its caliphate. So also did Jamil Murad of the Syrian Social Nationalist Party (SSNP) and Kassem Shaghoury, a student turned colleague and friend, who always has been my guiding hand in ideological politics. The formidable Farah Akel, my former research assistant at the Carnegie Middle East Center in Beirut, also took time to read through the book and offer her insights, as did my seasoned colleague Professor Joshua Landis, one of the finest Syriatologists today. A big thank you goes to my trustworthy personal assistant Abeer Jamal, whose time and efforts have proven a treasure – time and again, in everything I do.

I would like to thank my students, who have served as field reporters for this book, gathering data and conducting interviews from dangerous locations in the Syrian battlefield. A huge thank you goes to the editor of this book, Fadi Esber. Also a former student turned friend, Fadi left behind a promising career in the United States and a thundering success story at the London School of Economics to return to his native Damascus. He arrived in the middle of a grinding war, wanting to help his country rise from the ashes. He was a perfect example of a good citizen and a good son to a wonderful mother. Both she and Damascus were awaiting him with open arms. He gave to them both with tremendous passion. Fadi read four drafts of this book, did all the editing with a surgeon's eye for detail, added entire chunks, and helped polish the manuscript into its final form. This book is as much his as it is mine.

Finally, I would like to thank my mother and father, who watched the rise of ISIS with tears and fears. I always assured them that tomorrow would be better. They rarely believed me. It was painful for their generation, having known Syria at the height of its glory, to see it collapse into war, chaos and lawlessness. Beneath the layers of fear and despair, however, I still see hope. Nothing lasts forever. This is the golden rule of life. One day, all the current players on the Syrian battlefield will be gone. Jabhat al-Nusra and ISIS will disappear. Light prevails at the end of every tunnel, and dark clouds – no matter how vicious – eventually disappear. A country that has seen so much will certainly rise from its ashes. It always has, every single time, for nearly 10,000 long years. Politicians make mistakes. Regimes miscalculate. But history doesn't. History always gets it right.

Preface

A GRUESOME VIDEO MADE THE ROUNDS ONLINE IN MID-February 2015, sending shockwaves across the globe. The scene was coastal Libya, near the city of Sirt, hometown of the former Libyan dictator Muammar al-Gaddafi. Twenty-one Egyptian Christians dressed in orange jumpsuits were lined up on the shore, kneeling on the ground, the waters of the Mediterranean washing against their trembling feet. Behind each of the orange-clad men was another line of twenty-one men. At the centre stood a man dressed all in black, to his left ten men in battle camouflage, to his right another ten in battle camouflage, all of the men wielding shining razor-sharp knives. They grabbed their helpless hostages by the collar as the man in black spoke in a North American accent addressing 'the crusaders'. He promised to break the cross, kill the swine and conquer Rome. Then before him his henchmen slit the throats of the men kneeling before them. The video now cut to an image of the Mediterranean, just a few miles south of Europe, its waters soaked in blood. Before taking the knife to his victims, the man in black told the world:

> Oh people, recently you've seen us on the hills of al-Sham [the Levant] and on Dabiq's Plain [near Aleppo], chopping off the heads that have been carrying the cross of delusion for a long time, filled with spite against Islam and Muslims.

He was referring to the original 'man in black', Jihadi John, the chief executioner of the Islamic State of Iraq and the Levant. Jihadi John, a British-born jihadi, had horrified the world, appearing in one video after another slitting the throats of helpless Westerners, dressed, of course, in the trademark orange jumpsuit. ISIS's reign of terror now extends from the deserts of Iraq and the hills of the Levant to the shores of the Mediterranean.

The Islamic State of Iraq and the Levant (ISIS/ISIL/IS) is a relatively new organization, born after the US occupation of Baghdad in 2003. Daesh is the Arabic acronym many Arabs and foreigners use to refer to ISIS. Its adherents hate that name, as it sounds quite comical. Instead they prefer to simply call it '*al-Dawla al-Islamiyya*' (The Islamic State). Its ideological roots, however, are much older. In fact they can be traced back to the early years of Islam and the generation of the first Muslims. Islamists believe that the ultimate goal of true believers is to establish a state ruled by the laws of Islamic Shari'a and governed by a caliph as in the earliest days of Islam, immediately after the death of the Prophet Muhammad in 632. This is the crux of ISIS ideology. The idea of a caliphate has been a sacred dream, passed down from one generation of Islamists to the next. Celebrated jihadis like Osama bin Laden and Abu Musaab al-Zarqawi have harboured that same dream. From the very beginning, Syrian jihadis wanted to re-establish a caliphate in Damascus, the former capital of the glorious Umayyad dynasty over 1,200 years ago. This is where Islam had its first empire, with a proper bureaucracy, internal security, a navy and a postal service. It is from there that Islam expanded to reach territories as far away as China and Spain, converting 'infidels' along the way. Syrian jihadis see themselves as a continuation of those powerful Muslim leaders, such as the orthodox Sunni Muslim line of successors to the Prophet Muhammad: Abu Bakr al-Siddiq, Umar ibn al-Khattab, Uthman ibn Affan and Ali ibn Abi Talib. That generation of the first Muslims, the four true caliphs of Sunni Islam, provided the epitome of true Islamic practice. In Arabic, they are referred to as the '*Salaf*', or 'predecessors', meaning the early Muslims. Those example are called 'Salafi'.

Modern-day Salafi jihadis claim to want to within, helping to free and purify the faith of un-Islamic These 'reforms' range from demolishing false idols such as statues and gravestones to banning: the use of toothbrushes in favour of *miswak* – a tooth-cleaning twig used by the Prophet; the wearing of neckties – considered an emulation of Western infidels; and the practice of smoking – an affliction compared to drinking alcohol, which is strictly forbidden in Islam. In effect they want to see the Islamic world revert in its ethics, pieties and practices to the prism of the early Muslim era as represented by the first caliphs. The concept of Salafism first emerged in the nineteenth century in response to the rise of European influence in the Muslim world, which challenged and eroded long-standing social, cultural and religious norms. Not only were the European consuls and merchants having an increasing influence, but there were also a rising number of missionary and foreign schools in the empire, ranging from Dutch and Russian to American, French and British. The most famous of them, of course, was the Syrian Protestant College, established by American Protestants in 1866. The extent of the Muslim-ruled territories had shrunk under Ottoman rule. They had once included parts of Eastern Europe, the Balkans, Crimea and the Caucasus. Serbia, Montenegro, Romania, Bosnia, Herzegovina and Cyprus were lost. Even parts of North Africa, which had been steadfastly Muslim – such as Egypt and Tunisia – were embracing a degree of secularism, which was shunting aside traditional regions of Muslim rule. The Ottoman Sultan compensated for the dramatic decline in land by imposing his iron rule on the Arab provinces of the Empire, positioning himself as a divine leader who ought to be neither questioned nor challenged. In today's world, Salafis aim for a global theocracy, ruled by a firebrand version of the Muslim faith. Their version of Islam excommunicates the Shi'a and other non-Sunnis like the Alawites and allows the beheading of so-called 'infidels'. Mainstream Muslims regard their actions as a distorted version of Islam.

When ISIS overran vast swathes of territory in Syria and Iraq during the summer of 2014, many predicted that this was a short-lived phenomenon that would soon vanish. Born out of the chaos of the Syrian Civil War, it was assumed that it would disappear once the guns fell silent in Syria. Many analysts claimed that the ideological roots of ISIS were shaky, as was its power base. At the time of writing in mid-2015, ISIS has not disappeared – far from it. The terror group has solidified control of its captured territory, surviving the massive bombing campaign led by the United States since September 2014. It has set up its own functioning government with all the trappings of statehood: a court system, an efficient police force, a powerful army, a sophisticated intelligence service, a national anthem and a flag – the black banner of al-Qaeda. More importantly, its coffers are buoyed by revenue from oil, enabling it to function as a proper state. ISIS has taken control of land in Syria and Iraq, fighting against both the Syrian and Iraqi armies, and has outflanked similar groups in the jihadi movement. Its caliph, Abu Bakr al-Baghdadi, has received pledges of support from deadly groups reaching as far as Nigeria and Egypt – Boko Haram of Nigeria and Ansar Bayt al-Maqdis in the Sinai Peninsula. ISIS is extending its reach into Europe as well, hoping to re-establish the Islamic empire that once ruled Spain. ISIS has not vanished. Its ideological roots and power base have proved stronger than many observers once claimed them to be.

*　　*　　*

This book will delve into the ideological foundations of the Islamic State and the caliphate, taking the reader from the late Ottoman era up to the present. It will try to shed light upon the true nature of ISIS: where it came from, how it has flourished and where it might be heading in the years ahead, using first-hand interviews with ISIS members and people living within ISIS-held territory, as well as presenting the observations of field reporters from within ISIS-held territory. Who were the shadowy figures behind ISIS's formation in 2013? Were they only ex-Baathists from Saddam Hussein's army, who turned to jihad after 2003? Was it born out of the Obama administration's reluctance to intervene in the Syrian conflict since 2011? Was it the brainchild of Iran, as the Syrian opposition has claimed? Did it originate in Turkey and Saudi Arabia, as the governments of Tehran and Damascus claim? Or was it a combination of all of these factors that grew out of control and has now become a 'gun for hire', willing to work with anyone in the region, against everybody else? The truth, of course, is still unknown – and it may take years, if not decades, for any convincing answers to emerge.

I originally hesitated before writing this book. It was a dangerous project which could have cost me my life. By training, I am a Syrian historian specializing in pre-Baathist Syria. I found it hard to write a book about post-Baathist Syria. In the Syrian north, where ISIS rules today, the state has vanished into thin air. The pre-Baathist Syria of the 1950s will never return – nor will the Baathist one of 1963–2011. The Damascus I know is a place of fabled beauty, in which secular statesmen charted their country's future at the founding conference of the United Nations. I have no sympathy with Islamists and power-hungry soldiers. What is happening today is a completely new chapter in the history of my country. It is an ugly chapter, but one that will last much longer than any of us desire. One cannot view ISIS, however, only through the clear-cut black and white frames of post-9/11 and pre-Arab Spring politics. It is simply not as straightforward as it seems to the Western world. A serious look at the early years of Muslim history is needed, taking readers into the inner thoughts of Abu Bakr al-Baghdadi and his ambitions, which are all deeply rooted in the past. It is in that ancient history that one might find some answers as to why ISIS emerged in 2014, and what its leaders hope to achieve in the years ahead.

Sami Moubayed
BEIRUT

ONE

All Rise for the Caliph

THE CALIPHATE IS DEPOSED.

With these four powerful words, the secular Turkish president Mustafa Kemal Atatürk abolished the last official caliphate of Islam on 3 March 1924.[1] The controversial decision was announced by the Turkish National Assembly five years after the Ottoman Empire's collapse towards the end of World War I. Part of the caliph's duties, some of his functions and what remained of his funds were transferred to the secular Turkish parliament. Atatürk explained: 'I must make it clear that those seeking to keep Muslims absorbed in the illusion of the caliphate are the enemies of Muslims.'[2] Never did he imagine that exactly 90 years later, the caliphate would be resurrected in a dusty forgotten city along the Euphrates, 1,400 km south of Istanbul.

The term 'caliph' literally means successor to Muhammad, the Prophet of Islam. On paper, the caliph rules over a sovereign state that encompasses the global Muslim community, known in Arabic as the '*ummah*'. According to Sunni Muslims, the position was first occupied by the Prophet's neighbour, friend and trustworthy companion Abu Bakr al-Siddiq in 632. People called him '*Khalifat Rasoul Allah*' (Successor of the Messenger of God). The caliph had to be chosen by consensus, through the global Muslim community. Sunni Muslims say that the caliph must be able to trace his lineage directly back to the powerful Quraysh clan of Mecca or any of its sub-branches, given that Mecca is the birthplace of Islam. The Prophet himself belonged to the

Banu Hashem clan of Quraysh. The Hanafi 'school' of Islam, however, says that non-Qurayshis can also assume the caliphate, which explains how Ottoman sultans came to rule a Muslim empire despite the fact that none of them hailed from Meccan notability. Shi'i Muslims claim that being a Mecca notable by ancestry is not enough to become caliph. Potential contenders need to hail strictly from *Ahl al-Bayt* (the family of the Prophet). This explains why Abu Bakr al-Baghdadi insists on using two important additional last names whenever making a public statement or appearance. One is *al-Qurashi* (hailing from Quraysh), and another is *al-Hassani* (descendant of the Prophet's grandson, al-Hasan ibn Ali). Western journalists and non-Muslims tend to drop both titles for practicality, but ISIS media *never* refers to him without both affiliations. Al-Baghdadi wants to draw as much historical, religious and popular legitimacy as he can; yet this should not be seen as an attempt to placate either the Shi'a or the Sunnis who oppose him.

IDEOLOGICAL FOUNDATIONS FOR THE CALIPHATE

The cornerstone of Islamic jurisprudence is the Prophet's Hadith, a meticulous compilation of Muhammad's words and actions which comes second in importance after the Holy Qur'an for all Muslims. The Prophet is quoted referencing the resurgence of the caliphate, saying:

> There will be Prophethood for as long as Allah wills it to be, then He will remove it when He wills, then there will be a caliphate on the Prophetic method and it will be for as long as Allah wills, then He will remove it when He wills, then there will be biting Kingship for as long as Allah wills, then He will remove it when He wills, then there will be oppressive Kingship for as long as Allah wills, then He will remove it when He wills, and then there will be caliphate (once again).[3]

The respected Hadith compiler Imam Muslim in his *Sahih Muslim* quotes the Prophet's Companion Abu Huraira saying: 'There will be no Prophet after me. There will be Khalifahs [caliphs] and they will number many.' Another Hadith quotes the Prophet saying:

> Leaders will take charge of you after me, where the pious (one) will lead you with his piety and the impious (one) with his impiety, so only listen to them and obey them in everything which conforms with the truth (Islam).

In the Qur'an itself, the word 'caliph' appears three times. The first is in the first *Surat al-Baqara* (verse 30) where God identifies Adam as his *khalifa* on earth. The second is in *Surat Sad* (verse 26) where God addresses King David as his *khalifa* on earth, reminding him of his obligations to rule with justice. The third is in *Surat al-Noor* (verse 55):

> God has promised those of you who have attained to faith and do right-eous deeds that, of a certainty, He will make them *Khalifa* on earth, even as He caused [some of] those who lived before them to become Khalifa; and that, of a certainty, He will firmly establish for them the religion which He has been pleased to bestow on them; and that, of a certainty, He will cause their erstwhile state of fear to be replaced by a sense of security [seeing that] they worship Me [alone], not ascribing divine powers to aught beside Me. But all who, after [having understood] this, choose to deny the truth – it is they, they who are truly iniquitous!

It must be noted that although Islam begins with Muhammad, all of the Qur'anic references to a 'Khalifa', God's successor on earth, are from the pre-Islamic Abrahamic tradition. The Qur'an makes no mention of any of the Prophet's successors, or caliphs.

WHO CAN BE A CALIPH?

Apart from lineage, conditions for becoming a caliph are fairly straightforward. The caliph must be a Muslim male. Women are not allowed to assume the rank. The caliph is required to lead the masses during prayer, and in Islamic tradition a woman cannot lead, or even appear, in an all-male mosque. The caliph must be knowledgeable in Islam; he must be just, trustworthy and have high morals. He must also be physically fit, spiritual, brave and capable of protecting the *ummah* against its enemies.[4] Both Sunnis and Shi'a agree that a caliph is a temporal ruler, expected to rule 'by justice' within the boundaries of Islamic Shari'a. He passes laws penned on his behalf by an Islamic jurist, and citizens have to obey them. The caliph, however, is never above the law of the Qur'an. If he breaks Qur'anic teachings, he can be impeached by a Shura Council – a small group of learned men mandated to debate affairs of state and take decisions on behalf of the Muslim nation. One reason justifying the impeachment of the caliph, for example, would be if he doesn't call Muslims to prayer.

After the first caliph Abu Bakr al-Siddiq's death in 634, Umar ibn al-Khattab (r. 634–44) was chosen to become caliph. He was an exceptional figure in the history of Islam: wise, just, pious and politically sharp. When Umar ibn al-Khattab spoke, his words became laws which were handed down from one generation of Muslims to the next. He was also an old friend of the Prophet and the father of his wife, Hafsa. To avoid the redundancy in saying '*Khalifat Khalifat Rasoul Allah*' (Successor of the Prophet's Successor), Umar ibn al-Khattab took on the title *Amir al-Mu'minin* (Commander of the Believers). This became both his title and that of his two successors, Uthman ibn Affan (r. 644–56) and Ali ibn Abi Talib (r. 656–61). Both were Mecca notables who were married to the Prophet's daughters. All the first four caliphs, according to Sunni Hadith, were chosen by the Prophet for an afterlife in heaven. This was an exclusive position to which none of the Prophet's family were admitted, not even his beloved first wife Khadijah, their daughter Fatima, or his favourite wife, the teenage Aisha. With the exception of Abu Bakr al-Siddiq (r. 632–4), who died a natural death at the age of 61, all the early caliphs were murdered. A Persian stabbed Umar ibn al-Khattab at a mosque; Uthman ibn Affan was slaughtered at his home; and Ali ibn Abi Talib was assassinated by a *Kharijite* (defector from Islam). All three were praying at the time of their death. The history of their lives is a focal point for the Muslim world. It is a history that Abu Bakr al-Baghdadi knows off by heart. Not only has he memorised it, but al-Baghdadi also believes that theirs is the path that the Islamic State and all of its personalities should follow today in the twenty-first century, and it is how he would like them to be remembered many years from now. These first four caliphs are the iconic role models for any good Muslim, and al-Baghdadi claims to be walking in their footsteps.

Under the first three caliphs, the capital of Islam was Medina, which houses the Prophet's grave at the Masjid al-Nabawi (Prophet's Mosque). Medina was also the place where the final chronological verses of the Qur'an were revealed to the Prophet. During the short tenure of Muhammad's son-in-law, Ali ibn Abi Talib, the fourth caliph, the Muslim capital was moved to al-Kufa in present-day Iraq, 170 km south of Baghdad. Then Ali ibn Abi Talib's successor, Muawiya ibn Abi Sufyan, Muawiya I (r. 661–80), moved the capital yet again, this time to Damascus, to prevent Ali ibn Abi Talib's heirs from claiming the caliphate for themselves. His sons, Hasan ibn Ali and Hussein ibn Ali, had declared themselves the sole rightful heirs of Muhammad, as blood relatives of the Prophet – their grandfather. Muawiya I, on the other hand, hailed from the aristocratic Banu Umayya clan, hence the designation 'Umayyads'. He originally refused to accept the new faith and dismissed its prophet as a charlatan. He took up arms against Muhammad, but after realizing that the latter was winning, Muawiya I converted to Islam. He then married his sister Ramla to the Prophet and became a reciter of the Hadith.

When he became caliph, Muawiya I persuaded Ali ibn Abi Talib's first son Hasan ibn Ali to abandon his claim to the caliphate. He then made history by transforming the caliphate into a hereditary dynasty, bequeathing the position to his own son, Yezid. The crisis of succession was passed down from one generation to another. Muawiya's son Yezid killed Ali ibn Abi Talib's second eldest son Hussein, along with his entire family, at the Battle of Karbala, 100 km south-west of Baghdad. To justify their actions, the Umayyads made use of the famed statement of the Prophet, 'If the pledge of allegiance is given to two caliphs, kill the latter.' They chopped off Hussein ibn Ali's head and sent it as a gift to Yezid's palace in Damascus. This single event inflamed the Sunni–Shi'a divide, which has lasted for 1,400 years and still continues today. The Shi'i faith is founded on the idea that Ali ibn Abi Talib and his line of successors, the Prophet's bloodline, are the rightful heirs of the Prophet. They believe that Muawiya and all consecutive caliphs of Sunni Islam have robbed them of this inheritance. The Shi'a still commemorate Hussein ibn Ali's martyrdom annually with a ten-day ritual – the Mourning of Muharram. Abu Bakr al-Baghdadi grew up hearing the stories of all these wrongdoings to Ali ibn Abi Talib and his family by the Umayyads. Like many Sunni Muslims, he isn't fond of the Umayyad dynasty and has a lot of respect for Ali ibn Abi Talib, whose name is carried by one of al-Baghdadi's own children. Another child is named after Ali ibn Abi Talib's son, Hasan.

The Sunni Umayyads were Islam's first dynasty. They created an empire that grew rapidly in territory, incorporating the Caucasus, Sindh, the Maghreb and the Iberian Peninsula, known as al-Andalus. At its peak, the Umayyad caliphate covered 13.4 million km^2. The fall of the Umayyad dynasty at the hands of the Abbasids in 750 ushered in centuries of strife within the Islamic world and invasion from without. The Abassids, a clan descending from the Prophet's younger uncle, Abbas ibn Abd al-Muttalib, moved the caliphate to Baghdad. The Abbasid period, however, saw other caliphates established in Umayyad Andalusia and Fatimid Cairo, as well as the Crusaders' capture of Jerusalem and other Muslim territory. In 1258, the Mongols invaded Baghdad and reduced the crown jewel of the Abbasid Empire to rubble. The caliphate was soon re-established in Cairo by the Mamluks, descendants of Turkic slaves who had served in the Abbasid army, until they themselves were overrun by the Ottoman Turks at the turn of the sixteenth century. The Ottomans then moved the caliphate yet again, this time to Istanbul, and from there, the Muslim world was ruled continuously until Atatürk abolished the caliphate in 1924. These tumultuous years for the world of Islam, just before the consolidation of Ottoman rule, saw the birth of one scholar whose ideas would resonate throughout the centuries and influence Islamic radicals from the medieval period to present-day ISIS fighters: Ibn Taymiyya.

DEEP ROOTS IN HISTORY

Born in Harran on the southern edge of present-day Turkey, Ibn Taymiyya (1263–1328) was raised by his father Shihab al-Din, who was a theologian. Ibn Taymiyya grew up in Mamluk Damascus hearing the horrifying stories of human suffering in Baghdad at the hands of the Mongols. The two cities had once been the capitals of two glorious Muslim empires, and their fates seemed inseparable. The reason for this excessive misery, Ibn Taymiyya later wrote, was because Muslims had strayed from the true meaning of Islam. It should have come as no surprise to the Muslim world, he added. Moral corruption and social decay were the reasons behind the God-sent collective punishment for the people of Baghdad. A rebirth could only be achieved, he wrote, if Muslims returned to the earliest interpretations of the Holy Qur'an, and to the life and practice of the *Salaf* (first Muslims). The Mongol sacking of Baghdad was God's justice, he claimed. Something was horribly wrong in the Muslim world and unless it was addressed properly, once and for all, more disaster would soon befall Muslims around the globe. Ibn Taymiyya called for a holy jihad to create an Islamic state, ruled by a caliph, according to the basic guidance of the Holy Qur'an:

> It is obligatory to know that the office in charge of commanding over the people (i.e. the *Khalifa*) is one of the greatest obligations of religion. In fact, there is no establishment of religion except by it. This is the opinion of the salaf (first Muslims).[5]

Only then would justice prevail in the Muslim world.

Ibn Taymiyya's views earned him a colourful assortment of powerful enemies. Kings and sultans despised him because he challenged their authority and accused them of being weak. Sufis, Christians, Shi'a and Alawites abhorred him because Ibn Taymiyya collectively wrote them off as agents of foreign powers and infidels, deserving of nothing but the sword. He wrote polemics against them all and argued vociferously with the ruling of jurists and theologians of his day.[6] Ibn Taymiyya spent 15 years in the prisons of Damascus and Cairo. His last tenure in prison was in 1320 when he issued a *fatwa* (religious decree) banning Muslims from visiting the Prophet's grave in Medina. Graves and tombstones were un-Islamic, he argued; they were Christian habits, and reflected attention to a material life. He demanded that the authorities tear down the Prophet's grave at the Masjid al-Nabawi in order to cleanse the Holy Land. On the subject of jihad, Ibn Taymiyya wrote: 'It is in jihad that one can live and die in ultimate happiness, both in this world and in the afterlife. Abandoning it means losing entirely or partially both kinds of happiness.' True to his teachings, his disciples took up arms to fight the invading Mongols, who arrived at the gates of Damascus in 1330. Ibn Taymiyya did not live to see the Mongols destroying his city. He died in Damascus in 1328, at the age of 65.

THE BIRTH OF WAHHABISM

The ideas of Ibn Taymiyya loomed long after his death; they were preserved and taught by scholars in Damascus, Cairo and Arabia. He had inspired two central Muslim figures who single-handedly influenced the biggest transformations in Sunni Islam. Muhammad ibn Abd al-Wahhab (1703–92) and Muhammad ibn Saud (d. 1765) were the founders of modern Wahhabism that, in turn, formed the backbone of ISIS theory.

Muhammad ibn Abd al-Wahhab detested anything and anybody that did not adhere to the orthodox interpretations of Islam. He was invited to settle in Diriyah, a small town on the north-western outskirts of Riyadh, by its ruler, Muhammad ibn Saud, who had watched his career with great interest. The two men saw things eye-to-eye when it came to the future of Islam; both were obedient pupils of Ibn Taymiyya, and they worked together brilliantly to expand their power and influence over the Arabian Peninsula and beyond. Both Abd al-Wahhab and Ibn Saud opposed Ottomanism and all post-Muhammadian interpretations of Islam. They excommunicated Jews, Christians, Shi'a and Alawites. The crux of Wahhabi thought is that only Allah is to be worshipped and loved. No idols were allowed in their version of Islam, not even the Prophet's Companions. No graves or representations of human or animal forms were tolerated. There should be no religious celebrations, not even to celebrate the birthday of the Prophet.

By 1790, the two men had taken over most of what is now known as Saudi Arabia, except for Mecca and Medina. They spread fear and obedience throughout the Arabian Desert, using brutal punishments such as the severing of feet, hands and heads. In the absence of mass communication, stories of their brutal campaigns were handed down from one generation to another, a gruesome form of oral history. When reaching the holy Shi'i city of Karbala (in modern-day Iraq) in 1801, the forces of Ibn Saud butchered 5,000 Shi'a. Uthman bin Bashir al-Najadi, a historian of the first Saudi state and a contemporary of Ibn Saud and Abd al-Wahhab, wrote: 'We took Karbala and we slaughtered. We took its people *sabaya* [as booty and slaves]. With the permission of Allah, we will not apologize for what we have done and we tell all *kuffar* [unbelievers], "You will receive similar treatment."'[7]

WAHHABISM TODAY

In 1812, the Ottomans struck back through their viceroy in Egypt, Mehmet Ali Pasha, retaking all the lost territory in the Arabian Peninsula by the winter of 1818. Mehmet Ali's son Ibrahim Pasha arrested Ibn Saud's grandson and had him deported to the Ottoman imperial capital Istanbul, where he was interrogated and beheaded, putting an end to the Saud dynasty's first kingdom. At the turn of the twentieth century, one of Ibn Saud's direct grandchildren, Abdul-Aziz, breathed renewed life into the Wahhabi project. The collapse of the Ottoman Empire after World War I and its withdrawal from the Arab world left a power vaccum that allowed Abdul-Aziz to revive the House of Saud and launch an aggressive war against the other tribes of the Arabian Peninsula. Armed with swords and surrounded by fearless warriors, he launched a military campaign to regain cities and towns once ruled by his ancestors, retaking one after another. In 1932, Abdul-Aziz formed the modern kingdom of Saudi Arabia, named after Ibn Saud and ruled at first by Abdul-Aziz and then by his male children after him. The descendants of Abd al-Wahhab, now known as the 'al-Sheikh' family, were given control of the kingdom's spiritual and religious institutions, upholding the alliance of the founders. At the time of writing in 2015, Abd al-Wahhab's descendant, Abdul-Aziz ibn Abdullah al-Sheikh, is the Grand Mufti of Saudi Arabia while Ibn Saud's great grandchild Salman is the seventh king of Saudi Arabia.

Thanks to Saudi Arabia, Wahhabism has survived much longer than its original authors and engineers. For the past 80 years, the works of Abd al-Wahhab and Ibn Taymiyya have been taught extensively in Saudi educational institutions. Abd al-Wahhab's classic book, *Al-Tawhid* (Monotheism), is compulsory at all state-run schools. Their thoughts and writings have had a profound influence on generations of Saudis, and on all Arabs who have lived and worked in Saudi Arabia since the 1970s. Although extremely critical of the House of Saud, Osama bin Laden, himself a Saudi citizen, was also influenced by the teachings of Ibn Taymiyya. At least once, back in 1996, Bin Laden paid tribute to the inspiration behind Wahhabism, saying: 'Real believers will instigate the *ummah* against its enemies, just like the *ulema salaf* Ibn Taymiyya.'[8] Spreading the faith by the sword, killing infidels and purifying the Islamic world from foreign ideas and lifestyles is the crux of Wahhabism and forms the cornerstone of jihadi thought and doctrine. It is the ideological blueprint for all the Sunni jihadi movements that have dominated world affairs over the last generation, namely al-Qaeda, Jabhat al-Nusra and ISIS.

All of these Islamic groups are loyal students of Ibn Taymiyya. When asked for justification as to why they kill Christians, for example, members of ISIS point to the ancient works of Ibn Taymiyya as the foundation for their ideology. The invisible connection between eighteenth- and nineteenth-century Wahhabism and twenty-first-century ISIS does not necessarily mean that Saudi Arabia is directly behind the rise in all jihadism in today's world. Contemporary jihadis, however, are the intellectual product of a school of thought founded in the Arabian Desert back in 1744. This school thrives in the psyche of Saudi officialdom and in the books of Saudi theorists. Without Wahhabism, there would be no Saudi Arabia, no Islamic State in al-Raqqa today and no talk of al-Qaeda or ISIS.

Oil-rich Saudi Arabia has been marketing its own vision of Islam for years. Under the long rule of King Fahd (r. 1982–2005), for example, Saudi Arabia financed 210 Islamic centres around the world, as well as 1,500 mosques, 202 Islamic faculties and 2,000 schools. All of them, from Nigeria to Malaysia, were packed with Wahhabi scholars and books. Saudi teaching and influence has spread far and wide, reaching deep into Bosnia, Chechnya, London, Canada and the United States. When the president of Algeria, Chadli Bendjedid, came to Riyadh seeking money in the early 1980s, the Saudis complied, but also sent him an aeroplane filled with books by Ibn Taymiyya and Muhammad Abd al-Wahhab. In 2013, the Saudis allocated $35 billion for schools in south Asia, where one billion of the world's 1.6 billion Muslims live.[9] With Wahhabi views deeply imprinted in their minds and hearts, an estimated 35,000–40,000 Saudis went to jihad in Afghanistan in the late 1980s.[10]

In 2007, Stuart Levey, the US Under Secretary for Terrorism and Financial Intelligence in charge of monitoring terror trafficking, spoke to ABC about al-Qaeda, saying: 'if I could somehow snap my fingers and cut off the funding from one country, it would be Saudi Arabia.'[11] Not a single individual identified by the United States as having funded terrorism was prosecuted by Saudi Arabia, he added. According to a cable revealed on WikiLeaks, the Secretary of State Hillary Clinton wrote in December 2009, 'Saudi Arabia remains a critical financial support base for al-Qaida [...] and other terrorist groups.'[12] Saudi donors were the 'most significant source of funding to Sunni terrorist groups worldwide,' she added.[13]

THE CALIPHATE FROM 1924 TO 2014

The Ottoman caliphate that ended in 1924 was a symbol of Islamic unity and power. During World War I, it had shrunk to a semi-symbolic and very lightweight religious authority. By the early 1920s, gone was the pomp and power vested in the position of the Ottoman Sultan, the last of whom was Mehmed VI, also known by his birth name, Wahiduddin. His army was crushed and his empire lay in ruins. His capital was occupied by Western powers after the Great War (1914–18). Having once commanded wide respect reaching as far as Muslim Spain and India, the defeated caliph was now forced to obey the dictates of Great Britain and France. He had to give up parts of Anatolia, relinquish all of Syria and Iraq, and unconditionally release Allied prisoners. The caliph also had to surrender control of the famed Ottoman railway and telegraph routes of communication. On 17 October 1922, Mehmed VI left his throne in Istanbul; he travelled aboard a British liner headed to Malta, with orders never to return. He never did, and nor did the caliphate of Islam as the world had known it.

Two years later, in March 1924, President Mustafa Kemal Atatürk officially abolished the caliphate. Some of Atatürk's aides had advised against such a move, suggesting that it could be separated from the sultanate, and thus maintained. Doing away with the sultan's divine authority was one thing, but abolishing a title once held by Muhammad's Companions was something totally different. They argued that keeping the caliphate would serve the interests of the new Turkish republic, uniting the world's 15 million Muslims behind its authority.[14] It would be similar to the Vatican's hold over Catholicism, they argued. The staunchly republican and secular Atatürk, however, had different plans for Turkey. A caliphate strongly contradicted republicanism, he said. The two simply couldn't mix. According to the new constitution, the Turkish people were the source of legislation and not Islam, nor the caliph. Muslims around the world, former subjects of the caliph, were unhappy with Atatürk's decision. Many tried to save the caliphate from collapse, but with little success. In 1919, for example, the Khalifat Movement of India was created to lobby global Muslim support against Great Britain, attracting senior figures to its events, including Mahatma Gandhi. It was short-lived and unsuccessful, as were other bids for the caliphate. In Damascus, a Caliphate Movement was established by the Algerian notable Emir Said al-Jazairi, but it too had died out by the late 1920s.

One caliphate aspirant was King Ahmad Fouad I of Egypt, and another was Sharif Hussein ibn Ali, the emir of Mecca and commander of a British-backed Arab uprising against the Ottoman Empire during World War I.[15] Hussein ibn Ali positioned himself as the natural successor to the last Ottoman caliph, Wahiduddin. He pointed to his family tree, saying that his great ancestor was the Prophet Muhammad himself, making him perfect for the job. Hussein ibn Ali announced his bid for the vacant caliphate on 11 March 1924, just two weeks after it had been abolished in Turkey.[16] One year later, his kingdom in the Hejaz was overrun by Abdul-Aziz al-Saud and he was banished to Cyprus. His claims to the caliphate vanished with his political demise. On 25 March 1924, the king of Egypt called for a pan-Islamic conference to discuss the future of the caliphate. The aim was to 'unite all Muslims' under authority of the new caliph-in-waiting, and it was endorsed by al-Azhar, the highest religious authority in Egypt. Both initiatives failed.[17]

The issue was hardly forgotten in the century that followed. The Muslim Brotherhood, founded in Egypt in 1928, called for the restoration of the caliphate. The Brotherhood's founder and chief ideologue, Hasan al-Banna, declared:

You [the Muslim Brotherhood] are neither a welfare organization nor a political party, nor a local association with strictly limited aims. Rather you are a new spirit making its way into the heart of this nation. A new light is dawning.[18]

This new light would only shine once an Islamic state was firmly in place throughout the Arab and Muslim worlds. Although al-Banna didn't speak much about it, the end objective of a caliphate was at the core of his guiding ideology and principles. According to al-Banna's *ijtihad* (intellectual discourse), the root problem of the Muslim world was the individual corruption and moral decay of society. Both were perceived to be the direct result of Western-imposed lifestyles and ideas brought by foreign occupiers to the Arab world. Muslims, therefore, had to rid themselves not only of the physical forms of occupation, but also of Western influences that contradicted Islamic morality and behaviour: 'No revival for a nation without manners.' Liberation came first, reform came second, and only then would the time be ripe for an Islamic form of government. Hasan al-Banna said that after the Muslim world was liberated from colonial rule, the time would come to establish the Islamic State. It would carry its mission 'to all mankind'. He added, 'Without its establishment, every Muslim would be living in sin and would be responsible before Allah for the failure to do so.'[19] This is how the Syrian Muslim Brotherhood justified its decision to run for parliament in the 1950s, claiming that the chamber's pulpit would be used to raise the call for an Islamic state.[20]

The demand for a caliphate has therefore been deep-rooted in the rhetoric of political Islam and within conservative Muslim societies ever since the Ottoman caliphate collapsed. In 2007, for example, a Gallup Poll found that 71 per cent of respondents from four Muslim countries wanted the laws of Islamic Shari'a to apply in every Islamic country. They were of different age groups and backgrounds, coming from Egypt, Morocco, Pakistan and Indonesia. Additionally, 65 per cent wanted unity of Muslim states under a caliphate and 74 per cent wanted to keep Western values out of Islamic countries.[21] Also that summer, 100,000 people filled a major stadium in Jakarta to 'push for the creation of a single state across the Muslim world.'[22] In mid-2006,

Osama bin Laden called Baghdad the 'home of the caliphate'.[23] It wasn't clear if he was referring to the old Abbasid dynasty or if this was where he wanted the new caliphate to be based. Wahhabis, after all, recognize only four caliphs in Islam and they completely reject the caliphs who ruled Damascus and Baghdad under the Umayyad and Abbasid dynasties.

Although al-Qaeda leaders believed in the caliphate, they saw it as a distant aspiration, used for PR and motivational purposes. When asked by the journalist Robert Fisk what kind of system he would like to live under, Osama bin Laden famously replied, 'All Muslims would like to live under Shari'a Law.' He did not mention the caliphate per se. In 2001, Bin Laden said that it was obligatory for all Muslims to establish 'an Islamic State that abides by God's laws.'[24] He also made no mention of the caliphate and only started using the term more frequently after the 2003 occupation of Iraq. Osama bin Laden's mentor Abdullah Azzam, the leader of the Afghan Arab Islamists from 1979 to 1989, added that the jihad of today is 'individually obligatory for every Muslim.' Jihad needs to occur, he said, 'until the last piece of Islamic land is freed from the Disbelievers.'[25] Only then will a caliph rise to rule the Islamic State, he adds. In 1982, Ayman al-Zawahiri, Osama bin Laden's right-hand man and his successor as the global leader of al-Qaeda, wrote that two Islamic states were emerging: one in Afghanistan and another in Chechnya. He made no mention of the caliphate.

Despite this, the rhetoric of the caliphate was returning in Western discourse. In 2006, US President George W. Bush mentioned the caliphate 15 times, including four times in a single speech.[26] The US Vice-President Dick Cheney warned that al-Qaeda wanted to 're-create the old caliphate', while Defense Secretary Donald Rumsfeld added that al-Qaeda wanted 'to establish a caliphate' instead of mainstream Muslim regimes.[27] Meanwhile, the British Chief of General Staff Sir Richard Dannatt explained that British troops were needed in Afghanistan because the long-term objective of the Islamists was restoring 'the historic Islamic Caliphate'.[28] In August 2011, the US Representative Allen West added: 'this so-called "Arab Spring" is less about a democratic movement, than it is about the early phase of the restoration of an Islamic caliphate'.[29] The Western obsession was not unfounded. All of this came in the aftermath of 9/11, when fear of Islam heightened as a reaction to the threat of terrorism from al-Qaeda under Bin Laden's leadership.

Shortly after they won the post-Arab Spring elections in Tunisia in October 2011, the Secretary-General of the Islamic al-Nahda party, Hamadi al-Jabeli, said: 'We are in the sixth caliphate, God willing.' By sixth he was referring to the four *Salaf* caliphs (Abu Bakr al-Siddiq, Umar ibn al-Khattab, Uthman ibn Affan, Ali ibn Abi Talib) and adding a fifth, Umar ibn Abdul-Aziz of the Umayyad dynasty. Tunisian leader Rashid al-Ghannouchi added that a caliphate was the hope and desire of all Muslims.[30] When asked how seven armies were unable to defeat Israel during the war of 1948, veteran Syrian scholar Sati al-Husari once replied that this was precisely because they were seven armies.[31] One army was needed, with one caliph running the Islamic State. The leader of the Egyptian Muslim Brotherhood, Mohammed Badie, went further, saying that an Islamic state governed by the laws of Shari'a and headed by a caliphate was his ultimate goal, and that of his party.[32]

Yet it was 90 years after Atatürk that the first serious contender for the 'caliph' emerged. Rising from obscurity, Ibrahim Awwad Ibrahim al-Badri (aka Abu Bakr al-Baghdadi), a veteran leader of al-Qaeda in Iraq and a former inmate of the US prison facility Camp Bucca in Iraq, was declared by ISIS as the new Caliph of Islam. In a propaganda video posted on 29 June 2014, a day laden with religious significance as it is the first day of the Muslim holy month of Ramadan, ISIS spokesman Taha Subhi Falaha (aka Abu Muhammad al-Adnani) announced the re-establishment of the caliphate to the world in a communiqué read in Arabic and translated into English, French, German and Russian. He also announced that from now on, ISIS would be referred to as the Islamic State (IS) and that Abu Bakr al-Baghdadi would assume the title Caliph Ibrahim. Following al-Adnani's announcement, al-Baghdadi appeared, speaking at a mosque in Mosul a few weeks after Iraq's second largest city fell to

ISIS. In his 20-minute speech, the 43-year-old turbaned al-Baghdadi spoke with a strong commanding voice, capturing the minds of many in the Arab and Muslim worlds. The announcement was followed by celebrations in ISIS-captured cities and towns. In ISIS's Syrian stronghold, the city of al-Raqqa, a large parade was organized. ISIS fighters, all in uniform, marched in the streets astride Russian-made tanks that they had captured from the Syrian army, and US-made Humvees and trucks captured from the Iraqi army. The parade even featured a defunct Scud missile that the group had captured from a Syrian army facility. The body of the missile was inscribed with the words: 'The Islamic State of Iraq and Levant', written in curvy Arabic calligraphy. The celebrations lasted into the night, with ISIS fighters standing on street corners, AK-47s hanging from their shoulders, to hand out sweets to the joyful crowds.

A CALIPHATE DECLARED NULL AND VOID

When Abu Bakr al-Baghdadi proclaimed himself caliph, ISIS spokesman Abu Muhammad al-Adnani described it as 'a dream that lives in the depths of every Muslim believer.'[33] He added: 'The legality of all emirates, groups, states, and organizations becomes null by the expansion of the caliph's authority.'[34] In other words, with a single verdict, he rejected all other Islamic groups as invalid. The declaration was sharply criticized by Islamic scholars worldwide. Most weren't critical of the concept, but of the person himself. Before establishing ISIS, Abu Bakr al-Baghdadi had worked his way up in the ranks of the Islamic State of Iraq (ISI), becoming its leader in 2010 after a short term in an American prison in Iraq. He was largely a shadowy figure whose name was either mentioned briefly in the news or on the United States' Most Wanted list. The military defeats that ISIS had suffered at the hands of Iraqi Sunni tribes, known as the 'Sahawat' (awakenings), pushed al-Baghdadi and his organization to the backbenches as the Arab Spring began to topple long-standing Arab regimes left, right and centre.

The exiled Syrian Muslim Brotherhood said that the caliphate could not be assumed by a political and religious 'nobody'. Even Salafi clerics had few good things to say about ISIS. The Saudi-based Syrian preacher Adnan al-Aroor labelled them 'modern-day *Khawarij*'. In Islamic terms, this refers to Muslims who have deviated from mainstream Islam. The Saudi government official Saleh al-Fawzan added that ISIS is the creation of 'Zionists and Crusaders'.[35] While the notion of an Israeli or Western hand being involved in the creation of ISIS may seem far-fetched, this choice of labels from the Saudi spokesman is an indication of the levels of venom that the most traditional representatives of the Islamic order were prepared to level at this ISIS upstart. Many, including Abu Muhammad al-Maqdisi, the one-time spiritual mentor of Abu Musaab al-Zarqawi, who was the Jordanian leader of al-Qaeda in Iraq from 2004–6, share this view.[36]

The harshest criticism of all, no doubt, came from Abu Mohammad al-Golani, the al-Zawahiri-backed commander of Jabhat al-Nusra, the al-Qaeda branch in Syria, and one-time close friend and protégé of al-Baghdadi. Al-Baghdadi had despatched al-Golani shortly after the war in Syria started, in order to establish a branch of ISIS in Syria. Al-Golani, however, broke off from his mentor's organiza-tion and established Jabhat al-Nusra, with al-Qaeda's leader Ayman al-Zawahiri's blessing. Appalled by his ex-friend's audacity, al-Golani announced: 'Abu Bakr is a usurper. Even if he were to declare the caliphate a thousand times, no one must be deceived.' He added that ISIS's move 'destroys the jihadi project that the nation has been dreaming over for 1,400 years.'[37] In a communiqué broadcast by Al Jazeera TV, al-Golani said that al-Baghdadi 'was wrong when he announced the Islamic State in Iraq and the Levant without asking permission or receiving advice from us and even without notify-ing us.'[38] When the al-Qaeda leader Ayman al-Zawahiri challenged Abu Bakr al-Baghdadi's claim to the caliphate, he too was not spared from the violent rhetoric of ISIS. He refused to recognize Abu Bakr al-Baghdadi, prompting an ISIS spokesman to say:

> If it's God's fate for you to ever set foot in the Islamic State, you have to
> give the *ba'ya* to its leader and to become one of its soldiers, under the flag
> of its emir, Abu Bakr al-Baghdadi. [...] This applies to you, O' Zawahiri
> and to you, O' Mullah Omar.[39]

On 20 September 2014, over 120 Sunni clerics from the Sufi order signed an open letter to Abu Bakr al-Baghdadi, challenging his interpretations of the Holy Qur'an and the Prophet's Hadith. 'You have misinterpreted Islam into a religion of harshness, brutality, torture and murder,' they said. 'This is a great wrong and an offense to Islam, to Muslims and to the entire world.'[40] The group was accused of instigating *fitna* (sedition). The heavyweight Doha-based Egyptian theologian Yusuf al-Qaradawi added: 'The declaration issued by the Islamic State is void under Shari'a and has dangerous consequences for the Sunnis in Iraq and the revolt in Syria.'[41] The title of caliph, he noted, can only be given by the entire Muslim nation, and not by a specific group or individual.

Further attempts have been made to de-Islamify and de-Sunnify ISIS. In France, thousands of Muslims rallied at a mosque to say: 'Not in our name.' In Egypt, Dar al-Ifta, the religious authority in charge of issuing *fatwa*s (religious dictums) ruled to stop calling the group 'Islamic State'. Instead, it ought to be referred to as 'Al-Qaeda Separatists in Iraq and Syria' (QSIS). In October 2014, the Islamic Society of Britain, the Association of British Muslims and the Association of Muslim Lawyers proposed coining the term 'Un-Islamic State' (USIS). An article was widely circulated in the online *Middle East Eye*, saying that, before bombing ISIS, the world should acknowledge that they are neither Muslims nor Sunnis, so as not to permanently associate the group's terror agenda with innocent Muslims around the world.

At the time of writing in mid-2015, the Western media is still busy trying to explain the strange and rising phenomenon of the caliphate, often misleadingly describing al-Baghdadi as successor to the first caliph of Islam, Abu Bakr al-Siddiq. Entire chunks of al-Baghdadi's sermon in Mosul, after all, were taken directly from al-Siddiq's speeches. Western journalists communicating the story to an uninformed audience have wrapped up their articles with a historical brief, saying that the caliphate of Islam was established after the Prophet Muhammad's death in 632 and lasted until 1924 when it was abolished by Kemal Atatürk after World War I. Whether intentionally or not, this flawed argument implies that Abu Bakr al-Baghdadi is the natural successor to Abu Bakr al-Siddiq and a line of great men like Umar ibn al-Khattab, Ali ibn Abi Talib and Ottoman sultans like Suleiman the Magnificent, Abdülmecid I, Murad I and Abdul Hamid II.

Abu Bakr al-Baghdadi's rise to prominence in mid-2014 was expedited by the absence of galvanizing leaders in the Sunni community across the Arab world. In the twentieth century, the Shi'a had found a great leader in Ruhollah Khomeini, the central figure of Iran's 1979 Revolution. He lifted the Shi'i communities in Iran and the Arab world from sentiments of oppression and victimization; he built a strong state in Iran, with influence beyond its borders; Ruhollah Khomeini became the Shi'i world's *vali e-faqih* (guardian of the faith). He was succeeded in Iran by another charismatic figure, Ali Khamenei, while strong leaders also emerged in other Shi'i communities in the region, such as Hasan Nasrallah of Hizbullah in Lebanon and the Shi'a-affiliated Abdul Malik al-Houthi in Yemen. By comparison, the recent war has left Syria with no unifying, single Sunni leader. There has been no Sunni leader in Lebanon since the murder of Rafik al-Hariri in 2005. There has been no Sunni leader in Iraq since the execution of Saddam Hussein in 2006. All the Sunni figures who have emerged since then, from Vice-President Tariq al-Hashimi in Iraq to Prime Minister Saad al-Hariri in Lebanon, are spiritless, to say the least. And more importantly, there is no leader in the Sunni world who proclaims a Sunni message. None of the secular leaders has fit the bill. Sunni Muslims of today are where the Shi'a were 35 years ago: they feel weak, leaderless, victimized and abandoned. So it is no wonder that the most fervently pious of them are seeking a different Sunni solution. They feel that they *need* a caliph. The Turkish President

Recep Tayyip Erdogan has tried to play the role of Sunni leader, but his political ambitions have got in the way. Because he is a non-Arab, he has always had a language and a cultural barrier with Arab Muslims. The House of Saud tried to play the role of Sunni leadership in the Arab and Muslim worlds, but their form of radical Wahhabi Islam has always got in the way of their success, as has the advanced age of their monarchs, who have all been way past retirement age. As they didn't come from Quraysh and were not related to the Prophet, they weren't able to assume the title of 'caliph'. This is what makes Abu Bakr al-Baghdadi and the ISIS phenomenon so important. They are filling a vacuum at the leadership level of what was once an '*ummah*' (nation) stretching from the Atlantic coast to the borders of China under one caliph. Al-Baghdadi did not have to hail from the clergy to lead the Sunni world. As long as mainstream Sunnis were leaderless and feeling victimized, al-Baghdadi's actions and ideas would linger, perhaps even beyond his own lifetime, as we shall see in Chapter 5.

TWO

Gentlemen to Jihadis

THE JIHADI GROUPS OPERATING IN SYRIA TODAY ARE NOT NEW. Although many were born after the outbreak of hostilities in Syria in 2011, their ideological roots can all be traced back to the Syrian branch of the Muslim Brotherhood, established in the mid-1940s. This is when the idea of a 'caliph-led Islamic State' began to take shape in people's minds long before it saw the light of day in parts of northern Syria nearly 70 years later. As explained in Chapter 1, it has also been present in Sunni Islamic discourse for centuries. It was the Muslim Brotherhood, however, not ISIS, which in modern times first introduced the new terms of Islam into the Syrian dictionary. Terms like 'Islamic State' and 'caliphate' were widely discussed by Syrian intellectuals in the 1920s, at the time of Atatürk's controversial decision to abolish the Ottoman caliphate. Articles debating the subject appeared on the front page of Syrian newspapers. The topic slowly disappeared from public discourse and was restricted only to Islamic journals and salons. It was simply written off by the mainstream public as démodé – something of the past that was more folkloric than real. Examining Syrian newspapers from the 1940s to the 1960s, one finds almost no mention of the caliphate, except in the Brotherhood daily *al-Manar*. In the 1980s, celebrated playwright Muhammad al-Maghout even penned a play that was performed on the stages of Damascus, poking fun at the caliphate's indulgences and depicting the caliph as a fat, turbaned buffoon chasing a concubine.

Colonialism, Baathism, Arab nationalism, secularism and all the upheavals of the twentieth century prevented the Salafis from inching closer to their dream project. The first generation of the Brotherhood tried to gain power through democratic practice during the 1940s and 1950s. The second generation tried, and failed dramatically, to achieve their aim militarily, both in 1964 and during the bloody years from 1976 to 1982. The Baathists responded with unprecedented force, eradicating the Islamic movement from public life throughout Syria for nearly three complete decades. Their mosques were demolished, their publications suspended and their underground bases bulldozed.

An entire generation of Syrian Islamists was killed, exiled or imprisoned in Syrian jails. Some remain in prison even today. Those released by presidential pardon in the early 2000s were generally too old and mentally disoriented to lead the Islamic masses. A third generation was born and raised in the faraway cities of Europe. Although now in their mid-thirties, most of them have never visited Syria. The fourth generation appeared after 9/11, carrying arms in Kabul, Peshawar and Baghdad. By then, many were no longer affiliated with the Syrian Brotherhood but instead with more radical groups like al-Qaeda. The fifth generation, now members of Jabhat al-Nusra and ISIS, are taking dramatic steps towards their ancient dream, with the help of comrade jihadis from Iraq and Europe. To understand where this generation comes from, we need to delve into the origins of political Islam in Damascus and the history of twentieth-century Syrian jihad.

GENTLEMAN POLITICS AND EARLY FANATICS

The father of political Islam in modern Syria was a fair-skinned preacher from the central city of Homs named Sheikh Mustapha al-Sibaii (1915–64). He studied Shari'a law at the prestigious al-Azhar University in Cairo, where, like many of his generation, he fell under the spell of the charismatic founder of the Egyptian Brotherhood, Imam Hasan al-Banna. In 1930, al-Sibaii officially joined the Brotherhood, shortly before Egyptian authorities deported him back to Syria for taking part in clandestine anti-British activities. One year later, he founded Shabab Mohammad (Muhammad Youth), a paramilitary group of religious teens modelled after the Egyptian Brotherhood. Shabab Mohammad monopolized the Islamic street scene in Damascus and Homs, feeding off the commitment of the Syrian youth to bringing an end to the French Mandate, which had ruled Syria since 1920. Al-Sibaii recruited a handful of young men from the Syrian middle class, and formed the nucleus of what later became known as the Syrian Muslim Brotherhood.

In 1944 and 1945, al-Sibaii worked closely with Hasan al-Banna to found the Damascus branch of the Egyptian Brotherhood. At 30 years old, al-Sibaii became the leader of what was to become the most powerful Islamic group in twentieth-century Syria. He led the Syria branch of the Brotherhood through their most active parliamentary campaigns. In 1948, he volunteered for jihad in Palestine, leading a small group of Brotherhood fighters. One year later, al-Sibaii was voted into the Constitutional Assembly that drafted a new legal charter for Syria. He also served as a member of parliament from 1949 until 1951. During his tenure, he famously tabled a bill calling on the state to enforce an additional layer of black to the thin *melaya* that women wore in public, and demanded the prohibition of the albums of the Cairo-based Syrian pop singer Farid al-Atrash, who was adored by Syrian teenage girls. Al-Sibaii and his supporters lobbied hard to prevent the erection of a statue of General Yusuf al-Azma in downtown Damascus, the minister of war who was killed confronting the invading French army in 1920, on the grounds that statues were reminiscent of the pre-Islamic *jahiliyya* era (the era of ignorance) and were pagan habits that ought to be eradicated. This after all is what the Prophet had done when he took Mecca over one thousand years previously. Idol worship was prohibited in Islam. Such rhetoric resonates with the Taliban's notorious actions in March 2001 when they destroyed the ancient statues of Buddha, carved into the side of a cliff in the Bamiyan Valley in Hazarajat, central Afghanistan. A few years later, ISIS and its proxies would encourage similar activities in northern Syria. In 2013, for example, Jabhat al-Nusra rebels beheaded a statue of Abbasid-era poet and philosopher Abu Alaa al-Maari in Muarret al-Nouman in north-western Syria. He was celebrated for his criticism of all religions, Islam included. In February 2015, ISIS released a five-minute video of its warriors smashing ancient statues into tiny fragments at the Mosul Museum. The destroyed statues were thousands of years old, dating back to the Assyrian and Akkadian empires. In the video, another man is shown drilling through the statue of a winged bull, an old Assyrian deity, dating back to the seventh century. In March 2015, Abu Bakr al-Baghdadi called for the destruction of both the Great Sphinx and the Pyramids in Egypt, claiming that they were un-Islamic.[1] When Jabhat al-Nusra overran Idlib in early 2015, they also beheaded the statue of Ibrahim Hananu, a celebrated anti-French leader of the 1920s. For Syrian Islamists, this is not new. As mentioned above, they tried to do the same to Yusuf al-Azma's statue back in 1950.

In 1955, Mustapha al-Sibaii co-founded the Faculty of Islamic Shari'a at Damascus University and became its first dean. This was during the heyday of democratic rule in Syria, where civil politicians ran the state and allowed various political currents to operate in Syrian society, with no restrictions on political Islam. They failed to realize how powerful and influential this faculty would prove to be. The Shari'a department single-handedly groomed generations of Syrian clerics, many of whom went on to become Salafi leaders or ideologues. One of its most celebrated students was Abdullah Azzam, the ideological father of al-Qaeda. Al-Sibaii also worked in journalism, founding the Brotherhood newspaper *al-Manar* and serving as its chief editor in 1947. In all of his writing, al-Sibaii spoke of the core principles of Islam and preached about an Islamic state which would be based on the legacy of the *Salaf*. Al-Sibaii himself never resorted to the sword to make it happen. During the brief intervals of military rule in Syria, officers did try to clip the wings of Salafi preachers, jihadi theorists and even ordinary mosque clerics. In 1949, for example, General Husni al-Za'im banned clerics from publicly wearing the white turban and black *jubba* (religious gown). In 1950, the government took control of the country's mosques, even those which had been built with private funds. When General Adib al-Shishakli rose to power in 1953, he allowed clerics to wear their traditional garb, but only once they had obtained security clearance and an official ID from the government. This was done, al-Shishakli said, 'to protect men of religion from charlatans trafficking in the name of God.' Those who defied orders and paraded in public with their white turbans – without prior clearance – were arrested on the spot.[2]

TURNING TO THE UNDERGROUND

Mustapha al-Sibaii opposed the military regimes of both al-Za'im and al-Shishakli. Both generals had him arrested and both outlawed the Muslim Brotherhood. When the Baath Party came to power, via a military coup in March 1963, the Brotherhood offices were once again shut down, for the fourth time in just a decade. Al-Sibaii's books, along with the works of the Egyptian ideologue Sayyid Qutb, were banned from Syrian bookstores. Al-Sibaii's newspaper, *al-Manar*, was closed and al-Sibaii himself was put under house arrest; he was classified by the Baathists as 'dangerous'. Informers were stationed at his doorstep to monitor his activity; his phone was tapped and his state pension suspended. He suffered a stroke that left him partially paralysed and he died shortly after, in October 1964. His death marked the end of 'gentleman' politics among Syrian Islamists. The first generation that he embodied had tried – and failed – to achieve an Islamic state in Syria through ballots, not bullets. Clearly, this strategy had not worked. Al-Sibaii's successors were already turning to arms, trying to right the wrongs which they perceived had been done to them by consecutive Syrian governments since the 1940s.

The first elements of Salafist military Islam began to appear in Syria during the final months of al-Sibaii's own lifetime, in mid-1963. Underground cells had started to form first in Aleppo, the industrial capital of Syria's north, and in the ancient city of Hama, perched on the River Orontes. This is where a young Salafi named Marwan Hadid was recruiting teenagers into what he called Kata'ib Mohammad (Phalanges of Muhammad), which later took the name al-Tali'a al-Mukatila (Fighting Vanguards). They were preparing to launch a holy war – jihad – against the Baathists, who were principally made up of Alawites, Isma'ilis, Druze and secular Sunnis from the Syrian countryside. For the jihadis, all of these were infidels. Once they were eliminated, a true Islamic society would emerge, based on the core values of the founding fathers of Islam – the Companions of the Prophet. The Baathists were too distracted by infighting during the early weeks of their rule to pay attention to the subterranean rumblings of the growing Syrian Islamist movement.

Between March and July 1963, the Baathists were locked in a vicious war with Nasserist elements within the Syrian army, which culminated in a failed coup – and bloodbath – in Damascus that summer. While Baathists were setting up local tribunals to try the so-called 'traitors', the Islamists were busy stockpiling arms and training young men in their use. In a manner similar to that which emerged with the Palestinian resistance a few years later and with al-Qaeda in the 1990s, these men took on secret *noms de guerre*, always starting with 'Abu-' to avoid being tracked by the intelligence services. Often their choice of names was taken straight out of Muslim history books: Abu Bakr, Abu Omar, Abu Talha and Abu Ubaida. Their last names indicated which region from Syria they came from: al-Hamwi (Hama), al-Homsi (Homs), al-Yabroudi (Yabroud, in the Damascus countryside) and al-Jisri (in reference to Jisr al-Shughour, a city in north-western Syria).

The Baathists, meanwhile, were drawing on their massive membership base in the Syrian countryside, calling on teachers and village officials to come to the cities to take up government jobs. This left the rural areas free as vast playing fields for the Syrian Brothers, where they were able to teach, recruit and train young men, with little competition from the Baathists. This is similar to what happened in 2011, when the Baathists found out that their power base in the Syrian countryside was being completely overrun by mosque clerics and Islamic politicians, whose rhetoric was far more appealing to the masses than the by now archaic and bankrupt Arab nationalist rhetoric of the Baathists. Their headquarters were local mosques, whose imam was usually either a Brotherhood member or secret sympathizer. Young boys would go to the mosque after school for evening recitals of the Holy Qur'an. Brotherhood teachers would single out potential recruits, and train them in how to hide, load or strip a gun. The next stage in their training would be to engage in 24-hour surveillance of local Baathists, and then report on their movement and activities to the Brotherhood cells. Finally, the boys would be taught how to use their firearms. The Brotherhood found easy targets for shooting practice in the state-employed street-sweepers, who were often at work before dawn when nobody else was around. From the rooftops of carefully concealed huts, they would practise shooting at these wretched innocents, killing many in a ruthless training exercise.³

THE GODFATHER, MARWAN HADID

If Mustapha al-Sibaii was the father of political Islam in Syria, then Marwan Hadid (1934–76) was the godfather and founder of the militant jihadism which today influences thousands on the Syrian battlefield. Tall and red-haired, Hadid was born into a wealthy family of Albanian origin in 1934. One of his brothers, Kenaan, was a Baathist, while another, Adnan, was a communist – the classic fault lines in twentieth-century Syrian politics. Marwan disapproved of both, joining the Muslim Brothers instead during his college years. He wasn't studying Islam, like al-Sibaii, but rather industrial agriculture at the prestigious Ayn Shams University in Cairo.⁴ Although he lacked the Islamic credentials to teach, Hadid started delivering sermons at the local Barudiya mosque in his native Hama, shortly after returning to Syria. His followers gave him the honorary title of 'sheikh' when he began teaching at the Barudiya mosque, despite the fact that he had never been officially educated in Islamic Shari'a. He had no academic certificate – either from the Grand Umayyad Mosque of Damascus or from al-Azhar. By all accounts, he was never an 'alim' (a man of knowledge and science). He was immensely charismatic, however, and a gifted orator who captured the minds and hearts of his followers. Hadid warned regime-friendly clerics: 'if the worshippers of God launch the struggle against His enemies, you behave as spectators, without fighting, and therefore the enemies of God will crush you while you are in your homes, and then you will go to Hell.'[5] He spoke with particular venom about the Alawites, a splinter group of Shi'i Islam, from which Syria's military strongmen in the Baathist government hailed, including the Chief of Staff, Salah Jadid, and Air Force Commander Hafez al-Assad.

THE ALAWITES

A close-knit esoteric Shi'i community dating back to the tenth century, the Alawites followed the teachings of Muhammad ibn Nusayr al-Namiri – hence the designation 'Nusayris' – who was a contemporary of the tenth Shi'i imam. The Alawite faith stops at the tenth imam, diverging from mainstream Shi'ism, which believes in the 12 ordained imams, and the last imam, Mahdi, who lives in occultation and will reappear at the end of time. The Alawites lived in the rugged mountains surrounding the coastal city of Latakia on the Mediterranean; additional clusters lived in the towns surrounding Homs and Hama in central Syria, and within the Sanjak of Alexandretta, a narrow coastal plain along the lower valley of the River Orontes. Ibn Taymiyya had issued a religious *fatwa* (*c*.1303), accusing the Alawites of being 'greater infidels than Jews and Christians'. War against them would 'please' God Almighty, he added, because they did not believe in the Prophet of Islam. This controversial dictum became a cornerstone of hardline Sunni Muslim attitudes towards the Alawites during the 400 years of Ottoman rule. During most of their four centuries in Syria, for example, the Ottomans deliberately ignored the Alawites, acting almost as if the community did not exist. Their predecessors, the Mamluks (who ruled Syria from the mid-thirteenth to the mid-sixteenth centuries), had periodically attempted to steer them away from what they considered to be the schismatic heresy of the Shi'i faith, by resorting to the sword. And when that failed, they tried to exterminate them completely. Mass arrests, flogging, hanging in public and torture in jails were common – terrible stories of brutality and injustice have been passed down through the generations in the Alawite community.

By World War I, the Alawites numbered 100,000 and lived almost entirely off agriculture, primarily as landless serfs.[6] Many were coerced into the Ottoman army, but they were never promoted past the rank of foot soldier. The Ottomans used them as military fodder, despatching them to the frontlines with mediocre weapons – clearly to perish – so that the Empire could survive. Absentee Sunni landlords, mainly in the vicinity of Hama in the Syrian midland, abused them as a workforce. The more they disappeared from the public eye, however, the more stories were spun about their peculiar ways of life. With the passing of time, their seclusion resulted in something of an Alawite enclave within Syria – a place that was dramatically backward and medieval. Neither government clerks, schoolteachers nor policemen wanted to serve in the Alawite districts. Electricity came to Damascus in 1907, but it did not reach the Alawite villages until the late 1940s.

When the French came to Syria in 1920, they created an independent state for the Alawites, protected by the mandate regime until 1941. Its borders stretched to Greater Lebanon's northern and northeastern boundaries. It was the first time that the term 'Alawite' was coined, in parallel with 'Muhammadian', which was used by Western Orientalists to describe Sunni Muslims. Thus one community was distinguished by its reverence of Muhammad and the other by its allegiance to Ali, the Prophet's son-in-law: for the majority Sunnis, the fourth successor to the Prophet (caliph) and for the minority Shi'a, the Prophet's direct legitimate successor. The Alawites welcomed their newly found autonomy and executive powers because, for the first time ever, they were allowed self-government, although in a limited sense, and were thus freed from the burden of obeying the Sunni leaders of Damascus, Homs and Hama. The jobs provided by the French provided them with a good income, which relieved them from having to harvest crops in the vast plantations of Syrian landowners. By 1925, the Alawites had achieved all the symbols of nationhood: a police force, a government headquarters and a local municipality which served as a mini-parliament. They also had their own IDs and their own national flag – a yellow sun on a white background; they even had their own postage stamps. The French encouraged the Alawites to join the newly formed Army of the Levant, which was set up in 1921. They were now given good salaries, smart military uniforms and weapons to defend their towns and villages. This service taught them discipline, introducing them to new ideas and ushering in a military tradition to Alawite families that was to become vital to the community's future after Syrian independence was achieved in 1946. It was this tradition that the Muslim Brothers faced when they discovered, in the early 1960s, that the armed forces were packed with Baathist Alawite officers, from top to bottom, including Hafez al-Assad and his brother Rifaat.

GENTLEMAN POLITICS IN REVERSE: HAMA 1964

Marwan Hadid was greatly inspired by Ibn Taymiyya. At his urging, the Islamists of Hama began preparing for their first official holy jihad against the Alawites and the Baathists. It was the opposite of Mustapha al-Sibaii's gentleman politics. In April 1964, Sheikh Mahmud al-Hamid of the prominent Sultan Mosque in Hama put up roadblocks and delivered a fiery sermon targeting the increasingly liberal and entirely secular lifestyle that the Baathists were leading, and the rising influence of the Alawites in the Syrian army. Stores serving alcohol were ransacked and wine bottles were smashed in public and then spilled into the gutters of Hama.[7] Hadid's men captured a young Alawite militiaman, Isma'il Munzer al-Shamali of the party's National Guard. He was killed in public. The Baath soldiers responded by killing a Hama notable from the once powerful Azm family.

President Amin al-Hafez, himself a middle-class secular Sunni Muslim from Aleppo, described the events in Hama as 'a major military revolution against the state of the Baath'.[8] The army was called in, and Hadid's men fled to the Sultan Mosque, along with their leader. President Amin al-Hafez gave orders to kill them all. The mosque was shelled; its minaret was brought crashing to the ground. Hadid was arrested and 70 people died.[9] Speaking about the event in 2001, Amin al-Hafez challenged the death toll, saying that only 40 civilians were killed.[10] He added, 'Marwan [Hadid] was not as important as we claimed him to be; we exaggerated his role.'[11] Perhaps this is what Amin al-Hafez actually thought, and it explains why he set Hadid free a few months later, and why Hadid was then free to travel to Jordan in 1969. When Hadid's supporters tried to repeat the same scene at the Grand Umayyad Mosque of Damascus, soldiers broke into the ancient mosque – one of the most sacred in the entire Muslim world – and shot the rebels. Gentleman politics would no longer do, seemingly on both sides of the power spectrum. Both sides were willing to kill, either to seize power or to retain it.

The swift defeat in Hama came as a huge surprise to the Syrian jihadis. It reminded them of how poorly trained they were to take on the Baathists. It also showed them how far their enemy was willing to go to eliminate their opposition. Seventy people had been killed in Hama in one single day. It was the largest death toll the country had known since the French had bombarded the Syrian capital back in 1945. Clearly, something had gone wrong and they wouldn't try their hand at regime change again until 1976. By then, the Alawite officer that Hadid detested so much – Hafez al-Assad – had come to power in Damascus.

COLLUSION WITH HAFEZ AL-ASSAD

The new president Hafez al-Assad was well versed in history and he knew the Brotherhood well. He grew up interacting with their student members in Latakia in the late 1940s and early 1950s. This is where they had engaged in street fights during student demonstrations: Baath vs Brotherhood. He knew that they were indoctrinated politicians who would stop at nothing to achieve their goal. From the start of his rule, Assad tried to court Sunni *ulama* (scholars) to fight the Brotherhood with their own weapon and strip them of the very banner they were using to rally people against him: Islam.

In 1971, Hafez al-Assad created a parliament of appointed deputies, who were all hand-picked by him. It included the top people in Syrian society, with prominent doctors like Mohammad al-Shami and president of the Women's Syndicate, Adila Bayhum al-Jazairi. Assad insisted on bringing three Sunni clerics into the chamber: Sheikh Ahmad Kaftaro, the veteran mufti of Damascus; Sheikh Mohammad al-Hakim, the seasoned mufti of Aleppo; and Sheikh Abu al-Faraj al-Khatib, the popular preacher at the Great Umayyad Mosque of Damascus.[12] Al-Khatib had been fired from his job by Salah Jadid, who wanted to shut down the Umayyad mosque and transform it into a museum. Assad cancelled the order and welcomed al-Khatib with red carpets, restoring him to the pulpit of the Umayyad mosque, where his ancestors had taught since the late nineteenth century. He and his colleagues were strongly rooted in Damascene society. They had excellent relations with the city's mercantile elite and hailed from prominent families of great social standing in the old quarters of Damascus. All of them had been close to the first generation of Syrian Islamists under Mustapha al-Sibaii. All of them frowned upon the idea of military rebellion, and all of them saw promise in Hafez al-Assad.

In a carefully calculated move, President Assad increased the wages of the country's 1,138 mosque *imams*, 252 religious teachers, 610 *khatibs* (preachers), 1038 *mu'azzins* (prayer call men) and 280 Qur'anic readers.[13] He increased their pay three times: in 1974, 1976 and 1980. In 1976 alone, Assad spent S£5.4 million on mosque construction throughout Syria. From then until his death in 2000, he made it a habit to break his fast during the month of Ramadan – every single year – with the country's religious scholars (Sunnis, Shi'a and Alawites included). So thrilled were the Sunni notables of

Syria with Assad's gestures that they did not object when in 1973 he passed a draft constitution that omitted a clause proclaiming 'Islam is the religion of the state'. That phrase had been included in every Syrian constitution since 1920. Assad kept a clause that said: 'Islamic jurisprudence is the principal source of legislation in the Syrian Arab Republic.' The two muftis in parliament, Kaftaro and al-Hakim, did not object to the draft constitution, nor did the scholars dining at Assad's table. The only real opposition came from a respected scholar from the conservative al-Midan quarter of Damascus, Sheikh Hasan Habanakeh, himself a long-time critic of the Baath. Less prominent *ulama* rallied around him, as he was immensely popular with the city's poor; so also did the Salafis and jihadis. Wanting to avoid a confrontation, Assad backed down. On 20 February 1973, he reintroduced the clause to the constitution – in order to keep the Sunni Muslim *ulama* of Damascus happy.

In 1976, Hadid's men, by now known as the 'Fighting Vanguards of the Muslim Brotherhood', assassinated the Alawite chief of intelligence in Hama, Major Muhammad Gharrah. It was a declaration of war against Hafez al-Assad. Assad responded swiftly, abducting Hadid and sending him to jail, where he went on hunger strike. Assad didn't give up; he called on Hadid's brother Kenaan, then serving as a diplomat in Tehran, and asked him to visit Hadid in prison.[14] Hadid was offered clemency if he gave up his militant activity, but he refused. Hadid died at the Harasta Military Hospital, east of Damascus, in June 1976 at the age of 42. Assad's Islamic opponents found great inspiration in Hadid's martyrdom. Thirty-seven years later, a small militia carrying his name emerged in Syria, the 'Marwan Hadid Brigades'.[15] Affiliated to Jabhat al-Nusra, it was founded in Hama in 2013 and claimed responsibility for a rocket attack on Hermel in Lebanon's east Bekka Valley. Assad, however, had not wanted Marwan Hadid dead. He realized that a martyred Hadid would be a far greater problem for the government than one kept under lock and key. A 26-year-old zealous engineer from al-Quneitra in the Syrian Golan succeeded him at the helm of the Fighting Vanguards. The son of a town baker, Adnan

Uqla was to mastermind one of the most famous terror operations in modern Syrian history.[16] It happened in Aleppo during the summer of 1979.

On 16 June 1979, a 29-year-old Baathist officer named Ibrahim Yousef assembled 300 of his men in a dining room at the Aleppo Artillery School. He came from a peasant family in Tadaf, a small town north-east of Aleppo, and was working secretly with the Fighting Vanguards. Eleven of the Vanguards were smuggled into the academy and given army uniforms, guns and open access to bullets. Once Yousef's men were bundled into one place, the militants broke into the dining hall where Yousef had collected his men. 'Death to you!' he screamed as the jihadis opened fire on everything and everybody inside. Reports of the death toll vary, from 32 dead and 54 wounded to 83 killed. All of the victims were Alawites. The state began a manhunt through every home throughout every town and city in Syria. Scores of suspects were hauled before ad hoc military tribunals and executed on the spot. In the troubled years of 1979 to 1981, the state killed 2,000 people – mostly members of the Brotherhood and anybody associated with them, no matter how tenuously.[17] Syrians were appalled by Yousef's horrific attack in Aleppo. The state blamed it squarely on the Brotherhood. The Aachen-based Brotherhood chief Issam al-Attar retorted that this accusation was a 'barefaced lie unsupported by any fact or proof.'[18]

From here, the Brotherhood leaders took their terror to new heights, assassinating Alawite and Christian doctors and engineers. Abdul-Aziz Adi, a ranking Baathist, was gunned down in front of his wife and children and his body thrown into the street in his native Hama. In October 1976, the Fighting Vanguards killed the Alawite commander of the Hama garrison, Colonel Ali Haidar. Four months later, they murdered Mohammad al-Fadel, the rector of Damascus University; he had a brilliant legal mind and was one of the co-founders of the Baath Party. In June 1977, the Vanguards shot Brigadier Abdul Hamid Razzouq, commander of missile corps in the Syrian army. Five months later, they assassinated Professor Ali al-Ali of Aleppo

University, and in March 1978 they killed Ibrahim Na'ama, the doyen of Syrian dentists. Colonel Ahmad Khalil, director of police affairs at the Ministry of the Interior, was murdered in August 1978, and in April 1979 the Vanguards shot Syria's public prosecutor, Adel Mini. Assad's own neurologist, Mohammad Shehadeh Khalil, was assassinated in August 1979. Assad's friend and cardiologist Yousef al-Sayyegh was killed in December 1980, along with Darwish al-Zuni of the National Progress Front (NPF), a parliamentary coalition of socialist parties headed by the Baath. Anybody working with the Baathists became an open target, a scheme that was carried out with similar success 35 years later during the era of ISIS and Jabhat al-Nusra. The Vanguards even killed ten Soviet technical advisers based in Damascus, in January 1980.[19] When the Vanguard commandos were cornered by the security services, they would blow themselves up using explosives strapped to their waists. It was incredibly painful for the President to see some of Syria's best men – the leading lights of his Alawite community – fall to the guns of the Muslim Brothers.

The Brotherhood then tried to make cities go on strike by forcing all shopkeepers to shut down in the suburbs of Damascus, Aleppo and Hama, and those who refused had their premises set ablaze.[20] Between 1976 and 1979, at least 300 state-affiliated citizens were killed in Damascus, Aleppo, Hama and Idlib. Even Sunni clergymen were not spared their wrath, if they spoke out against the terror campaign. The most prominent to fall was the respected preacher Sheikh Mohammad al-Shami of the Sulaymaniyeh Mosque in Aleppo. The veteran cleric had travelled to Damascus with the city's main *ulama* a few days earlier, for an audience with the President. He asked al-Shami to: 'Go and speak to them [the Brotherhood]. See what they want. Do they want to take part in government?'[21] Assad offered to give them all cabinet portfolios except the ministries of education, defence, interior and finance. Before walking out, he warned them: 'Our army is trained for vicious warfare against the Israeli enemy. It is a strong army. If it appears on the streets, it will be extremely painful. Go and tell them just that.' As the Aleppine clerics were walking out of the palace, one of them scoffed: 'Our friend [Assad] is about to fall. Two weeks of pressure and he has already agreed to give us half the government. Tell the boys to carry on. He will collapse any minute now.'[22] Sheikh al-Shami exploded in a fit of rage against his colleagues, saying that this would be an open invitation to disaster. Days later, he was slain at his own mosque in Aleppo, on 2 February 1980.[23] The murder had the Brotherhood's fingerprints all over it.

One month later, the Islamists tried to bring their jihadi war to the streets of Aleppo, shutting down the city's commercial district for two full weeks. Open allegiance to their campaign was recorded in Idlib, Homs, Hama and Deir ez-Zour. Leaflets were dropped at night in the old Hamidiyah Market of Damascus, demanding nothing less than absolute solidarity with the Brotherhood. The Damascenes were lukewarm, having seen the fate of Hama in 1964. The city, run by a state-affiliated commercial elite, wanted to avoid such a fate at all costs. Some Brotherhood sympathizers, however, did close down. Assad then called on Badr al-Din al-Shallah, the 77-year-old president of the Damascus Chamber of Commerce. Sunni Muslim merchants swore by his name. Wearing his crimson Ottoman fez and a snow-white coat, Shallah marched down the arcaded markets of al-Hamidiyah and al-Harika, knocking on the cranked shop shutters one after another, asking owners to break the strike.

In January 1980, Assad appointed Abdel Raouf al-Kassem, an old-time Damascene Sunni Baathist, as prime minister. His father was Sheikh Atallah al-Kassem, a former mufti during the immediate post-Ottoman era. One-quarter of his cabinet posts went to Damascene Sunnis from the old bourgeoisie. Assad then raised the percentage of Sunni Muslims in the Regional Command of the Baath Party from 57 to 66.7 per cent, and decreased that of the Alawites from 33.3 to 19 per cent, before convening the seventh Baath Party Regional Congress in January 1980.[24] His brother Rifaat, commander of the elite all-Alawite Defence Corps, called for an all-out war against the Islamists. He snarled, 'Why is it that only they kill? We need to kill as well!'[25] Rifaat added, 'Stalin sacrificed ten million to preserve the Bolshevik

Revolution and Syria should be prepared to do the same.' Rifaat al-Assad said that he personally was willing to 'fight a hundred years, demolish a million strongholds, and sacrifice a million martyrs' to finish off the Syrian Brotherhood.[26] He began by doing just that, distributing arms to local militias, known as the Popular Committees, and to pro-government students at university campuses throughout Syria. Ordinary citizens, until then neutral in the war, were now forced to choose: either they were with the state or they were with those whom the state described as 'terrorists'. Rifaat's women soldiers, a hallmark of his Defence Corps, took to the streets of Damascus and began to rip the veils off the heads of Muslim women. This was his way of making a point, but it infuriated Hafez al-Assad, who came on television a few hours later with a public apology for the outrageous act.

On 9 March 1980, helicopter-borne troops were sent to the Brotherhood stronghold of Jisr al-Shughour (105 km to the north-east of Latakia), where 97 soldiers had been killed by jihadi militias. Days later the entire Third Division of the Syrian army, with 10,000 men and 250 armoured vehicles, was sent north to fight the Brotherhood in Aleppo. They were joined by Rifaat al-Assad's Defence Forces.[27] Hafez al-Assad himself began to develop grand orator skills, appearing on television night after night to drum up anti-Brotherhood sentiment. He would break into an animated monotone, seated before a camera with the Syrian flag right behind him. On the 16th anniversary of the Baath Party takeover, Assad spoke with a noticeable Islamic overtone, saying: 'Yes, I believe in God and in the message of Islam... I was, I am, and I will remain a Muslim, just as Syria will remain a proud citadel flying high the flag of Islam! But the enemies of Islam who traffic in religion will be swept away!'[28] He spoke again, with the exact same message, on 10, 11, 17, 22, 23 and 24 March, appearing at all kinds of populist rallies with peasants, teachers, students, writers and athletes. The Brotherhood and its Fighting Vanguards responded on 26 June 1980 with a failed attempt to assassinate Assad. A hand grenade was thrown at his feet and armed men opened fire at him as he was welcoming an African guest at the gates of the Presidential Palace. He kicked one grenade out of harm's way and another exploded after his body-guard had thrust himself upon it. Ten days later, Assad passed Law No. 49, making membership of the Brotherhood a capital offence, punishable by death.[29]

In August 1981, a car bomb went off outside Prime Minister Abdel Raouf al-Kassem's office. In September 1981, the Brotherhood set off a bomb at the army's headquarters in Umayyad Square, and, one month later, another at a Soviet expert's office in Damascus. On 29 November 1981, a massive explosion rocked the al-Azbakieh neighbourhood on Baghdad Street in Damascus. A Honda loaded with TNT exploded at 11.20 a.m. at the gates of a recruitment office of the Syrian army, killing 175 civilians.[30] This was a turning point in the Brotherhood's tactics: that is, inflicting maximum violence on the civilian population. The Assad government transformed Damascus into an army barracks, with checkpoints and armed men on street corners, along with full-body checks. The Brotherhood continued their campaign of violence, setting fire to food stores and gunning down Baathists on the streets.

HAMA 1982

The situation was most troubled in the conservative city of Hama, in the Syrian midland. At 2 a.m. on 3 February 1982, an army unit was ambushed in the Old City of Hama. As snipers on rooftops began to shoot at them, the soldiers realized that they had stumbled upon the hideout of a local Fighting Vanguard commander named Omar Jawad – better known by his *nom de guerre*, Abu Bakr. He was linked by radio to other cells throughout Hama, and gave orders for all Islamists to rise. Lights were switched on in all mosques and preachers rose to the minaret, grabbed their loudspeakers and started their call for jihad. It was the moment the Vanguards had all been waiting for since 1964. At the signal, hundreds emerged from their secret hide-outs, and started to attack government buildings, overrunning army posts and police departments. Two Alawite female soldiers were slain in their beds by militiamen who had sneaked in via the rooftops.[31] By the morning, 70 Baathists had been killed in Hama and the city was declared 'liberated from Alawite control'.[32]

Assad sent 12,000 men from Rifaat al-Assad's Defence Corps to retake Hama.[33] It was a test of loyalty both for the official Syrian troops and for the Islamists. The rebels retreated into the old quarters of Hama, such as al-Kaylaniya and al-Barudiya, preparing themselves for a long siege. The Syrian army simply flattened them to the ground. Some rebels hid in the city's two-metre-high water canals. Assad threw dynamite into the French-made canals, sealed them off, and had them blown up, with the jihadi rebels inside. Some hid in the mosques. Assad brought the buildings crashing down over their heads.[34] Three weeks later, on 28 February, the state declared that Hama was 'Brotherhood-free'.[35] Almost a third of the historic city was destroyed by those events of 1982.[36] The government said that 3,000 people were killed. The Syrian opposition puts the number at somewhere between 35,000 and 50,000 dead – all civilians. Assad's biographer Patrick Seale puts the number at 5,000–10,000.[37] The real number was never known, but it was horrifically high by any count. On the government's side, 1,436 men were killed and another 2,150 were wounded.[38]

Hafez al-Assad blamed the entire ordeal on fellow Arab states and the CIA. News of the Hama bloodbath was at first kept secret. Both the Brotherhood and the Syrian government held their silence for an entire week. Neither television, radio nor any foreign journalists were allowed into Hama during the month of February 1982. The news was first broken through the Department of State in Washington DC in early March. Automatically, the Brotherhood, awakened from the shock of defeat, issued a powerful statement, accusing Assad of genocide. Assad saw the back-to-back statements as clear evidence of US compliance with the Brotherhood and Fighting Vanguards. His response was a victory speech on 7 March 1982. On the 19th anniversary of the Baath Party Revolution, he appeared in public for the first time in months, carried shoulder-high by the masses from the old Presidential Palace in Abu Rummaneh Street to the historic parliament building on Abed Street. It was a stone's throw away, but it took hours for the entourage to pass, because of the crowd that the state had assembled for the occasion. 'Brothers and Sons [...] Death to the Muslim Brotherhood! Death to the hired Muslim Brothers who tried to bring havoc to the homeland. Death to the Muslim Brotherhood!'[39]

GHOSTS OF HAMA

The events of Hama and the bloody struggle between the Baathist state and the Muslim Brotherhood play a central role in the jihadi narrative of today, whether discussing ISIS or Jabhat al-Nusra. Lest we forget, the new jihad originally began in 2011 to bring down the Syrian regime, before growing more complex and expanding to other parts of the region. At the start of hostilities in 2011, thousands of opposition youth, many of whom were the children and grandchildren of those slain in 1982, demonstrated in Hama, occupying urban spaces. The state moved quickly to quell the uprising and has since mid-2011 tightly controlled the city. No armed rebellion occurred in Hama, yet its rural areas have turned into a hotbed for al-Nusra and other Islamist groups. In the summer of 2014, the state and al-Nusra fought a desperate battle in rural Hama, on the road to the city, in which the regime threw its elite forces to defend the city of Hama and the concentration of Alawite, Christian and Isma'ili villages in its countryside against al-Nusra's offensive. The Syrian army succeeded in halting al-Nusra's advance; a rebel invasion of Hama, however, is still a clear and present danger.

ISIS too is not a stranger to the historical struggle with the Syrian regime, even though it plays a less central role in its rhetoric than in that of al-Nusra. When ISIS captured the ancient city of Palmyra, in the heart of the Syrian Desert, ISIS media proudly showed how al-Baghdadi's troops demolished the notorious Tadmour military prison, in which hundreds of Muslim Brothers had been incarcerated and systematically tortured since the 1970s.

THREE

The Islamic Rebound in Syria: 1982–2011

THE HAMA 'BLOODBATH' OF 1982 DEALT A SEVERE BLOW TO THE Brotherhood and was a turning point in the life of Syrian jihadis. Hundreds of members were hauled before military courts and were either executed or sent to prison. The few who did survive fled to Saudi Arabia, Jordan or Iraq. The monarchs of Saudi Arabia and Jordan and the president of Iraq all refused to give them access to the media. It was feared that their defeat would inspire the spite and ambitions of Brotherhood sympathizers in these countries. When the Brotherhood leaders did manage to appear on radio or Arab television channels, they complained about having been denied justice, calling on Syrian jihadis to regroup, assess what went wrong and avenge what had happened to them in Hama. However, it was too late. The entire apparatus of Syrian jihadis had begun to collapse from within. Accusations were traded back and forth, with the Fighting Vanguards accusing the Brotherhood command of having abandoned them in battle, while men like Issam al-Attar, the Aachen-based Brotherhood chief, retorted that the Vanguards had dragged the Brotherhood – and Syria as a whole – into an ill-planned confrontation with drastic consequences for the Islamic nation. This chaos lasted well into the late 1980s.

From that time both the Brotherhood and the Vanguards officially ceased to exist in Syria. Divided and weak, a few reconciled with the regime, seeing that they had been completely crushed and outsmarted by Hafez al-Assad. Others went into a haunting silence, refusing to talk about the subject. A handful went to Afghanistan and Pakistan, from where they declared, in March 1982, that Hama had been 'the tragedy of the century', and that they would not rest until they had taken full revenge. To do that, they needed many things that they completely lacked: money, arms and a new leader. The ageing commanders and theorists of the Muslim Brotherhood would no longer do. By 1984/5, however, the entire command of the Brotherhood in Syria was in ruins. Despite this, some remaining Vanguard fighters were able to find the funds, weapons and leadership that they had been looking for in a 28-year-old Saudi tycoon who welcomed them with open arms at his rugged hideouts in Afghanistan. He was spirited and young – the opposite of what the Muslim Brothers had become. His name was Osama bin Laden.

THE SYRIAN CONTINGENT AND ABDULLAH AZZAM

Much has been written about the birth and evolution of al-Qaeda, and its founding years are not the subject of this book. It is, however, important to remember some of its key aspects and central figures, as this book is interested in tracing the roots of ISIS's ideology and organization. The terrorist organization was informally created by Saudi Arabia and the United States in direct response to the Soviet invasion of Afghanistan in 1979. It manifested into its present form after the Soviets withdrew in 1989. Bin Laden treated the Syrian jihadis lavishly. They were well-educated urbanites, with plenty of fighting experience. Ninety per cent of them were university graduates and almost all of them spoke conversational English or French. This meant that they could find their way around Europe for secret missions when needed. Most came from middle-class families and were not there for the money, but rather for the holy jihad experience. They were seemingly God-sent to the *mujahideen* in Afghanistan.

Taking charge of the Syrian Islamists was a Palestinian theologian named Sheikh Abdullah Azzam, the spiritual 'godfather' of al-Qaeda.

Some have called him 'imam al-jihad', and even veteran ex-al-Qaeda members refer to him as 'father'. He was the real founder of the global jihadi group that came to world prominence on 11 September 2001. He was the strategist, theorist, fundraiser and chief ideologue. Bin Laden was the organization's chequebook and public face. The jihadis who flocked into Afghanistan came because of Abdullah Azzam, not because of Osama bin Laden.

Azzam was born in a small West Bank village in 1941 and joined the Egyptian Muslim Brotherhood in the mid-1950s. In 1963, Azzam travelled to Syria, where he enrolled at the Faculty of Islamic Shari'a at Damascus University. Smart and charismatic, he automatically attracted the attention of firebrand Syrian Salafis, namely Issam al-Attar, Said Hawwa and even Marwan Hadid himself. Azzam was an eyewitness to the 1964 debacle in Hama. He even hid teenage Islamists fleeing from the *mukhabarat* (intelligence services) at a secret apartment in the Yarmouk Palestinian refugee camp in the Syrian capital. His four-year stay in Syria not only cemented his hatred for the Baathist government, but it also made him many friends in the Damascus underground. He took note of why the Islamic project had failed so drastically in Syria.

After graduating from Damascus University with high honours in 1966, Azzam went to Egypt for his PhD and then moved to Saudi Arabia, where he was employed as an instructor at the King Abdulaziz University in Jeddah. His political views, mainly his criticism of pro-Western monarchies, angered Saudi authorities, prompting him to flee in 1979, when he went to Peshawar, near the Pakistani–Afghan border. Azzam saw striking similarities in the Soviet occupation of Afghanistan and the Israeli occupation of his native Palestine. All Muslims were obliged to fight foreign occupiers, he said. This was a *fard ayn* (religious obligation), as dictated in the Holy Qur'an. Azzam set up a recruitment office in Peshawar, welcoming scores of *mujahideen* coming from all four corners of the Muslim world. Some came at will; others were 'nudged' into making the journey by Abdullah Azzam himself. The messages he sent to old friends in Damascus were almost always verbal, to avoid falling into the hands of Syrian informers. When something had to be written down, it was woven into the soles of their sandals, or carefully written on the interior of their cigarette packs. 'Come join me in Pakistan. A new world awaits you; one that pleases Allah.' He would add, 'From here we will return home one day, hand-in-hand. First, we will return to a liberated Damascus and then, to a liberated Jerusalem.' In total, between the years 1979 and 1985, 35,000 jihadis registered at Azzam's 'Service Office' (*Maktab al-Khadamat*), located at a house owned by Osama bin Laden himself.

One of those who took Azzam's invitation at face value was Osama bin Laden. The two men had first met in Jeddah in the mid-1970s. Bin Laden's wealth came in handy, as he began to invest part of his family's significant funds in the jihadi movement, at the urging of Abdullah Azzam. The Syrian analyst Hassan Hassan and the American journalist Michael Weiss penned the following description of the two men:

> If Azzam was the [Karl] Marx, a grand philosopher articulating the concept of a new revolutionary struggle and drawing in the necessary disciples to realize it, then bin Laden was his Engels, the wealthy scion who paid the bills and kept the lights on while the master toiled on texts that would change the world.[1]

Azzam manipulated Bin Laden and the Syrian jihadis who came knocking on his doors from 1984–6. Bin Laden at the time was primarily anti-communist, while the Syrian jihadis were anti-Alawite. They didn't have the ideological foundations for a global jihad, and were uninterested in liberating territory beyond their immediate borders. Azzam on the other hand had an ambitious project; even at this early stage, he wanted an Islamic state, ruling an empire that spread far and wide to all corners of the globe – just like the Umayyads. He made Syrian Islamists a vehicle for his thinking, and they willingly submitted to his leadership. It was a two-way relationship of convenience and trust.

Azzam would tell Bin Laden and the Syrians: 'Jihad and the rifle alone! No negotiations, no conferences, no dialogue!' Bin Laden himself knew the Syrians as well, but he let Azzam handle them. Bin Laden's mother was Syrian, and so was his first wife Najwa Ghanem, whom he married in the coastal city of Latakia back in 1974.[2] This made Bin Laden half-Syrian, half-Saudi. Taj al-Din al-Mawazini, a retired accountant and former associate of both men, recalled:

> Sheikh Azzam would often break into lengthy stories about the virtues of Marwan Hadid. 'Marwan did this...' and 'Marwan did that.' The Damascus years were vital for him and had shaped plenty of the man we saw before us. This is why he blended perfectly well with the *mujahideen* who came from Syria. There were some stories about his Syria experience – like memories of Syrian cuisine and evening walks in the old city – that he would repeat over and over. Damascus had a special place in his heart. Sheikh Osama, however, never knew Marwan Hadid in person. In fact, he never spoke about anybody but himself.[3]

Bin Laden and Azzam created a military camp in Jordan for Syrian jihadis. Called the 'Mu'askar al-Sheikh' (Sheikh's Camp), it was one of the few non-PLO (Palestine Liberation Organization) camps in Jordan. Other camps soon followed in Peshawar and Kandahar. One of those to travel to Peshawar during the hot summer of 1986 was Farouk Abdul-Rahman (aka Bilal al-Dimashqi). A resident of Qabr Atkeh, a lower-middle-class neighbourhood of Bab Srijeh in Old Damascus, Farouk dropped out of school to work at the local bakery, where he took responsibility for his family of six sisters and his widowed mother after his father's death in 1972. He was burdened with poverty, and found great solace in Islam. Farouk was an easy target for the Salafis, who lured him into the Damascus branch of the Muslim Brotherhood in 1976 at the tender age of 16. Farouk was enlisted at the Danqiz Mosque on Nasr Street during the month of Ramadan. Soon after, he was carrying arms with the Fighting Vanguards.

An impassioned Salafi, Farouk chose the name of the Prophet Muhammad's legendary *mu'azzin* Bilal, himself a slave who was liberated by the Prophet and fought with the early Muslims. The original

Bilal had died and was buried in Damascus. Like his namesake, the young Damascene soon found himself freed from the chains of slavery, fighting not with the Prophet but with Adnan Uqla in 1979–80. He fled arrest, first to Irbid, 20 km south of the Syrian border, and then found his way to Afghanistan, travelling with a fake Syrian passport under the name Ali Munzer Raslan.

Speaking about the subject 30 years after Hama, 'Bilal al-Dimashqi' didn't look like a one-time guerrilla warrior, once 'wanted' by the Syrian government. He was skinny and short, with dark-rimmed glasses and permanent three-day stubble, looking more like Woody Allen than Osama bin Laden. Bilal recalled:

> The *mujahideen* treated us with the same brotherly warmth that the people of al-Madina showed the Prophet Muhammad when he first went there, fleeing persecution in his native Mecca. We were kept in a guest house near the Afghan border for two nights, where we were given a full medical check-up by a Libyan doctor and his Sudanese nurse. This was to make sure that none of us were carrying any disease. They were very forthcoming, especially when I told them that I came from Damascus. Before being given an audience with Sheikh Osama and Sheikh Abdullah, we were drilled by a Palestinian brother named Abu Qays al-Nabulsi, who asked us all sorts of questions and took down detailed notes. I was asked to recount family events dating two or three generations back. They asked me about mosque-going and the history of Islam in my family. They asked if any members of my family drank alcohol, and whether any sisters or cousins were unveiled. They wanted to know everything about us and did not hide their smiles when I said that I had carried arms with the *mujahideen* in the weeks ahead of Hama. My stint with the Vanguards was my passport to Abdullah Azzam. A few hours later, I was taken to meet him in a simple office overlooking a deserted parking lot. Its windows were half-broken. The room was filled with flies and the temperature was extremely hot. I didn't feel any of that. I couldn't believe that I was coming face-to-face with the glorious leader who had led the resistance against the wretched Soviet Union.[4]

Nostalgia got the best of 54-year-old Bilal, and he almost choked when remembering Abdullah Azzam. He did not have the same affection, clearly, for 'Sheikh Osama'.

> Sheikh Abdullah was the real imam. He was the real leader. Sheikh Osama was the person you see on TV. He was always kind, but the rich boy in him could still be felt – not in appearance, but in attitude. Sheikh Abdullah was more humble; more down-to-earth. He treated us as a father, and we were his obedient children. Sheikh Abdullah drew grand inspiration from glorious figures in the history of Islam, and from contemporaries like Imam Hasan al-Banna, Sayyid Qutb, and Mustapha al-Sibaii. Sheikh Osama felt threatened by these big names. He preferred not to talk about them, so that he would remain the focus of everybody's attention. He was immensely egocentric, may God have mercy on his soul.[5]

One day, Abdullah Azzam gathered his Syrian troops and told them that Afghanistan was going to be their new home, and the *mujahideen* their new family. Monthly stipends would be discreetly delivered to their families back in Damascus and Amman, he added. Depending on how big the family was, this could reach up to S£10,000 (back then equal to approximately US$200) per month. This is what an upper-level managerial job in the private sector would make in the late 1980s.

> But you have to leave that material life behind. We will make sure that your dependants don't need anything or anyone in your absence. Your children will go to the best schools and your daughters will be wed into the finest families. We guarantee that they will receive a sound Islamic education. Your ageing parents will receive gentle care and attention, and access to the finest hospitals. You have to trust us, after placing your full faith in Allah. All of them will be in safe hands.[6]

Initially, the Syrian *mujahideen* were not allowed to bring their wives to Pakistan and Afghanistan. They were also forbidden from telling them of their whereabouts. 'Beware of women,' said one teacher named Abu Omar al-Akkawi from Palestine. 'Whenever there are women, the Devil is around.' He added, 'Women cannot keep secrets, and that is why you cannot tell them about our location.' Only after spending two to three years in the camps, and having proven their value and trustworthiness, were some jihadis allowed to bring their wives along. Those complaining during the probation period were married on the spot to young girls from local Afghan communities, sometimes 20 years their junior. Of the entire generation that lived in Afghanistan from the mid-1980s until 9/11, not a single one of them took one of these girls for permanent marriage. It was more of a temporary arrangement to satisfy their needs and to avoid any distraction in their thinking. Polygamy – although allowed in Islam – was strictly off-limits for the jihadis. 'One woman can keep a secret, but four certainly cannot.' A jihadi warrior was allowed to marry as many times as he wished, but only after divorcing his previous wife. Abdullah Azzam and Bin Laden feared spies and informers, and they believed that Arab regimes would infiltrate the camps through women posing as kin of the *mujahideen*.

The secrecy that Azzam was asking for would not only apply to one's wife and children. The *mujahideen* now got a new house, a new name, a new ID and a new mission in life. Recruits were no longer allowed to introduce themselves by their old names, or to answer if anybody addressed them as such. Old photos and documents were destroyed. They were also asked not to delve into forgotten memories about life back home in Amman, Ramallah or Damascus. That life was now officially history, and remembering it would only bring heartache. With heartache comes pain and with pain, emotional weakness – and the jihadis had to be strong, from the inside as well as out. A soft heart would not do. They had to have just one guide in life and it was the Holy Qur'an. The only link to their former lives was what they had learned at university: mechanical engineering, chemistry, mathematics and geometry. Mechanical engineering was needed for the making of missiles, for example, chemistry for poisons, geometry and topography for maps, etc. The *mujahideen* were expected to expand upon these sciences while training at the camps. These were the only tools they were asked never to forget.

ABU MUSAAB AL-SOURI:
A NEW LEADER OF SYRIAN JIHADIS

In late 1989, the Syrian contingent of al-Qaeda was ready. It was led by two men, Abu Musaab and his second-in-command, Abu Khaled, both of whom took on the suffix 'al-Souri' (The Syrian). This was done to differentiate them from other *mujahideen* from different Arab countries carrying the same first names. Both men travelled to Afghanistan sometime between late 1986 and mid-1987. During the set-up phase, they reported directly to Abdullah Azzam, until his assassination in November 1989. Afterwards they reported to Bin Laden and his Egyptian deputy, Ayman al-Zawahiri. Both Abu Musaab and Abu Khaled were natives of Aleppo and ex-members of the Fighting Vanguards. Both were loyal disciples of Abdullah Azzam. Although the world knows Abu Musaab better, it is Abu Khaled who joined the Islamic rebels in the north after 2011 and became the intermediary between Jabhat al-Nusra and ISIS.

According to Abdullah Anas (Azzam's son-in-law and the commander of Arab Afghans) the first Syrian cell of al-Qaeda was made up of 20 to 30 Salafis. Ninety per cent of these were born between 1960 and 1966, and were in their mid-20s when they set up a permanent base in Afghanistan.[7] The eldest Syrian jihadi was 30 years old. Ninety-five per cent had studied either at the state-run Damascus or Aleppo universities. A small handful had been educated in Lebanon, Egypt or Sudan. Sixty per cent hailed from Aleppo and its countryside, and the rest came from Damascus and its countryside, Homs and Hama. Only one came from the port city of Tartous. All were ex-members of the Fighting Vanguards, but only 20 per cent were official members of the Muslim Brotherhood. All of them, with no exceptions, had nothing but spite for the Alawites and Christians and were determined to drive them out of Syria.

Mustapha al-Setmariam Nassar (aka Abu Musaab al-Souri) was the most famous of Syrian jihadis to emerge during this period. He was deeply influenced by Abdullah Azzam, whom he first met in Peshawar in July 1987. Abu Musaab wasn't always famous. CNN commented in March 2006 that he was probably 'the most dangerous terrorist you have never heard of.'[8] Abu Musaab was born in Aleppo in October 1958 to a family that claimed lineage to the Prophet's grandson Hasan, and who originally came from Egypt. He was one year younger than Osama Bin Laden. The two men became good friends between 1989 and 1992. Bin Laden treated him as an equal, never as a subordinate, and as a trusted confidant.[9] So close were they that Abu Musaab named one of his children Osama.[10] In fact, their relationship was so informal that in April 1998, the two friends went live on air on Radio Kabul, with Bin Laden playing the guest and Abu Musaab the show host.[11] With his ginger hair and deep blue eyes, Abu Musaab looked more German than Syrian. He had studied mechanical engineering at Aleppo University and had joined the Fighting Vanguards at the age of 23 on 11 June 1980.[12] He mentioned the date with precision, since it had had a life-changing effect on his thought and career. He never met Marwan Hadid but tried to copy him in speech, rhetoric and actions. He was a big fan of martial arts and had a black belt in karate. He also enjoyed football and closely followed the 1987 Mediterranean Games on television; they were held in the coastal city of Latakia. When the Syrian team defeated France 2-1, he was overcome with euphoria. Friends describe him as 'bookish, with an encyclopaedic memory' and a fondness for the Beatles – very unusual for a jihadi.

During his early career in Syria, before joining al-Qaeda, Abu Musaab was known by his first code name, Omar Abdul Hakim. He was instrumental in trying, with little success, to revive jihad inside Syria after 1982. From Syria he moved to Jordan, where he joined the Muslim Brotherhood, but quickly quarrelled with its leadership, seeing them as 'good for nothing other than flawed intellectual chatter.' After a brief tenure in Pakistan, he travelled to Europe in 1995, where he established the Islamic Conflict Studies Bureau at his home in London. This 'office' arranged for Bin Laden's famous interview with CNN's Peter Bergen in March 1997. Bergen recalls that Abu Musaab was 'tough and really smart. He certainly impressed me more than Osama bin Laden.' In Bergen's book on al-Qaeda, *Holy War, Inc.*,[13] Abu Musaab appears as CNN's tour guide in Afghanistan, billed as 'Ali'. Abu Musaab also sat in on Bin Laden's interview with Abdel Bari Atwan, the celebrated Palestinian journalist and editor of the mass circulation London-based Arab daily, *al-Quds al-Arabi*. In 1996, Atwan travelled to the Tora Bora cave complex in Afghanistan to meet him. Abu Musaab felt comfortable enough to interject to correct Bin Laden on Arabic grammar, prophetic Hadith, and even verses of the Holy Qur'an. Bin Laden nodded, took notes, and corrected his mistakes – trusting Abu Musaab's judgement fully.[14] In 1994, Abu Musaab started to pen articles for the immensely popular Islamic periodical *al-Ansar*. Most of his early articles focused on how to undermine Arab dictators and replace them with a theocracy. Issues of the magazine were photocopied and distributed to the *mujahideen*, to enhance their Islamic awareness.

Abu Musaab was not only a fighter. He was a gifted orator and seasoned politician; he lectured his followers on politics, history, strategy and guerrilla warfare. Throughout the 1990s he wrote extensively, both for personal use and to indoctrinate his disciples, often occupying himself with intellectual affairs, more so than hands-on military training. He would stay up late, sitting at his desk reading and penning lengthy essays – most of which he never published. When one of his aides referred to him as *alim*, or scholar, Abu Musaab corrected him: 'I am not a scholar or a sheikh. I have no training in Islamic jurisprudence. I am a pious Muslim with a sacred mission, nothing more.' The Hama fiasco of 1982 was a classic case that ought to be studied, he would tell his followers, because it showed how far the infidels were willing to go to obstruct the Salafi objective of an Islamic state. 'From it, you should draw your inspiration.'[15]

Abu Musaab claimed that failure in 1982 was due to several factors: lack of arms, improper ideological indoctrination, weak communication channels and denial of proper access to international media and mainstream Arab newspapers. In May 1991, he published a manifesto which would become a blueprint for al-Qaeda strategy for the next decade. Thirteen years later, he published a 1,600-page tome called *The Global Islamic Resistance Call*. It was released online on al-Qaeda-affiliated websites in December 2004. It speaks of macro-jihad and barely mentions al-Qaeda. His online jihadism needed no introduction; he was by far the most widely read and downloaded contemporary Islamic jihadi. 'The establishment of an Islamic State is the strategic goal of the resistance,' he wrote. He praises the Taliban, which ruled Afghanistan from September 1996 to October 2001, and claims that it was the only true embodiment of Salafi Islam. It was the only true Islamic movement that Abu Musaab found worthy of praise, and in 2000 he swore allegiance to its leader, Mullah Omar. That same year, Mullah Omar of Afghanistan invited him to edit the Taliban's official newsletter, *al-Shari'a*. From the airwaves of Radio Kabul, Abu Musaab called for leaderless jihad: 'global jihad without any *tanzim*' (order). It was the duty of each and every Muslim to take up arms, regardless of hierarchy and party structure or affiliation. 'Every infidel, be he Alawite or Christian, is a target, and every plot of land a battlefield.' This would only work if the *mujahideen* pursued '*nizam, la tanzim*' (order, not organization). It was the religious duty of every individual to strike out on his own, without waiting for orders. In other words: 'Centralization of thought and decentralization of execution.' This would be the only path towards the creation of an Islamic state with a proper caliph. And only then would real Muslims be on the right track towards paradise.

Although now becoming a pan-Islamic celebrity, Abu Musaab never lost interest in Syria. Toppling the Assad government was temporarily 'on-hold', he would say, until the jihadis were strong enough to take on the Baathists and Alawites once again. A glimmer of hope arose in June 2000, when Hafez al-Assad died after 30 years in power and was replaced by his son, the ophthalmologist Bashar al-Assad. The young president started his tenure with a general amnesty, setting 300 prisoners free, mainly from the Brotherhood and Fighting Vanguards. It was too little, too late for the Syrian jihadis. Abu Musaab published a strongly worded pamphlet that summer reminding his followers that Syrian jihad had been the focal point of global jihad since 1982. He encouraged his countrymen to rise up against Bashar al-Assad, and 'finish off what we started in 1982.' He added: 'We either remain or disappear. Do we, all Sunnis in Greater Syria [Bilad al-Sham] remain guardians of the religion of Allah, or shall the heretical sects, comprising the Jews, the Crusaders, the Alawites and other remaining sects [Shi'a] remain in it?'[16]

Abu Musaab was a strategist who didn't mind resorting to methods of guerrilla warfare to achieve his goals. He persistently engaged in criticism of al-Qaeda from within the ranks, before he officially drifted apart from Bin Laden in 1992. The reason for dispute, seemingly, was Bin Laden's theatrical stunts. Abu Musaab claimed that 'Sheikh Osama' was more interested in making world headlines than doing anything useful for the jihadi cause. 'I think our brother has caught the disease of screens, flashes, fans, and applause.'[17] Abu Musaab was extremely critical of the 9/11 attacks on the World Trade Center, which led to the downfall of the Taliban that October. This was one of the greatest tragedies to fall on the global jihadi movement since Hama, he told his aides. The US-led war did actually lead to the destruction of 80 per cent of al-Qaeda warriors and installations in Afghanistan. 'People come to us with empty heads and leave us with empty heads.'[18]

Before the two men parted ways, Bin Laden had asked Abu Musaab to set up the al-Ghuraba military camp near Kandahar, on the outskirts of Kabul. Located next to military barracks, it was well guarded by the Taliban's 8th Division. *Al-Ghuraba* means 'foreigners' in Arabic. The camp was funded and controlled by the Taliban's Ministry of Defence. At this camp, Abu Musaab spent long hours indoctrinating jihadis and personally trained them in poison, chemical weapons and guerrilla warfare. The al-Ghuraba camp had a mosque, fully equipped classrooms and its own media office, which was run by Abu Musaab personally. It was his project. Pictures of Bashar al-Assad, King Fahd of Saudi Arabia and Husni Mubarak of Egypt were placed before young recruits and used as target practice in firearms training. Abu Musaab's role in the global jihad movement eventually earned him a 'WANTED' position on the US Department of State's list of terrorists, with a $5 million bounty for anybody who could provide credible information on his whereabouts. Abu Musaab was arrested at a camp near the Pakistani city of Quetta on 31 October 2005. From her new home in Qatar, his wife had reportedly tried to reach him by telephone, which alerted Pakistani and US intelligence to his whereabouts. He was handed over to the United States, and then extradited to his native Syria in 2008. Despite rumours of his release in 2011, Syrian authorities claim that he is still in custody. Yet, even locked away in jail, his influence continues to thrive in the minds of jihadis on the Syrian battlefield, scattered around Aleppo, Idlib and Deir ez-Zour.

A NEW JIHAD

The world changed twice in one decade, on 11 September 2001 and with the US invasion of Iraq in March 2003. After 9/11, Syria's state-run media said that Damascus and Washington DC were now in the same boat, fighting the same jihadis. To properly combat radicals, Syrian authorities assumed that they needed moderate Sunni clerics on their side. Syrian state-run media depicted al-Qaeda as the biological offspring of the Muslim Brothers. Syrian security furnished the FBI with its databank, having kept close watch on Brotherhood members who had fled to Afghanistan after 1982. That cooperation halted after the US invasion of Iraq. Syrian officialdom refused to join the US-led coalition, claiming that the war on Iraq was unjust, and slowly a chorus emerged in the United States lobbying for regime change in Damascus. Damascus suspended its intelligence cooperation and looked the other way as jihadis started crossing the border to fight against the Americans in Iraq. The more inflamed Iraq became, the less likely it seemed that the Americans would seek serious change in Damascus. Ultimately, the Syrians hoped that one day US officials would come knocking on their door, asking for their help in counter-terrorism intelligence in Iraq.

The Syrian government saw a potential, if unorthodox, ally in the Islamic groups in the wake of the US invasion of 2003. This was not new. The Syrian government had tried to court the Islamists before, back in the mid-1990s. In 1995, for example, President Hafez al-Assad permitted the return of the 80-year-old ex-Brotherhood leader Abdul Fattah Abu Ghuddah to his native Aleppo. When he died in February 1997, Assad offered his condolences to the Abu Ghuddah family and news of his passing was broadcast on Syrian television's prime 8.30 p.m. news bulletin. In September 2001, Bashar al-Assad allowed Abu al-Fateh al-Baynouni, a prominent Brother from Aleppo, to return home after decades of long exile. He was the brother of the brethren's new leader, Ali Sadr al-Din al-Baynouni. President Assad also issued a general amnesty, releasing 300 political prisoners from jail. Ninety per cent of these were former members of the Fighting Vanguards and Muslim Brotherhood. Another amnesty followed in November 2001, releasing 113 inmates serving prison time for their role in the 1979 massacre at the Aleppo Artillery School. Similar amnesties followed in December 2004 and February 2005. In 2003, the Ministry of Information lifted a three-decade-old ban on the books of the Brotherhood's founder, Sheikh Mustapha al-Sibaii. They hadn't been available in Syrian bookstores since 1963. Books about an Islamic state, Salafi thought, Qur'anic interpretations and jihad suddenly appeared in windows of Syrian libraries. They sold well at the annual book fair at the Assad Library, held under the patronage of the Ministry of Culture. Baathism and Arabism were now démodé – only Islam would mobilize the masses against the United States in Iraq.

The US invasion and the need for Islamic allies prompted the Syrian government to huddle closer to Islamic figures. It was already allied to the Islamic resistance in Palestine embodied by Hamas, the

Palestinian branch of the Egyptian Muslim Brotherhood. After their exodus from Jordan in 1997, Hamas leaders had been invited to set up a political base in Damascus. Their chief, Khaled Meshaal, was a guest of the Syrian government, with open access to the mosques of Damascus. This is where crowds would gather to hear him speak every Friday in the months after the US invasion, lecturing on Islam, its state and the core principles of jihad. Unlike other mosque preachers, he didn't receive a printed copy of the officially sanctioned version of his sermon and was allowed to lecture freely, with no interference from the Syrian *mukhabarat*. His model of jihad was supposed to be different from the one preached by Marwan Hadid in the 1970s. This was a jihad aimed exclusively against the Israelis in Palestine and the Americans in Iraq. Government authorities, rather short-sightedly, failed to realize that there was no such thing as good Islamists and bad Islamists. Jihadis think alike, and ultimately, they all have one target: an Islamic state, governed by the rules of Shari'a. It was, in fact, Khaled Meshaal who first parted ways with Bashar al-Assad, shortly after the outbreak of the Syrian crisis in 2011. Having planted disciples and aides at every juncture of the Yarmouk Refugee Camp, on the outskirts of the Syrian capital, where he once reigned, he began to openly call for a holy war against the very same government that had protected him for so many years. His stalwarts continued to preach jihad, only this time within Syria, and went as far as to smuggle arms and distribute them to Syrian rebels in Yarmouk. This of course was only after the Egyptian Brotherhood had risen to power in Cairo and Brotherhood-affiliated parties had swept elections in Tunis, Morocco and Libya.

Before any of that happened, however, Syrian officialdom started speaking a language that sounded hauntingly similar, if not identical, to that of the Islamists. They refused to acknowledge Hamas as a terrorist organization or expel it from Damascus. Both stressed the need to liberate the Syrian Golan and Jerusalem from Israeli occupation. And both were supportive of the Sunni insurgency that swept through Iraq after the downfall of Saddam Hussein in 2003. In fact, shortly after the war, Syria's Grand Mufti Ahmad Kaftaro – now in his early nineties – issued a religious *fatwa* calling on Muslims worldwide to mobilize and fight the American occupiers of Iraq. Although there was nothing but distrust and scorn between him and the Brotherhood, this was exactly what they too had been calling for. When the Danish cartoon controversy tore through the Muslim world in October 2005, the state responded to the public outrage, allowing massive demonstrations in Damascus which attacked and set fire to the Danish and Norwegian embassies. Turbaned clerics were encouraged to speak to the masses and to drum up anti-Westernism. On the anniversary of the Prophet's birthday in April 2006, colourful Islamic banners decorated the Old City of Damascus for the first time in years. The celebrations were state-approved, but not state-monopolized and engineered as they had been since 1982. In April 2006, the head Qur'anic reciter of Damascus, Sheikh Krayyem Rajah, came out with a powerful statement, saying that the enemies of God ought to know that 'Damascus and Syria will be the vanguards of the jihad that will brush them aside. Syria stands firmly against the unbelievers.'[19] He too became a mosque celebrity and was among the first Islamic scholars to defect in 2011. He had also endorsed the sending of Arab fighters into Iraq after 2003.

MONEY IS MONEY

In the weeks that followed the US invasion of Iraq, scores of fighters arriving from Syria crossed the border to join the then-called Sunni insurgency. One of those Syrian jihadis, Qutaiba al-Omari, hailed from the oil-rich city of Deir ez-Zour. He himself was not rich – far from it. After fighting briefly in Iraq, he gave up arms and worked for a short time as a small contractor before returning to a life of early retirement in Syria in mid-2009. Having crossed the Syrian border and returned on fake travel documents, he was neither harassed nor questioned upon his return. At the outbreak of Syrian hostilities in 2011 al-Omari was working as a cab driver at the Yarmouk Refugee Camp in southern Damascus. Al-Omari recalls that the 2003 trip to

Iraq was facilitated by a go-between named Ahmad Rawayeh from the Damascene Jobar neighbourhood. He met them at the Iraqi consulate office at the Damascus International Fairgrounds, overlooking the Barada River and just opposite the Four Seasons hotel. The consulate was still made up of Saddam Hussein appointees, who had stayed on at their jobs after the occupation of Baghdad in April 2003. 'Iraqi diplomats knew we were there but looked the other way, acting as if we were invisible.'[20] Rawayeh furnished them with maps, telephone numbers inside Iraq, real Iraqi passports with fake names and a stipend of US$200. 'On that day, there were 15 of us only,' al-Omari said. 'The arms came much later, only after we were settled inside Iraq.' They were driven off in a variety of old buses, all carrying Iraqi licence plates. When reaching the border, Syrian authorities stamped their documents without delay. They didn't have to bribe their way through Syrian border security. On paper, all of them were Iraqi citizens returning home. 'On the Iraqi side, there was total chaos. We went through easily,' he recalled many years later.

When asked what prompted him and his colleagues to go to Iraq, al-Omari didn't have a coherent answer. The common mumble was, 'We wanted to fight the occupation.' It was a catchy slogan that obviously sold well among family and friends back in 2003. The middle-aged man would suddenly joke about how unlucky he had been, stuck behind the wheel of his cab while colleagues in the Iraqi resistance were 'making millions'. He almost sounded envious of them – he too ought to have made millions, it seemed, but he hadn't, returning home empty-handed. The jihadi experience was not as rewarding as it had promised to be. Iraq had been a cash cow for many Syrian jihadis. It wasn't all about principle; some of it was about money as well. Al-Omari was asked what kind of money his friends had made in Iraq.

I won't mention names, but at least two of them returned to buy property at Yarmouk [Camp] and to the Idlib countryside. They now trade with marble villas and nobody in Syria ever asked them where the money had come from.[21]

'Was it al-Qaeda money?' Al-Omari just shrugged his shoulders, ignoring the question at first and then casually remarking, 'And what if it was, who cares? Money is money whether it comes from Bin Laden, Saddam or Bashar.' Have any of those jihadis returned to join ISIS? Al-Omari smiled, 'Who hasn't joined ISIS?'[22]

Nobody knows for sure how many jihadis crossed the Syrian–Iraqi border during the years 2003–6. We don't have records of names or nationalities, as officials in Iraq and Syria still refuse to admit having permitted any such border traffic in the immediate aftermath of the occupation. Qutaiba al-Omari says that not all of them were Syrian:

> On the contrary, most were Palestinian members of Hamas from the Neirab Camp near Aleppo. They came with the full blessing of Khaled Meshaal, the chief of Hamas. In our bus, we were a total of 24; nine of them had missed the bus on the previous day and joined us on our journey. Only eight of us were Syrian. None were from the Muslim Brotherhood or al-Qaeda. We were ordinary Muslims carrying out our religious duty against the occupiers of Iraq. Before going to Iraq, I was a contractor; I refurnished apartments in the al-Ghouta countryside of Damascus and took commissions off the sale of brick, paint and building material. One of my friends installed satellite dishes and cable television in rural Damascus. A third was a plumber. One brother was from Libya, and two were from Saudi Arabia. One of them barely spoke Arabic; he was from Albania.[23]

Al-Omari adds, 'Once inside Iraq we disembarked from the bus, and walked in the desert for nearly three hours, guided by the moonlight.' Three black jeeps came out of nowhere to transport them to Mosul. They were driven by Bedouins from Arab tribes in the Iraqi desert. In Mosul they were taken to a shabby apartment and given traditional Arab garb, to blend in with the locals. The arms were delivered only months later – and they were distributed not by bearded jihadis, but, ironically, by ex-members of the Iraqi Baath

Party. The arms had been salvaged from the warehouses of the Iraqi army. Al-Omari adds:

> One of the Iraqi Baathists looked familiar. I had seen him in Damascus during the US war, wearing a pin of Saddam Hussein. He had now abandoned the pin and was wearing a Bedouin *galabiya* [traditional Bedouin garment], after growing a full beard. When we asked him what had become of Saddam, he replied: 'You will hear good things about Abu Uday [Arabic for father of Uday, i.e. Saddam Hussein], very soon.'[24]

JIHADIS COME HOME

A decade later, many of those Syrian fighters had started returning home, inspired by the military insurgency and the rise of ISIS and Jabhat al-Nusra. Their return halted all previous cooperation between Islamic groups and the Syrian government. Iraq had changed their lives completely and was bound to revamp Syrian society as a whole. On 27 April 2004, four unmasked Islamists carried out a terrorist operation in broad daylight in western Damascus, at an abandoned UN building on the Mezzeh Highway, occupied on both sides of the road by senior officials of the Syrian Baath Party. Although the initial report claimed that the terrorists were from different nationalities, in mid-May Damascus announced that all of them were Syrian citizens from the town of Artouz, 15 km south-west of Damascus.[25] They had trained and worked with Sunni rebels close to al-Qaeda in Iraq. In May 2005, Syrian authorities announced that they had discovered a terrorist cell in the Daf al-Shok neighbourhood of the southern Damascus countryside. Its members were Syrian fighters who had also trained with ex-Baathists in Iraq. That same year an attack was thwarted at the Damascus Palace of Justice, reportedly planned at peak-time by Abu Musaab al-Souri's accomplices.[26] Weeks later, gunfire was exchanged between the security services and Islamic cells in Mount Qassioun, overlooking the Syrian capital.[27] On 12 September 2006, attackers tried to drive two explosive-filled trucks into the US embassy compound in the posh al-Rawda neighbourhood, a stone's throw from the presidential palace. Three of them were killed and a fourth was arrested. Fourteen people were injured, including two security officials, one local embassy employee and a Chinese diplomat, who was hit by a stray bullet. The US Secretary of State, Condoleezza Rice, said that she 'very much appreciated' Syria's efforts in thwarting the attack.[28]

On 2 June 2006, Islamic militias tried to overrun Umayyad Square in central Damascus. The specific targets were unknown, since the roundabout was surrounded by important government buildings like the Assad National Library, the Damascus Opera, the Syrian television and radio offices and the army's headquarters. One security official and one guard at the television premises were shot. Four militiamen were killed and another four were arrested. The next morning their photos were shown on Syrian television along with the arms that they had carried. They were carrying CDs with inflammatory speeches by the Aleppo-based Salafi preacher Abu al-Qaqa. In the recordings, Abu al-Qaqa was addressing a crowd worked up into a frenzy. The scene looked more like Kabul or Tora Bora, rather than Aleppo: 'We will teach our enemies a lesson. Are you ready?' The bearded crowd shouted in unison: 'Yes, we are.' Abu al-Qaqa, thrilled with the reaction he was generating, screamed back: 'Speak louder so that George W. Bush can hear you!' The audience broke into chants: 'Foreigners have come to our land! Slaughter them like cattle. Burn them!'[29] This was in broad daylight in pre-2011 Syria. Jihadi pockets were mushrooming throughout the country, with or without the knowledge of the Syrian authorities.

The notorious Abu al-Qaqa, whose real name was Safwat Aghassi, was born into a Kurdish family in al-Foz, a small village north of Aleppo, in 1973. If one describes the years 2003–11 as the interwar years (coming between the Iraq War and Syria War), then Abu al-Qaqa was one of the most prominent Syrian figures of this period. He recruited men, trained them in how to use arms, and indoctrinated them with anti-Americanism and fanatic Islamic ideology.

Like everybody else associated with the Syrian jihadi movement, he had studied at the Faculty of Islamic Shari'a at Damascus University, before obtaining his PhD from the University of Karachi. He taught at the Alaa al-Din al-Hadrami Mosque in Aleppo and rose to fame in 2003 after inciting his audience to jihad in Iraq.[30] A cleric with his impressive following would not have made it to a mosque pulpit after 2003 without the blessing of Syrian authorities. Abu al-Qaqa said good things about the widely hated *mukhabarat,* which prompted doubters to write him off as a creation of the Syrian intelligence services. He advocated unifying the efforts of the security services and the religious establishments, saying: 'Every believer must see that security is positive. The objective of every believer is to prevent harm. This prevention is done by the security services.'[31] He became something of a celebrity in Aleppo, driving a Mercedes-Benz 600, with full security usually reserved for senior Baath Party officials. The identity of the Umayyad Square attackers, however, signalled that Abu al-Qaqa's followers had gone astray. He swore that although originally his students, those attackers were carrying out terrorism at their own will, inspired not by him but by al-Qaeda in Iraq.

The Syrian authorities hadn't wanted it that way. They had encouraged the jihadi penetration of Iraq, wanting them to fight only the Americans. They didn't imagine that a battlefield would emerge in Syria ten years after the fall of Saddam Hussein and that these same jihadis would one day bring the battle back home. The Syrian government began a crackdown on Islamic groups and figures throughout the country, but they struck at the wrong people. The radicals embedded themselves in society, waiting for the right time to emerge. None of them were affected by the crackdown of 2006–10. The Syrian government forced all clerics to resign from charity NGOs suspected of sending money to Iraq or bankrolling Islamic societies at home. A travel ban was placed on all Islamic preachers, and those who had radio shows were taken off the airwaves. Prayer rooms at malls were shut down and religious symbols were banned from personal use on cars. It had become a habit to decorate cars with Qur'ans, the sword of Ali, or a curved fish, a symbol of Jesus Christ. The government went a step further, banning women wearing the niqab from teaching or studying at school, and in December 2010 it threw sand in the eyes of the Islamists by reopening the Damascus Casino, which had been closed since the early 1970s. It was the government's way of brandishing its secular character and declaring that it was parting ways, once and for all, with the Islamists. In 2010, President Assad didn't break his fast with the *ulama* of Damascus, as customarily done since the early 1970s. On 28 September 2007, a gunman stepped out of a car next to Abu al-Qaqa's mosque in Aleppo after Friday prayer. The anti-al-Qaeda and anti-US cleric was shot dead. He had outlived his usefulness.

The state was trying to undo what it had very willingly allowed to happen, creating an Islamic genie within Syria, which soon emerged in the form of Jabhat al-Nusra and ISIS. It was already too little, too late. The 'wolf' that Syrian authorities had been trying to fend off for years was now clawing at the doors of Damascus.

FOUR

The Rise of Jabhat al-Nusra

ENTIRE GENERATIONS OF SYRIAN SALAFIS DREW STRONG INSPI-
ration from the Prophet Muhammad and all his Companions
(*al-Sahaba*). It is often the case that modern jihadis have seen themselves as continuations of *al-Sahaba*. The early Muslims (*Salaf*) divide
their history into four stages. The first is the pre-Islamic *al-Jahiliyya*
(ignorance). This was the period when – according to early Muslim
traditions – people drank alcohol, enjoyed lewd poetry and worshipped idols rather than the Prophets and one God. Sexual prom-
iscuity was common in pre-Islamic Mecca. Women dressed immod-
estly with their faces exposed, dancing, drinking and consorting with
strangers. This 'moral decay', according to the Salafis, is very similar to
where the Arab world stands today, so every true Muslim is obliged to
fight *al-Jahiliyya* in society. The second stage was marked by the revelation of Islam. Following an internal struggle (a jihad within oneself)
pious Muslims, 'awakened' by the light of the Qur'an, embarked
on a holy war (an outward jihad) to promote their new faith and to
cement its rule throughout the Arabian Desert. The persecution of the
first Muslims famously led to *hijra* (migration), where men of social
standing fled from persecution at the hands of Mecca's elite and followed the Prophet to Medina, thus joining the jihad for Islam. This
is an ongoing stage in the life of the Salafis. They have passed from
al-Jahiliyya into jihad and *hijra*. They leave the comfort of their homes
behind them to join in the struggle for Islam, under the banner of

Allah and his messenger Muhammad. The final stage, the culmination of the struggle, is the setting up of an Islamic state and the founding of a caliphate to rule a united Islamic world.

Historical parallels gave the Salafis of today, whether ISIS, Jabhat al-Nusra or the many other organizations, a sense of purpose and a feeling of spiritual immortality. It also gave them a delusion of grandeur, because it transported them into an imaginary world that was extremely detached from the real one in which they were living, forcing them to walk blindly towards an illusion. Islamic theorists taught them that the only way forward in life was to copy the Prophet and his Companions in every single aspect, regardless of how compatible or not this was with the rapidly changing world of the twenty-first century. So instead of following the conventional route, extolling Muhammad's wisdom, compassion and vision, they took the nitty-gritty details of early Muslims, and abandoned what really mattered in terms of statesmanship and nation-building. The students of Syrian jihadi chief Abu Musaab recall that he saw prophetic parallels between himself and that generation of first Muslims. These daydreams always put him in a trance, which usually lasted for several hours.

Muslims are taught that the Prophet was 40 when, while meditating at Mount Hira near Mecca in 610, he received his first revelation via the Angel Gabriel. It was a soul-shaking experience that was to change his life, and that of billions after him. Abu Musaab was 40 when he first set foot in Afghanistan, which also was a life-changing experience. He too had meditated and he too had seen the light in the form of angels. Like the early Muslims, Abu Musaab had abandoned an urban life of comfort to take part in a jihad for the spread of Islam. The early Muslims had migrated from Mecca, fleeing persecution by its then rulers, while he had left his homeland in Syria. The struggle was no different and nor was repression of 'The Truth'. This is how Abu Musaab saw himself through the eyes of history. The Taliban who welcomed him in Afghanistan, he would say, were much like the 'noble people of al-Medina', who welcomed Muhammad and his Companions with open arms when they came seeking refuge in 622. Before converting to Islam, the Medinians were hailed as 'al-Ansar' (Supporters of Islam). This was the same name given to Afghan warriors by the Arab jihadis (including Abu Musaab) in the 1990s, and to Syrians by foreign fighters flocking to Syria after 2011. Abu Musaab often said that he was heavily burdened with a divine mission to combat moral decay, to overthrow infidels, to govern with the laws of Islamic Shari'a and to right all the wrongs done to the Muslim world by centuries of colonialism and military rule. He had no other life and he had no other goal.

Abu Musaab's views laid the ideological foundations for Jabhat al-Nusra and ISIS. Although the man had long been jailed when the two groups emerged, his thoughts lived in the minds and actions of his many supporters. Many of those who joined the al-Qaeda branch in Syria or defected to join ISIS in 2014 were one-time students of Abu Musaab al-Souri. Apart from ISIS, the *Jabhat al-Nusra li-Ahl al-Sham* (The Support Front for the People of the Levant), often called the al-Nusra Front, was at one point the single most powerful and deadly jihadi organization to emerge in post-2011 Syria. It was founded by four Salafis in December 2011 and announced on 23 January 2012, just ten months after the start of the Syrian uprising. The four co-founders were Abu Mohammad al-Golani, Abdulmuhsen Abdullah Ibrahim al-Sarikh, Hamid Hamad Hamid al-Ali and Abu Yusuf al-Turki. One of the founders, al-Sarikh (aka Sanafi al-Nasr), was a Saudi citizen who had been living in northern Syria since 2013. He travelled to Nusra-held territory weeks after the group was announced in 2012. Born in 1978, he previously lived in Pakistan, worked with al-Qaeda and briefly served as head of its underground operations in Iran. He is a third cousin of Osama bin Laden and his six brothers are all members of al-Qaeda. Two of them were held in Guantanamo Bay after 9/11,[1] after planning to attack US troops at the Prince Sultan airbase in Saudi Arabia. Another founder, Hamid al-Ali, from Kuwait, works as Jabhat al-Nusra's 'secret-keeper', or as something of an informal 'secretary'. Additionally, he is al-Nusra's fundraiser and certified accountant. Hamid al-Ali specialized in the science of Hadith, obtaining an MA from Saudi Arabia. He also earned a PhD from the University of Edinburgh in Scotland, returning to work as a mosque imam at the Kuwaiti Ministry of Religious Endowments. As recently as June 2015 he tweeted support for Abu Mohammad al-Golani, describing his responses to an interview on Al Jazeera as 'balanced'. The third, Abu Yusuf al-Turki, was a skilful sniper, who boasted of training over 400 snipers during a 20-year career. He came to Syria from his base in Bursa, Turkey in 2013 to fight alongside Syrian rebels. He was killed at the age of 47 in September 2014, when the US-led coalition began striking jihadi posts in northern Syria. Abu Musaab was to these men, and to Jabhat al-Nusra, what Abdullah Azzam had been to the second generation of Syrian jihadis and to al-Qaeda. Both left the scene shortly before their organizations came to life – Azzam was killed in 1989, Abu Musaab was arrested in 2005.

Khaled al-Fahl (Abu Ayyub), a 32-year-old Nusra member based in the al-Raqqa countryside, said:

> All of our brother *mujahideen* were raised on the teachings of Abu Musaab al-Souri. We read his works and many of us attended his classes, either in Pakistan or Afghanistan. We never knew Osama bin Laden; Abu Musaab was our sheikh, our leader and our spiritual mentor. It is a pity he is not with us today to see his dream manifesting itself in cities and towns throughout northern Syria – the very same places where he grew up as a child and young adult. He would have been very proud.

Abu Ayyub, a graphic designer by training and education, claims that in his prison cell in Syria, Abu Musaab is deprived of any access to the outside world: no visits, no radio or television and certainly no internet. As of the time of writing in 2015, the only person to have visited him is a state-appointed Baathist lawyer. When asked if Abu Musaab knew if Jabhat al-Nusra existed, his comrade Abu Ayyub replied:

> If he is still alive, I am sure he feels it. I don't think he is aware of any of the details. Our brother Abu Musaab was a man of Allah (*min rijal Allah*).

He feels things that ordinary people cannot possibly grasp. Alas, we lost all contact with him.

Abu Musaab's attorney, however, confirms: 'Abu Musaab al-Souri knows exactly what is happening in Syria today. He even prophetically warned me, shortly after his extradition to Syria, "Rivers of blood are going to be gushing through this country – just wait and see."' Abu Ayyub notes that 'the Syrian revolt was the moment Abu Musaab had been waiting for since 1982'. Nusra fighters didn't just learn military tactics from Abu Musaab, they were also taught how to establish schools, operate a charity/welfare system, run a media campaign and, ultimately, how to set up a state and how to get its agencies working based on the laws of Islamic Shari'a. According to Sami al-Oraidi, a member of al-Nusra's Shari'a Council, Abu Musaab left behind 19 written recommendations on how to run an Islamic state. 'We have been able to implement some,' he wrote on his Twitter account in March 2014. 'When in doubt, since our mentor is no longer with us, we turn to the Holy Qur'an for guidance.'

The name of their front was inspired by Abu Musaab al-Souri's classic book, *The Global Call for Islamic Resistance*. In the last passage, Abu Musaab says: 'From the blessed Syria in the early 1960s was the beginning of the jihadi movement. Jihad flourished [in Syria] in the 1980s and returns now, God willing. *Al-Nusra! Al-Nusra!* Oh Brothers.' On 20 June 2012, Jabhat al-Nusra released its founding charter online, explaining its ideology to both a jihadi and non-jihadi audience. It needed little clarification, completing a sequence started by the Muslim Brotherhood in the 1940s and taken up by al-Qaeda in the 1990s. Any male Muslim could join. No specific age, nationality or academic qualification was required, not even an Islamic family background or lineage. Fighting skills were not even a prerequisite; they could be learned later. Piousness and 'fear of God' were essential, along with a commitment to uphold the teachings and legacy of the first Muslims (the *Salaf*). The text introduced the group as a 'blessed front' with 'the best *mujahideen* from various parts of the earth'. Their ultimate goal was to 'establish the rule of Allah in the Levant.' Real deep-rooted change was what they aspired to, 'not phoney change, as happened in Yemen, Egypt, Tunisia and Libya.' Their objective, it added, 'is to change the whole governance system and bring justice, freedom and equality in the country, as ordered by Allah.' In one of their YouTube videos, a spokesman for al-Nusra says: 'We are Syrian *mujahideen*, back from various jihad fronts to restore God's rule on the Earth [...] Jabhat al-Nusra has taken upon itself to be the Muslim nation's weapon in this land.'[2] Abu Ayyub adds that Nusra fighters 'know exactly who their enemies are. Our number one enemy is the United States, followed by its agents in the Muslim World, the non-believers: Alawites, Shi'a and Christians. With Allah's help, we will eliminate them all.'

ABU MOHAMMAD AL-GOLANI

The man who breathed life into Abu Musaab's vision was Jabhat al-Nusra's official founder and emir, Abu Mohammad al-Golani. His *nom de guerre* implies that he hails from a small village in the occupied Golan Heights (which was seized by Israel during the Six-Day War of 1967). When al-Golani announced the creation of al-Nusra in an audio message posted on the internet in early 2012, senior figures in the Syrian opposition were sceptical. At the time, they were desperately trying to prove that no Islamists existed in the Syrian rebel community – only secular soldiers who had defected from the Syrian army. If Jabhat al-Nusra was real, then it threatened to do away with all that they had been working for since March 2011. Some argued that al-Nusra fighters were former inmates of Syria's prisons, released by the state to infiltrate the rebel community. This was partially true, since among those set loose by the 2011 amnesty were Abu Khaled al-Souri and Zahran Alloush, commander of the Islamic army in al-Ghouta.[3] Others insisted that the entire organization was imagined, produced and then marketed by the director of national security in Syria, General Ali Mamlouk. One Dubai-based dissident went so far as to claim that Abu Mohammad al-Golani was none other than Ali Mamlouk himself.

They were soon proven wrong, as Western intelligence confirmed that such a man actually existed, but he wasn't from the Golan, as his name indicated. His mother was from the Golan region, but al-Golani himself is actually a native of oil-rich Deir ez-Zour in eastern Syria, and was born in al-Shuheil, a small village famed for its agricultural produce, in 1979. A protégé of Abu Musaab al-Souri, his associates refer to him as 'al-Sheikh al-Fateh'. This translates from the Arabic roughly as 'The Conqueror Sheikh' or 'The Victorious Sheikh'. His real name is Usama al-Hadawi, although Western reports say nothing about his background and education. The Doha-based Al Jazeera channel says that his real name was Usama al-Wahidi. His father was a state-employed driver and a petty farmer who owned a small plot of land, while Usama – or al-Golani – studied at state-run schools in Deir ez-Zour. This is where he first learned to use a firearm, at the age of 12, with Baath Party cadets at summer camps. Friends describe him as bookish, preferring to spend evenings browsing the internet rather than drinking coffee with friends at the local cafeteria. He only ventured into the common room when a soccer match was on television. Football was his only indulgence and he watched everything, ranging from local Syrian teams to international ones like Barcelona and Real Madrid. The 2003 occupation of Iraq fuelled his religious zeal and so did his older brother Ammar al-Hadawi (aka Abu Yaarob), a Saudi-based cleric reportedly close to the Hama-born preacher Adnan al-Aroor.

Al-Golani studied medicine at Damascus University but dropped out in 2005. He lodged in the university dorm and was registered as 'mildly religious' but 'anti-government'. At the age of 20, al-Golani taught Arabic grammar and poetry at local high schools in Deir ez-Zour. His choice of poetry is rather strange, since hardline jihadis frown upon poetic verse, seeing it as Satanic. Poets, they claim, are influenced to write by the Devil himself. Al-Golani's students knew nothing about his Islamic ideology or his critical views of the Syrian government. Very professionally and with a completely straight face, he taught them the sexually flamboyant works of the ancient poets like al-Mutanabbi and Abu Nuwas. These famous poets gave al-Golani a cover to protect himself from Syrian intelligence – an Islamist, after all, could not possibly be teaching pre-Islamic poetry about lust, sex and a woman's body. Although he never met Abu Musaab in person, al-Golani became obsessed with his writings. By 2005, he had memorized entire chunks of his jihadi literature. We don't have many details about how and when he was recruited into al-Qaeda. Clearly, it was after leaving Syria in 2005 – facilitated through a 50-year-old Syrian member of al-Qaeda in Iraq named 'Abu Hamzah'. Al-Golani left Syria legally on official documents but entered Iraq on a fake Yemeni passport provided by Abu Hamzah.

It was in Mosul that he first met his friend, the future caliph of ISIS, Abu Bakr al-Baghdadi. The two men 'clicked' almost automatically, with al-Baghdadi admiring al-Golani as being 'shrewd, and highly intelligent'. Only a few years apart in age, both men were well versed in Islamic history, both enjoyed poetry recitals and both were avid soccer fans – much like Abu Musaab al-Souri himself. Al-Golani returned to Syria in the autumn of 2006, after a brief stopover in northern Lebanon, where he lived in Tripoli on fake ID papers as 'Mohammad Fathallah'. He spent ten months in Syria, working part-time at a printing press in the town of al-Mleihah in the al-Ghouta orchards on the outskirts of Damascus, to make a living. He would sometimes travel to Aleppo to attend sermons by the regime-friendly Salafi sheikh Abu al-Qaqa, becoming one of his early admirers. Al-Golani returned to Iraq in early 2007, where he was briefly arrested by the Americans and held at Camp Bucca on the Iraqi–Kuwaiti border. US prison authorities mistook him for an Iraqi Kurd from Mosul. In jail, he again taught Arabic poetry, this time to other prisoners. Al-Golani had not engaged in combating US troops in Iraq. His only 'crime' was his visible association with murky Islamic figures, who were suspected of being members of the Iraqi underground. The Americans released him in 2008 and he stayed in Iraq using the very same ID papers, working closely with Abu Bakr al-Baghdadi, who by then was a top figure in the Islamic State of

Iraq, as an unofficial consultant. The post-Saddam Hussein rulers of Baghdad brought no charges against him. It was during this period in Iraq that he trained in guerrilla warfare, but he never took part in any real combat. Al-Baghdadi appointed him as director of al-Qaeda operations in Mosul. It was a civilian job that required strong administrative skills, rather than a sound military record.

Shortly after creating al-Nusra, just months after Bin Laden's death in May 2011, al-Golani pledged loyalty to al-Qaeda's leader, Ayman al-Zawahiri. Thus Jabhat al-Nusra became al-Qaeda's official branch organization in Syria. As recently as late May 2015, al-Golani declared, in an interview with Al Jazeera, that he still receives guidance and advice from al-Zawahiri.[4] By 2012, al-Golani was already recruiting troops and creating a powerful army. He even designed a black flag for al-Nusra, like the one used by al-Qaeda in Iraq. There was very little al-Baghdadi could do to actually stop al-Golani, let alone join him. Al-Baghdadi's pride would not allow him to become a subordinate of his former protégé, nor would he diverge from his main objective: the battle for Iraq. By February or March 2012, Jabhat al-Nusra made up roughly 1 per cent of the rebel community in Syria. The proportion grew to 3 per cent in August and reached an impressive 7 to 9.5 per cent (6,000–10,000 fighters) by November 2012.[5] The breakdown in numbers was: 2,000 troops in al-Bab (north-east of Aleppo), 3,000 in the Idlib countryside west of Aleppo, 2,000 in Deir ez-Zour (eastern Syria) and 750–1,000 in the Damascus countryside. According to al-Nusra's own account, it currently stands at 60,000 fighters, although this number is impossible to verify and sounds greatly inflated. According to the global policy think-tank RAND, they stood at no more than 5,000–6,000 in 2014. *The Economist* says that their peak was 7,000 troops in 2013.[6]

Regardless of the precise numbers, finding recruits was always relatively easy for Abu Mohammad al-Golani. Young men came knocking on his door, wanting to join Jabhat al-Nusra. In fact, many *begged* to join. The media attention the West was giving to al-Golani was the greatest advertisement he could ever have hoped for. And it was free.

People came to al-Golani for different reasons. Some saw real promise in his jihadi programme. Others wanted arms to protect their homes and neighbourhoods. Many needed the umbrella of a local militia, as all manifestations of statehood had collapsed throughout northern Syria. With no police and no official army, people had to run their own affairs and protect their own lives and belongings. People needed arms and al-Golani had plenty to distribute. According to one of his men,

> 60 per cent of his weapons came from government storehouses in Iraq. Parts were stolen after sporadic attacks on Iraqi military bases and others were sold by intermediaries, and sometimes by Iraqi officers themselves. The rest were either stolen from the battlefield or storehouses of the Syrian army. They had automatic weapons, rifles, pistols, grenades and soon obtained missiles and rockets, but no tanks and no aeroplanes.

Before fully accepting recruits, al-Golani had them undergo a ten-day religious training course (since the bulk of those who joined him were either non-religious or only mildly religious). A full graduation ceremony came next, modelled on that of modern universities but with no caps and gowns, after which al-Nusra members undertook a month of military training. Only then were they given a personal sidearm, a quota of grenades and a monthly portion of ammunition. His men never fully penetrated the Damascus countryside, but pretty soon became kings in rural Aleppo and in al-Golani's native Deir ez-Zour. His army was organized along semi-conventional military lines, with units divided into brigades, regiments and platoons. At a micro-level, however, these units were given great autonomy in battle. Platoon commanders were allowed to make on-the-spot decisions without awaiting instructions from higher command. They had the liberty of firing at will, invading villages, taking captives from the Syrian army or shooting anybody they perceived as obstructive to al-Nusra's victory. All targets were valid. All Syrian soil was legitimate jihadi land. No need to wait for orders. It was the military strategy of Abu Musaab al-Souri coming to life: *nizam, la tanzim.*

RUNNING A 'STATE'

On a social level, al-Golani founded the Public Management for Services in Aleppo in mid-December 2013. This institution was charged with administering the day-to-day affairs of residents living in Nusra-held territory. Part of its job was regulatory governance, incorporating a police department, a ministry of supply, a ministry of agriculture and local municipalities, all in one. It included overseeing the distribution of flour to bakeries, for example, and regulating the price of bread. With a bundle of white bread selling for S£15 (7 US cents), anybody charging a higher price would be arrested and flogged by the Nusra police. Ironically, this was the same state-subsidized selling price fixed in regime-held territory. At the time of writing in spring 2015, al-Nusra controlled small pockets of land and their fiefdoms fluctuated throughout the Syrian conflict. In early 2015, ISIS successfully drove al-Nusra out of north-western and eastern Syria (namely Deir ez-Zour, al-Hassakeh and al-Raqqa), but the control of several towns in the provinces of Idlib, Aleppo, Homs and Daraa in the Syrian south still lay with al-Nusra. It was also able to maintain its presence in the Aleppo countryside, along the mountains dotting the Syrian–Lebanese border and in some opposition-held areas in rural Damascus, like al-Ghouta and al-Yarmouk.

Al-Nusra's Public Management for Services has run electricity, water and municipality affairs in all of these Nusra-held territories. It has clipped trees, mowed lawns and collected garbage, in addition to administering schools, mosques and courts. It has also overseen the sale of heating fuel (*mazot*) to local residents, which is also fixed at the same price as Damascus (S£125 per litre, which equals 32 US cents). Residents have bought and sold with the official currency of the Syrian government. The only paper money declared null by al-Nusra has been the green and yellow S£1,000, because it is decorated with a picture of President Hafez al-Assad. The Public Management for Services has even created a Facebook page in Arabic with a colourful logo where residents are able to read daily updates on price control, currency fluctuations and Nusra services.[7] According to al-Nusra, its 'good behaviour' towards the locals has been the main reason why residents support it more than other Islamic groups.[8]

To administer al-Nusra, al-Golani created a small *Majlis al-shura* (Consultative Council). With himself at the top, this council has taken strategic macro-decisions, such as when and how to launch a major offensive against a particular city or town, who to accept into the front and when to retreat from a battlefield. At this level, top decisions were made on how to handle other jihadi groups like ISIS and how to coordinate with veteran al-Qaeda figures like Ayman al-Zawahiri. This council was also charged with screening foreign jihadis wanting to fight with al-Nusra. Al-Golani knew his personal shortcomings and hand-picked clerics for the council, who were often older than him and far better versed in Islamic jurisprudence and theology. He surrounded himself with veteran Islamic scholars. He listened well to what these men had to say, preferring to abide by the time-honoured Islamic tradition of *shura* (consultation). He was bold enough to admit his mistakes and confident enough to let others make decisions on ideological matters that were far beyond his academic learning. He followed the same approach with senior generals, giving them full power and authority.

Beneath the clerics, or sheikhs, the council appointed religious commissioners (*dubbat shari'a*) to carry out its vision within Nusra ranks. Learning from Abu Musaab's experience with the al-Ghuraba Camp in Afghanistan, al-Golani established a media outlet for Jabhat al-Nusra called *al-Manara al-Bayda* (The White Minaret). It handled all official communications, interview requests and online propaganda via the leading jihadi forum, *Shamoukh al-Islam*. It was through *al-Manara al-Bayda* that Abu Mohammad al-Golani gave his first television interview to Al Jazeera's anchor Tayseer Allouni in December 2013. This was the very same journalist who had been accused by the Spanish courts of being an al-Qaeda affiliate back in 2001. Allouni was a good friend of Abu Musaab al-Souri, the man who helped him set up an office for Al Jazeera in Afghanistan and who had ensured that his press credentials were certified by the Taliban regime. He said that he was searched thoroughly before being given an audience with al-Golani. 'The security measures were far stricter than those taken by the security team of Bin Laden.'[9] The interview did not show al-Golani's face and his voice was distorted for security reasons. He sounded strong, tough and extremely delusional. 'The battle is almost over. What is left is small. We will achieve victory soon. It's only a matter of days.'[10]

Jabhat al-Nusra was designated as a terrorist group by the US Department of State in 2012. Al-Golani claims, 'This is a medal on our chests, of which we are extremely proud.'[11] Instead of scaring locals away from al-Nusra, the US designation only magnified their aura and expanded their power base. In December 2012, locals in rebel-held territory famously said, 'We are all Jabhat al-Nusra.'[12] They called on people to raise al-Nusra's flag in order to express gratitude to the organization, seemingly for turning the tide against the the Syrian army. Twenty-nine Syrian groups opposed to the regime signed an online petition calling for demonstrations in support of al-Nusra. Not only did Islamists sign the document, but so also did civilian organizations impressed with Jabhat al-Nusra.[13] 'These [Nusra fighters] are the men of the people of Syria. These are the heroes who belong to us in religion, in blood, and in revolution.' Opposition figure Mulham al-Jundi said: 'It's terrible timing on the part of the United States. By calling Jabhat al-Nusra terrorists, the United States is legitimizing the Syrian army's bombardment of cities like Aleppo. Now the government can say it is targeting terrorists.' The moderate Damascus cleric Mouaz al-Khatib, by then heading the Syrian National Coalition, also came out in their defence, hailing them as jihadi fighters who should be left alone. He called on the United States to reconsider its decision. A spokesman for the secular Free Syrian Army (FSA – the original defectors from the Syrian army) added: 'We might not share the same beliefs as Jabhat al-Nusra, but we are fighting the same enemy.' After all, some of al-Nusra's suicide operations were very useful for the FSA, helping them overrun several Syrian army checkpoints and bases. Some FSA members even defected to join al-Nusra, making it the most attractive and powerful organization in northern Syria.

THE KINGS OF PAIN

Shortly after the US occupation of Iraq, Osama bin Laden said to his troops: 'Don't be afraid of their tanks; they are *kuffar* [non-believers]. If you launch martyr attacks, you will see fear in the soul of Americans all over the world.'[14] His followers did just that during the uprising in Baghdad and copied the orders verbatim after the outbreak of hostilities in Syria. Al-Nusra claimed responsibility for 57 of the 70 suicide attacks in Syria between March 2011 and June 2013. The earliest happened even before the group was officially formed, in December 2011. On this occasion, a suicide bomber struck a bus filled with riot police in Damascus, killing 26.[15] Al-Golani was already planning attacks on Syrian targets and managed to detonate two other coordinated bombings in Damascus, killing 44 people and wounding 166. One month later, an al-Golani affiliate named Abu Baraa al-Shami blew himself up in the conservative al-Midan neighbourhood of Damascus, once a hotbed for the Muslim Brotherhood. Also in January 2012, al-Nusra followers attacked security headquarters in Idlib. In May, a huge common grave was discovered near Deir ez-Zour filled with the decomposing corpses of 13 men. All of them had been shot. Jabhat al-Nusra claimed responsibility for the attack on 5 June 2012. The bodies belonged to soldiers in the Syrian army. They had been arrested, interrogated and 'justly' punished for working with 'the Alawite regime'.

Most of the car bombs used by al-Nusra were made by Walid Ahmad al-Ayesh, an explosives expert who was arrested and executed by the Syrian government in June 2012. Syrian television described him as al-Golani's 'right-hand man'. On 27 June 2012, al-Golani sent his men to attack the offices of al-Ikhbariya, a state-run television station in the town of Drusha, south of Damascus. The studios were destroyed by explosives and three journalists were killed. Al-Golani claimed responsibility and even published photos of the eleven state employees captured after the raid. In mid-July 2012, they kidnapped Mohammad al-Said, a well-known anchor working with state-run Syrian television. On 3 August 2012, al-Nusra's media branch announced that he had been executed. 'The heroes of western Ghouta imprisoned the *shabih* [pro-government militia] presenter on July 19. He was then killed after he had been interrogated.'[16]

Al-Nusra's violence didn't stop there. The month of October 2012 was seemingly their most destructive phase, with several mass casualty urban attacks. On 3 October, three car bombs exploded at the eastern corner of the Saadallah al-Jabiri Square in central Aleppo. They had multiple targets: the nearby Officers Club, the historic Jouha Café, a small hotel and the statue of Saadallah al-Jabiri, a secular statesman who had led Syria's struggle against French occupation in the 1930s and 1940s. In total, 48 people were killed and more than 100 were injured. Al-Golani's media office laid claim to the attack. Nine days later, al-Nusra struck again at an air defence base, also in Aleppo, completely destroying its radar system. That same month, they attacked a government military base in Wadi al-Deif, near Maaret al-Nouman, 33 km south of Idlib. Syrian troops engaged them in fierce battle, leading to a prolonged siege by the Nusra Front. They also attacked the Taftanaz airbase, 17 km north-east of Idlib, grounding then destroying its 48 helicopters. They then seized three army checkpoints around Sarakeb, east of Idlib, prompting the army's headquarters in Damascus to order a retreat from the entire area to minimize its losses. Already, 28 army troops had been killed in the battle, as opposed to five Nusra fighters. Those captured were executed immediately on al-Golani's orders, accused of being 'dogs'. Not only did they film the massacre, but they also posted it on YouTube. Worldwide condemnation followed, with the United Nations referring to al-Nusra activities as 'war crimes'.

In November 2012, al-Nusra carried out two suicide attacks which rocked both Syrian officialdom and the entire rebel community. The first was in the cross-sectarian and fertile Sahl al-Ghab valley near Hama, the second in the upmarket Mezzeh neighbourhood of Damascus. The first led to the death of 50 soldiers, the second to a total of eleven civilians. On 23 December 2012, al-Nusra unilaterally declared a 'no-fly zone' over Aleppo, using 23mm and 57mm anti-aircraft guns to shoot the Syrian army jets.[17] They threatened to do the same with commercial flights, prompting all major airlines to drop Syria from their itinerary and drastically increasing flight times as a result.

As the world was adjusting to how horribly wrong the Syrian war had gone, al-Nusra began to fall apart. The victory spark of late 2012 was almost all but gone less than two years later, in early 2014. Al-Nusra had bloated in size, becoming much larger than its leaders and founders could handle. Not all of its troops were listening to al-Golani any more. As a result, al-Nusra units became wild and chaotic. With power, corruption crept in. No longer were al-Nusra fighters pure and utopian, as they had portrayed themselves back in 2012. Many started kidnapping citizens and exchanging them for ransom money. The ransom varied from one 'customer' to the next, ranging from S£1 million (approximately US$5,000) up to as much as S£20 million (US$100,000). Others made money by stealing flashy new cars and then selling them, either for spare parts inside Syria or to crime gangs in neighbouring Lebanon and Iraq. Crime became easy and it paid well. A new breed of recruits was rapidly emerging in the group, feeding off criminals and self-seekers.

In June 2013, a 49-year-old Catholic priest named Father Francois Murad was captured and shot dead at his church in the Christian village of Ghassaniyeh in the Homs Governorate. The murder was claimed by Jabhat al-Nusra. In December 2013, they abducted 13 nuns from a monastery in the ancient Christian town of Maaloula. Before taking the hostages, they terrorized the village, trying to convert some Christians to Islam. They also struck at the ancient St Thekla Convent, and then smashed a beautiful statue of the Virgin Mary in Maaloula's central square. The nuns were held in Yabroud in rural Damascus until March 2014.[18] Jabhat al-Nusra's deputy commander in the Qalamoon

Mountains, Abu Azzam al-Kuwaiti, handled the negotiations for their release with Qatari and Lebanese officials. They were eventually released unharmed, only after Jabhat al-Nusra was paid US$16 million in ransom money. In return, the Syrian authorities released 150 women from jail, namely the families of al-Nusra members on the battlefield. In contrast to ISIS, which boasts of its female recruits, al-Nusra says nothing about its women and gives them no role in the movement, abiding by puritan interpretations of Islam that insist on keeping women in the background of public life. In April 2013, al-Nusra kidnapped Boulos Yazigi, the Orthodox Bishop of Aleppo and Iskenderun, and Yohanna Ibrahim, the Syriac Orthodox Bishop of Aleppo. Both men remain missing. In February 2013, al-Nusra fighters seized two clerics, Michel Kayyal (Armenian Catholic) and Maher Mahfouz (Greek Orthodox) on the main road between Damascus and Aleppo. In August 2014, they kidnapped 45 Fijian UN peacekeepers in the Syrian Golan. All of them were part of the United Nations Disengagement Observer Force. Al-Golani said that they would only be released if the UN removed Jabhat al-Nusra from its list of terrorist organizations. The soldiers were later released after unconfirmed claims that Qatar paid al-Nusra a ransom for their release.[19]

As Jabhat al-Nusra expanded horizontally in rebel-held territory, Abu Bakr al-Baghdadi was biting his lip in anger and disbelief. His former protégé, al-Golani, was now controlling more territory, towns and foot soldiers than the Islamic State of Iraq (ISI) ever did. Furthermore, al-Golani was in control of oilfields in eastern Syria and lucrative border crossings in northern Syria; all would have put a pretty penny in al-Baghdadi's war chest. In May 2013, unable to hide his frustration any longer, al-Baghdadi showed up in Aleppo, and started to personally recruit al-Nusra members into his newly formed ISIS, luring them with double wages. This is how ISI had 'stolen' members of the Free Syrian Army – with incentives, promotions and money.[20] Al-Golani was paying his men up to $400 per month; al-Baghdadi raised it to $800. That certainly encouraged many to defect, along with the fact that Jabhat al-Nusra's popularity had started to decline. A bad reputation topped with joint US and UN sanctions, hostile local communities and lack of funds all helped destroy everything al-Nusra founders had been working for since 2011. According to Al Jazeera TV, over 70 per cent of al-Nusra fighters defected to join ISIS in mid-2013.[21] Many were interested in the high pay which ISIS offered, others bought into its more radical approach, and some just accepted al-Baghdadi's leadership as a fait accompli following military defeats at the hands of ISIS, especially in eastern Syria. Locals who had been supportive were now protesting against the organization, with a huge demonstration staged in Deir ez-Zour where residents chanted: '*Bara! Bara! Al-Nusra Bara, bara!*' This is translated as 'Out! Out! Al-Nusra Out!' Al-Golani's enemies were seemingly increasing as rapidly as his adherents once had. His rapid success had roused jealousy and anxiety among other Syrian Islamist factions. Also, many moderate Syrian rebels did not want to be associated with the stigma of terrorism that al-Nusra painted, as they hoped for more Western-funded military assistance. Secular activists accused al-Golani of 'hijacking the peaceful revolution'. One of the leaders in Aleppo said: 'We are not fighting Bashar al-Assad to go from living in an autocratic to a religious prison.'[22] Despite the dramatic reversal of fortunes, al-Qaeda remained firmly committed to al-Golani. Its higher command disavowed any relationship with ISIS in February 2013. This served Golani well in jihadi circles, but completely destroyed him among secularists, moderates and ultra-radicals. That same month, al-Zawahiri's mediator in the al-Golani–al-Baghdadi feud, Abu Khaled al-Souri, was killed in Aleppo. Each of the al-Qaeda leaders blamed the assassination on the other. Al-Golani claimed that al-Baghdadi had killed him because of al-Zawahiri's sympathy with Jabhat al-Nusra.

On 16 April 2014, al-Baghdadi sent al-Golani another strongly worded message – by killing his top chief in Idlib, Abu Mohammad al-Ansari, along with his wife. He appeared to be saying: 'If we can reach your top lieutenants, we can kill you anytime.' One month later, the two sides fired at each other in al-Golani's native Deir ez-Zour, leaving hundreds dead. By now, however, it was al-Baghdadi's men who were getting the upper hand, having firmly established ISIS. By July 2014, al-Nusra was barely to be found in Deir ez-Zour. All of its bases, checkpoints and ammunition stockpiles had been occupied by ISIS. Al-Golani hid low for a few months and then came out with an audio statement in early July 2014, saying that al-Nusra wanted to establish an Islamic Emirate in all parts of northern Syria. It was a poor PR stunt aimed at polishing his crumbling image. He summoned al-Nusra's Shura Council and announced: 'We will not allow any person to reap the fruits of your jihad, regardless of whatever happens to us.'[23] Explaining his vision for the Islamic Emirate, al-Golani said:

> There will be an army and Shari'a courts in every city. There will be an army in Aleppo and an army in Idlib. Your brothers in Daraa [in southern Syria] will join you. The same goes for besieged al-Ghouta [in the Damascus countryside]. The Front has formidable power, and few can rival it in the Levant. We will never withdraw from any region [we control].[24]

Despite the grand announcement, which created a stir on jihadi websites, al-Nusra's state has not been created as of late 2015. Nor has al-Golani kept his army in every town and city in northern Syria. On the contrary, it has retreated significantly as ISIS has swept into cities and towns stretched between Iraq and Syria. In June 2014, for example, al-Nusra's branch in the Syrian town of Al-Bukamal pledged allegiance to ISIS. On 13 November 2014, ISIS and al-Nusra finally announced a truce. Al-Golani and al-Baghdadi met in the town of Atareb, west of Aleppo, for the first time since early 2012. The meeting lasted for four hours, after which they announced an ending to hostilities, saying that now was the time to join forces against both the Syrian regime and the US-led international coalition, which had started to bomb rebel-held territory in September. Addressing Muslims worldwide in an audio message, al-Golani said: 'Muslims, your [Islamic] state is in good hands!'[25] The past, present and future were in the hands of al-Qaeda, he seemed to be saying. He soon realized that al-Nusra's grip was not really as strong as he wanted it to be. This is the trend of Syrian jihad. The Fighting Vanguards one day are dwarfed and swallowed up by the Muslim Brotherhood. Then came al-Qaeda to absorb them both. Jabhat al-Nusra was born out of Bin Laden's network, but made al-Zawahiri and his team look like amateurs – yet they too were outflanked by ISIS. Al-Golani's al-Nusra and al-Baghdadi's ISIS overshadowed the old al-Qaeda with their organizational prowess and their ability to conquer and hold territory. While al-Qaeda in Afghanistan and Pakistan is still scattered in mountainous hideouts, al-Nusra and ISIS openly control vast swathes of territory, raising the black flag over many towns and cities of the Fertile Crescent.

On 5 March 2015, al-Nusra suffered a harsh blow in the Idlib province when the Syrian Air Force struck, killing several of their top commanders. Among the dead were al-Nusra's military commander Samir al-Hijazi (aka Abu Hummam al-Shami), also known as al-Farouk al-Souri, along with Abu Umar al-Kurdi, Abu al-Baraa al-Ansari and Abu Musaab al-Filastini. Both Abu Hummam and Abu Umar were early founding members of al-Nusra. They were all together in one place, planning an offensive on the Abu Duhour Military Airport, the last government base in Idlib. Abu Hummam was one of the Syrian field fighters in Afghanistan who commanded Kandahar Airport during the rule of the Taliban. He swore allegiance to Bin Laden in 1998, shortly before arriving in Kabul to join al-Qaeda. In 2003, he joined the jihadis in Iraq and worked closely with the two Abu Musaabs (al-Souri and al-Zarqawi). Abu Umar al-Kurdi was a member of ISIS who defected to join Jabhat al-Nusra. Yet the loss did not seem to slow al-Nusra down. In late March, al-Nusra fighters expelled Syrian government forces from the southern city of Bosra. An even more dramatic event took place in northern Syria around the same time when hundreds of al-Nusra fighters alongside other rebel factions launched a massive assault on the city of Idlib. After less than a week of fierce battles, the city fell to al-Nusra and its allies, becoming Syria's second provincial capital to fall completely outside of government control after al-Raqqa. The success was due to a coordinated effort between many factions (all unaffiliated with ISIS) over a two-month period and the use of sophisticated missiles provided by the United States to moderate rebels, which had been snatched by al-Nusra and its affiliates.[26] Government forces claimed that their exodus was tactical, but they took all the civil service records and documents with them to the nearby province of Jisr al-Shughour. Al-Nusra tried its best to promise its new subjects that 'this won't be another al-Raqqa', meaning that they wouldn't let it fall into the hands of ISIS. Indeed, al-Nusra seemed wiser this time than when it first took al-Raqqa in 2013. They didn't fire government bureaucrats, for example, and they created a human corridor for army troops to withdraw safely from the city. But whether al-Nusra will be able to hold on to the city is still a matter of question. Furthermore, will al-Nusra be setting up its own capital in Idlib, the way ISIS had in al-Raqqa? Or will it coexist with other rebel factions in managing the city? Nevertheless, al-Nusra has solidified itself as a major player on the Syrian scene and as a significant stakeholder in the country's future.

FIVE

The Jihadis of Iraq

IN 2014, A FORMER PALESTINIAN RESIDENT OF BAGHDAD picked up the phone to call old friends in the Iraqi capital. She had lived in Baghdad throughout the 1990s and knew the 'who's who' of Iraqi high society under Saddam Hussein. Her milieu had been doctors, engineers, regime-affiliated businessmen and officers in Saddam Hussein's army. Speaking to the author from Beirut, she said: 'Time and again, I got a chilling answer: "*He*? Oh, well hmmm ... he's joined Daesh!"' Quietly, she would ask about another person, and the reply would be: 'He is no longer reachable – he has changed all his numbers. Authorities are on his track; his son joined Daesh!' This applied to former Iraqi VIPs, including members of Saddam Hussein's own family.

Daesh of course is the Arabic acronym for ISIS, which as of mid-2015 has somewhere between 35,000 and 50,000 fighters inside Syria and Iraq and controls approximately 90,000 square kilometres of territory. This is huge, given that according to US intelligence ISIS had no more than 200 warriors in Syria as of August 2012.[1] With an area as large as Great Britain and comprising approximately six million people, the Islamic State has a larger population today than countries such as Finland and Denmark.[2] ISIS has erased the boundaries of the Middle East, which were drawn up a century ago by the British and French during World War I. The nation states of the post-Ottoman order have fallen apart; there is no longer a boundary between Syria and Iraq, thanks to the flow of arms, men and ideas between Mosul and al-Raqqa. ISIS has achieved more for Salafi jihadism than the Muslim Brotherhood, the Fighting Vanguards, al-Qaeda and Jabhat al-Nusra combined.

The organization has gone through several important stages before reaching its present form. It started out as a mini al-Qaeda-affiliated militia founded in Jordan yet operating exclusively from Iraq, first under the name Jama'at al-Tawhid wa al-Jihad (Group of Monotheism and Jihad) in 1999. Its original goal was neither jihad in Syria nor the downfall of President Bashar al-Assad. Rather, its initial objective was to bring down the Jordanian monarchy of King Abdullah II, which it accused of being a vehicle for Western penetration into the Arab world. Unlike Jabhat al-Nusra, which linked directly to an older generation of Syrian Islamists who had survived the Hama debacle of 1982, ISIS had few links to Syria. Al-Qaeda in Iraq was headed by a Jordanian Salafi leader, Abu Musaab al-Zarqawi, and composed mostly of Iraqi jihadis. They all coalesced into the so-called Sunni insurgency after the US occupation of Iraq in 2003. In October 2004, al-Zarqawi swore allegiance to Osama bin Laden. From here the group took on the name Tanzim Qaidat al-Jihad fi Bilad al-Rafidayn (The Organizational Base for Jihad in Iraq). Westerners preferred to refer to it as 'Al-Qaeda in Iraq'. The story of ISIS would not be complete without a sketch of the man who made it happen. Al-Zarqawi was to ISIS what Abu Musaab al-Souri was to Jabhat al-Nusra – and what Abdullah Azzam was to al-Qaeda. Like them, he departed the scene several years before ISIS was born, when he was killed by an American air strike on his hideout in Iraq in 2006.

Abu Musaab al-Zarqawi lacked all the assets and qualities that Abu Musaab al-Souri had in abundance. He had no pre-jihad Islamic credentials on his CV, had written nothing substantial in his entire life and received little formal education. Born Ahmad Fadel al-Nazal al-Khalayleh in 1966, he hailed from the Jordanian city of Zarqa, approximately 21 km north-east of the capital Amman. He was a troublesome teenager and a heavy drinker, with a criminal record of up to 37 felonies.[3] He could barely read and write, and dropped out of school in 1984. This was the year of his father's death, and he sank into a life of crime. Trying to tame her delinquent child, Abu Musaab's mother enrolled him at a religious course at the al-Hussein Bin Ali Mosque in Amman. This was a soul-shaking experience that changed his life, and it was where he was first introduced to Salafism.

In no way was al-Zarqawi's jihadi career the product of intellectual evolution, unlike that of Abu Musaab al-Souri. It was initially born out of a thirst for vengeance on the ruling Hashemite family in his home country Jordan, which was brought to the throne with British backing in the early 1920s and has been in power ever since. Fleeing persecution at home, al-Zarqawi travelled to Afghanistan in 1989, with the aim of joining the war against the Soviet Union. Unlike his Syrian namesake, he never met Abdullah Azzam. He did come across Osama bin Laden, however, eventually becoming one of his many aides. Apart from street fighting, al-Zarqawi didn't have much experience with arms, which explains why Bin Laden first appointed him to a civilian job – as editor of an al-Qaeda-affiliated Islamic newsletter. Unlike Abu Musaab al-Souri, who skyrocketed to fame by travelling Europe to recruit Syrians into al-Qaeda, al-Zarqawi did little for the jihadi cause throughout most of the 1990s.

The relationship between Bin Laden and al-Zarqawi started off on a bumpy road when they first met in Kandahar in 1999.[4] Al-Zarqawi's arrogance simply got in the way. Bin Laden suspected him of being a spy, and the many tattoos obtained during his wild days only added to Bin Laden's disgust. Al-Zarqawi had tried to erase them using hydrochloric acid, but with no luck.[5] His rigid views were frowned upon by Bin Laden, who up until then had not been in favour of slaughtering Alawites, Shi'a and Christians. Bin Laden didn't have an axe to grind with the Alawites, given that his Syrian mother was from the Alawite community. Al-Zarqawi, however, had nothing but spite for them. Ayman al-Zawahiri was present, and he said that al-Zarqawi would not make good material for al-Qaeda. A former officer in the Egyptian army turned explosives expert at al-Qaeda, Seif al-Adel, advised otherwise. He convinced Bin Laden that al-Zarqawi's contacts in the Middle East would prove useful to al-Qaeda. When asked to offer the *ba'ya* (the pledge of allegiance) to Bin Laden, al-Zarqawi arrogantly refused. The relationship only healed after 9/11 when al-Zarqawi was charged with bringing al-Qaeda properly into Iraq.

During a brief return to Amman in 1992, al-Zarqawi was arrested after guns and explosives were found at his home; he spent the next six years at the Jordanian Swaqa prison, 70 km south of the capital Amman. Jordanian authorities accused him of trying to blow up a five-star hotel in Amman frequented by American and Israeli tourists. While in jail, he called on fellow inmates to join him in overthrowing the Jordanian monarchy. After his release in 1999, al-Zarqawi went to Peshawar, where he met Abu Musaab al-Souri. The two never got on. The veteran Syrian jihadi saw him as irrational, wild and intellectually inferior. Al-Zarqawi didn't care; he was already firmly established as a favourite of Osama bin Laden. So impressed had Bin Laden become with al-Zarqawi that he paid homage to him by name in a December 2004 audiotape, describing the young Jordanian militant as the 'Emir of al-Qaeda in Iraq'. Bin Laden asked 'all our organizations' brethren to listen to him and obey him in all his good deeds.' Through Bin Laden, al-Zarqawi received a subsidy of US$200,000 to establish a military training camp near Abdul Mehdi, close to the north-eastern Iranian border.[6] The banner at its entrance read: *'Tawhid wa Jihad'* (Monotheism and Jihad). The camp specialized in poison and explosives, while offering classes in Islamic history and Shari'a. This is where al-Zarqawi began to expand his jihadi knowledge while training his students. He avidly read all of Abu Musaab al-Souri's jihadi literature and made it mandatory reading for his students as well, regardless of what he personally thought of the author. It was an all-Jordanian camp, with few Syrians and no foreigners. Jordanian intelligence infiltrated the group, however, and it fell apart shortly before the US war on Afghanistan in October 2001.

The US government put al-Zarqawi on its 'wanted' list, with a $25 million reward for any information leading to his capture. This was the same amount offered for Bin Laden's head in 2004. More important than his role in Afghanistan was al-Zarqawi's involvement in the 2002 assassination of a senior Amman-based US diplomat named Laurence Foley. Three suspects confessed that they had been paid by al-Zarqawi to eliminate Foley. Al-Zarqawi was also charged with planning a series of attacks in Casablanca and Istanbul in 2003. One year later, he tried to sabotage a NATO summit in Turkey. He was also accused of masterminding the Amman bombings of 2005, which killed 60 people in three hotels, including Palestinian and Chinese officials and the Hollywood-based Syrian director Mustapha al-Akkad.

THE IRAQI INSURGENCY AFTER 2003

These years of terrorism in Amman and Afghanistan were a transitional phase in al-Zarqawi's thundering career. He is remembered most for his role in Iraq after the US occupation of 2003. In May 2004, the CIA claimed that al-Zarqawi appeared in a video of the beheading of the American civilian Nicholas Berg in Iraq.[7] Berg was killed, according to al-Qaeda, in response to the Abu Ghraib prison scandal, where inmates had been photographed in humiliating torture scenes by American officials. The Abu Ghraib scandal had permeated all corners of the Muslim world and fuelled a hatred of the West in jihadis and non-jihadis alike. Al-Zarqawi was believed to have personally beheaded another American, Owen Eugene Armstrong, in September 2004. In the video Armstrong is shown kneeling before his death, with a black al-Qaeda flag in the background.

In total, the United States claimed that al-Zarqawi was responsible for the killing of 700 people in Iraq during the years 2003–6.[8] Additionally, his name was linked to 42 per cent of all suicide attacks during the same period. In August 2003, he was accused of bombing the UN Headquarters in Iraq, killing 22 people including the UN Secretary-General's special envoy Sérgio Vieira de Mello. Al-Zarqawi said that he targeted de Mello personally because the UN diplomat was 'embellishing the image of America, the Crusaders and the Jews'.

That same month, his men attacked the Imam Ali Mosque in Najaf, a supremely holy site for Muslim Shi'a, killing 95 people including the veteran Shi'i cleric, Mohammad Baqir al-Hakim, commander of the Supreme Islamic Council in Iraq. The operation was carried out by al-Zarqawi's father-in-law.[9] In March 2004, he was accused of masterminding the attack on Shi'i shrines in Karbala and Baghdad, which resulted in over 180 deaths.[10] The Shi'a were among his main targets and he often quoted the thirteenth–fourteenth-century Islamic cleric Ibn Taymiyya, who called on Muslims to excommunicate both Alawites and Shi'a, putting them on an equal footing with Jews and Christians. Al-Zarqawi was also blamed for the December 2004 car bomb attack in Karbala, the most sacred site in the world for Shi'i Muslims, which claimed 60 lives. He ordered the blowing up of the al-Askari Mosque in Samarra, another Shi'i site, on the east bank of the Tigris River, triggering massive Sunni–Shi'a sectarian conflict. After the attack, death squads emerged, with Sunni gangs roaming Shi'i neighbourhoods, shooting clerics and community leaders. Shi'i militiamen slaughtered Sunni leaders in response.

Al-Zarqawi recruited fighters from the disbanded Baath Party of Saddam Hussein. They turned to him for arms and support while he used them as fuel to spread havoc and bring down the post-Saddam Hussein US-appointed government. Apart from having a common enemy, the Baathists and al-Zarqawi had very little in common. The Sunni insurgency started off with 50,000 ex-Baathists taking up arms against the US occupation.[11] It wasn't initially an Islamic uprising and had nothing to do with al-Qaeda or setting up a theocracy in Baghdad. When al-Zarqawi arrived on the scene, he stole the spotlight from the Baathist rebels. By virtue of their experience with Saddam Hussein's army, his men were better equipped and better trained. They were also driven by jihadi thought, making them more effective on the battleground. US propaganda helped inflate his image, no doubt, because it justified the continuation of military operations in Iraq. The *Telegraph* went as far as to describe the al-Zarqawi phenomenon as a 'myth' that suited all stakeholders in Iraq.[12] Quoting an unnamed

US military intelligence source, the newspaper said that al-Zarqawi's inflated role was originally the product of faulty intelligence. The United States accepted and promoted it, however, because it suited American goals in the Middle East. So did the governments in Amman, Baghdad and Damascus. At least one Iraqi Baath rebel came out saying that al-Zarqawi was 'an American, Israeli and Iranian agent'. The prominent Shi'i cleric turned leader of an anti-American militia, Muqtada al-Sadr, made similar accusations, saying: 'I believe he is fictitious. He is a knife or pistol in the hands of the occupier.'

Abu Musaab al-Zarqawi was no myth. For three years he stormed and overtook the Iraqi underground, until he was killed by US warplanes on 7 June 2006. The US dropped two 230 kg laser-guided bombs on his hideout near Baqubah in north-east of Baghdad, eliminating the al-Qaeda chief along with five aides, his wife and child. Iraq's new prime minister, Nouri al-Maliki, an ally of the United States, announced the death saying: 'Today, Zarqawi has been terminated. Every time a Zarqawi appears, we will kill him. We will continue confronting whoever follows his path.' President George W. Bush added, 'Now Zarqawi has met his end and this violent man will never murder again.' Al-Qaeda, of course, honoured him as a martyr of the global jihad and described his death as a 'great loss'. On 23 June 2006, Ayman al-Zawahiri described him as a 'soldier, a hero, an imam and the prince of martyrs.'[13] One week later, Bin Laden himself paid tribute to al-Zarqawi:

> Our Islamic nation was surprised to find its knight, the lion of jihad, the man of determination and will, Abu Musaab al-Zarqawi, killed in a shameful American raid. We pray to Allah to bless him and accept him among the martyrs.[14]

In his last public address, al-Zarqawi said: 'Muslims will have no victory or superiority over the aggressive infidels such as the Jews and the Christians until there is a total annihilation of those under them.'[15] He of course was referring to Arab Christians, the Shi'a of

Iraq and the Alawites of Syria. Al-Zarqawi's elimination did not end the Sunni insurgency. The death toll in Iraq was still an average of 90 Iraqis per day. Within four months of his death, 374 coalition soldiers and 10,355 Iraqis died in the war, proving that al-Zarqawi lived on in the minds and hearts of Iraqi jihadis.[16] In Jordan, his memorial services were made public and they were attended by Islamic MPs in the Jordanian parliament.[17] In Syria, al-Zarqawi's brand of jihad had deep effects on many, especially on disenfranchised youth living in the poorer urban areas. DVDs of his organization's operations in Iraq were sold undercover by street vendors in Damascus and other Syrian cities. The minute-long videos of exploding IEDs repeated in slow motion with motivational jihadi songs playing in the background were a sensational hit and they only cost S£50 (US$1). Anybody could buy them. Within the old streets of Duma, Daraya and the Yarmouk Camp on the outskirts of Damascus, informal mourning circles were set up after al-Zarqawi's death was confirmed. The state wrote him off as a terrorist, but many ordinary Syrians – future adherents of ISIS – were saddened by his demise, seeing him as a 'glorious martyr'. To them, al-Zarqawi and his band of warriors had challenged the world's strongest military, blowing up its armoured vehicles and shooting its soldiers in broad daylight. This was the same military that a few months ago had been able to swiftly occupy an Arab capital in a matter of weeks. Al-Zarqawi's success showed that jihadi Islam was working, and clearly it was keeping the Americans awake at night. This bloodstained inspiration is al-Zarqawi's lasting and lethal legacy.

THE ISLAMIC STATE IN IRAQ

Shortly before his death, al-Zarqawi merged several small insurgent groups under the umbrella of what he called the 'Mujahideen Shura Council', in January 2006. It had only one Syrian on board, Suleiman Khalid Darwish (aka Abu Ghadia). Born in 1976, he grew up in the Damascus countryside and studied dentistry at Damascus University.

Al-Zarqawi met him at one of his classes in Afghanistan, where he was studying topography and jihadi thought. Abu Ghadia became al-Zarqawi's main fundraiser prior to the Afghan war of 2001. He channelled US$10,000–12,000 to al-Qaeda every two to three weeks, tapped from Islamic circles around the world. He travelled freely, using two fake Syrian passports.[18] Along with another protégé named Abu Omar al-Baghdadi, al-Zarqawi established the Islamic State of Iraq (ISI) five months before he was killed in the summer of 2006. Al-Zarqawi by now had become kingmaker of Iraqi jihadis; he no longer contented himself with leading any of the small militias operating in the Iraqi battlefield. He was one step short of doing what Abu Bakr al-Baghdadi did later in 2014: self-appointing himself king of the Islamic State. He could not proclaim himself caliph, however, because according to Sunni tradition, the caliph strictly had to be a descendant of the clan of Mecca notables, which al-Zarqawi was not. He could have played with his background, as some have accused al-Baghdadi of doing, in order to link himself directly to one of the clans of Quraysh. Had he lived on for another three months, recalls an aide, then this is exactly what he would have done. American bombs, however, came sooner, ending al-Zarqawi's life and his aspiration. The role of al-Zarqawi's ISI was to seize power in central and western areas of Iraq and turn them into a Sunni Islamic state, ruled by the guidelines of the Qur'an and following the example of the first Muslims (*Salaf*). 'Syria was not on their agenda,' confirms a top al-Zarqawi aid.

At the time of his death in 2006, al-Zarqawi was busy mapping out what his state would look like. He had sketched out hierarchy charts and maps, and had written abstracts and synopses for his new state. He had even roughly calculated the economy of the state, its expenditure and income, through taxation based on Islamic Shari'a. Al-Zarqawi went as far as to ask his aides to come up with a 'vision paper' on surplus, deficit and potential revenue from oil. The concept remained primitive, however, and never reached the leverage later enjoyed under Abu Bakr al-Baghdadi in al-Raqqa – although it did enjoy significant support in al-Anbar, Nineveh, Kirkuk, Babil, Diyala,

Baghdad and the Salahuddine province. It claimed Baqubah as its capital city, 60 km to the north-east of Baghdad.

The experiment was short-lived and had fallen apart by late 2007. The kiss of death was al-Zarqawi's elimination in the summer of 2006. His successor Abu Omar al-Baghdadi tried and failed to develop the project. The efficient top-to-bottom chain of command collapsed after al-Zarqawi's death, leading to chaos among the foot soldiers, fighters and local clientele. Many took the law into their own hands and ceased to obey al-Zarqawi's deputies, thereby alienating the local population. Once seen as Islamic heroes, they were now viewed as thugs, pirates and crooks. Theft, kidnapping, looting and blackmailing became common within al-Zarqawi-controlled areas. Al-Zarqawi's 'institutions' disintegrated, failing to provide services like price control and police enforcement. Instead, his appointees ruled by the sword, demanding nothing less than full obedience and allowing no complaint. Those who dared to challenge the Islamic State in Iraq were arrested, tortured and flogged. The central al-Qaeda administration, suffering from consecutive setbacks after 2001, was no longer in a position to send money to its Iraqi branch: 'This is why many of our brothers turned to stealing cars and taking hostages. They needed to earn money. With Abu Musaab al-Zarqawi gone, outside money stopped coming. They had no other choice.'

Additionally, non-stop US and Iraqi raids had helped eliminate large al-Zarqawi bases throughout Iraq. Foreign fighters had stopped coming, thanks to better control of the Syrian–Iraqi border. Instead, al-Zarqawi's men had to rely more and more on locals to help in his battle. Many of them had received no military training in their lives. They just added to the prevailing chaos in al-Qaeda ranks. The United States then created local Awakening Councils, arming citizens to defend themselves from al-Qaeda advances. They paid more than al-Zarqawi and provided better-quality arms. Many of al-Zarqawi's top lieutenants were soon killed and those who survived fled central Iraq to a relatively safe haven, the northern city of Mosul. On 18 April 2010, two of his top successors, Abu Ayyub al-Masri and Abu Omar al-Baghdadi, were killed in a joint US–Iraqi raid near Tikrit. By June, the United States announced that 80 per cent of ISI's top 42 leaders, including officers and financiers, had been either killed or captured.[19] Only eight survived and their lines of communication to al-Qaeda in Pakistan were cut off completely, thus isolating them from the global jihad movement.

On the eve of the Syrian uprising, the Islamic State of Iraq had become a minor player on the Iraqi scene. It no longer posed a grave threat to Nouri al-Maliki's government in Baghdad. Iraq was, it seemed, no longer a major battlefield in the war on terror. Most of ISI's leadership was eliminated; many of its foot soldiers had defected to join the higher-paying Awakening Councils. Few people worried about what Abu Omar al-Baghdadi might do or say, as his name was just another on the target list. Yet it was this dislocation of ISI's command that allowed Abu Bakr al-Baghdadi to consolidate his grip on power. The struggle in Syria and the receding power of its central government allowed ISI to find a breathing space in eastern Syria. Money, men and weapons from Syria rekindled the Iraq insurgency. Al-Maliki's sectarian policies alienated Iraq's Sunni population once more and the Awakening Councils began to collapse. This across-the-board dislocation from Damascus to Baghdad created the space in which Abu Bakr al-Baghdadi was about to launch his devastating project: The Islamic State of Iraq and the Levant.

SIX

The Birth of ISIS

THE ISLAMIC STATE OF IRAQ WAS IN DIRE STRAITS. AL-ZARQAWI'S elimination, topped with successful US counterterrorism operations via the Awakening Councils, hit al-Qaeda badly. So did Osama bin Laden's death in 2011. The man to turn the tide and preserve Abu Musaab al-Zarqawi's legacy in Iraq was one of his disciples, Abu Bakr al-Baghdadi. He was not the obvious candidate to succeed al-Zarqawi. At the age of 39, he became the Islamic State's new emir on 16 May 2010, voted for by nine out of eleven members of the Shura Council. He was originally known by the informal name of 'Abu Du'aa' (father of prayer) but began using the current 'Abu Bakr' as of 2010. Different sources say different things about the self-appointed caliph of Islam. They all agree on his date and place of birth, but practically on nothing else. Because of the contradictory information, sketching his profile is extremely difficult. Much of the confusion is al-Baghdadi's own doing. The little information written about him during the years 2003–13 is all quite consistent. Those bits and pieces were authored before the growth of his political ambitions from militia leader to pan-Islamic caliph. In other words, he didn't try to modify – or hide – entire chunks of his past because he had nothing to prove and nobody to please. This changed the minute al-Baghdadi declared himself caliph. Dust and doubt needed to be thrown on everything ever written about him in the past. Confusion and conflicting information had to prevail, mixing the truth with fiction and fantasy.

A STAR IS BORN: ABU BAKR AL-BAGHDADI

Abu Bakr al-Baghdadi was born Ibrahim Awwad Ibrahim al-Badri, to a middle-class Iraqi Sunni family that links itself directly to the Prophet Muhammad, via his eldest grandson Imam al-Hasan – a historical figure respected by Sunni Muslims but worshipped by the Shi'a. Al-Baghdadi's father was a cleric who used to teach the Qur'an at the Ahmad Bin Hanbal Mosque of Samarra. The story of his ancestry is strongly disputed by Islamic scholars at the Umayyad Mosque of Damascus, where ancient scrolls documenting the Prophet's lineage have been stored for centuries. They show no reference whatsoever to al-Baghdadi's family, and the 'caliph' himself has provided no evidence through his various social media networking channels. 'Ibrahim Awwad Ibrahim al-Badri' was born in 1971 in the city of Samarra in the Salhuddine province, 125 km north of Baghdad. The city itself is historically important to all Muslims and had a tremendous influence on al-Baghdadi. Between the years 836 and 892 it housed the seat of power of the Muslim Empire – the caliphate's throne. The residents of Samarra take great pride in how the Abbasid Caliph al-Mutassim transferred the caliphate from Baghdad to Samarra, seeing it as more fit to serve as the Muslim capital. This is carved into their collective consciousness, and references to al-Mutassim in Samarra can be found in poetry books, house paintings in Arabic calligraphy and in Friday sermons. Al-Baghdadi grew up hearing endless stories about the fabled virtues of his native city, and how glorious and beautiful it had been during the Abbasid dynasty.[1] Deep inside he longed for the day when he could restore its lost glory.

Although predominantly Sunni, Samarra is also home to the magnificent al-Askari Mosque, containing the mausoleums of Shi'i imams Ali al-Hadi and Hassan al-Askari. Al-Baghdadi walked by this holy site almost daily as a child. We don't know whether it really meant anything to him at the time, or if he saw it simply as part of the city's furniture. His grandfather Hajj Ibrahim was a respected elder in Samarra who died shortly after the US occupation of 2003, well into his nineties. Al-Baghdadi was his favourite grandchild. The Samarra elder must have lectured him on the city's past and the greatness of its Islamic monuments. During the 1950s, when Hajj Ibrahim was an active adult, the Sunnis and Shi'a lived side by side in Samarra. They worked together, studied together, served in the armed forces together and often intermarried. Friction between the two communities did not erupt until after the American invasion of 2003. Stories of this coexistence are repeated daily over dinner in many Iraqi households. If al-Baghdadi did hear such arguments as a child and young adult, he must have deleted them from memory after proclaiming himself 'caliph' in 2014. Part of his programme, after all, was exterminating non-Sunni sects like the Shi'a, including Isma'ilis and Alawites.

Ibrahim Awwad Ibrahim al-Badri, or Abu Bakr al-Baghdadi, was the youngest of three children: himself, Shamsi and Jumaa al-Badri. The eldest, Shamsi, is currently in jail in Iraq over financial affairs and embezzlement. He is not a Salafi and is critical of his brother's career path. The middle brother, Jumaa, is a fervent jihadi and currently serves as his younger brother's private bodyguard. All three studied at state-run high schools in Samarra. Schools and hospitals were free of charge under Baath rule. Every morning, al-Baghdadi would attend military drill wearing the khaki uniform of Saddam's Youth (the Baathist youth corps). While saluting the Iraqi flag, the superintendent would bark: '*Kiam*' (Stand Up!). The students would respond: '*Aash al-Ka'ed Saddam*' (Long Live the Leader Saddam). The Baath official would wave his hand sternly: '*Julous*' (Be Seated). Al-Baghdadi and his friends would chant: '*Al-Mawt lil Fars wa al-Majoos*' (Death to the Persians and the Shi'a). Abu Bakr al-Baghdadi uttered this exact same line throughout his school education, which coincided with the Iran–Iraq War (1980–88). Unsurprisingly, he copied the exact same technique in the Islamic State, forcing students in al-Raqqa and Mosul to swear by his name and call out for his long life, every single morning at school.

Living under the harshest years of Saddam Hussein's dictatorship taught him plenty of lessons in life. When al-Baghdadi was nine, many of his family members and neighbours were hauled off to battle in the devastating Iran–Iraq War. Some returned with an amputated leg or having lost an eye. Thousands returned in wooden caskets – a lifeless corpse 'martyred' for the glorious Iraqi nation. Nobody in Iraq dared question the wisdom of such a prolonged war, launched over the disputed sovereignty of the Shatt al-Arab waterway dividing the two countries. Those who criticized the war were 'taken away' by Saddam Hussein's security services, or shot in front of family members. The United States, Saudi Arabia and other Gulf states bankrolled Saddam Hussein during the eight-year conflict, hoping to weaken or break Shi'i Iran and its founder, Ayatollah Ruhollah Khomeini. The war ended in stalemate in 1988, with the borders practically unchanged. An estimated one million people died in the Iran–Iraq War. It left a permanent scar in the psyche of an entire generation of young Iraqis, al-Baghdadi included. It ended on his 18th birthday. Had it lasted for another year, he too would have been hauled off to battle, since military service was compulsory for able-bodied men aged 18 and above.

As a young man, al-Baghdadi admired Saddam Hussein's ability to shake off troubles and move on. He also admired his unwavering commitment to bringing down Shi'i Iran. Iraqis of this generation grew up surrounded by Saddam Hussein's cult of personality. 'The Glorious Leader' Abu Uday (father of Uday, Saddam Hussein's nickname) was to be found everywhere, on shop windows, on buildings, war murals, in classrooms, on the front page of textbooks and newspapers, and on Iraqi television 24 hours a day. Streets, mosques, schools and universities were all named after him. People feared him, but later they began to respect the stability associated with his era, after experiencing the chaos of post-2003 Iraq. From Saddam Hussein's example, al-Baghdadi learned persistence and brutality. Saddam Hussein was the Iraqi alpha male: cruel, unforgiving and uncompromising. The years of Saddam Hussein's rule taught al-Baghdadi how tough leaders can survive even the harshest of defeats – and move on by turning a blind eye and deaf ear to everybody around them. When Saddam Hussein assumed power in 1979, he gathered the Baath Party command and had one 'conspirator' read the names of 'traitors' to be taken away and executed. The event was broadcast on television to solidify Saddam Hussein's terrifying reputation. Punishment was always harsh – and always public, to spread fear throughout society. In 1988, for example, he infamously gassed approximately 5,000 civilians to death in the Kurdish town of Halabja, using mustard gas and nerve agents. An estimated 10,000 people were seriously injured: burned, deformed or maimed. Saddam Hussein did not even blink and he didn't look back. Al-Baghdadi liked that in him. Following his ascent to power in 2013, al-Baghdadi carried out similar atrocities; he too did not blink. Like Saddam Hussein, he crushed any domestic challenge to his authority. The mere mention of Saddam Hussein's name was enough to send shivers down the spines of his allies and opponents. Al-Baghdadi loved that, and he copied it to the very last detail. Instead of the trademark khaki military uniform, Cuban cigar and Baathist rhetoric, al-Baghdadi chose Islamic garb and religious overtones to market his leadership. Baathism, after all, had outlived its usefulness.

SEE YOU IN NEW YORK

Al-Baghdadi moved from Samarra to Baghdad with his family in 1989. He was of university age and his family was searching for new work opportunities. They rented a small apartment in the overcrowded middle-class al-Tobaji neighbourhood in north-west Baghdad. The district started off as a vast orchard during the 1950s and was urbanized with modern apartments under President Abdul Karim Qasim. By the 1980s, it housed a school for the blind, a jail and a popular market (*souq*). As a teenager in al-Tobaji, al-Baghdadi briefly and secretly joined the Egyptian Muslim Brotherhood, as confirmed years later by Sheikh Yusuf al-Qaradawi, chairman of the Worldwide Association of Muslim Scholars.[2] He nevertheless found them to be more talkers than doers and he therefore left the Brotherhood in mid-2000. He was also close to the Iraqi Brotherhood chief Mohammad Hardan, who fled to Afghanistan in the 1990s and fought with al-Qaeda, returning to fight the Americans in Iraq after 2003.

Al-Baghdadi enrolled at the Saddam University for Islamic Studies shortly after it was established in 1998, obtaining a BA and an MA in Islamic Studies and a PhD in the science of *tajwid*: rules of pronunciation while reciting the Holy Qur'an. His university life was painfully slow and he only got his PhD in June 2006 – ironically, the very same month that Abu Musaab al-Zarqawi was killed. At university, al-Baghdadi sharpened his articulation, speech and stage charisma. Reciting the Qur'an required a strong clean voice and good performance skills. A neighbour recalls that al-Baghdadi would practise public speaking before a mirror, often breaking into animated monologues. While studying at university, he worked part-time as the al-Zaghal Mosque custodian in al-Tobaji, located right next door to his family home. Sometimes he would take to the pulpit wearing glasses to lead evening prayers (*Salat al-Ishaa*).[3] After al-Baghdadi skyrocketed to fame, the mosque's later custodian was taken in by Iraqi intelligence and drilled with endless questions about his relations with the ISIS leader. Because of the non-stop intimidation, the elderly Hajj Zeidan now denies any links to al-Baghdadi, trying to erase the entire episode from his life and that of the mosque. In addition to leading prayer at the mosque, al-Baghdadi also provided Qur'anic lessons to neighbourhood children, free of charge. This was done at the request of his mother, a woman from the Bodari tribe to whom the young al-Baghdadi was greatly attached. He carried a photograph of her wherever he went, eaten away at the corners with the passing of time. It accompanied him to Baghdad and to prison. According to aides, it remains in his wallet today.

Residents of the al-Tobaji district remember al-Baghdadi as a polite young man who was not envious of rich people, with an ambition of finding employment at the Ministry of Religious Endowments. He was also an avid football player and fan. Al-Tobaji is a hotbed for soccer fans; two of its natives are the prominent sports commentators Asaad Lazem and Ra'ed Nahi, while a third, Abdul Wahab Abu al-Hail, is a celebrated midfielder who played with the national Iraqi football team. Inspired by Abu al-Hail, al-Baghdadi went as far as to create a soccer team for mosque regulars, with himself as captain. He joked with friends, saying that he was Iraq's Maradona, in reference to the world-famous Argentinean star. This fascination with football among jihadis is interesting. Abu Mohammad al-Golani was a football player and so was Jihadi John (Mohammed Emwazi), the famed ISIS executioner. During al-Qaeda's years in Pakistan, the terrorist group had its own football team, with lead players being Seif al-Adel and Mohammad Abdul Rahman, both from Egypt. Abdul Rahman is the son of Sheikh Omar, the Egyptian mastermind of the first bombing of the World Trade Center. In the 1980s, when he was in Sudan, Bin Laden formed two football teams.[4] Hamas fighters have also bonded over the game, having first met at a football club in Hebron in the West Bank. Abu Bakr al-Baghdadi was and remains fascinated by the sport.

Al-Baghdadi's family left al-Tobaji in 2003 after quarrelling with their landlord, seemingly over rent. In the same year, al-Baghdadi began his official Islamic career, with a brief involvement in a small militia, Ahl al-Sunnah wa al-Jamaah. It was formed directly after the American occupation of Baghdad in April 2003. Going by the name Abu Du'aa, he served as head of its Shari'a Committee. He joined al-Zarqawi's Mujahideen Council in 2006 and was also on this Shari'a Committee. Following the formation of the Islamic State of Iraq, he became chair of its Shari'a Committee and a member of its Shura Council (the deliberative body of the organization). In late January 2004, al-Baghdadi was captured when American forces raided a home near Fallujah during the turbulent offensive against the Iraqi Sunni insurgency. A Pentagon official described him as a 'street thug' and he was held at Camp Bucca, near the Iraqi–Kuwaiti border, until 6 December 2004. He was arrested at the home of his friend Nessayif Numan Nessayif in Fallujah. The camp, which became a hub for future ISIS terrorists, was named after Ronald Bucca, an American firefighter killed on 9/11 in New York City. Among the prominent terrorists who met within its high walls were Abu Muhammad al-Adnani, the Syrian spokesman for ISIS, and Isma'il Najm (aka Abu Abdulrahman al-Bilawi), a member of ISIS's Shura Council.

Al-Baghdadi used to lead them at Friday prayer. They were dangerous men and 'wanted' terrorists, who had to escape from jail to join ISIS. Al-Baghdadi, however, was released alongside a large group of other prisoners all deemed to be a low-level threat.[5] This is where he met his good friend and future rival, Abu Mohammad al-Golani. In jail, his Islamic credentials came into use, with prison authorities using him to settle disputes between squabbling prisoners. Upon his release, al-Baghdadi patted the American guard on duty, smiled and looked him straight in the eye saying: 'See you in New York!' This chilling statement is both a celebration of al-Qaeda's biggest achievement, the 9/11 attacks, and a reminder of the ongoing struggle against the United States. The jihadi in him was now ready to roll.

When Abu Omar al-Baghdadi became emir of the Islamic State of Iraq in 2006, the world paid little attention to him. This was seven years before the birth of ISIS. He faced a tremendous task: pulling the militia together after so many of its top officials – including its leader al-Zarqawi – had been killed. Deprived of real Islamists, he started recruiting ex-Baathists from Saddam Hussein's army. Although previously seen as secular Sunnis, these officers were willing to grow their beards and take on an Islamic character to blend in with al-Baghdadi's forces. All of them had been collectively discharged from the Iraqi army with no pension when Paul Bremer, President George W. Bush's envoy to Iraq and the practical ruler of the country at the time, disbanded the Iraqi army after the fall of Baghdad in 2003. Many had even spent time in US prisons and many had been humiliated by the post-Saddam rulers of Iraq. They had vengeance in their hearts and empty pockets. Fighting with al-Qaeda gave these ex-Baathist officers a chance to confront two old enemies at once. The first was the American military, which had inflicted two great defeats on the Iraqi army in 1991 and 2003, and was now occupying Baghdad. Secondly, they had a chance to challenge and destroy the new Iraqi government, which, in their view, came into power on the backs of American tanks. Also, they saw the post-2003 government as predominantly Shi'i and therefore as a proxy to Iran, the Baath regime's mortal enemy. In fact, some members of the new government were Iranian operatives during the Iran–Iraq War, like the Badr Brigades or the Supreme Iraqi Islamic Council of the powerful Shi'i al-Hakim family. Many of the ex-Baathists and now ISIS members were veterans of the Iran–Iraq War, having fought with Saddam Hussein's forces.

Abdul Karim Muta'a Kheirallah is an ex-officer from Saddam Hussein's intelligence service who works with ISIS. Now aged 57, he no longer engages in combat due to both his advancing age and a fractured shoulder, but he serves as more of a battle coach. All of his 'case studies' are derived from the Iran–Iraq War and so is his entire battle memory. His lectures are filled with venom for the Iranians and the Shi'a. Kheirallah's son explained:

> They killed our people, [...] they slaughtered some of our finest young men. My father carried young deformed soldiers to hospital; he watched comrades gasping for breath, and dying within his own two hands, sometimes with a missing arm or leg. The young generation must not forget what the Iranians did to them in the 1980s.

This sounds identical to what al-Qaeda preachers told Syrian recruits arriving in Afghanistan after 1982, vis-à-vis Hama. Once Kheirallah had been a staunch secularist, like many Baathists. He listened to popular singers like Charles Aznavour, drank whisky, mingled with foreigners, and sometimes travelled abroad for summers with his family. His wife wore make-up, smoked a long, slim cigarette and went out with her friends unveiled; his children dabbled in English. During the last decade of Saddam Hussein's rule, Kheirallah's wife put on the hijab and he began to attend mosque prayers on Friday. Kheirallah says that two experiences changed his life. One was a hajj pilgrimage he made to Mecca in 1989. The second was a series of gatherings at the home of Izzat Ibrahim al-Douri, Saddam Hussein's vice-president, who by the mid-1990s was spearheading the Islamic camp within the Baath regime. Sunni clerics would attend, sharing books with guests and lecturing them about the virtues of being a good Muslim. His son explains: 'My father didn't join al-Baghdadi for the money – he doesn't need it, thanks to Allah. He did it because he was convinced it was the right thing to do.' It was a combination of religious awakening and nationalism that brought Kheirallah into the hands of ISIS.

Having been pensioned off prior to the US invasion, he was neither harassed nor forced out of the country after 2003. Kheirallah watched the emergence of the Islamic State in Iraq with meticulous interest. He learned to use the internet in order to browse al-Zarqawi-affiliated forums in 2005 but didn't reach out to al-Qaeda until the outbreak of the Arab Spring. Kheirallah saw the speedy collapse of secular regimes as a golden opportunity for Arab Islamists. In early 2012, he told his family that he was off for a short business trip to Beirut. Instead of showing up on the Mediterranean coast, he contacted them the next morning, saying: 'Don't be afraid. I am safe. Money is in the bank for all of your needs. I have joined the resistance!' In other words, he had joined ISI. Kheirallah was not alone – other former colleagues in Iraqi intelligence were already working with al-Qaeda. Since then he contacts his family infrequently from different hideouts inside Iraq. As of spring 2015, they do not know his exact location.

Other ISIS members are far less committed to the cause but see no other vehicle through which to fight the Americans and Iranians. All of these men were furious with the post-Saddam Hussein status of the Sunni community in Iraq. They felt abandoned and persecuted by the Iran-backed Shi'i regime of Prime Minister Nouri al-Maliki. The Iraqi premier had systematically punished the entire Sunni community, blaming them collectively for having produced Saddam Hussein. Anywhere between 65,000 and 95,000 men from Saddam Hussein's praetorian divisions, republican guards, intelligence and Fedayeen Saddam (Saddam Hussein's commandos, an elite group of Iraq's republican guard) were discharged from service by the Americans in Iraq.[6] All of them were Baathists and most of them were Sunnis. Al-Maliki kept them away from government office, and did nothing about the Shi'i death squads that were gunning down their community leaders. Not only that; when recruiting into the post-Saddam Hussein

Iraqi army, he relied heavily on the Shi'a, tapping into the reservoir of militias that had mushroomed in recent years. Sunnis were left out. Al-Maliki had sentenced scores of leading Sunni figures to death, the most prominent of which – no doubt – was Saddam Hussein himself, who was hanged by Shi'i militiamen on the eve of the Muslim festival Eid al-Adha in December 2006. As he rose to the hangman's noose, the masked men chanted '*Muqtada*' (in reference to the Shi'i warlord Muqtada al-Sadr). Additionally, the American raid that killed al-Zarqawi occurred during al-Maliki's first tenure at the premiership. Iraqi Sunnis, both secular and non-secular, had a score to settle with the new prime minister. They saw no better platform than Abu Bakr al-Baghdadi's militia, regardless of whether they agreed with its Islamic programme or not. The two-way relationship suited both al-Baghdadi and the Baathists extremely well. He was looking for experienced troops to revamp the Islamic State. He found them in very un-Islamic officers – but it didn't really matter.

By early 2011, these men accounted for one third of al-Baghdadi's top 25 commanders. Least known among the ex-Baathists working with al-Baghdadi are Assel Tabra, a billionaire and former business partner of Saddam Hussein's eldest son, Uday Hussein, who spent the years 2003–5 jailed at Baghdad Airport. Another low-profile associate is Bashar, the son of Sabawi Ibrahim, Saddam Hussein's half-brother and former director of security. Sabawi was hanged in 2013, but his son Bashar remains a ranking member of ISIS. There is also Walid Jassem al-Alwani, an ex-captain in the Iraqi army, who now serves as chairman of al-Baghdadi's Military Council, and Mohammad al-Jabbouri, the council's chief-of-staff, who, like Kheirallah, once worked in Saddam Hussein's intelligence. A third is Abu Mohammad al-Suwaidawi, also on the Military Council and considered a protégé of Izzat al-Douri. A prominent heavyweight to join al-Baghdadi's team was Colonel Samir al-Khlifawi (aka Hajj Bakr), a native of the al-Anbar province. Before 2003, he had served as an air force intelligence officer under Saddam Hussein and was charged previously with weapon development in the Iraqi army. He was discharged from service and arrested in Camp

Bucca, where he met both Abu Mohammad al-Golani and Abu Bakr al-Baghdadi. Khlifawi was an early member of al-Zarqawi's militia in Iraq and endeared himself to al-Baghdadi who first appointed him commander of Aleppo operations and then chairman of ISIS's Military Council. He helped Abu Bakr solidify his power within ISIS, promoting those who swore allegiance to the new emir and assassinating those who questioned his command. In 2013, he became al-Baghdadi's top deputy in Syria. Khlifawi was killed in the northern Syrian town of Tal Rifaat during clashes between ISIS and Syrian rebels from the Syrian Martyrs' Brigade in February 2014.[7]

In April 2015, German news magazine *Der Spiegel* obtained 31 pages of Khlifawi's documents. The documents confirm the major roles the ex-Baathists are playing within ISIS ranks and the degree of military precision with which the organization is run. The documents show how Khlifawi had tried to build a clandestine service for ISIS, modelled on the one he served with in Baathist Iraq. Surveillance, espionage, murder and kidnapping were a top priority for him. In each provincial council of the ISIS caliphate, Khlifawi had planned for an emir to be in charge of murders, abductions, snipers, communication and encryption, as well as having an emir to supervise the other emirs, in case they didn't do their jobs well. As the *Der Spiegel* article outlined, 'From the very beginning, the plan was to have the intelligence services operate in parallel, even at the provincial level. A general intelligence department reported to the "security emir" for a region, who was in charge of deputy-emirs for individual districts. A head of secret spy cells and an "intelligence service and information manager" for the district reported to each of these deputy-emirs. The spy cells at the local level reported to the district emir's deputy. The goal was to have everyone keeping an eye on everyone else', just like in Baathist Iraq.[8]

The documents also revealed multiple plans, organizational structures and operational dictates, some already tested and others newly devised for the purposes of invading Syrian rebel-held territories in rural Aleppo.[9] The blueprint that the documents revealed was implemented with astonishing accuracy. Khlifawi's modus operandi would usually begin with the same detail: ISIS recruited followers under the pretence of opening a Da'wah office (an Islamic missionary centre). Of those who came to listen to lectures and attend courses on Islamic life, one or two men were selected and instructed to spy on their village, in order to obtain a wide range of detailed information about the village, its notables and its ordinary residents. Khlifawi then compiled lists of powerful families, influential individuals and their sources of income, names of rebel factions in the village and its leaders, and those leaders' activities that went against Shari'a law;[10] the information would then help him set the appropriate plan and tactics to capture the targeted town before launching his deadly, usually successful, offensive.

Another top ex-Saddami was Lieutenant Colonel Fadel Ahmad Abdullah al-Hyali (aka Abu Muslim al-Turkmani). After a long career in Iraqi intelligence, he was transferred to Saddam Hussein's elite Republican Guard and remained pro-Saddam Hussein until the end of the regime. The Americans fired him from service and had him arrested at Camp Bucca in 2003. Al-Baghdadi appointed him governor of the 'liberated' territories inside Iraq in 2014. He oversaw local ISIS-appointed government councils and tracked down potential collaborators in territories on ISIS's hit list. He was killed in the coalition air strikes in November 2014. A third is Adnan Isma'il Najm (aka Abu Abdulrahman al-Bilawi). Al-Bilawi studied at the Iraqi Military Academy and graduated in 1993. He joined the Iraqi army as an infantry officer, rising to the rank of captain. When the US occupying force fired him from service, he moved to the underground, working closely with al-Zarqawi in 2003–5. He too was detained at Camp Bucca and then moved to Abu Ghraib prison. He escaped from prison in 2013 to join ISIS, pledging loyalty to al-Baghdadi. Al-Bilawi, who was in his early forties, became a member of ISIS's Military Council. He was killed by Iraqi troops in Mosul on 5 June 2014. He and al-Baghdadi were good friends from their joint days at Camp Bucca. After his death, al-Baghdadi honoured the slain officer by naming the military operation of Mosul after him: 'Bilawi

Vengeance'.[11] ISIS occupied Mosul four days after Bilawi's death, on 9 June 2014. Bilawi was succeeded by retired lieutenant colonel Adnan al-Sweidawi, another ex-officer in Saddam Hussein's army. He in turn appointed another officer, ex-general Adnan Latif Hamid al-Sweidani, as 'governor' of al-Anbar.

Abu Bakr al-Baghdadi's Iraqi advisers include: Far'e Rafa'a Nu'emi (Abu Shayma), who specializes in weapon procurement and reserves, Khayri Mahmud al-Tai (Abu Kifah), an expert in explosives and mines, and Abdul Rahman al-Ofari (Abu Suja), who handles the families of ISIS martyrs.[12] All of them are ex-officers from Saddam Hussein's army. So also are his governors: Wissam Abu Zayd al-Zubeidi (Abu Nabil) of the Salahuddine province, Nimer Abdul Latif al-Jabouri (Abu Fatima) of Kirkuk, Ahmad Muhsen Khalal al-Jouheishi (also Abu Fatima) of the south and central Euphrates Region, Adnan Latif Hamid al-Suweidani (Abu Abdulsalam) of al-Anbar, Ahmad Abdul Qader al-Jaza (Abu Maisara) of Baghdad, and Radwan Taleb Hussein al-Hamadani (Abu Jumaa) of the cities and towns along the Syrian–Iraqi borders.[13] Abu Bakr's first 'cabinet' was formed in July 2014 as follows:

Shawkat Hazem al-Farhat (aka Abu Abdul Kadir):
   Minister of General Administration

Bisher Isma'il al-Hamadani (aka Abu Mohammad):
   Minister of Prisoner Affairs

Abdul Wahab Khatmayar (Abu Ali):
   Minister of Public Security

Muwafak Mustapha al-Karmoush (Abu Salah):
   Minister of Accounting (Finance)

Mohammad Hamed al-Duleimi (Abu Hajar):
   General Coordinator of ISIS Provinces

Abdullah Ahmad al-Mashadani (Abu Qassem):
   Minister of Arab and Foreign Fighters' Affairs

All of these ex-Saddamis were born between 1955 and 1965. All of them were from middle-class Sunni families who, with no exception, were part of Saddam Hussein's son Uday's wide circle of associates. All were very wealthy under Saddam Hussein and lived a very liberal, secular lifestyle before growing their beards and placing the white turban upon their heads. These men were extremely useful for al-Baghdadi, on more than one level. First, they came from Sunni families and helped him tap into the 'old money' of the Iraqi elite. For years, they had worked with a wide variety of regime-affiliated Iraqi businessmen. During the Saddam Hussein years, these men 'protected' business figures in exchange for a pre-set commission from any business deal. Khatmayar (Abu Ali) handled the export of fruits and vegetables while Hamadani (Abu Mohammad) controlled the import and sale of cars – in addition, of course, to their military duties. When they came knocking on the business community's doors, seeking financial aid for the resistance, many were not turned down. Many were actually married into this old elite and knew its internal politics inside out. Second, they knew the terrain well from years of service under Saddam Hussein. They also knew where weapons and ammunition – and money – were stored. This is how they obtained brand-new AKM assault rifles, PK machine guns, RPG-7s, stingers and surface-to-air missiles for ISIS. When overrunning Mosul Airport in June 2014, these officers enabled ISIS to operate Black Hawk helicopters, along with MiG-21 and MiG-23s. They knew where the keys to Iraqi prisons were hidden and have systematically freed dozens of ex-officers held in jail. Forty-seven prisoners, for example, were rescued from Tikrit prison in September 2012.[14] Automatically, these released prisoners joined ISIS.

In July 2013 alone, the ex-Baathists were able to release 500 prisoners from Abu Ghraib prison. They fired dozens of mortars at the jail and detonated suicide bombers. This was planned and executed by Abu Murad al-Baghdadi (no relationship to Abu Bakr), a former prison officer himself who had served at Abu Ghraib prior to the US invasion. He furnished ISIS with the timetables of guard shifts and the names of the soldiers on duty. So many prisoners were released in this carefully orchestrated operation because at the time of the raid all of the inmates were in the prison yard for an open-air communal *iftar*, the meal that ends the day-long fast during the month of Ramadan.[15] In total, ISIS broke into eight major jails across Iraq in an operation called 'Breaking the Walls'.[16]

These ex-Baathist officers were experienced soldiers, well trained in war, communications, discipline and siege. During the battle for al-Bab north-east of Aleppo in 2012, they employed something usually done by official armies – a gripping starvation campaign. The town of al-Bab was starved into submission. Before 2003 Saddam Hussein had trained them to fight off either an Iranian invasion or a new Shi'i uprising. An entire underground system was charted for Saddam Hussein's officers, which all of them had knowledge of and made use of after his fall. The *New York Times* chief military correspondent Michael Gordon wrote extensively about pre-2003 Iraq, authoring two classic books with the retired Marine Corps general Bernard Trainor, *Cobra II* and *The Endgame*.[17] The two experts say that Saddam Hussein created: 'Networks of safe houses and arms caches for the paramilitary forces, including materials for making improvised explosives [...] It was, in effect, a counterinsurgency strategy to fend off what Saddam saw as the most serious threats to his rule.'[18] Saddam Hussein never realized that these networks would come into use one day not to fight the mullahs of Iran, but to fight the jihadis of al-Qaeda.

Saddamis working with ISIS knew how to obey a chain of command, unlike the famed '*nizam, la tanzim*' theory of Abu Musaab al-Souri and Abu Mohammad al-Golani (order but no organization). They also knew how to use sophisticated weapons and how to read military manuals in English and Russian. Many of them had undergone military training abroad during the Saddam Hussein years, either in France, Algeria or Moscow. Running a disbanded and reorganized army was certainly more effective for al-Baghdadi than training troops from scratch, as al-Qaeda and Jabhat al-Nusra had done. Seasoned men know how to fight and when to retreat in battle to minimize losses of arms and lives. Classical jihadis embrace death, seeing it as destiny. This explains why the death toll for ISIS members, after al-Baghdadi's ascent, is much lower than that in Jabhat al-Nusra and other jihadi groups. ISIS was able to marry classic military tactics, terrorist tactics and guerrilla warfare to wage a mechanized jihad with considerable firepower. In its operations, ISIS still uses the al-Qaeda method of starting its offensive with a suicide bombing before its infantry charges enemy fortifications. In addition to foot soldiers, however, ISIS employs heavy artillery, rocket launchers, mortar fire and tanks to decimate the enemy, before armoured troop carriers and plated 4x4s haul its troops to battle.

In the battle for Mosul in the summer of 2014, ISIS put on a brilliant series of diversionary attacks throughout the country, totally confusing the Iraqi army as to their true target. First, a column of vehicles entered al-Baghdadi's native Samarra in the Salahuddine Province on 5 June. Iraqi troops were rushed to the scene with helicopter reinforcements, only to find that ISIS was striking elsewhere, this time at a university campus in Ramadi, capital of the al-Anbar province. As Iraqi troops prepared to take down the terrorists in Ramadi, ISIS struck yet again, this time in Baquba, 50 km north-east of Baghdad. The Iraqi army was being stretched to its limits, asking for an entire week to send reinforcements to all of these cities. The assault on Mosul started with five suicide bombers, backed by heavy mortar shells and the dismantling of Iraqi army checkpoints. On 8 July, they seized Police Headquarters. On 9 July, three top generals defected to Iraqi Kurdistan, leading to the complete collapse of morale among Iraqi troops, thus enabling ISIS's swift victory. It should be noted that the leadership of the Iraqi military and security services back then, especially in Mosul, was in the hands of corrupt and inept generals busy taking commissions and defrauding on expenses. They were not leaders interested in a spirited defence of Mosul. They fled and left their troops to their fate; these young men had no choice but to drop their military uniforms and make a run for it. The same happened again in Ramadi, the capital of Iraq's al-Anbar province, in the spring of 2015. The Iraqi generals fled, leaving their troops no choice but to withdraw from the city, abandoning thousands of civilians to their fate.

CHARTING NEW TERRITORY

Al-Baghdadi's tenure with ISIS began a surge in violence in different parts of Iraq. By July 2013, monthly casualties stood at 1,000 dead – the highest since April 2008.[19] The writing had been on the wall since international media moved its attentions elsewhere after the outbreak of the 'Arab Spring' in 2010. In March–April 2011, for example, ISIS carried out 23 attacks south of Baghdad, all directly supervised by al-Baghdadi. At this point, the disturbances had just started in Syria and the world was more focused on Damascus than Baghdad. Very few Arabic newspapers picked up the daily attacks in Iraq. On 5 May 2011, al-Baghdadi personally masterminded an operation in Hilla, 100 km south of Baghdad, in response to the killing of Osama bin Laden on 2 May. More than 20 policemen were killed and 72 others wounded. Al-Baghdadi pledged to carry out another 100 operations in revenge for Bin Laden's death.

Because of the similarity in programme and tactics, many in the West have tended to depict the Nusra Front and ISIS as two sides of the same coin. Both are looked at as terrorist organizations that threaten the West's security and interests. At first glance, they might seem similar, each marketing a Salafi/jihadi agenda with the end objective of setting up an Islamic state. A closer look, however, shows the great differences in approach, structure and vision. The Nusra Front members really believe in what they are doing and are influenced strongly by their al-Qaeda past. Its top command and fighters are all indoctrinated Islamists, as the Fighting Vanguards had been in the 1980s. With ISIS, there is a clear mix between hardline Salafis and secularists wearing an Islamic mask. They are only using Islam to frighten people into submission – convinced that they can repeat the Saddam Hussein experience in a different shape and form. Secondly, ISIS fighters are far more experienced on the battlefield than al-Nusra, because of their former lives in the Iraqi army. ISIS is more interested in consolidating its rule in 'liberated territories', and doesn't really care if Assad stays in cities like Damascus, Homs or the coastal port cities of Tartous and Latakia. Jabhat al-Nusra has said that ISIS is a product of the Syrian regime, claiming that the two sides didn't fire a bullet at each other in 2013–14.

In territories that it does control, however, ISIS is more ruthless than Jabhat al-Nusra. ISIS runs its territory like Saddam Hussein used to administer Iraq – with brute force. Al-Nusra tried to blend in with Muslim communities and did not enforce a strict and literal interpretation of Shari'a law immediately; ISIS wants to jump straight to Islamic Shari'a, with brutal enforcement tactics. And finally, although packed with foreign fighters, Jabhat al-Nusra is generally regarded as more Syrian than ISIS. Abu Bakr al-Baghdadi and his team are still viewed as 'imported' Islamists and he doesn't hide his preference for Iraqi commanders. According to field reporters in rebel-held territory, over 60 per cent of Jabhat al-Nusra fighters are Syrian, while the number stands at only 10 per cent with ISIS.

In April 2013, al-Baghdadi made this superiority and favouritism clear by saying:

> When the people of Syria asked for help and everyone abandoned them we [al-Baghdadi] could not but come to their help so we appointed al-Golani, who was one of our soldiers, along with a group of our sons, and we sent them from Iraq to Syria. We set up plans for them and we advised policies for them and we supported them with help from our treasury every month. We also provided them with men with long experience. We didn't announce this, for security reasons.

There were way too many 'we's' in al-Baghdadi's speech, coming across as patronizing and striking a raw nerve with Jabhat al-Nusra. His obvious message was that Jabhat al-Nusra was never meant to be, that al-Golani was ordered to establish a branch of ISIS but went rogue, disobeying his master, al-Baghdadi. Syrians after all don't like to be ruled, or patronized, by non-Syrians. At schools, at home and in popular culture they are systematically taught to have a superiority complex, in that they are the only good Arabs and the only good Muslims. This was evident throughout history. In 1918–20, the Hashemite emir Faisal was brought to Damascus to set up a government, backed initially by the British and the French. Faisal spoke with a different accent, dressed differently and was unfamiliar with the ways of life and culture of the Damascenes. When he was toppled in 1920, the Syrians didn't lift a finger to protect him, arguing that Faisal was no good because he was not Syrian. The same happened in 1958, when President Gamal Abdul Nasser came to Damascus to set up rule during the short-lived Syrian–Egyptian Union of the United Arab Republic. The Syrians liked Nasser but never accepted Egyptian officers running their lives and affairs. With variations in time and substance, this still applies to the local attitude towards non-Syrians in the north – especially Iraqis and Abu Bakr al-Baghdadi himself.

In the long decade separating the events of 9/11 from the first shots of the Syrian jihad, a global war on terror was waged. Following the twin attacks on US soil, the Bush administration accused Saddam Hussein of having contacts with al-Qaeda, sponsoring terrorist activities and even plotting 9/11. These accusations, among others, provided the excuse for the US-led invasion of Iraq in 2003. Although these allegations were a fabrication, they became, hauntingly, a self-fulfilling prophecy. When Paul Bremer disbanded the Iraqi army following the fall of Baghdad, there was no al-Qaeda organizational presence in Iraq, but tens of thousands of frustrated Sunni officers from Saddam Hussein's once-secular Praetorian Guard who overnight found themselves jobless, leaderless and futureless without Saddam Hussein. The atmosphere was ripe for al-Qaeda in Iraq to rise from the ashes of the Baath regime, to feed off the chaos and the sectarian onslaught that ensued, and to incorporate those disgruntled and unemployed ex-Baathist men of war. The movement that began with a fringe Jordanian jihadi snowballed into today's caliphate. ISIS fed off the chaos and sectarian hatred in Syria and Iraq, and was able to develop a new form of jihad that combined a vengeful militarism with unabated fanaticism. Saddam Hussein was not a jihadi and nor was he a sponsor of al-Qaeda terrorism. The irony is that the consequence of the US war to bring him down was actually to produce Islamic terrorism in Iraq in the form of ISIS.

AL-GOLANI VS AL-BAGHDADI

The relationship between al-Golani and al-Baghdadi remained warm during the first few months of the Syrian war. When al-Golani formed Jabhat al-Nusra in 2012, al-Baghdadi complained, viewing it as a 'soft defection'. He considered al-Golani to be both his creation and his protégé – it wasn't easy letting go of a good friend and a promising successor. They met in a small village near the Syrian–Iraqi border in late December 2011. It was to prove their last meeting until November 2014. It was candid, frank and stormy. After a brief marriage, the two comrades were parting ways, each after their own personal glory. 'What is this *Jabhat al-Nusra*?' snapped al-Baghdadi. Clearly, he had not been consulted on its formation. 'This front [Jabhat al-Nusra] cannot live on its own. It doesn't have the means of survival. Assad and the Shi'a will crush it. Stay with me; together we can bring down this axis [Assad–Iran].' Al-Baghdadi was jealous – Jabhat al-Nusra should have been *his* idea. He was older, more experienced, and because his country, Iraq, was larger and richer, he had more money than al-Golani. Al-Baghdadi also considered his Islamic credentials far superior to those of al-Golani.

The rivalry between Baghdad and Damascus was not new. The two cities alternated as the heart of the Muslim Empire during the Umayyad and Abbasid dynasties in the early centuries of Islam. One dynasty put the other to the sword. Under the Baath, Saddam Hussein and Hafez al-Assad inherited the rivalry in a different form. Each considered himself to be the real embodiment of Baathism and the true champion of Arabism. Now, the Syrian–Iraqi competition reached new heights with al-Baghdadi and al-Golani. Al-Baghdadi wanted to either hijack al-Golani's group or destroy it altogether. It was no use. Al-Golani had already made up his mind. Like so many Islamists in Syria, he wished to chart his own path in life. He did not wish to remain subordinate to an Iraqi commander, arguing that the Syrian war was not al-Baghdadi's to wage. If the jihadi war failed, al-Baghdadi could easily pack up and return home, or head elsewhere to continue his journey in international jihad. Al-Golani was not a global jihadi – he didn't have targets beyond the Levant (Syria, Lebanon, Jordan and Palestine). Iraq was important to him as long as it was occupied by the Americans and dominated by Iran and its Shi'i proxies. Al-Golani wanted to establish an Islamic state in Greater Syria, with Damascus or Aleppo as its capital. Al-Baghdadi, he claimed, was more interested in Iraq and parts of Deir ez-Zour. In late December 2011, al-Golani cited a Qur'anic verse from *Surat al-Bakara*: '*Imsakun Bi Maarouf aw Tasrihon bi Ihsan*.' In other words, 'Hold on with benevolence, or let go with grace.' The Qur'anic text was in reference to marriage, of course, and not jihadi partnership.

Furious with al-Golani's stubbornness, al-Baghdadi decided to let go. The break-up was filled with spite, however, and was anything but graceful. Al-Baghdadi spent a few months devising sweet revenge, which came in the form of the Islamic State for Iraq and Bilad al-Sham, or the Levant (ISIS). It was a direct response to the creation of Jabhat al-Nusra. Since they had now gone separate ways, al-Golani was neither consulted nor informed. He heard of it through jihadi media channels, just like everybody else. The Jabhat al-Nusra fighter, Abu Zakariya, recalls:

> When watching the news on TV, al-Sheikh al-Fateh [as they called al-Golani] just shook his head in frustration. Banging both fists on the table in a temper outburst, he shouted: 'Abu Bakr doesn't know what he is doing. He is more interested in cameras than in obeying the commands of Allah. This new front will prove disastrous for the Syrian Revolt, and for al-Qaeda.'

Not only did this reflect a serious rift in al-Qaeda, but also sharp divisions within the entire jihadi rank operating in Syria. Shortly after creating al-Nusra, just months after Bin Laden's death in May 2011, al-Golani pledged loyalty to al-Qaeda's leader, Ayman al-Zawahiri. Al-Zawahiri endorsed al-Nusra and frowned upon the creation of ISIS, seeing it as 'childish rivalries between two mature adults. It came in reaction to al-Golani's initiative.' In June 2013, al-Zawahiri sent a letter to both men, ruling against such divisions within jihadi ranks and describing them as 'very wrong'.[20] Deep inside, Ayman al-Zawahiri probably felt worried by ISIS's dramatic rise. It soon threatened to completely dwarf al-Qaeda. Abu Bakr al-Baghdadi was young and charismatic while al-Zawahiri was dogmatic, lacklustre and 20 years his senior. Additionally, while al-Zawahiri and the older generation of al-Qaeda had become obsessed with their security and were hiding in caves and communicating with their men through audio recordings only, al-Baghdadi was on the battlefield, working hands-on with his soldiers. His youthful activism exposed how démodé al-Zawahiri had become – or perhaps always was. Even during the Bin Laden era, al-Zawahiri never tried to climb the jihadi ladder, satisfied fully with being al-Qaeda's number-two man. Should al-Baghdadi's movement succeed, the young emir threatened to make him completely insignificant.

Ayman al-Zawahiri appointed Hama veteran Mohammad Bahaiah (aka Abu Khaled al-Souri) in May 2013 to mend broken fences between the two friends-turned-rivals. Abu Khaled, an ex-member of the Fighting Vanguards, was a 50-year-old Syrian Islamist living in Spain since 1982. Al-Zawahiri also recommended a merger 'under Abu Mohammad al-Golani's leadership'.[21] Joining Abu Khaled in his mediation efforts were the Saudi cleric Abdullah Bin Mohammad al-Mahaseni and the Shari'a expert Abu Suleiman al-Muhajir. Both Abu Mohammad al-Golani and Abu Bakr al-Baghdadi rejected their ruling. Al-Baghdadi released an audio message, saying that al-Nusra was nothing but an extension of al-Qaeda in Iraq and should be treated only as such. In short, no merger was needed since both groups, on paper, ought to report directly to him. Al-Baghdadi went further, saying that it was he who had first sent al-Golani into Syria, furnishing him with plans and strategies for the jihadi war. He added that he had been paying all of al-Golani's expenses on a monthly basis, trying to completely discredit his former friend and ally. Furious, al-Zawahiri retorted: 'The Islamic State in Iraq and Bilad al-Sham is not a branch of al-Qaeda. We are not responsible for its actions and there is no coordination between us.'[22]

As troubling as ISIS's successes are for the world, they are even more troubling to Ayman al-Zawahiri. Although the al-Qaeda leader might be expected to rejoice at the emergence of a strong jihadi group, in reality ISIS's rise is eclipsing the old al-Qaeda. Al-Baghdadi, hungry for power and authority, could not put up with al-Golani's betrayal. This explains the ferocity of the fighting that broke out between the two groups; al-Golani admitted in an interview with Al Jazeera that al-Nusra had lost 700 men in the fight against ISIS.[23] Al-Baghdadi's ego would not allow him to accept any reconciliation effort; he even killed al-Zawahiri's messenger, Abu Khaled al-Souri. But this is more than just a clash of egos. ISIS was, and still is, eager to capture as much territory and resources as possible. Al-Baghdadi would not accept that his former protégé, whom he despatched to expand ISIS's reach in Syria, would end up creating a separate entity that controlled eastern Syria, the strategic oil-rich area that al-Baghdadi had coveted. Abu Bakr al-Baghdadi's final rejection of al-Qaeda's authority came in his declaration of a caliphate. From that moment on, he electively split the jihadi movement. Al-Qaeda and ISIS are now competing for more than the leadership of the jihadi movement: they are competing for its soul.

ISIS and al-Qaeda fundamentally differ on whom they see as their main enemy, which strategies and tactics to use in attacking that enemy and which social issues and other concerns to emphasize. ISIS does not follow al-Qaeda's 'far enemy' strategy, preferring instead the 'near enemy' strategy, albeit on a regional level. As such, the primary target of ISIS has not been the United States but the 'Shi'i' regime in Baghdad and the Baathist/Alawite regime in Damascus.' While al-Qaeda never amounted to more than splintered cells across the world, trying to plot a hit here or there, ISIS is effectively establishing a functioning army and a proto-state to serve as a beacon for Islamists across the world. Al-Baghdadi favours harsh tactics to purify the Islamic world. Al-Qaeda considers ISIS's killing sprees too extreme and thus counterproductive.

Having learned from al-Qaeda in Iraq's disaster when the population turned against it to join the Awakening Councils, Jabhat al-Nusra, under al-Golani's leadership and al-Zawahiri's guidance, tries to advise first rather than inflicting outright terror to convince Muslims to embrace Shari'a law. Furthermore, al-Nusra has, mostly, extended a helping hand to other Syrian Islamist factions, while al-Baghdadi demands complete allegiance – anything short of this merits death.

The future of this relationship is highly unpredictable. An alliance between ISIS and Jabhat al-Nusra seems unlikely at the moment, but it can never be completely ruled out. ISIS might successfully incorporate al-Nusra by force. Also, if the United States wages an extended campaign against al-Nusra, this might push the group closer to ISIS. Finally, if regional machinations lead to a Syrian rebel alliance (whether Islamist, secular or both) to eliminate al-Nusra, the group might choose to join forces with ISIS to fend off existential threats. In any case, it is impossible for al-Baghdadi to meet al-Golani half way – but it should not be ruled out that al-Golani might choose to go back under his old master's wing.

SEVEN

The House of Blood

THE SUMMER OF 2014 WAS A PERIOD OF DRAMATIC SUCCESS for ISIS and Abu Bakr al-Baghdadi. During the months of June and July, ISIS swept into Mosul and other cities along the Syrian–Iraqi border. The caliph chose Mosul's main pulpit to announce the creation of the Islamic State – the same mosque once used by his jihadi predecessor and boss Abu Musaab al-Zarqawi during the Iraqi insurgency. The weakened Iraqi army stood at just 350,000 soldiers, which had cost US$41.6 billion to train and equip since 2011. It easily collapsed at the feet of ISIS in just 100 days.[1] Within Iraq, ISIS took Fallujah, west of Baghdad, and reached as far as Saddam Hussein's hometown of Tikrit, 140 km north-west of the Iraqi capital. Tikrit succumbed without a fight, and so did Baiji, a city of 200,000 inhabitants in northern Iraq. In August, ISIS captured the towns of Zomar, Sinjar and Wana, also in the Iraqi north. As ISIS crept dangerously close to the gates of Baghdad, scores of disaffected young Sunni men came flocking to join its ranks. ISIS warned its warriors: 'Don't fall prey to your vanities and ego but go march toward Baghdad.'[2] By September 2014, the number of European jihadis working with ISIS rose to 2,000, backed by 100 Americans.[3] By October, 2,400–3,000 Tunisians had joined ISIS, along with 1,000 Turks. By winter 2014, ISIS had overtaken Deir ez-Zour in eastern Syria and several smaller jihadi groups in the Damascus countryside had sworn allegiance to al-Baghdadi. ISIS membership was estimated at 6,000 fighters in

Iraq and somewhere between 3,000 and 5,000 men in Syria, 3,000 of them being foreign fighters (1,000 from Chechnya, 500 from the UK, France and other EU countries).[4] At the beginning of 2015, estimates put their overall numbers at 31,000 fighters. Of that number, 20,000–25,000 were seen as core members, ideologically trained full-timers, and the rest as affiliates and civilians.[5] Their rallying motto has been: '*Bakiyya wa tattamaddad*' (staying and expanding).

ISIS's strategies became highly versatile, combining terrorist tactics with insurgent activities and a professional infantry. Commanders of ISIS's army use suicide bombers to shock their enemies, while their troops advance in well-prepared formations, supported with armour and preceded by an artillery barrage. Abu al-Waleed al-Daghestani, an ISIS fighter from Deir ez-Zour, put the number by early 2015 at 50,000 troops. 'Not all of them are ISIS-bred and trained,' he said. Many were inexperienced fighters who pledged allegiance to ISIS out of practicality, 'seeing that we are the strongest and most sincere jihadi group in Bilad al-Cham [Syria].' Unlike Jabhat al-Nusra, there were no requirements for membership in ISIS. Anybody who believed, or claimed to believe, in the need to establish an Islamic state and caliphate was eligible for membership. In July 2014, US Deputy Assistant Secretary of State for Iran and Iraq Brett McGurk said: 'They are worse than al-Qaeda.' They were no longer a terrorist organization, he added, 'but a full-blown army!'[6]

Underground military groups in the Arab world have historically swollen in size after victory in battle. This happened for example when Yasser Arafat's Fatah Movement fought the Karameh Battle against Israel from Jordan in March 1968. Fatah didn't win the battle, but managed to survive the Israeli offensive. Not losing to Israel was in itself a grand feat and it brought thousands of non-Palestinians scrambling to join the ranks of Fatah. Syrians, Iraqis, Jordanians and Egyptians were anxious to join Yasser Arafat. Among them, of course, was the founder of Syrian militant jihad, Marwan Hadid. A similar case was repeated in June 2014, when, in just three weeks, over 6,000 Arabs from different cities and towns applied for ISIS membership. Not all of them were jihadis and not all of them were Iraqi. Some were actually secular Syrian officers who had defected from the official army to join the Free Syrian Army. Others were ordinary Iraqis or Palestinians from the camps of Syria and Lebanon. Many were Saudi and Jordanian youth, attracted by ISIS's thundering success story. In November 2014, militants controlling the Libyan city of Derna swore allegiance to ISIS, thus making it the first non-Syrian/Iraqi city to become part of al-Baghdadi's 'Islamic State'.[7] Derna, a city of 100,000 inhabitants on the Mediterranean coast, had been largely independent of the central government in Tripoli since the start of the Libyan Revolt in 2011. On 10 November 2014, an Egyptian Islamic group, Ansar Bayt al-Maqdis, also pledged allegiance to ISIS in the Sinai Peninsula. In March 2015 the al-Qaeda-affiliated terrorist group Boko Haram pledged allegiance to ISIS. It is active in north-east Nigeria, Chad, Niger and northern Cameroon.[8] Boko Haram's leader Abubakar Shekau released an online video in which he proclaimed: 'We announce our allegiance to the Caliph of the Muslims!'

ISIS'S CAPITAL IN AL-RAQQA

With its membership reservoir firmly secured, ISIS began to consolidate its power in the territories now under the control of Abu Bakr al-Baghdadi. This was done through high pay to tribal leaders and individuals, along with fear, blackmail and both direct and indirect intimidation. First, ISIS created a new province, merging territory around the eastern Syrian town of al-Bukamal with adjacent areas around al-Qaim in Iraq.[9] The new *vilayet* was named 'Al-Furat' (The Euphrates). ISIS's 'capital city', its seat of power, was declared in the agricultural city of al-Raqqa, located on the north bank of the Euphrates River, 160 km east of Aleppo. With a pre-2011 population of approximately 300,000 people, al-Raqqa was the sixth largest city in Syria. It was late to fall into the hands of Syrian rebels; indeed, President Bashar al-Assad prayed at one of its mosques during the

Eid holiday as recently as June 2012. Nine months later, the city was occupied by Jabhat al-Nusra, ironically, on the tenth anniversary of the US occupation of Baghdad. In 2003, the US occupiers had torn down a statue of Saddam Hussein and draped it with the Stars and Stripes. Ten years later, Jabhat al-Nusra tore down a bronze statue of Hafez al-Assad, replacing it with the black flag of al-Qaeda. Jabhat al-Nusra, under the leadership of al-Golani, controlled al-Raqqa for 18 months until, in the summer of 2014, it fell under al-Baghdadi's authority. Al-Baghdadi chose an emir to run every province, or *vilayet*, ruled by ISIS. For al-Raqqa he chose Awwad al-Makhlaf, from the town of al-Mayadeen in the Deir ez-Zour province. Because it was ISIS's first urban conquest, al-Baghdadi decided to run al-Raqqa's affairs himself, which left al-Makhlaf as more of a ceremonial figurehead. Strangely and purely for security reasons, ISIS emirs are forbidden from residing in the provinces that they rule. Al-Makhlaf lives in Mosul, for example, and rarely travels to Syria, while the *vali* (governor) of al-Bab resides in Deir ez-Zour.[10]

Al-Baghdadi divided al-Raqqa into three provinces. The east established its capital in the city of Madan, with a population just below 40,000, while the north formed its capital in Tal Abyad, located along the Balikh River, with a population of 10,000. The west, being the richest part of al-Raqqa, was awarded to Abu Huraira al-Jazrawi, a Saudi national reporting directly to Awwad al-Makhlaf. He was appointed in late 2014, after US air strikes killed his predecessor, Abu Sara. Northern al-Raqqa is vital for ISIS because it contains Lake Assad, the Euphrates and the prized Euphrates Dam, 60 metres high and 4.5 km long, constructed by Hafez al-Assad and the Soviet Union in the early 1970s. Together, these provinces form what became officially known as 'al-Raqqa State'.

During the Abbasid dynasty the renowned Caliph Haroun al-Rashid ruled an empire from al-Raqqa between 796 and 809. His era was marked by scientific, cultural and religious prosperity and is often referred to as the Islamic Golden Age. The city was strategically important because it lay on the crossroads linking Damascus,

Palmyra and the temporary seat of the Abbasid caliphate in Resafa. Al-Baghdadi chose al-Raqqa as his capital for two reasons. One was pure coincidence – it happened to be the first city to fall under his complete authority. Another was historic symbolism; it reminded him of his native Samarra – a city that was also once capital of the Abbasid dynasty. During its heyday, the Abbasids controlled a Muslim empire stretching from North Africa to Central Asia from their capital al-Raqqa. Al-Baghdadi hoped to revive its bygone glory by imposing a strict form of Islamic government, although he had little respect for the flamboyant and hedonistic Abbasid caliph Haroun al-Rashid. ISIS member Abu al-Waleed al-Daghestani says, 'The Caliph Ibrahim [al-Baghdadi] was very excited about al-Raqqa.' Locally appointed emirs send him regular intelligence reports about daily life in the city. They are printed on A4 paper with the black and white header 'Al-Raqqa State'. The caliph doesn't have time to read much, and asks his emirs to limit their reports to one page per day. He trusts these reports absolutely, especially when coming from Afghanistan veterans who worked with the Taliban and know how to run a state.

Al-Baghdadi communicates with his officials through a variety of tools, ranging from Thuraya mobile phones to WhatsApp and Skype. He writes in both Arabic and English, using the latter only when dealing with foreign fighters. Al-Baghdadi has a relatively good command of English, which he learned as a second language at school. Thanks to years of British colonialism, English was taught at Iraqi schools, something that lasted throughout Saddam Hussein's era, when al-Baghdadi was growing up. Al-Baghdadi browses the internet, reading whatever is written about him in the Western press, always resorting to Google. He insists that he needs to be able to find any emir or official he needs on the spur of the moment. 'He doesn't like to wait to speak to somebody,' said one of his aides, Abu Mansour al-Libi. To achieve that, all top officials are required to furnish him with up-to-date telephone numbers, and the most recent home address. One aide said: 'He loves to ask questions. He goes into the most specific of details, often overriding the local emir and his entire entourage by calling up local governors or summoning them to his home, even in the middle of the night.' He doesn't have work hours, and ISIS officials have to expect a call from him at any moment. 'It's almost like he is living with us. He watches us from afar, almost as if he had cameras in every room.' Al-Baghdadi bought three Arabic books about the history of al-Raqqa and read them with meticulous interest, taking down notes. One of them, authored by the scholar Saleh Hawwash al-Muslet, covered the years 1916–46. It was out of print, as it had first been published in 1956. Al-Baghdadi had it photocopied in Beirut and shipped by courier to him in al-Raqqa, noted al-Daghestani. When asked about the caliph's PO box, al-Daghestani smiled: 'He doesn't need a postal address. Just write "Al-Khalifa Ibrahim: Al-Raqqa". Be sure it will arrive safely.'

An efficient postal service is no doubt one of the many manifestations of a functioning government, and there are plenty of others in al-Baghdadi's al-Raqqa. One of course is the black flag of ISIS. Another is Islamic State's own anthem, 'Dawlat al-Islam Qamat' (The Islamic State has Risen). The four-and-a-half-minute anthem's official English title is 'My Ummah Dawn has Appeared'. It is one among many in the Islamic State. The singer is 29-year-old Ghaleb Ahmad Bak'ati (aka Abu Hayar al-Hadrami), from Hadhramout in Yemen. He dropped out of high school to join al-Qaeda in Iraq and then came to Syria, where he was arrested and deported to Yemen, only to flee jail in May 2011 and head back to Syria, joining ISIS in 2014. He has a pure and clear voice, which resonates hypnotically as he lengthens the articulation of certain words for emphasis. Al-Hadrami sings a cappella drenched in a reverberant echo, since all musical instruments are banned in Islam. The ISIS icon, Ibn Taymiyya, once said that music was like alcohol to the soul. Digital remastering is allowed, however, to mimic the sound of percussion and to create overtones. Instead of brass and wind instruments, one hears clips of ISIS-related sound effects: gunfire, the thumping of soldiers' boots and the unsheathing of swords – all added for jihadi emphasis. The ISIS anthem is often heard from the windows of 4x4 jeeps, driven by ISIS fighters. Anthems, *nasheed* in Arabic, are the only form of music allowed in the Islamic State.

The caliph runs his territory with a three-man war cabinet – himself and two deputies. Abu Muslim al-Turkmani deputizes on Iraqi affairs, while Abu Ali al-Anbari runs Syrian affairs and handles intelligence cells (*khalaya amniyat*). He is an ex-general in the Iraqi army, originally from Mosul. Twelve governors have been hand-picked by al-Baghdadi to govern Iraq and Syria. They work closely with local councils on finance, welfare, media and military affairs. These local councils are responsible for the foreign fighters based in each city and town run by ISIS. They report to the governors on how these fighters are doing: how well they are performing on the battlefield, and how effective they are at running the state and mixing with its locals. An independent Shura Council runs ISIS's legal affairs and is charged with all Islamic jurisprudence. They are the courts of ISIS and they handle everything, even cases dated prior to mid-March 2011. Currently twelve Saudi judges run the court system of al-Raqqa. These judges have ruled, for example, that Christians who are living within the Islamic State have three options. One is to convert to Islam by announcing that there is only one God and Muhammad is his Prophet. Another is to pay a religious levy – *jizya* – (approximately 20% or more of an individual income), which is calculated as part of the city's tax. The third option is to be put to the sword. They are given 48 hours to flee the city.[11] This is based on Qur'anic verses 1–5 from *Surat al-Tawbah*. The Christians of Mosul refused to comply with the new ruling and all of them were uprooted from their homes during the hot summer months of 2014. Many fled to Iraqi Kurdistan and other parts of the country, while others chose to leave Iraq altogether.

THE CALIPH WEARS BLACK

Abu Bakr al-Baghdadi has told his deputies that al-Raqqa will make or break them. If they succeed in running the city, then other 'God-sent conquests' will follow. Depending on who one talks to, results have been either a total catastrophe or an impressive progression towards creating a so-called Islamic society. Al-Baghdadi himself is 'extremely pleased' by what he has achieved so far. The colour black covers ISIS-held al-Raqqa. The government headquarters are painted in black. The black al-Qaeda flag is to be found everywhere: on windows, lampposts and draped on walls. Black is a special colour for ISIS – women are forced to wear black from head to toe. Black was reportedly the colour of the Prophet Muhammad's flag during the early Muslim battles. It was also the official colour of the Abbasid dynasty, chosen for its contrast with white – the colour of their predecessors, the Umayyads. This explains why the 'caliph', Abu Bakr al-Baghdadi, wears nothing but black. He spends a significant amount of time in front of the mirror, fixing his black cloak and black turban.

Unlike in Christian culture, black is not the colour of death and mourning for ISIS. On the contrary, Sunni Muslims associate death with the colour white – signifying purity of the afterlife and cleansing of both body and soul. During burial, all Muslims are removed from their clothes; they undergo a ritual washing and are then covered with a thick white cloth (*kafan*). While burying their dead, old Sunni families also dress in white, which can also symbolize the colour of the angels that are supposed to hover around the deceased during burial. In ISIS-held territory, mourning the dead is not allowed. Dead people are better off in the hands of the Creator and therefore tears should not be shed on their behalf. ISIS does not observe the three days of mourning which is common in many Muslim societies. They also refuse to erect marble graves for their dead, considering it a pagan tradition that didn't exist during the times of the Prophet. They don't even allow tombstones for their martyrs. White, therefore, is only allowed in times of sorrow, while black is the colour of daily life. Such behaviour is in accordance with the strict teachings of Ibn Taymiyya. It is also adopted by the Wahhabi tradition in Saudi Arabia, where the deceased (be he a king or commoner) is buried without any headstone or even a nameplate; there is only a small sign with a number on it to mark the burial spot. Erecting a tombstone is strictly forbidden, as is visiting graveyards or mourning the dead. Ibn Taymiyya's devout student Muhammad ibn Abdul al-Wahhab went as far as to demand the destruction of the Prophet's grave in al-Medina back in the nineteenth century.

Qur'anic verses are plastered all over the walls of al-Raqqa, mostly on black backgrounds. ISIS chooses Qur'anic phrases that remind people of God's wrath and punishment, instead of those that speak of compassion and mercy. Civil servants on ISIS's payroll are only allowed to celebrate Islamic holidays, like the Prophet's birthday, the Islamic New Year and the two Eids, Eid al-Adha and Eid al-Fitr. All holidays which were celebrated in pre-ISIS Iraq and Syria have been cancelled, including the anniversary of the Baath Party Revolution (8 February in Iraq and 8 March in Syria). Other celebrations which have been removed by al-Baghdadi include 7 April (founding of the Baath Party) and 18 January (anniversary of Saddam Hussein's first rocket attack on Israel in 1991). The annual celebrations of the October War of 1973 have also been cancelled, as has the celebration of Syria's official Independence Day (17 April), which marks the 1946 evacuation of French troops. ISIS has also given the Islamic State a six-day working week, with only Friday as a day of holiday. Any homage, let alone mention of pre-Islamic State political personalities, such as Hafez al-Assad or Saddam Hussein, is a serious offence, punishable by arrest and whipping. All photos of President Bashar al-Assad have been removed, as have the Syrian and Baath Party flags. The statues of the Assads have also been smashed, on the direct orders of al-Baghdadi himself. Loyalty from here onwards is to be to the Islamic State and Islam. During the holy month of Ramadan in 2014, the 'caliph' ordered that each family pledging loyalty to ISIS receive a stipend of S£20,000 (US$66 in mid-2015).

THE ISIS POLICE AND ITS CIVIL SERVICE

Former employees of the Iraqi and Syrian government have been allowed to maintain their jobs in ISIS territory, but only after pledging loyalty to ISIS. This applies to civil servants, teachers, municipality workers and technicians who fix phone lines, roads and electricity. The Iraqi and Syrian police have been fired, however, and have been replaced with a moral vice squad, similar to the one in Saudi Arabia. Non-Arab foreign fighters are prevented from joining the ISIS police force because of the language barrier. They need to be able to communicate with the locals and this is close to impossible with their substandard Arabic. Al-Raqqa residents are also not allowed to join the ISIS police force, because they might lose impartiality and sympathize with relatives or friends when 'imposing the law'. As a result, only Tunisians, Palestinians, Saudis and Iraqis are allowed into the ISIS police, in addition of course to Syrians from cities other than al-Raqqa. The police force's official name is Diwan al-Hisbah (the Verification Bureau), or simply al-Hisba.

In total, there are 75 policemen in al-Raqqa, 'all above the age of 30'. They get a monthly salary of S£30,000 (US$100), along with 'perks' that include free education for their children, free bus fares and free medication. They patrol the streets of al-Raqqa and make sure that all adults and children aged seven and above attend local mosques for the five mandatory prayers of Islam. This is their most important task. They also make sure that no trade takes place during prayer time, forcing residents to run errands during prayer intervals. When not on the streets, these policemen work at the same offices once used by the Syrian government and are lodged in the homes of ex-Baathist officials. ISIS policemen enforce a speed limit on roads and highways, hand out traffic tickets to drivers, arrest vagabonds and beggars, regulate shacks and kiosks and supervise law and order on the streets.

A prime task for ISIS police is to make sure that bakeries are fully operational and are supplied with daily wheat. Those who hoard bread or sell it at unregulated prices are flogged in public. Those who are fined for exceeding a speed limit or for parking in the wrong place are expected to pay their fine within a given grace period, or suffer a multiplied fine. The revenue goes to ISIS's al-Raqqa Treasury. Bribing an ISIS policeman is a serious offence, punishable by 30 lashes in public – so also is verbally insulting an ISIS policeman. 'Neither transgression has happened since *we* came to al-Raqqa,' said an ISIS member proudly. 'People respect the Islamic State and its Caliph, and they abide by our laws and regulations.'

Only ISIS troops are allowed to carry guns on the streets of al-Raqqa. Although checkpoints are infrequent, both men and women are body-searched for illegal arms and a wide assortment of prohibited products, including Western items like iPods, nail polish, mascara, bottled fragrances, condoms, tampons, deodorant and cigarettes. Shisha pipes are banned at local cafés, because they corrupt the mind and are un-Islamic. In al-Bab near Aleppo, ISIS carry out beheadings at the gates of a famous – now shuttered – shisha café, making the venue forever synonymous with pictures of decapitated corpses and a blood-soaked pavement.[12] ISIS citizens are expected to clean their teeth with the wooden *miswak,* a rough stick used by early Muslims in the pre-toothbrush age. ISIS police inspect laptops and mobile phones at checkpoints. For example, mobile phones should not have songs for ringtones, since songs and music are absolutely forbidden, as are smartphone games like *Angry Birds.* Such entertainment 'corrupts the mind and distracts people from their prayer.' No punishment applies here; ISIS policemen simply delete the applications. Additionally, both men and women are regularly quizzed at ISIS checkpoints, with questions from the Prophet's Hadith and verses of the Holy Qur'an. Those who give incorrect answers are assaulted verbally as ignorant and forced to attend religious schools. In the mixed territories of Deir ez-Zour, which are only partially ruled by ISIS, Christians hide their crosses and any images of Jesus Christ. They also put on an Islamic hijab and memorize Islamic sayings in order to pass through ISIS checkpoints. A common question has been: 'What are the differences between the five prayers of Islam?' Another question was: 'Name three *souar* (verses) that were revealed to the Prophet in al-Medina and three from his time in Mecca.' Sometimes policemen just ask citizens to recite a particular short *sura* from the Holy Qur'an.

ISIS police have also interfered with how people dress on the streets: with the length of women's skirts and the thickness of their veils. Tight clothes are off-limits for both men and women. For women, cleavage is a taboo, as are tattoos and high heels. Such decrees are either posted on walls, as in medieval times, or announced at mosques. People are asked to spread the decree by word of mouth. Women are prohibited from being seen on the streets without a male companion. These companions may only be the woman's husband, brother, son or father. No other man is allowed to walk with them, even if by consent of the male chaperone. Two female garrisons, known as the al-Khansaa Brigade, have been set up to inspect women on the streets – opening their bags and fixing their veil if it reveals too much of their face. One woman, Samar, tried to object politely: 'The wives of the Prophet used to join him in battle unveiled. What you are doing is un-Islamic.' She added that during the times of the Prophet, women and men used to cleanse for prayer using the same well, and all of them were not covered. The ISIS policeman snapped: '*We* teach *you*; you don't teach us!'

Stores, buses, schools and bakery lines are segregated in al-Raqqa. Shops selling women's outfits can only employ female salespersons. Lingerie shops are banned from displaying bras and underwear in shop windows. Female mannequins in department store windows have been covered with the Islamic hijab. Between fashion seasons, a naked mannequin must be taken off public display until properly dressed by store owners. Photos of celebrities (whether Muslim or not) cannot be displayed in public. The Islamic State does offer an easy low-cost housebuilding programme for newly-weds unable to purchase a home on their own, free vaccination for children and a consumer protection office to monitor the quality and price of goods. During the one week of chaos in between Jabhat al-Nusra's exodus and ISIS's entry into al-Raqqa in 2014, bundles of bread skyrocketed to S£200 (80 US cents). ISIS made sure that the consumer price was reduced to S£35 (1 US cent), to match its selling price in regime-controlled Damascus. In Mosul, they have set a limit on how much landlords can charge their tenants – no more than US$85 for an apartment per month, regardless of its furnishing, size or location.

Additionally, al-Baghdadi has set up an 'orphan's bureau' and a Taliban-inspired 'Complaints Box' where residents of the Islamic State can reach him directly via the regular postal service.

DVDs are strictly forbidden by ISIS, and especially banned are the comedies of stars such as Egypt's Adel Imam and Syria's Duraid Lahham. Both have been accused of spreading public vice, for raunchy scenes in some films and for slapstick comedy that 'portrays shallow people' in comedies from the 1960s and 1970s. More importantly, both actors were critical of the uprisings in their countries – Imam having supported the ousted President Husni Mubarak and Lahham still being supportive of President Bashar al-Assad. Also on ISIS's blacklist is the music of Egyptian diva Umm Kalthoum and Egyptian crooner Abdel Halim Hafez. All kinds of music – even patriotic songs – are considered blasphemous by ISIS. Music is described as Satanic and is banned at home, in schools, in cars and in cafés. Once an icon for teenage romance in the 1960s, Abdel Halim Hafez is now described as an 'adultery advocate and pimp', while Umm Kalthoum is considered an 'outrageous whore who drugged the masses with her music and unveiled face for forty long years.' Mustapha, a local resident who refused to leave after ISIS took over his city, spoke to the author by Skype: 'It's no different if you are caught with a bottle of whisky or with a CD of Abdel Halim. Music and comedy are big "no"s in al-Raqqa.' An ISIS fighter commented,

> Comedy is nonsense. It is a waste of time, money and mental powers. It is a drug that distracts people from their duties towards Allah and the Islamic State. Instead of watching a funny and useless television show, one would better serve his cause by memorizing and learning from the Holy Qur'an.

CRIME AND PUNISHMENT

Public executions and decapitations are common in ISIS territory, and they usually take place in al-Raqqa's main square. Usually, those executed are 'infidels, spies, doubters and prisoners of war.' ISIS deserters have also been executed, with 120 being sent to the gallows so far in 2015 for trying to flee ISIS territory.[13] The only seemingly petty crimes that merit execution are adultery and the private sale of alcohol. The unfortunate accused are herded into the main square in chains, where their verdict is read out loud. Locals are encouraged to watch the scene – women and children included. ISIS fighters display the severed heads on poles or on park fences, to maximize fear and keep them on display until they rot. Some are just left on the ground. This looks and sounds hauntingly similar to something Saddam Hussein would have done when trying to instill deep fear and terror into any delinquent city or town during the 1980s. It also serves ISIS well during its military offensives, as enemy soldiers flee before the troops of the caliphate, fearing the dreadful punishment if captured. The objective is also to inflict maximum shock on the international community and frighten ISIS's subjects into submission. It is a calculated cry for attention, similar to how Palestinian militants used to hijack aeroplanes and storm embassies in the 1970s – only with more gruesome tactics. In the 1980s, they turned to car bombs, followed by suicide attacks in the 1990s. Beheading, therefore, is just the latest of jihadi 'trends' – psychological warfare at its finest.

When asked why they behead prisoners, ISIS always has answers, pointing to a referenced Hadith by the Prophet Muhammad and to the Qur'an itself: 'When you encounter the unbelievers on the battlefield, strike off their heads; then bind the prisoners tightly.' This has been universally translated as: 'When you meet the believers; strike their necks' (Holy Qur'an 47:4). In the Hadith, the Prophet is quoted saying: 'When you kill, kill well and when you slaughter, slaughter well.' In Arabic, the term is '*Darb al-rekab*' (hitting the neck). ISIS seemingly forgets that the Prophet adds: 'Let each of you sharpen your blade and let him spare suffering of the animal he slaughters.' In other words, Muhammad was talking about sheep and cattle – not human beings.

ISIS members also argue that the Prophet Muhammad ordered the execution of prisoners captured in the Battle of Badr in 624. This is documented in the earliest biography of the Prophet, written by the Muslim scholar Ibn Ishaq. Future dynasties that claimed the caliphate did the same as the Umayyads and the Ottomans. When defeating Ali's son, the Damascus-based Caliph Yezid ordered the beheading of al-Hussein ibn Ali. At the Battle of Varna in 1444, for example, the Ottomans beheaded King Ladislaus of Hungary.[14] In 1456, they decapitated King Stephen of Bosnia and his sons, although they had surrendered to them. Beheading is also common in Saudi Arabia; it is one form of capital punishment enacted by the Saudi criminal code. In 2003 alone, the Saudi government beheaded more than 50 people for various offences, ranging from theft to witchcraft and apostasy.[15] More recently, speaking at an election rally, the Israeli Foreign Minister Avigdor Lieberman spoke of Israeli Arabs, who account for 20 per cent of the population, saying: 'Whoever's with us should get everything. Those who are against us, there's nothing to be done – we need to pick up an axe and cut off his head.'[16]

Beheadings, however cruel and savage, are not the only method of execution implemented in ISIS-held territory. Several propaganda posts by the organization show execution by gunfire. In June 2014, ISIS fighters summarily executed over 1,000 Iraqi soldiers captured at the Speicher airbase in Tikrit. Sabawi Ibrahim, Saddam Hussein's half-brother now working with ISIS, drove the bus carrying the ten ISIS militiamen. Another propaganda video featured an ISIS child soldier of central Asian descent shooting two alleged Russian spies in the head. Even after the person is shot, ISIS sometimes hangs the body on a cross for three days in a public square, in order to terrorize and intimidate the local population. Many Syrian rebels captured by ISIS were crucified after being shot. Another method of execution is to throw a person from the tallest building. This particular form of capital punishment is reserved by ISIS for presumed homosexuals. Several women accused of adultery were stoned to death by ISIS. No male adulterers have been punished so far. According to ISIS 'religious authorities', the aforementioned forms of capital punishment are founded in Qur'anic texts and the Hadith. ISIS propaganda videos tend to include the religious text upon which the sentencing was based.

Perhaps the most distasteful of ISIS's executions came in February 2015, when 26-year-old captured Jordanian fighter pilot Mutah al-Kassasbeh was burned to death. Al-Kassasbeh's F-16 crashed near al-Raqqa on 24 December 2014 during a bombing raid against ISIS positions. Jordan and the United States maintained that the fighter jet crashed due to a mechanical failure, while ISIS claimed it had shot the plane down using a heat-seeking missile. According to the execution video posted by ISIS on 3 February 2015, al-Kassasbeh was executed in early January. ISIS, however, spent the month of January negotiating with the Japanese and Jordanian governments in hopes of exchanging captured Japanese journalist Kenji Goto and al-Kassasbeh for Sajida al-Rishawi, an al-Qaeda suicide bomber held in Jordan since 2005, along with other convicted terrorists. The negotiations reached a dead end, and Goto was beheaded on 30 January 2015. Four days later, ISIS posted a propaganda video showing al-Kassasbeh in a steel cage wearing an orange jumpsuit before he was set ablaze by masked ISIS warriors. The video was shot and edited to professional standards. It also featured the names and addresses of hundreds of Jordanian pilots and the coordinates of several military airbases in Jordan. ISIS placed a financial reward on each pilot's head. Another feature of the video was several excerpts from Ibn Taymiyya's texts justifying the type of punishment that al-Kassasbeh received. The next morning, Jordan executed al-Rishawi and another convicted al-Qaeda member in retaliation.

Under ISIS, there have been reported cases of the execution of men and women, and the enslavement or rape of Christian and other non-Muslim girls who refused to convert to Islam. In September 2014, the UN Human Rights Council said that ISIS had killed innocents on 'an unimaginable scale'.[17] Earlier in June, the UN accused ISIS of executing hundreds of prisoners of war and killing over 1,000 civilians.[18] In August, ISIS was blamed for the mass execution of over 250 Syrian army troops near the al-Tabqa airbase in al-Raqqa.[19] In the Shaer gas field they shot over 200 Syrian soldiers, and at Camp Speicher they murdered somewhere between 1,000 and 1,700 Iraqi soldiers, most of them Shi'a.[20] Amnesty International has accused ISIS of 'ethnic cleansing on a historical scale'. In September 2014, it published a report saying that ISIS was to blame for 'killing or abducting hundreds, possibly thousands, and forcing more than 830,000 others to flee the areas it has captured since 10 June 2014.'[21]

In Sinjar, northern Iraq, ISIS massacred 70–90 members of the Yazidi community, an ancient ethno-religion linked to Zoroastrianism. ISIS declared them 'devil worshippers'. Another 200–500 were killed in their native Sinjar, and 20,000 were uprooted from their homes and forced to climb the rugged high mountains, seeking refuge in Dohuk in Iraqi Kurdistan. In Beshir, 700 Shi'i Turkmen were slaughtered, and another 670 inmates were murdered at the Badush prison in Mosul.[22] In the three Syrian towns of Ghareneij, Abu Haman and Kashkiyeh, 700 Sunni tribesmen were gunned down for attempting an uprising against ISIS.[23] All of them belonged to al-Sheitat, a prominent tribe in the Deir ez-Zour province. They were beheaded, crucified or shot at close range in three days of mass murder. At least six of ISIS's victims have been non-Muslim children, and one was a 102-year-old man, shot in the Hama province. The UN estimates that more than 1,000 Iraqis were killed between 5 and 22 June, and another 5,000 Yazidis were killed in the month of August 2014.[24] All of these murders were proudly claimed by ISIS.

Older women who refuse to convert to Islam or pay the *jizya* (the tribute tax paid by non-Muslims to their Muslim rulers) are sold in local markets as slaves and young ones are married off to fighters. These marriages are often brief, but on paper they are official. If the fighter dies during the tenure of the marriage (regardless of how short it is) his 'wife' is entitled to her inheritance of his material possessions, as clearly stated by the Qur'an. Those women who do not convert are subjected to physical and sexual violence, often treated like sheep. Those sold on the market are chained in a row and put on display with price tags. At least one case has been recorded where Yazidi girls jumped to their death from Mount Sinjar, after being raped by ISIS fighters. According to a UN report of October 2014, ISIS took 450–500 women to Iraq's Nineveh region in August. Approximately 150 of them were unmarried Christian and Yazidi girls, and they were sold as sex slaves.[25] ISIS didn't even try to hide the story, which was drawn up by the UN based on 500 interviews.

JIHADI JOHN

On 19 August 2014, ISIS posted an online video showing the beheading of the 41-year-old US photojournalist James Foley. On 2 September, it posted another video, this time of the execution of another American journalist, Steven Sotloff. Eleven days later, a third video appeared, this time of the beheading of David Haines, a British aid worker. On 16 November ISIS executed Peter Kassig, an ex-US soldier turned aid worker. Kassig had converted to Islam, taking on the name Abdul-Rahman, but this didn't save him from ISIS's verdict. In the same video, Syrian soldiers were slaughtered as well. In January 2015, two Japanese citizens were also beheaded on camera. These were Haruna Yukawa, a private military contractor, and Kenji Goto Jogo, a freelance video journalist. In all the videos, one man, nicknamed 'Jihadi John', carried out the beheadings. In one video, he spoke to the camera with a flawless and heavy British accent, saying: 'To Obama, the dog of Rome. Today we are slaughtering the soldiers of Bashar, and tomorrow we will be slaughtering your soldiers. And with Allah's permission we will break this final and last crusade.'[26] By Rome, Jihadi John was actually referring to Washington DC, the capital of the Western world, just as Rome had been during ancient times. All foreign prisoners were forced to wear orange jumpsuits, similar to the ones worn by jihadi prisoners at Guantanamo Bay. In the second film, Jihadi John says:

I'm back, Obama, and I'm back because of your arrogant foreign policy towards the Islamic State, because of your insistence on continuing your

> bombings. [...] just as your missiles continue to strike our people, our
> knife will continue to strike the necks of your people.

He then warns the US-led international alliance to 'Back off and leave our people alone!'[27]

These videos were not released randomly. They always appeared just before and after any bombing campaign against ISIS, either by the Syrian or Iraqi army, or the US-led international coalition. If before, the air strikes were aimed at spreading fear among their enemy ranks; if after, they were to muzzle ISIS citizens into haunting silence. ISIS sought to blackmail the United States and its allies with hostage videos prior to the international coalition air strikes in September 2014. Once the bombing campaign began, these executions (and the threat of future ones) became a sort of retribution and a warning against future strikes. As of spring 2015, the strikes had failed to frighten ISIS and the beheadings have failed to stop the international bombing campaign. In the case of the Japanese hostages, for example, the videos came after Japan had pledged financial support for the countries fighting ISIS.

In February 2015, Jihadi John, the infamous executioner who appeared in all the videos, was identified as 26-year-old Mohammed Emwazi, a British citizen of Iraqi origins. His family had moved to London after the second Gulf War in 1994, where he was raised in a middle-class neighbourhood.[28] Those who knew him say he was polite, liked to wear stylish clothes and loved to play football, pretty much like both Abu Mohammad al-Golani and Abu Bakr al-Baghdadi. Adhering strictly to the teachings of Islam, he sported a light beard and was mindful of making eye contact with women.[29] After graduating from the University of Westminster with a degree in computer programming in 2009, Emwazi and two friends travelled to Tanzania. Once they landed in Dar es Salaam, they were detained by police and later deported to Amsterdam, where Emwazi claimed that an officer from MI5, Britain's domestic security agency, accused him of trying to reach Somalia, where the al-Qaeda-linked militant group al-Shabab operates. Emwazi denied the accusation and claimed that

MI5 representatives had tried to recruit him.[30] A former ISIS hostage said Jihadi John was obsessed with Somalia and made his captives watch videos about al-Shabab.[31] In 2010 Emwazi moved to Kuwait for work. He came back to London twice: the first time to visit family and the second time to finalize his plans to marry a woman in Kuwait. In June 2010, however, counterterrorism officials in Britain detained him once again. When he tried to fly back to Kuwait the next day, he was prevented from doing so.[32] Emwazi felt harassed by authorities, leading him to contact CAGE, a human rights and Muslim advocacy organization, to seek legal help. In one email to CAGE, he wrote: 'I told them that I want to be left alone, as I have an ambition of moving from the UK and settling in Kuwait. That is why I found a job and a spouse!! But they laughed.'[33]

It is unclear exactly when Emwazi reached Syria or how. One friend said he believed Emwazi wanted to travel to Saudi Arabia to teach English in 2012 but was unsuccessful. Soon afterwards, the friend said, he was gone.[34] Once in northern Syria, Emwazi contacted his family and at least one of his friends. Emwazi was part of a team guarding Western captives at a prison in Idlib in 2013. Two other men with British accents joined Emwazi in Idlib. The trio became nicknamed after the Beatles – Emwazi was 'John' and another British man was 'George'. Anybody who heard Emwazi speaking, with his heavy British accent, would remember his voice among the multitude of ISIS members in Idlib. A former hostage said Emwazi participated in the waterboarding of four Western hostages. Others described George as the leader of the trio. Jihadi John, they said, was quiet and intelligent. 'He was the most deliberate,' a former hostage said. An ex-ISIS fighter told the BBC that Emwazi struck him as odd the first time he met him. 'He was cold. He didn't talk much. He wouldn't join us in prayer,' he said. 'He'd only pray with his friends [...] the other British brothers prayed with us, but he was strange.' He added: 'The other British brothers would say "hi" when they saw us on the road, but he turned his face away.'[35] Beginning in early 2014, the hostages were moved to a prison in al-Raqqa, where the three men visited them often. They appeared to have taken on more powerful roles within the Islamic State.[36]

Jihadi John became the masked face of ISIS propaganda, making an appearance in every high-profile beheading video. Not all ISIS beheadings were captured on camera. In February 2015, the Libyan branch of ISIS posted a video of its fighters beheading 21 Egyptian workers taken hostage. The Jihadi-John-styled video featured a masked man dressed in black delivering a message in English. The execution took place on a beach, with the hostages dressed in orange jumpsuits, an ISIS fighter standing behind each one. In the video, the executioner said: 'The sea you have hidden Sheikh Osama bin Laden's body in, we swear to Allah, we will mix it with your blood.'[37] He went on to threaten Italy and Europe: 'Today we are south of Rome [...] We will conquer Rome with Allah's permission.'[38] The inspiration behind this sheer brutality was neither a Syrian nor an Iraqi jihadi, but a Londoner. It speaks volumes about how far and wide ISIS's influence has spread in a matter of months.

ISIS EDUCATION

In schools, ISIS has imposed strict forms of Islamic Shari'a. Classes, of course, are now fully segregated. The last of the official state-run public schools was closed down in November 2014, and now all students have to study at ISIS centres, which are mostly in mosques. Students no longer hail the tricolour of the Syrian and Iraqi Flags but the black flag of ISIS. Student parades swear allegiance to the Prophet Muhammad. ISIS has also banned the teaching of art, music, Syrian and Iraqi history, Arabic literature, chemistry, physics, trigonometry, and, of course, Christianity. These subjects have been replaced by a heavy focus on learning the Qur'an, Shari'a and Hadith. A total of 104 teachers are employed at schools across ISIS-held territory in Syria, with an average salary of US$400 per month. Seventy-five of them are male and 29 are female. Schools are gender-segregated, with male teachers teaching in all-male schools and female teachers teaching in all-female schools. Good teachers, it must be noted, are prized in ISIS territory – even more so than strong foreign fighters. Approximately 90 per cent of ISIS schoolteachers were trained at state-run Syrian schools and the remaining 10 per cent are university-educated, with degrees in physics, mathematics and engineering. ISIS values training in the sciences in order to prepare future soldiers to handle artillery, the maintenance of vehicles and perhaps to use more sophisticated weaponry. All teachers, however, undergo extensive training in Shari'a law and Qur'anic studies before they are allowed to interact with students.

Women are not allowed to go to school without a male chaperone to accompany them to and from school, resulting in an approximately 45 per cent drop-out rate for girls in middle and high schools for the academic year 2014–15.[39] There have been cases of forced conscription of male children below the age of 15 into ISIS ranks. ISIS denies this report and its spokesman, Abu Muhammad, confirms: 'Children need to go to school. With or without the war, children have to be in school. They have to get a sound Islamic education, to grow into strong, wise and capable jihadis.'

In the academic field, there have been some cases of rather striking cooperation between Islamists and the central government in Damascus. It was born out of necessity. During the summer of 2013, students in al-Raqqa and Deir ez-Zour sat for their annual baccalaureate exam. Classrooms were monitored by Jabhat al-Nusra fighters with guns. Nusra fighters could make sure that cheating didn't occur, but they were certainly incapable of grading the exams. They didn't have a recognized legal authority to pass or fail students. Unless they were stamped by the Damascus-based Ministry of Education, those exams would have been null and void – unacceptable at foreign universities across the world. Nusra troops therefore carried the exams to the nearest checkpoint for the official Syrian army to collect. They in turn sent them to Damascus, where the papers were graded, authenticated and then sent back to al-Raqqa. Likewise, telephone lines, electricity and the internet are all still functioning in al-Raqqa today, although

Syrian authorities in Damascus could switch them off in the blink of an eye. They haven't done so yet, and in exchange, al-Raqqa's ISIS authorities have not damaged the Euphrates Dam in west al-Raqqa.

ISIS FUNDING

The Islamic State is rich. Unlike al-Qaeda, which relied on donations from members and sympathizers, ISIS earns its own money. Thanks to the oilfields under its control, ISIS has collected tens of millions of dollars in less than one year. It has produced crude oil from captured fields, and even sold electric power to the Syrian government through third parties. According to a US Treasury official, ISIS earns US$1 million per day from the export of oil.[40] Much of it is sold illegally to whoever is willing to buy – even to the central government in Damascus. One estimate actually put the combined oil revenue as high as US$3 million per day, just before the start of the international coalition's bombing campaign that began in the second half of 2014, reflecting the fact that 60 per cent of Syrian oilfields are under ISIS's direct control, or that of its proxies and allies. In total, they control eleven oilfields in Syria and Iraq, including al-Omar, with a production capacity of 75,000 barrels per day.[41] The same source adds that illicit oil production by ISIS stands at approximately 90,000 barrels per day.[42] The Syrian government and other parties buy it at slashed prices, at only 20 per cent of what it is actually worth on the global market.[43] In New York or Paris, crude oil traded at US$100 per barrel in 2014. ISIS sold heavy oil for US$26–30 per barrel and light oil for US$60.[44] This black-market oil is smuggled to refineries in Iran, and then brought back into regime-controlled territory. This means that ISIS is not making as much profit from oil as it potentially could, partly because of the discounted prices, but also because the oilfields are old, need plenty of maintenance and are only operating at 10 per cent of their pre-2011 output.[45]

When the US-led international coalition started bombing oil refineries in Deir ez-Zour and al-Raqqa in late 2014, ISIS's supply of fuel dropped significantly because its tankers and machines were incapacitated. Highlighting the importance of the oil trade to ISIS, the first US targeted killing of an ISIS commander was aimed at Abu Sayyaf, ISIS's 'oil minister'. Infiltrating deep into Syrian territory in May 2015, US special operations troops carried out the assassination at the al-Omar oilfield near the city of Deir ez-Zour, killing Abu Sayyaf and capturing his wife. To compensate for its losses, ISIS imposed electricity cuts on al-Raqqa, sometimes lasting as long as 20 hours per day. The price of diesel doubled to more than S£150 (60 US cents) per litre – suddenly selling at the same price as the black market in Damascus. Many bakeries stopped production for lack of power, so the price of bread skyrocketed from S£15 (6 US cents) to a staggering S£200 (US$1). The sharp drop in oil prices since the fall of 2014 exacerbated these problems, but it did not halt ISIS's oil economy. In fact, the drop in prices has pushed ISIS to try to control more oilfields in the Syrian Desert and in the al-Anbar province in Iraq. At the time of writing, ISIS is still pushing towards the Jazal oilfield near Palmyra in Syria and the Baiji oil refinery in Iraq.

ISIS has also actively engaged in smuggling historical artefacts outside of the country, which has generated impressive revenue. This includes gold coins, bronze artefacts and early Christian relics such as gold chalices and other valuables. Statues, crucifixes, Byzantine coins and iconography are however immediately destroyed no matter what their worth, since making money from them is 'haram' (prohibited by religion). ISIS, for example, looted the ancient Assyrian city of Dur Sharrukin in northern Iraq, selling most of its treasure, but it demolished the city of Hatra and bulldozed Nimrud, south of Mosul. ISIS justifies the sale by saying that such artefacts are alien to Islamic culture and need to be removed in order to purify the Islamic State. Reportedly, it made $36 million from selling stolen artefacts from al-Nabk, north of Damascus, in 2014.[46] Not all of the stolen material is found in ISIS territory. Some of the findings which have been shipped to ISIS for sale include boxes of pure gold Ottoman coins, found in Damascus and near the Daraa station in southern Syria, and ancient Shi'i scriptures from Baghdad. The gold boxes were buried by Ottoman officers fleeing Damascus at the end of World War I. Depending on the quantity of gold, they sell at $5,000–$10,000 per box, according to an artefact trader in Damascus. The original version of the Shi'i book *al-Jafr* is also reportedly in their possession and has a price tag of a staggering US$120 million. It was stolen from the Baghdad Museum, an antiquities dealer confirmed. *Al-Jafr* is a mystical book for Muslim Shi'a, which, according to their belief, was compiled by the fourth caliph Ali ibn Abi Talib and inherited by him from the Prophet Muhammad himself. In May 2015, shortly after capturing the ancient Syrian city of Palmyra, it was reported that ISIS had set up a 'ministry of antiquities', tasked with streamlining the process of selling looted artefacts from across the territory under ISIS control.[47]

ISIS has also enforced its own shadow taxation on cargo coming through the Syrian–Iraqi border. It currently stands at $300 for trucks carrying fruits and vegetables and $400 per truck carrying electronics (LCDs, air conditioners, refrigerators and mobile phones). Patrols monitor these trucks, ostensibly to protect them from bandits and to give them receipts to display at ISIS checkpoints. ISIS has also been known to demand 'protection money' from businessmen in the cities it occupies, such as Mosul, which can reach up to US$500,000 per month from each company.[48] In late 2014, ISIS announced that it plans to mint its own reservoir of gold, silver and copper, issuing coins identical to the ones used by the third caliph of Islam, Uthman ibn Affan (who was married to two of the Prophet's daughters).[49]

Although nothing official has ever been released regarding the foreign funding of ISIS, state-run Syrian media claims that many jihadis have confessed that they were visited by Kuwaiti, Saudi, Qatari and Libyan go-betweens. Pro-government journalists have accused Qatar and Saudi Arabia of bankrolling ISIS. This has been echoed by Iranian media and by the Iraqi prime minister Nouri al-Maliki. France's foreign minister did acknowledge foreign backing for ISIS, but stopped short of mentioning names.[50] The *Telegraph* reported in October 2014 that according to the US Treasury, a 49-year-old Qatari was raising money for ISIS.[51] Another report in November identified 20 Qataris as terrorist financiers and facilitators. Ten of them have been placed on the UN and US blacklist.

On at least one occasion, a Kuwaiti intermediary handed out salaries paid in cash in al-Raqqa during the second week of April 2014. Before showing up at the city's former Baath Party branch, he had been visiting Abu Bakr al-Baghdadi at an undisclosed location on the Iraqi–Syrian border. Abu Qays al-Hersh was one of the Syrian fighters present, and he recalled:

> The Kuwaiti man had a large Adidas sports bag and was accompanied by a Tunisian commander from ISIS. Our Tunisian brother read out a list of names and we came forward, one at a time, to get an envelope with our salaries. We don't know where the money came from, and honestly, we don't really care.

He added that al-Baghdadi takes salaries, pensions and funds very seriously. Al-Baghdadi insists that his men be paid on time, although he himself gets no salary for heading ISIS; he is taken care of by his loyal flock. When salaries were late because of intense fighting, al-Baghdadi was furious. 'He made a few phone calls, we were told, and shortly thereafter the Kuwaiti intermediary showed up at our offices. We never knew his name or where he came from. We never saw him again.'

Outside donations from ISIS sympathizers were almost non-existent before 2013/14. According to a RAND study, al-Qaeda in Iraq received only 5 per cent of their operating budget from outside sources. The rest was raised inside Iraq through kidnapping, theft and by other illegal means. Twenty per cent of the annual budget was provided by different cells scattered throughout Iraq. This is similar to a 'target' that branches of large franchises are asked to meet in the corporate world. Senior clerics within the organization would collect the money in one place and then redistribute it to local cells in financial need. According to an Iraqi intelligence report, ISIS had assets worth

US$2 billion.[52] Many of these assets were confiscated property in al-Raqqa and Mosul, all obtained in the summer of 2014. After sweeping Mosul, Iraq's second largest city, for example, ISIS seized $420 million in cash from the coffers of the city's Central Bank.[53] According to the UN, ISIS received $35–45 million in ransom money in 2014.[54]

Nobody can tell for sure what ISIS's monthly expenditures have been, because nobody knows exactly how many people are on its payroll. None of the ISIS fighters involved in any of the looting operations would agree to speak to the author. What we do know is that ISIS salaries are always paid in cash. All banks – even Islamic ones – are prohibited in ISIS culture. We also cannot tell for sure how much money they have in their treasury. According to Michael Knights, a Middle East expert at the Washington Institute for Near East Policy, ISIS is the 'world's richest terrorist organization' leading 'the world's poorest state'.[55] According to the *Financial Times*, before seizing Mosul in the summer of 2014, ISIS assets stood at US$875m.[56] The *Guardian*, however, puts its worth at US$2 billion.[57]

It is not clear whether ISIS will be able to develop a viable and fully functioning economy in the areas it now controls. It is certainly a necessity if ISIS wants to implement a 'state-building' project and sustain the nascent caliphate and its population, both residents of Syrian and Iraqi cities and towns and the thousands of foreign jihadis flocking to the Islamic State. This, however, depends on several factors – first and foremost, the ability of international and regional powers to stifle ISIS's funding sources worldwide, especially the lucrative donations it receives and its henchmen's ability to sell smuggled artefacts abroad. Another chief source of funds, ISIS's oil trade, depends largely on two crucial factors: first, Turkey's ability to control its border with Syria; and second, the continued and successful targeting of ISIS's oil trade infrastructure, logistics and key personnel by the US-led international coalition. Finally, the military operations currently conducted by several states and other groups against ISIS might curtail its ability to conduct quasi-normal economic activity by shrinking the territory and the size of the population it controls.

ISIS MEDIA

One reason why ISIS's rise to fame has eclipsed that of any other jihadi group has been the impressive propaganda that has accompanied all of its campaigns. In contrast, Jabhat al-Nusra waited for others to write about them and only launched their media channel *al-Manara al-Bayda* after they had achieved worldwide attention. Their job was to manage their image, rather than promote it. The ISIS media branch existed even before the group reached its present form. While still a local militia in Iraq, its leaders founded the Al-Furqan Institute for Media Production in November 2006. This was four months after the Israeli war on Lebanon, where the world had been amazed by the effectiveness of Hizbullah's media campaign. Al-Qaeda decided to copy what it had seen, producing CDs, DVDs, posters and pamphlets while also managing an active online campaign with ISIS-related material. After the war in Syria started, ISIS founded another outlet, the I'tisaam Media Foundation, in March 2013. In 2014, it founded the al-Hayat Media Center, targeting a Western audience with multi-language material in English, German, Russian and French. In 2015, ISIS began recruiting experts in sign language to help them reach an even wider audience – the deaf and mute curious to know more about the Islamic State. Foreign journalists visiting ISIS territory have to get their papers stamped by the media centre. They are also required to pledge allegiance to the caliph before starting work, after which they are told what they can do and what is not allowed. Freelancing for Al Jazeera TV is banned, for example, and any contact with Al Arabiya, Al-Dunia TV (semi-official Syrian channel), Syrian TV or the opposition platform Orient TV is also forbidden.[58] In July, al-Hayat Media started ISIS's glossy digital magazine, *Dabiq*, filled with interviews with fighters and stories of their conquests. By December, ISIS had successfully published six issues of *Dabiq*. The magazine's name comes from a town in northern Syria, which is mentioned in the Hadith and from which the Ottomans marched to Damascus in 1516. Dabiq is a small town near Aleppo where the Prophet Muhammad foretold that Muslims and the West would clash before the apocalypse. *Dabiq*'s success is one of the many reasons why foreign jihadis have abandoned al-Qaeda and joined ISIS. The prominent US magazine *The New Republic* compares al-Qaeda to AOL and the Islamic State to Google, when it comes to reputation.[59]

Downloadable in PDF form, *Dabiq* reads and looks like *TIME* and *Businessweek*. The font, the page layout, the colourful and cutting-edge production are extremely noteworthy, and so also is the flawless English. It aims at attracting recruits and legitimizing ISIS among the approximately eight million people who fall under its rule in Syria and Iraq. It serves as an important propaganda tool in attracting Muslims worldwide into ISIS's ranks, encouraging them to emigrate to Mosul and al-Raqqa. Every edition has a quote from Abu Musaab al-Zarqawi: 'The spark has been lit here in Iraq and its heat will continue to intensify – by Allah's permission – until it burns the crusader armies in Dabiq.' In its October 2014 issue, the front story reads: 'The Failed Crusade'. It shows a Photoshopped picture of ISIS's flag flying over St Peter's Square in the Vatican.[60] Their second issue is called *The Flood* and features the headline: 'It's either the Islamic State or the Flood.' In a lead editorial, they argue that the caliphate is Noah's Ark, here to save humanity from the coming flood.

Abu al-Nada al-Faraj is a 25-year-old journalist working with ISIS in al-Raqqa. He studied English at the University of Aleppo and graduated in 2007. Although conservative and mosque-going, he is not a fanatic and treats ISIS as just another well-paying employer. For them he translates Arabic articles into English for the four-man staff that runs *Dabiq*. All of its editors and journalists are European, he says. 'They monitor everything that appears online about their activity, and are more interested in critical stories than ones that praise.'[61] Abu al-Nada adds that *Dabiq* staff are 'Google addicts', who have 'favourited' the following websites for daily reference: the *Washington Post*, the *New York Times*, the *Huffington Post*, the *Wall Street Journal*, the *Financial Times*, *Foreign Policy* magazine, *Le Monde*, *Le Figaro*, the *Guardian*, the *Independent*, the *Daily Mail*, the *Sunday Telegraph*, *al-Hayat*, *Asharq al-Awsat*, *al-Quds al-Arabi*, *al-Ahram*, *al-Watan*, SANA (Syrian Arab News Agency), NINA (National Iraqi News Agency), in addition to the Jamestown Foundation's *Terrorism Monitor*, Carnegie Middle East, RAND, Middle East Institute and Brookings. They also subscribe, by proxy, to Agence France-Presse, Reuters, Associated Press and the Russian news agency Interfax. 'They also watch Hizbullah's al-Manar TV and the Iran-backed al-Mayadeen.'

Additionally, ISIS has relied heavily on social media, which has become their main recruitment tool, attracting foreign jihadis from across the world. They operate an Android application to share posts and photos called *Fajr al-Basha'er* (Dawn of Good Tidings).[62] ISIS also operates the Amaq News Agency and the al-Hayat channel, which broadcasts their reporting via YouTube. Al-Amaq is famous for its extensive coverage of ISIS's battles in Syria and Iraq, and has become a source of footage for many international and Arab television channels. One of al-Hayat's most prominent features is a series of reports by British hostage/journalist John Cantlie. Abducted in Syria alongside James Foley back in 2012, Cantlie has appeared since September 2014 in a series of filmed reports titled 'Lend Me Your Ears' to describe 'the facts on the ground' throughout the citites and battlefronts of ISIS, from Mosul to Kobani.

The Syrian government has not banned any of ISIS's Twitter or Facebook accounts – not even the *Dabiq* website or their YouTube videos – so that they can monitor who browses these channels. One of ISIS's YouTube videos, for example, released by al-Furqan Media on 17 March 2014, was watched 56,998 times within 24 hours. Two months later, it had been tweeted 32,313 times over a 60-hour period, an average of 807.25 tweets per hour.[63] After the seizure of Mosul in the summer of 2014, ISIS sent 40,000 tweets in 24 hours. ISIS has been exceptionally active on Twitter, distributing messages by organizing hashtag campaigns, despite repeated shutdowns by the online giant. In April 2015, Twitter responded with a single mass purge, deleting 10,000 ISIS-affiliated accounts in one day.[64] Briefly, ISIS tried to shift their messages elsewhere, using alternate social media sites like Quitter,

Friendica and Diaspora. ISIS fighters have also used Instagram to post photos of themselves in between battles. Sometimes the photos are of casual outings. ISIS fighters are seen smiling, giving high-fives, patting each other on the back – always with a rifle slung across their shoulder. It is the best manifestation of twenty-first-century jihadi propaganda, which the celebrated early online jihadis like Abu Musaab al-Souri would have loved to have experienced. It has also served as a great recruitment tool, attracting thousands of jihadis from Europe, the United States and the Arab world. On the other hand, ISIS's extensive social media presence was used by the US airforce to track and target many of its soldiers and commanders, according to General Hawk Carlisle, commander of the United States Air Combat Command.[65]

ISIS therefore has everything needed for a state to survive. It has its own flag, border parameters, a functioning civil service, an armed police force, media outlets, currency-in-the-making, a treasury and a president – or caliph. As we will see in Chapter 8, it is also developing values to give true foundations to its state.

EIGHT

Foreign Jihadis

ABU OSMAN AL-BARITANI (SUFFIX FOR 'THE BRIT') KNEW CLOSE to nothing about Syria before arriving in the war-torn country just before Christmas 2011. Growing up in Tower Hamlets, north of the River Thames in London, his father had converted to Islam back in the 1960s. This was during the heyday of the Palestinian struggle and at the apex of the civil rights movement in the United States. 'My father was inspired by Malcolm X. He worked as a nurse at a hospital in Saudi Arabia in the early 1970s. This is where he and my mum decided to convert to Islam.' Abu Osman's father came from a middle-class family of North African origins. Born in 1986, Abu Osman was an avid Michael Jackson fan, who learned to moonwalk at the age of seven and embraced the religion of Muhammad into which he was born. He grew up observing its main pillars: praying five times a day and fasting during the month of Ramadan. Speaking from Manbij, 30 km west of the Euphrates, Abu Osman said that it was online Muslim forums, and not the international media, that first brought Syria to his attention.

> I was always active in online discussions. We didn't talk politics, just religious affairs. Most of us lived in the Greater London area, and shared similar backgrounds. A Muslim brother from Spain told me that he was leaving his job in Madrid to fight for Islam in Syria. He sent me YouTube videos of the [Assad] regime's brutal treatment of Muslims. He asked me to join and I agreed.

His Spanish friend had lived briefly in Damascus and studied at the Sheikh Ahmad Kaftaro Institute from 2001 to 2002. The two men had been online pals since 2009.

Abu Osman was a waiter at a Turkish restaurant in central London, offering sizzling kebabs and *tawouk* to Arab tourists missing home cuisine. He didn't have much to lose. 'London was becoming too expensive for me, and there was little room for professional mobility if you weren't affiliated with one of the big private schools.' Abu Osman spoke with a heavy British accent and a deep commanding voice, similar to the one heard in ISIS videos of 'Jihadi John', who beheaded the American journalists. 'I hadn't carried a gun in my life and spoke no Arabic. I went to Syria to see for myself what this war was all about. I had no intention of joining the *mujahideen* in military warfare.' In other words, he was more of a jihadi tourist than a jihadi warrior. His Spanish friend – also an amateur in holy jihad – was killed just three weeks after arriving in Syria, in October 2013. 'My passport and travel documents were with him. We never retrieved his body. With him gone, I had no choice but to stay behind, and pretty soon, I started searching for a job in Syria.' Abu Osman had only informed his parents of his whereabouts after arriving safely in Manbij, via Turkey. 'Father offered to send me some money. I said no thanks; I will rely on myself.'

A Jordanian commander from Jabhat al-Nusra named al-Nasser al-Zarqawi (no relation to Abu Musaab al-Zarqawi) threw him a lifeline in the summer of 2014. He was asked to write English press releases for al-Nusra. 'We want to look like *Newsweek*,' said al-Nasser, showing him the latest edition of the American magazine, with a big green-eyed Muslim woman wearing the niqab on its cover. This was before ISIS came out with its first issue of *Dabiq*. The al-Manara al-Bayda agency offered to pay US$10 per press release, which amounted to roughly US$30 per day. They gave him an Acer laptop, a wireless internet connection and al-Nusra press credentials. 'They chose the name of Abu Osman for me (Osman being the third caliph in Islam). I liked it and didn't object. Since then, I have gone by this name.' Osman, sometimes spelled 'Uthman', is the name of the third caliph of Islam, an early Companion of the Prophet, who married two of his daughters. Abu Osman was still working with al-Manara al-Bayda as of mid-2015. He carried a gun for his own protection and worked out of a small apartment in the Aleppo countryside. The house is owned by Jabhat al-Nusra and Abu Osman doesn't pay any rent. 'I have only used the gun once: to scare off wild dogs in the wilderness. If I had to use it against infidels, spies or Assadists, I wouldn't hesitate.'

His story sounds almost identical to that of thousands who have come from Europe to Syria since 2013. It breaks the Arabic stereotype of these foreigners – not all of them are attracted to the idea of becoming a fighter. Some certainly are coming to kill in the land of ISIS. Others, however, stumbled across the project and found it convenient to stay. The Arab and Western press has incorrectly lumped all of them into one group: 'foreign jihadis' and 'foreign fighters'. All of them are indeed foreigners. Many of them, however, were neither jihadis nor fighters. And many of them work with different groups, including Jabhat al-Nusra, but all have been stereotyped as ISIS figures. In fact, over 90 per cent came to Syria with no previous fighting experience and learned to carry a gun only after setting foot in Aleppo, Idlib or al-Raqqa. This applies to all those recruited from Western Europe, who arrived starting from the summer of 2011. Their first target was Jabhat al-Nusra, not ISIS. It was the only jihadi franchise operating on the scene at the time. When ISIS surfaced, many started to defect to al-Baghdadi's new organization. The same cannot be said for battle-hardened warriors who came from previous frontiers in Afghanistan, Pakistan, Chechnya, Libya, Iraq and Algeria. They came with plenty of experience and knowledge, fully aware of what they were doing and whom they were joining.

Like Abu Osman, almost all the Europeans who first joined al-Nusra were originally employed as fundraisers, medics, interpreters, copy-editors and media advisers. Some took Arabic lessons, but it was not essential to do so. Foreign jihadis live in compounds where all their neighbours are non-Arab, and they communicate with each other in conversational English. These men have progressed within the jihadi establishment: growing long beards, training with explosives, practising marksmanship, and finally, learning to slit throats when needed. This explains why so many of them die while learning the craft – they are poor fighters and easy targets. Unlike Syrian jihadis, who know the terrain by heart, they are navigating territory that they know nothing about. Often they are sent to battlefields they have never seen in their lives, relying only on Google Maps for navigation.

OPERATION MUM

Pro-government media first reported foreign fighters in northern Syria as early as 2011. Opposition activists scoffed at the story, claiming that it was entirely untrue. The government stuck to its version throughout. Pretty soon the residents of al-Raqqa and Deir ez-Zour started arriving in Damascus, in search of relative calm and security. Terrified and shivering, they spoke of checkpoints patrolled by bearded men 'who didn't speak a word of Arabic'. Before 2010, tourists complained that locals spoke very little English on the streets of Syria. Now, although the tourists are gone, a colourful assortment of foreign languages can be heard on the streets of Syrian cities under rebel control: English, French, Turkish, Chechen, Tajik, Urdu, Persian, Chinese and Russian.

The world only began to take the government's claims seriously in 2012, when several Western governments admitted that many of their countrymen had indeed taken up arms and joined Islamic rebels in Syria. The prominent German weekly *Der Spiegel* was the first to report on a European fighting in the Syrian north, in mid-2012.[1] The first European foreign fighter to volunteer was a 24-year-old Frenchman from a wealthy family. In July 2013, an American-Egyptian named Amir Farouk Ibrahim went missing from his home in Pennsylvania. His passport was discovered at an ISIS base captured by Kurdish fighters.[2] Later that summer, two Lebanese-Swedish brothers were killed near Krak des Chevaliers, the Crusader castle 40 km west of the city of Homs. One of them died when he detonated a suicide vest at an army checkpoint.[3]

Significant global attention came in May 2014, when a 22-year-old from South Florida blew himself up in Idlib. Moner Mohammad Abusalha (aka Abu Huraira al-Amriki) grew up with a Jordanian father and American mother who converted to Islam and wore the hijab. He was polite and funny, a seemingly normal kid who played basketball and listened to the American rapper Jay Z. He travelled frequently to the Middle East with his family and decided to join jihad in Syria after the outbreak of the war. Jabhat al-Nusra posted a video of him loading rockets into a large truck, and then announced his 'martyrdom'. His choice of name, 'Abu Huraira', is deeply rooted in Islamic history. The original Abu Huraira was a Companion of the Prophet and one of the most prolific narrators of his Hadith, with over 5,000 stories carrying his signature. The original Abu Huraira liked kittens and cared for them at local mosques, thus earning his name, which roughly means 'of the kitten'.[4] The 2014 American jihadi bearing the same name was featured in online forums also caressing a cat.

After this, red flags were raised throughout the West. White House National Security Council member Bruce Riedel said: 'Syria is the new epicenter for the global jihad with would-be "martyrs" arriving from across the Islamic world to fight Assad. They are getting experience in the terror arts they will bring home.'[5] The UN noted that jihadis swarming into Syria were arriving at an 'unprecedented scale' from countries that had not previously contributed to global terrorism. The UN put the number at 15,000 and said that this was 'many times the size of the cumulative numbers of foreign terrorist fighters between 1990 and 2010.'[6] Countries like France, Great Britain and Saudi Arabia, which had previously gathered under the banner of 'Friends of Syria', bankrolling several Syrian rebel factions and embracing the Syrian political opposition, suddenly began to recalculate, seeing that the 'Syrian Revolution' had gone horribly wrong. EU countries in the 'Friends of Syria' consortium began to worry about returning jihadis, while Saudi Arabia feared the destabilizing effect of ISIS's ideology on its own society. But by 2013 this policy began to change. Saudi Arabia's highest religious authority, the Grand Mufti Abdul-Aziz al-Sheikh, has tried to talk young Saudis out of taking up the battle. 'This is wrong. It's not obligatory. I do not advise you to go there. What they [Syrian rebels] want from you is your prayer. There are feuding factions and one should not go there.'[7] The UK police went as far as to ask Muslim mothers to dissuade their children from going to Syria. This was officially passed as Operation Mum in April 2014.[8] At least four fathers (three Belgians and a Russian) have travelled to northern Syria to bring their sons back home.[9]

In January 2014, a European jihadi was arrested in Malaga, having just returned from Syria. In April, Spain arrested an Algerian-French man with dual citizenship who also had been in Syria, recruiting Europeans into both ISIS and Jabhat al-Nusra. Neither tried to hide their affiliations, showing up with their long beards and wearing short, white Muslim garb. In mid-March 2014, Spanish and Moroccan security targeted al-Qaeda recruiting networks and arrested four suspected members in Spain and three in Morocco. The network has spread far and wide, across Belgium, France, Tunisia, Turkey, Libya, Mali, Indonesia and, of course, Syria. In May 2014, Norway arrested three citizens from Oslo suspected of being members of ISIS. Two of them were Kosovars and one was Somali. Great Britain also arrested a former Guantanamo detainee for having attended a terrorist training camp in Syria. The EU's Director of Justice and Home Affairs estimated that 3,000 EU citizens were fighting in Syria, with the highest number coming from France.[10] The French Foreign Minister Laurent Fabius has put the number of Frenchmen at an estimated 500.[11] The Norwegian police estimated that 40 Norwegians were fighting in Syria. Five of them were officially declared dead in November 2013.

Many think-tanks and media outlets have speculated about the actual number of foreign fighters in Syria. Nobody has been able to give exact figures, since many foreigners made the trip using fake passports. Many were EU citizens with Muslim roots, usually second- or third-generation Arab emigrants. Many were Europeans, either by birth or immigration, shown clearly by their blue eyes and light-coloured hair. The Syrian government has a full log at its official archive in Damascus, which it presented to the United Nations. According to its data, the number of foreign troops currently engaged in the Syrian battlefield stands at a staggering 25,000. This is higher than any figure reported by the UN or jihadi-monitoring agencies. Historians must treat it with a pinch of salt, but at the same time it cannot be ignored. 'In total, they come from 80 countries around the world.' Only 5 per cent are currently languishing in Syrian jails, and just 7 per cent have been killed, either by the Syrian army, the US-led coalition or by rival rebel factions.

The average age of foreign fighters stands at 25. Most were children in 2001 when 9/11 happened. Nearly 60 per cent of them are single when they arrive in Syria. Most have married into local communities after setting up base. Many come from Muslim families. Traces of a troubled past can be found in most – a complicated relationship with parents, an abusive stepfather/mother, a failed love story or a crash in lifestyle due to economic hardship. None of the European jihadis, it must be noted, had ever met any of the legendary figures in global jihad: Abdullah Azzam, Osama bin Laden or the two Abu Musaabs. Abu Amro al-Filastini, a part-time medic, part-time jihadi with Jabhat al-Nusra, reveals a very interesting fact. He claims that foreign fighters who don't speak Arabic are generally perceived as gullible and naïve. Syrian jihadis see them as 'imported helpers' but never as committed to the cause as the Syrians themselves. This has resulted in something of a superiority complex in jihadi circles: Syrians vs non-Syrians.

> Some have been ripped off, charged astronomical sums for items that cost a fraction of what they are asked to pay in hard currency. Others are mocked with sarcastic Arabic jokes, and some of our brothers, sadly, get a good laugh at seeing foreigners completely dumbfounded at what is being said about them. Being polite, they just laugh with the crowd.

Arabs get a good laugh out of the entire scene. It must be noted that local fighters are resentful of the foreigners, who are better paid and better housed on the orders of the caliph. Foreign fighters get to live in cities where coalition air strikes are rare because of the high density of civilians, while local fighters are housed in the al-Raqqa countryside. The coalition has tried so far to avoid major civilian casualties, refraining from bombing any targets in densely populated areas, something that ISIS is exploiting rather successfully.

ISIS of course differentiates between two kinds of foreign fighters. Beneath all the layers of Islamic equality, ISIS is actually a very racist organization. The term 'foreigner' is applied both to non-Arabs, and to those Arabs who are neither Syrian nor Iraqi, who are the crux of ISIS. There are huge differences in how ISIS treats different kinds of foreigners. Europeans and North Americans are lumped into one group, and 'other foreigners' are put in another: Chinese, Indian, Nigerian, Pakistani and Afghan. To some local fighters, 'foreign fighters' can also refer to Algerians, Libyans, Sudanese and Yemeni fighters. The ones sheltered from battle, because of their know-how and experience in different fields, are the Europeans. ISIS prefers to keep them for media, engineering and technical affairs, and opts to send other 'foreigners' to war. On the battlefield, those with the least experience and the highest numbers (Syrian locals of civilian background, Sudanese, Nigerians) are ordered to the front lines. These frontline foot soldiers are the ones to die first. They are followed by Arab fighters with battle experience from Syria and Iraq. The last line is composed of and commanded by Syrian jihadis.

TRICKED INTO SUICIDE

Abu Amro al-Filastini, an ISIS fighter originally from the suburbs of Haifa in Palestine who grew up in Yarmouk in Damascus, points out that those who carry out suicide operations on ISIS's behalf are not always aware of what they are doing.

> Many are asked to run an errand, like delivering a bundle of papers, or picking up a parcel from a specific location. They are given a car to do the job, unaware that it is loaded with dynamite. When reaching the specific

target, be it an army checkpoint, a government office, or a café, they are asked to make a phone call so that somebody can meet them and collect the item. The minute they dial the number, the car explodes – pre-set automatic detonation.

Then they are hailed as 'glorious martyrs' in YouTube videos and online propaganda. Abu Amro claims that this is how the American citizen of Jordanian descent, Moner Mohammad Abusalha (aka Abu Huraira al-Amriki), died in Idlib.

One Arab fighter from Egypt gave another very haunting assessment of these foreign jihadis. 'They have no clue what they are doing,' he exclaimed via Skype from metropolitan Aleppo. He cites 'manipulation, hypnotization and blackmailing' as common tools used for recruiting European jihadis. When arriving in Syria, they are at first attracted with ordinary yet well-paid jobs and welcomed with open arms. When some decide that they have had enough and that it is now time to leave, they are prevented from doing so. Buses are not allowed to carry ISIS fighters outside their camps without the official approval of their commanders.

Their travel documents are confiscated by whoever is in charge of their unit. They are told that if they return to Europe, they will be killed by Western security agencies. Some are told that they can go back but only if they leave behind their wives and children, who will be 'given' to the *mujahideen*, as spoils of war. Abandoning a battlefield is a sin, after all, and no punishment is too harsh for those who sin.

Abu Amro confirms that at least two Frenchmen and one Lithuanian have been shot by ISIS for expressing a desire to return home.

PUNISHMENT BY *JINN*

One remarkable form of punishment to discourage jihadis from walking out on ISIS has been the use of *jinn* – supernatural creatures in

Islamic mythology who inhabit an unseen world. Their universe is beyond the one known to human beings and they can only be seen by certain animals. They are mentioned frequently in the Qur'an, with the 72nd Sura, *Surat al-Jinn*, dedicated fully to them. Islam says that *jinn* can and do interact physically with people, and that, like people, they can be good, evil or a combination of both. Generally, iniquitous *jinn* work against the goodness of angels. This is equal to demons in Christian culture. They travel long distances within seconds and settle in remote areas like farms, in caves and on mountains. *Jinn* are made of smokeless fire and they creep into cities, homes and into people's souls. Only when obsessed with a *jinni* (singular) can human beings see them, and this usually comes in the form of nightmares.

Jihadis are trained to embrace ISIS philosophy by reading books, digesting literature, listening to sermons and watching videos. Once the recruits are fully brainwashed, ISIS veterans start captivating them with *jinn*. It is a combination of black magic, hypnosis and psychological warfare all in one. The *jinn* are asked to torment young rebels in doubt, or those searching for a way out of ISIS, through metaphysical and psychological means. This applies to everybody – European and Arabs alike.

> The recruit hallucinates and starts seeing the *jinn* in the form of everybody around him; even his children and wives are transformed into demons. Any person inhabited by *jinn* will go into acute depression, distancing himself from everybody and everything. The *jinn* inflict both psychological and physical pain, and can order body parts to stop functioning completely. Some *jinn* have incapacitated the hands and feet of our comrades. Some have eaten away at the mind and soul. They strangle people at night; prevent them from sleeping, digesting and even going to the bathroom.

The narrator of this tale tells it with a completely straight face, fully convinced of ISIS's ability to control the underworld. 'The *jinn* are very, very powerful.' He mentions one case, where a young foreign jihadi was cursed with the disappearance of water. Whenever he picked up a bottle to drink, or turned on a tap to bathe or clean, the water would evaporate into thin air – thanks to the *jinni*'s command. The antidote for *jinn* varies, from magicians and sorceresses to pious men who read passages from the Qur'an to ward off the malice-filled *jinn*. Crooks have long maintained that *jinn* love to eat red mercury, because it gives them power and 'restores them to their youthful days'. ISIS only 'releases' the *jinn* after rebels in doubt are fully under their control: ready to fight, die – and slit throats – on their behalf. The *jinni* master in ISIS is a Moroccan zealot named Abu Yehya al-Maghribi.

ARAB JIHADIS

Arab jihadis from Sunni Arab countries account for a sizeable contingent of ISIS's foreign legions. The largest single Arab community of foreign jihadis in Syria, unsurprisingly, comes from Iraq, whose numbers vacillate, as the borders between the two countries have been largely erased by ISIS. Second is Tunisia, with 3,000 fighters as of late 2014, and Saudi Arabia is third, with 2,500 fighters. Fourth in rank is Jordan, with 2,000 fighters.[12] One of the Jordanian rebels was actually a captain in his country's air force before he defected in 2013 to join Jabhat al-Nusra in Syria. According to Jordanian jihadi leader Mohammad al-Shalabi (aka Abu Sayyaf), more than 700 Jordanian fighters came to Syria in 2014. In one of the documents presented to the UN, the Syrian government noted that it had arrested 26 al-Qaeda militants and 19 of them were from Tunisia.[13] In May 2013, the Tunisian foreign minister Othmane Jarandi admitted that 800 of his countrymen were actually fighting in Syria. A spokesman for the interim Tunisian president, Moncef Marzouki, himself a supporter of the Arab Spring, tried to find excuses, saying: 'Our youth have good intentions, but it is possible they fell into the hands of manipulators.'

Morocco comes in fifth with 1,000 jihadis, followed by Lebanon with 900 fighters – which is exceptionally high considering the country's small size. With regard to Lebanon, only Sunni Muslim jihadis fighting alongside the rebels are counted in government records. This number doesn't include Shi'i warriors from Hizbullah, who fight with the Syrian army and are estimated at around 10,000. Lebanese jihadis are mainly from the al-Qaeda-inspired Fateh al-Islam, which went to war against Lebanese officialdom in 2008 and was flushed out of Tripoli by the Lebanese army. A Tripoli-based ranking city cleric named Sheikh Masen al-Mohammad didn't hide his encouragement of the Lebanese jihadis: 'The struggle for freedom in Syria is our own struggle for freedom. We Lebanese are part of the Syrian Revolution, part of the rebellion.' He accused President Bashar al-Assad of being an infidel, adding: 'It is the duty of every Muslim, every Arab to fight the infidels. There is a holy war in Syria and the young men there are conducting jihad for blood, for honour, for freedom, and for dignity.'[14] Counter-intelligence between Syria and Hizbullah is high, explaining why Lebanese jihadis are found in high numbers in Syrian jails. They have been the easiest to track and kill by Syrian security.

The Libyan rebels based in Syria are led by a 41-year-old ex-brigade commander from the Libyan Revolution named Abdul-Mehdi al-Harati. Collectively, they number approximately 650–700 trained fighters. All of them have a certain level of military experience from the Libyan Revolution, and most are in their early to mid-thirties.[15] They have mainly been trained to use hand grenades and rocket propellers. Before the outbreak of the so-called 'Arab Spring' in December 2010, their commander al-Harati lived in Dublin with his Irish wife, teaching Arabic to Arab émigrés. He returned to Tripoli when an uprising erupted against Libyan leader Muammar al-Gaddafi in February 2011. He later became second-in-command of the Tripoli Military Council. When burglars broke into his home in Ireland, they stole expensive jewels and 200,000 euros. Irish authorities inquired about the substantial amount of cash. Al-Harati said that it had been given to him by the CIA to help topple Colonel Gaddafi.[16] Al-Harati left the Tripoli Council in October 2011 and went on a fact-finding mission to Syria.

He briefly formed his own militia, Liwaa al-Umma, but soon it merged with the Free Syrian Army. When arriving in Syria, he brought along money, cash and men-in-arms fleeing post-Gaddafi Libya. At least 5 per cent of the weapons seized from rebel strongholds, confirmed the Syrian security source, were all traced back directly to Libya. Al-Harati smuggled them into Syria in vegetable containers and on mules, via the 605 Syrian–Iraqi borders. According to Syrian sources, he doesn't reside permanently in Syria but comes and goes frequently to Libya.

Egypt ranks way behind Libya in its contribution to jihadism in Syria. Although repeated attempts were made by the Egyptian Brotherhood to nudge its cadres into the Syrian jihad, very few actually made the journey. Syrian sources put the number of Egyptians at a mere 200–250. Unlike their neighbouring Libyans, they are poorly trained and poorly equipped. Ranking further behind on the jihadi spectrum are Yemen, Somalia and Sudan with 100 fighters each, followed by Bahrain and Kuwait with 25 fighters. Palestinians have dotted the Syrian landscape and have fought on both sides of the conflict. Hamas militias aided the rebels, while pro-Assad Palestinians, loyal to Ahmad Jibril, fought alongside the Syrian army. Within the rebel community, Palestinian sub-groups could be found in the Lebanese and Jordanian rebel communities. These rebels came with varying degrees of experience, as well as with an axe to grind with Damascus, Hizbullah and their Iranian and Russian allies. According to Syrian official sources, approximately 700 of them were killed during the year 2014.

WESTERN WARRIORS

European fighters are plentiful in the Syrian jihadi war. The Quilliam Foundation puts the number of foreign fighters from Europe at 16,000.[17] The number of French jihadis has increased by 69.9 per cent between 2003 and 2014. The French prime minister, Manuel Valls, said that 90 Frenchmen have died in Syria and Iraq since the start of the conflict in 2011.[18] Germans have increased on the Syrian battlefield by 66.7 per cent (a total of 400 people). Roughly 600–700 male fighters come from Great Britain, followed by France and Turkey with approximately 400 fighters each. Britain's Home Secretary, Theresa May, recently said that '400 UK-linked individuals' have joined ISIS in Syria.[19] The International Centre for the Study of Radicalisation, based at King's College London, assessed that up to 366 British citizens had been involved in the war in Syria as of December 2013.[20] In October 2014, the Metropolitan Police Commissioner Bernard Hogan-Howe said:

> We still have an average of five people joining them [ISIS] a week. Five a week doesn't sound much but when you realise there are 50 weeks in a year, 250 more would be 50 per cent more than we think have gone already. [...] Those are the ones that we believe have gone. There may be many more who set out to travel to another country and meandered over to Syria and Iraq in a way that is not always possible to spot when you have failed states and leaky borders.[21]

Fourth on the list is Spain with roughly 300 jihadis. Fifth is Bosnia with 162 Islamists, and then Belgium with 212 Islamists, followed by Germany with 168 Islamists. The United States comes midway, with approximately 100 fighters, followed by Canada (70–75 men), Italy (35) and Finland (20). Scandinavian rebels are fewer: Sweden (80), Denmark (70) and Norway (40). Ireland has 21 rebels in Syria, and Austria has 60. In the first half of 2012, approximately 700–1,400 foreigners entered Syria through the Iraqi, Turkish and Jordanian borders.

LOOSE BORDERS

The biggest influx was via Turkey and Iraq, due to their extensive borders. Turkey was unwilling to stem the flow of these foreigners into Syria, and the situation in Iraq is more complex as ISIS has destroyed the borders between the two countries. The jihadis move back and forth into Syria almost with impunity. The Norwegian Defence Research Establishment estimated that in 2013 between 1,132 and 1,707 Europeans from 12 countries had joined the fight in Syria. The majority were from France (200–400), Great Britain (200–300) and Belgium (100–300). The lack of experience was noteworthy, given that of the 600 reported 'martyrs' in the first six months of 2013, less than 20 were experienced fighters from earlier battles in Afghanistan and Libya.

Because they speak little Arabic, however, these foreign fighters are forced to undergo major preparation before officially being admitted into jihadi groups like Jabhat al-Nusra or ISIS. First, fighters have to hand in all of their personal documents to the emir and then do 30–45 days of training. Exemptions are granted to jihadi veterans who have fought previously either in Chechnya or Afghanistan. Those exempted have to prove that they have at least one year's experience in the battlefield – any battlefield. Restrictions are placed on all of them; foreign jihadis are not allowed to travel outside Syria for the first four months of their enrolment. During this time a new recruit is watched closely for discipline, willpower and behaviour. Once they are given clearance, they can leave for personal reasons, but only after submitting a written application to the emir. They have to explain where they are going, the reasons for their departure and when exactly they will be returning.

Jabhat al-Nusra and ISIS pay for everything, starting with the foreign fighters' accommodation, food and expenses, including their one-way ticket to Syria. The leadership of *al-Muhajireen* (immigrants) consists of a military command, a Shari'a Committee, a Shura Council and a media arm – Liwa al-Muhajireen al-Ilami. This first emerged during the Bosnian War in 1992–5, and was revived in Syria after 2011. The Taliban has certainly encouraged fighters to travel to the Middle East and set up camps in northern Syria. According to Taliban commanders in Pakistan, the men were sent because 'our Arab brothers have come here for our support, we are bound to help them in their respective countries.'[22] The call was heard by jihadis worldwide.

CHINESE JIHADIS

Most of the material of the Western media focuses on Chechen and European foreign fighters, bypassing the Chinese factor in the Syrian battlefield. Middle Eastern Muslims, however, are of course linked to the Uyghurs of China by a common religion. The Uyghurs are a conservative Sunni Muslim ethnic group living in Eastern and Central Asia, mainly concentrated in China, where they are recognized as one of the 56 ethnic minorities. Islamic media, for example, paid great attention to Uyghur riots in Xinjiang's capital, Urumqi, on 5 July 2009. The Chinese authorities imposed a year-long communication blackout in Xinjiang, pushing its plight into the international spotlight. The Egyptian and Syrian Muslim Brotherhood compared the Chinese government to Husni Mubarak and Bashar al-Assad. The Turkish prime minister Recep Tayyip Erdogan said that China was 'almost committing genocide' in Xinjiang. Al-Qaeda threatened to carry out attacks against Chinese targets worldwide.[23] In August 2009, al-Qaeda described the Chinese 'regime' as being similar to the Zionist one in Israel, adding that Xinjiang was the Muslim world's 'forgotten wound'.[24]

China, along with Russia and Iran, has stood firmly behind the Syrian government since 2011. Its government claims that since 2012, Uyghur militants from Xinjiang have been fighting with rebels against the Syrian army.[25] In the summer of 2012, China said that an Istanbul-educated Uyghur militant who fought with the Free Syrian Army in Aleppo had returned to Xinjiang. He was arrested while planning to carry out terrorist attacks against the Chinese government. The Syrian battlefield has radicalized Chinese Muslim fighters, no doubt, and given them a wide network of allies and friends, who may be used in future years to spread havoc in China itself. Additionally, it has helped to internationalize the Xinjiang issue among jihadis and prompt them to travel to China – either when the jihadi war in Syria fails, or if it succeeds.

ISIS's predecessor, al-Qaeda in Iraq (AQI), expressed public

support for the Uyghur-led Turkistan Islamic Party (TIP), an affiliate of the Taliban and the Islamic Movement of Uzbekistan (IMU)
in Pakistan.[26] The TIP, like al-Qaeda, has declared its ambition to set
up an Islamic caliphate across Central Asia and to root out Chinese
communism. Among other things, the TIP accuses the Chinese government of assassinating Islamic scholars and of banning the hijab
for Chinese Muslim women. In February 2012, TIP carried out an
attack in Yecheng, 240 km north of Xinjiang's border with Pakistan,
where a group of Uyghurs killed up to 24 civilians in a commercial area
frequented by Chinese citizens.[27] On 1 October 2012, TIP claimed
responsibility for a motorcycle-borne suicide attack in Yecheng, which
led to the death of 21 border police.[28] When the Syrian war started,
TIP announced that it would be sending fighters to Syria. 'If China
has the right to support Bashar al-Assad in Syria, we have the full right
to support our proud Muslim Syrian people.'[29] Months later, Jabhat
al-Nusra started posting videos on YouTube showing Chinese rebels
side-by-side with their Syrian comrades. According to official Chinese
estimates, up to 100 Uyghurs travelled to Syria via Turkey, after having
received sophisticated military training in Pakistan.[30] In addition to
the Uyghurs, there are also a number of other Central Asians and
Caucasus natives fighting in Syria.

As well as Chinese rebels, Uzbeks have helped smuggle rebels
through the Syrian–Turkish border, and one of them has been leading an Islamic brigade in Aleppo since 2012.[31] Kyrgyzstan has said
that around 15 youths from the south of the country, including ethnic
Kyrgyz, Uzbeks and Tajiks, have also travelled to Turkey to fight in
Syria.[32] Syrian sources confirm that 30 Tajik fighters have crossed
the border from Turkey and eight Kazakh jihadis were arrested in
July 2013. They add that Muslim Tatars from Russia have shown up
in Aleppo, leading one of the numerous immigrant brigades under
Yusuf al-Sini, a Chinese convert to Islam. Another Chinese jihadi,
identified as Bo Wang, appears in a YouTube video apologizing to the
Syrian people for his country's support of Bashar al-Assad. He warns
Beijing to 'immediately stop all forms of aid to Assad' and urges fellow

Chinese Muslims to fight the 'infidels' in Syria. Azerbaijani jihadis have also been seen in Syria.

CHECHEN REBELS

The native Chechen community is one of the smallest, but most effective, of the foreign jihadi populations in the Syrian battlefield. Despite their low numbers, they are also the group to have received the most media attention since 2012. Rebel sources claim that Chechen fighters in Syria total 1,500, while Syrian officialdom puts the number at anywhere between 1,500 and 2,000. What we know for sure is that since the outbreak of hostilities in March 2011, approximately 500 North Caucasians have been killed in Syria. After the collapse of the Soviet Union, many of them left the North Caucasus to study Arabic and Islamic Shari'a in the Middle East. It was a means of rediscovering their Islamic identity and being taught by those who spoke the language of the Holy Qur'an. When the Arab Spring broke out, many were already based in Syria and Lebanon, and they played a crucial role in convincing others to come and join them. Returning home was impossible, after all, because the pro-Russian government of Ramzan Kadyrov was still pursuing all those allied to the Chechen independent movement. As a result, Syria became their new home, and their new battlefield.

The most famous Chechen to join the jihadi war was Omar al-Shishani. Born Tarkhan Batirashvili in 1986, he hails from the remote Pankisi Gorge in north-east Georgia. He served in the US-trained Georgian army and was posted in the disputed republic of Abkhazia from 2006–7. Symptoms of tuberculosis led to his discharge, and he was declared unfit for military battle. In 2010, he was arrested for the illegal purchase and storage of arms. Upon his release he went to Egypt, then Turkey, ending up in Syria in 2012. He immediately attracted the attention of Abu Bakr al-Baghdadi, who recruited him into ISIS and made him commander of its Northern Front. Three top Chechen jihadis followed in October 2013. They were Emir Muslim Margoshvili, Emir Seifullah (Ruslan Machaliashvili) and Abu

Musaaba.[33] These were experienced men in their early fifties, who had led battles against superior armies in Chechnya and Dagestan. Emir Seifullah was a protégé of Omar al-Shishani, who defected in September 2013 to form his own militia before officially joining Jabhat al-Nusra in December 2013.

Al-Baghdadi liked Omar al-Shishani because he was a fierce fighter and because he was not Syrian. As he spoke only a little Arabic, the chances of him staging an internal coup within ISIS were close to zero. He didn't aspire to rule ISIS territory in Syria. Additionally, al-Baghdadi knew that al-Shishani's jihadi credentials were much stronger than his. Instead of going on the offensive, he decided to make a close ally out of him – in anticipation of morphing him into a subordinate. Apart from al-Baghdadi's support and the inflated media attention he has received, Omar al-Shishani commanded a very thin power base within the rebel community in Syria. He complained that the Syrian jihadis had been 'ungrateful' and saw him as an 'imported alien' who came to teach them how to do things.

Al-Shishani's allegiance to ISIS alienated his closest supporters. In late 2013, his deputy commander Salahuddin al-Shishani denounced him and joined Abu Mohammad al-Golani in Jabhat al-Nusra. As Murad Batal al-Shishani describes in an article for *Terrorism Monitor*, 'While acknowledging that jihad is "easier in the Levant," Salahudeen said "it's better to wage jihad in the Caucasus, where Moscow and the Russian infidels fought us for centuries." Salahudeen also expanded on the priority that must be given to the jihad back home'.[34]

In March 2013, Omar al-Shishani's Brigade of Migrants merged with Kata'ibat al-Khattab and the Phalanges of Muhammad army.[35] Al-Khattab is not in reference to the second Muslim caliph Umar ibn al-Khattab but to a Saudi jihadi, Samir Saleh Abdullah al-Suwailem (aka Amir al-Khattab). He led the Arab jihadis in Chechnya until Russian security services poisoned him in 2002. The two small groups pledged their allegiance to Omar al-Shishani, taking up the name Jaysh al-Muhajireen wal-Ansar (Army of Migrants and Supporters). The Russians undoubtedly magnified this threat as, since 1999, they had been keen to find connections between Chechens and al-Qaeda. President Vladimir Putin wanted the world to believe that he was fighting international terrorism and not just Chechen rebels. Such an argument suited him well because it found answers to those questioning the superiority of the Russian army. That once-glorious army was being threatened by a small handful of Muslim rebels. Surely – so Moscow believed – the rebels must be connected to a far superior force. Al-Qaeda was gracing the world stage, and it was preferable for Russia to link them to Osama bin Laden.

The chance for a real affiliation came many years later, after Bin Laden's death in 2011. His deputy and successor Ayman al-Zawahiri knew plenty about the Chechen plight, through his own first-hand experience. Al-Zawahiri himself had visited the North Caucasus, where he was arrested by the Russians and deported. He even wrote a memoir about that period of his life. He had a sincere affection and respect for Chechen fighters, renowned for their ferocity, tenacity and military prowess as they have been fighting the Russian Empire in its various manifestations for centuries. The leader of the Caucasus Emirate, Sheikh Abu Muhammad, took the side of al-Zawahiri and al-Golani in their dispute with al-Baghdadi's ISIS. In fact, Sheikh Abu Muhammad called al-Zawahiri 'our sheikh'. Additionally, he criticized Omar al-Shishani's support of ISIS, asking him to refrain from speaking to the media since he possessed a 'poor command of the Russian and Arabic languages.' Abu Muhammad himself had lived in Syria.

CORRUPTING THE JIHADI COMMUNITY

The foreign jihadi element in the Syrian war is one that continues to attract plenty of media attention. Its direct ramifications are yet to be felt throughout Asia, Europe and the Balkans. The Syrian opposition was once sceptical of the existence of large numbers of foreign jihadis. Then they treated them royally, seeing them as a positive addition to the Syrian uprising. When beheading became common, and panic spread throughout Western Europe, the opposition distanced itself completely, asking these rebels to leave Syria. But by then it was already too late.

Those who survived the probation periods and the bombs of the Syrian army and the United States had started to get used to their new lives in Syria. Omar al-Shishani, for example, lived at one point in a luxurious two-floor villa in Hreitan, near Aleppo. It was confiscated from a wealthy Aleppine businessman, who ironically was also named Omar. When he came back to visit his home, he was stunned to find bearded guards from the Caucasus guarding its huge wooden doors with iron fittings. 'This is the home of Omar al-Shishani', they said to him, turning him away at gunpoint. Omar al-Shishani called him in, however, to hear his complaint. The businessman found that a decorator had been there and that the furniture and curtains had been replaced. Omar al-Shishani was enjoying the villa's jacuzzi but wanted to know why the chimney was not working. A jihadi indulging himself with such luxuries is not one passing in transit through Syria. This is someone who plans to spend a lifetime in ISIS-held territory.

Khaled al-Beel, who owns a mobile phone shop not far from Omar al-Shishani's new villa, spoke about the kind of life the foreign *mujahideen* were leading.

> We are told that once the war ends, these foreigners will pack up and leave. They cannot sustain themselves in times of peace. Society will excommunicate them. But the longer the war drags, the more entrenched they are becoming in Syrian society.

Al-Beel adds that the wives of these jihadis have set up their own communities, organizing weekly gatherings on Friday mornings. 'They do this early, before their husbands go off to prayer.' These women, from a variety of foreign countries, sip tea, gossip about social affairs, and sometimes go as far as playing cards or Scrabble.

Al-Beel, a young 25-year-old university dropout, who was studying electrical engineering prior to 2011, adds: 'I know these people well. They live in my neighbourhood and come to my shop to update their iPhones and to download applications. What they ban on check-points, like *Diamond Rush* and *Angry Birds*, are allowed inside their homes.' Al-Beel says that he sold ten iPhone 6s in the last two months of 2014, for US$800 each. 'They pay better than Syrian customers,' he chuckles. 'Early on, they didn't pay for anything. They just walked in with their rifles strapped on their shoulder and took whatever they coveted. Now they pay for things, which is good.' Al-Beel makes an interesting observation. The foreign jihadis have started to frame photos of their families on the walls of their new homes. 'You don't do that when you are in transit.' The previous lack of home decoration said something about the foreigners. Bare walls reminded them that these were temporary lodgings. Decorated ones with framed photos say the exact opposite.

NO PASSPORTS

In one of its propaganda videos of 2014, ISIS showed a group of foreign fighters gathered around a bonfire. It looked like a scene from medieval Europe. One by one, the fighters showed their passport to the camera and then threw it into the flames, almost with a vengeance. In doing so, they made a pledge of faith to their new country, the Islamic State. Some of the passports in the video were easily recogniz-able: green Saudi, burgundy British and navy blue Jordanian. The fighters' former lives were gone, and so were their borders and pass-ports. There is no way back. There is only one state for these fighters now, and it is that of Abu Bakr al-Baghdadi. One Canadian gave an ad hoc speech in English: 'This is a message to Canada and all American powers: we will come and we will destroy you!' The Jordanian spoke next: 'I say to the tyrant of Jordan [King Abdullah II]: we are the descendants of Abu Musaab al-Zarqawi and we are coming to kill you!' Also among the passports tossed into the flames were those of Bahrain, Egypt and Chechnya.

The purpose of the film was multifaceted. First, ISIS wanted to make one thing clear: in the absence of legitimate officialdom, ISIS was the only true state in the so-called Arab world. Its capital was al-Raqqa, its army was ISIS and its borders defined by whatever territory was under ISIS's control. Affiliation to anything else was standing on the wrong side of history. Second, ISIS wanted to further threaten the countries of the international coalition, choosing to show fighters of the very same nationalities as those bombing the Islamic State by air. Third and more importantly, ISIS was trying to show how much of an international organization it had become. This inflated sense of ego is a developing story in ISIS-led territory. They also don't like to be referred to as an Iraqi or Syrian organization any more. That too is now becoming too small for their ambition, both territorially and demographically. ISIS is very proud of its British, French and American members. They are the jewel in the crown of the terror organization, and they will take it from the level of militia to that of a nation state. ISIS is willing to give them more than just passports in return for what it expects from them as nation-builders in years to come.

NINE

Women in ISIS

FATIMA SOBBED HER HEART OUT ON THE NIGHT SHE ARRIVED
in al-Raqqa. The reality was not what she had expected. She collapsed
onto her purple lace bedcover, with fittings made exclusively for her
wedding night. Fatima was born in Cairo in 1990 but had been shuf-
fled frequently in life between Egypt and Moscow. Her father had
been a flight attendant for Egyptian Airways. The parents returned to
Egypt in the late 1980s, after her father's retirement. Then the family
lived for a brief period in post-Soviet Russia, where her father had
tried to set up a small business. Fatima was enrolled at an elemen-
tary school and she picked up conversational Russian. She wore the
Islamic headscarf from a relatively young age, taking after both of her
Egyptian grandmothers. At the age of 16, she met a young Palestinian
from Syria through an online forum. Mourad, who was a member of
Yasser Arafat's Fateh Movement, was two years her senior and was
studying law at Damascus University. He lived on 30th Street in the
Yarmouk camp in the Syrian capital. Mourad was religiously strict and
came from a well-to-do family. His father traded in used cars, making
enough money to buy him a brand-new one at the age of 18. It was a
life of relative comfort and privilege. 'The best thing about you is your
hijab,' he wrote to her, 'you look so beautiful with it.' Weeks after
they started dating, Facebook came to life in Syria and Egypt, taking
the relationship to new heights. In 2011, they switched to Viber – an
immensely popular instant messaging and voice-over IP application

for smartphones. The relationship was celibate. Very little photo exchange. No cybersex.

After hostilities started in Syria, Mourad asked to be transferred to Aleppo University, claiming that it was safer there. He was anti-Assad to the bone and wanted to escape harm's way in the Syrian capital during the difficult first months of the Syrian uprising. Fatima encouraged him, seeing the chaos in her own city after the resignation of Husni Mubarak that February. Then something started to change. Mourad was rarely online and wouldn't pick up the phone that frequently. He blamed it on the bad internet connection and electricity cuts, but Fatima knew better. When she demanded an explanation, Mourad replied that they had to stop speaking to each other because, being out of wedlock, their relationship was '*haram*'. Geography separated them, she tried explaining, as did her college education, but Mourad would not listen. She loved him dearly and didn't want to lose him but all of that didn't matter. He became erratic, loud and often rude, using swear words that he would never have uttered before starting his jihadi experience. He also became a chain-smoker, in spite of the fact that cigarettes are not allowed in Salafi communities. A few months later Mourad dropped out of university and moved to Idlib, joining the rebel forces of Hassan Abboud, known as *Ahrar al-Sham* (Free Men of the Levant). The further he drifted into Syrian jihad, the more Fatima feared that she would lose him forever. Fatima decided to visit Mourad and to get married secretly, without her parents' permission. She would then travel back to Cairo and visit him when possible, waiting for the Syrian war to end and for them to settle properly, either in Egypt or Syria. Mourad moved to al-Raqqa in April 2013. When ISIS took over the city in 2014, he pledged his allegiance to Abu Bakr al-Baghdadi and, given his knowledge of legal affairs, was appointed scribe at ISIS's al-Raqqa *Diwan*.

By the time Fatima first met him in person in November 2014, Mourad was wearing a short *galabiya* (traditional Arabic gown), a white cap typical of mosque-goers, and carrying a Kalashnikov. He had grown a thick black beard, whitened at the corners, which made him look older than his years. Fatima had been through a painfully long journey, travelling from Cairo to Istanbul and then crossing the border by bus, where a Syrian car had driven her into ISIS territory to meet her husband. She had lied to her parents, saying that she was on a field trip with friends. The picturesque image Fatima had kept of Mourad was shattered in an instant. So also was all the fantasy that came with high-school romances – there was no embrace sweeping her off the ground, no kisses of passion and no merry-go-round giggles. Fatima was wearing jeans and blue Converse sneakers with big white shoelaces. She was in the middle of nowhere, having never visited Syria before. Mourad didn't even shake her hand – let alone kiss her – and was as stiff as a log. Though cordial, he didn't want to make any physical contact until the marriage was officially authenticated by one of the sheikhs of ISIS. After the brief ceremony had taken place, Mourad started to smile and Fatima was relieved. This was the Mourad she knew and had met through online chats years ago. That Mourad was funny and full of life. The old Mourad had wanted to become a commercial lawyer one day, working with international firms. However, this new Mourad was only interested in one thing: arms, jihad and the future of ISIS.

On the night of their marriage, Mourad raped Fatima. He raped her over and over, and when he had finished, he broke into hysterical tears, apologising and weeping like a child. Fatima tried to find excuses for her young husband: 'He's been here all alone living in very hard circumstances, away from his university and family. He and the fighters haven't seen a woman in ages.' He stopped calling her by her first name and chose 'Um Mahmud' as her new name. Mahmud was the name of his father, and custom in Arab societies dictated that eldest boys would name their first male child after their father. Mourad was obviously going through a troubled experience and needed care, if not professional counselling. Fatima felt it was her duty to stand by him, but the madness did not stop. Days after their first encounter, Mourad showed up at midday at the couple's new apartment, overlooking a main street in al-Raqqa. It was a modern apartment with banana-yellow paint and green shutters. Fatima hadn't left the house since arriving from Egypt, refusing to go online so that her family couldn't find out her GPS location. Instead she texted them saying that she was safe. Mourad handed her a rifle and black armband, saying: 'Tomorrow, you have to join the Khansaa Brigade!' This was the all-woman police force created by Abu Bakr al-Baghdadi to patrol the streets of al-Raqqa. Fatima was terrified by the thought and by the damaged man standing before her. She was too afraid to challenge him but gathered the courage to speak up, claiming that she had never carried a gun in her life. 'Don't worry; we will teach you,' Mourad replied.

Fatima did join the Khansaa Brigade, but only briefly. Six months later, Mourad unilaterally divorced her and discharged her from the Brigade. He had discovered that she was incapable of conceiving children, and there was no room for infertile women in the Islamic State. Fatima remains trapped in ISIS territory, unable to return home and unable to reveal her true identity. Her ex-husband has confiscated her passport. Fatima's story is almost identical to the hundreds of women, all grouped as 'female jihadis', whose number is mushrooming within the Islamic State. Not all of them came for the jihadi experience. Many, in fact, are victims of manipulation. Very few came to fight with ISIS. The majority are like Fatima – they came for marriage and to raise children. And not all of them are 'foreign' in the Western sense of the word. Many come from Arab countries, but they don't get as much media attention since it's much more interesting to write about a European in al-Raqqa than it is to write about an Egyptian or Moroccan 'Mrs ISIS'.

Ten per cent of the European jihadi community in Syria are women aged 18–25. The Syrian government has no official number for them and, surprisingly, nor do the rebels themselves. Both seemingly feel that because they don't engage in actual battle, these women are not worth either counting or analysing. The London-based Quilliam Foundation, however, says that 200 European females have travelled to Syria since the outbreak of the war in 2011. All of them are married to fighters either from ISIS or Jabhat al-Nusra. At least 70 of them are French, 40 are German, 60 British, 20 Belgian and 35 Dutch.[1]

All the 13 women interviewed for this book reveal a thin and cosmetic understanding of the Syrian conflict and of Islam. In fact, most of them see it in black and white: good guys vs villains; Sunnis vs Shi'a; Muslims vs Christians. With only one exception, none of the interviewees knew anything about how Salafism started in Syria back in the 1940s. Most had heard of Hama 1982, but only from their husbands *after* arriving in Syria. None of them had any previous interaction either with the Syrian Muslim Brotherhood or al-Qaeda. Only one had carried a firearm before setting foot in al-Raqqa. Interestingly, although they had memorized certain verses of the Qur'an, especially pertaining to the veil and the role of women, these interviewees had a mediocre knowledge of Islam – its history, evolution and its codes of conduct. Fatima was the exception – not the norm.

This amateur understanding of religion is common among both European men and women coming to Syria, thus making them an easy target for ISIS recruiters and the perfect frontline infantry once they've joined the ranks of the organization. Two young ISIS recruits from Birmingham, for example, ordered *Islam for Dummies* and *The Koran for Dummies* from Amazon before travelling to Syria.[2] One ISIS recruit from rural Damascus couldn't tell the difference between *masjid* and *jamee'*. In English both are translated as 'mosque', but the first, *masjid*, is only for prayer, while the second is where both prayer and lessons are held, like the Umayyad Mosque of Damascus. Another recruit, a foreign jihadi based in al-Raqqa, couldn't differentiate between the Qur'an and the *Mashaf*. Again, in English both are translated as the book of Allah. In Arabic, however, Qur'an refers to what is read, while *Mashaf* is the actual book of what was recited verbally by Muhammad and his Companions. None of ISIS's European women can read the Qur'an in Arabic. All of them rely on English translations, published years ago in Saudi Arabia. Most of what they memorize is in Arabic, however. They are trained to repeat what they hear, word for word, articulating nouns with difficulty, and then repeat the phrases again in public, like parrots.

ISIS has actually become so deeply involved with the recruitment of foreign women that it went as far as to open a 'marriage bureau' in the town of al-Bab near the border with Turkey.[3] This is where incoming Western women are registered and officially married off to their jihadi grooms. Some have developed long-distance relationships like Fatima, but many flock to the land of the caliphate having never seen their husbands-to-be, or even heard their voice. Their profiles are sketched and then described to jihadis who are searching for a wife – the couples are not allowed to see each other's faces until after the marriage ceremony is complete. Obtaining parental approval for marriage is essential in Islam. This is a sticking point that has slowed down the process, says Jennifer, the American wife of ISIS officer Zain al-Abidin al-Shami. In some cases, ISIS appoints a guardian, usually from the city's elderly community, to 'bless' the marriage. This is valid in Islam, she points out, adding that the caliph himself, Abu Bakr al-Baghdadi, has married off one of his cousins to a foreign jihadi, deputizing on behalf of her deceased father during the religious ceremony.

Before joining ISIS, these women were normal schoolgirls. Apart from high-school parties and family outings, they hadn't had much experience of the real world. They literally didn't speak the street language and had very little understanding of the tricks and tools for survival. The youngest Western girl to join ISIS was just 13 years old.[4] When being interviewed these girls sometimes giggled, often joked, and communicated via SMS with a wide assortment of emojis and smileys. They didn't sound brutal at all. On the contrary, many were very forthcoming and wanted to share their Syrian experience. All of them had got prior approval from their husbands before speaking to the author. Many were eager to dispel the cliches of the Western media. 'We are not terrorists,' smiled Aisha, the Turkish wife of a Syrian jihadi from Hama. She points to her niqab and says:

> They [critiques of Islamic codes of practice] say that our dress code is a violation of social norms. Women are not allowed to walk the streets with their face, hair and body covered. Is she allowed then to walk the streets with her face, hair and body fully uncovered? Is walking around 90 per cent naked equal to walking 90 per cent covered?

She certainly seemed more interested in making a social point and cementing a counterculture than in killing people. Aisha adds:

> We didn't come here to fight. We came for marriage and to raise children. We came to support our men in a cause that unites us all as Muslims. If you want a Western audience to understand, let's say, we are the 'cheerleaders' of ISIS. Perhaps this is a term they will understand.

Cheerleaders, however, don't spend their entire waking hours drumming up support for their teams. Once their work is done, they revert to the routines of their conventional lives. The ISIS 'cheerleaders' – though the same age as their American high-school counterparts – have different priorities and routines. These young girls are armed with tools much more powerful than fluffy pompoms and batons – their iPhones! Day and night, they manage ISIS-affiliated pages on Facebook, along with their accounts on Twitter and Instagram. They are in charge of nearly all of ISIS's online media. Although ISIS has official media channels like the Hayat Center and I'tisaam Foundation, these outlets are generally run by an older generation of obsessively bureaucratic and rigid hardliners. Their journalists and editors are all young, but the administration is usually in the hands of an elderly ISIS commander, often in his mid-fifties. 'We decided to save them from themselves,' chuckled Umm Obada, a 23-year-old British wife of ISIS commander Abu Ahmad al-Anbari from Iraq.

> Sometimes if you read what they write and close your eyes, you will think you are reading something ripped straight out of the 1960s. Basically, they preach to the converted and don't try to reach out to those who are

neutral or undecided. Deep inside, all of our men still have a small Soviet commissar or tiny Baathist inside of them.

She is referring here to Syrian and Iraqi jihadis who grew up under parallel Baath regimes in Damascus and Baghdad. ISIS has often said: 'Don't hear about us; hear from us!'[5] and these social media platforms offer an effective way for would-be jihadis or jihadi wives to speak directly to those within ISIS territory.

The material that ISIS women post on social media is cutting-edge, trendy and well planned. It is far from amateur. They reach out to both Muslim and Christian women in Europe. To marry off a jihadi is a good deed: to couple him with a non-Muslim woman who has been converted to Islam is even better. European women are addressed as 'sisters' and told that if they come to Syria their task will be marriage – not to be free sex objects for the jihadis, as some in the West have reported. 'There is no such thing as *Jihad al-Niqah*,' said Fatima, angrily brushing off accusations that women came to ISIS territory only for sex with the jihadis. *Al-Niqah* is the Qur'anic Arabic term for sex. 'Matrimony, not martyrdom,' she adds. These women are persuaded to abandon their former lives in the West, not by telling them of how sinful it is, but rather by concentrating on how different and better their new life would be under the Islamic State. Photos try to promote a sense of purpose behind marriage into the jihadi community, along with the 'honour' of raising children to become new fighters for Islam. Nothing is said about beheading, strict dress codes or the many items that women are banned from owning under the government of ISIS. Instead, they paint a rosy picture of family life under the Islamic State. Some take 'selfies' wearing camouflage outfits and carrying automatic rifles; others post photos of themselves attending wedding parties, cuddling babies, sewing winter clothes, eating ice cream and making Nutella pancakes. They also share pictures of their husbands playing snooker or sunbathing by large swimming pools, making it look like jihad is merely a 'cool vacation'. During the 2014 World Cup, they always added game-related hashtags to make sure that their posts received maximum exposure, like #Brazil2014. For Europeans like Abu Osman al-Baritani, who worked as a waiter in London, the life of jihadism painted by the social-media-savvy cheerleaders of ISIS looked pretty exciting and warm – certainly better than the dead-end job he had back home. But, in contrast to the image they try to present, the women of ISIS live the average day-to-day life of a Syrian housewife: cooking, cleaning and taking care of children, away from the glitz and glamour posted on social media.

DIARY OF A MUHAJIRAH

Aqsa Mahmood (aka Umm Layth) is the most famous ISIS woman on social media. She travelled from Glasgow to Syria in November 2013 and now blogs daily for ISIS. With more than 2,000 followers on Twitter, she started an English-language 'Diary of a Muhajirah (Migrant)'. Reading like a *Lonely Planet* travel guide, it offers free-of-charge advice on how to reach Syria, how to bargain in its markets and what to expect from its peoples. One section is titled, 'Ask me Anything'. Since European parents usually oppose their daughter's decision to marry into an ISIS family, Umm Layth gives advice on how to convince them. 'Your love for Allah comes before anything and everything,' she reminds the girls. She advises them to talk to their parents about joining the *mujahideen* in Syria and, if necessary, to elope:

> The first phone call you make (to family) once you cross the borders is one of the most difficult things you will ever have to do. [...] When you hear them sob and beg like crazy on the phone for you to come back it's so hard. [...] Many people [...] do not understand [...] why a female would choose to make this decision. They will point fingers and say behind your back and to your families' faces that you are taking part in [...] sexual jihad.[6]

Umm Layth even advises what young girls should pack: 'For the winter you will most likely need a good pair of boots.' For medication, she says:

Get all the shots and vaccinations that you require. You are travelling half way across the world and your immune system will most likely be in for a shock. You will regret if you don't do this since the Health care here is funny [...] Try and bring painkillers and Diarrhoea tablets.[7]

There are only a few hospitals still functioning in ISIS-held territory, and even fewer trained doctors. Small clinics are more common, and they mostly tend to those wounded in battle and bombing raids. Childbirth is mostly done in the old-fashioned way, assisted by experienced midwives, the majority of whom are local Syrians and Iraqis. ISIS has recently opened its first medical school in al-Raqqa, with a three-year study term, in order to produce trained physicians. Umm Layth adds:

Most sisters I have come across have been in university studying courses with many promising paths, with big, happy families and friends and everything in the Dunyah [material world] to persuade one to stay behind and enjoy the luxury. If we had stayed behind, we could have been blessed with it all from a relaxing and comfortable life and lots of money.

Wallahi [I swear] that's not what we want [...]

Emotionally you will face many obstacles, from family to your everyday habits. I remember I thought I would be living in a camp in the middle of the desert so I tried my best to cut down on my favourite foods [...] Haha I find it very funny now when I look back.[8]

In September 2014, she appealed to other Europeans: 'To those who are able and can still make your way, [...] hasten to our lands [...] This is a war against Islam and it is known that either "you're with them or with us". So pick a side.'[9]

In addition to Umm Layth's diary, prospective ISIS women are encouraged to surf ask.fm, a Latvian-based Q&A platform. It answers questions on how to travel to and from the Islamic State in Syria and Iraq and has plenty of daily traffic. On 8 March 2015, a group of ISIS internet buffs launched 5elafabook.com (CaliphateBook), trying to imitate Facebook to work around the regular bans on their use of social media networking websites. The project, still amateur, was pulled down hours later and its Twitter-linked account was suspended. It appeared using Facebook's hallmark blue and white colours decorating a map of the world with the Islamic State's insignia. The website gave its home address as ISIS-held Mosul and wrote in its opening statement: 'To clarify to the whole world that we do not only carry guns and live in caves as they imagine [...] We advance with our world and we want advancement to become Islamic [...] We love to die as you love to live'.[10]

REBELS WITHOUT A CAUSE

In April 2014, two Austrian teenage girls, aged 15 and 16, were declared missing in Vienna. They were the daughters of immigrants from Bosnia. The two teenagers left behind a note to their parents that read, 'Don't look for us. We will serve Allah – and we will die for him.'[11] They later surfaced in Syria, posting pictures on Facebook where both looked perfectly happy, wearing the burka. Austrian police believe that the photos were doctored and that somebody else is administering their account, using them as 'poster girls' to encourage other European girls to join ISIS.[12] Shortly afterwards, two 16-year-old British twins (originally from Somalia) sneaked out of their homes in Manchester to become 'jihadi brides'.[13] In July 2014, ISIS recruited a 19-year-old Denver nurse who had converted to Islam. The FBI arrested her while she was boarding a plane to Syria.[14] Shannon Conley wanted to marry a jihadi she had met online: 32-year-old Yousr Mouelhi from Tunisia.[15] In court she pleaded guilty to providing material support for the Islamic State in al-Raqqa. There has also been the case of the half-German, half-Algerian Sarah, another 15-year-old, who ran away from school in Konstanz, southern Germany. She later posted pictures of herself on Facebook holding a machine gun, wearing a burka and black gloves. The teen then added a chilling post: 'By the way, I've joined al-Qaida!'[16] Moezdalifa El Adoui is another teenager, who was stopped at Dusseldorf Airport while en route to Syria at the tender age of 15. She was a Dutch-Moroccan girl born and raised in the Netherlands.[17] All of these cases were reported in the last six months of 2014.

Nora al-Bathy is yet another example. She was an ordinary 15-year-old French schoolgirl from Avignon who dreamt of becoming a doctor one day.[18] One of her pre-ISIS photos on Facebook shows her smiling in jeans, posing beneath the Eiffel Tower. She packed for school on one cold January morning in 2014 and never returned home. Nora took a train to Paris, withdrew 550 euros with her ATM card, and changed mobile phones to cover her tracks. She took a plane to Istanbul and then switched to another plane heading for the Islamic State in al-Raqqa. Her family, practising but moderate Muslims, were shocked. They later discovered that she had a second Facebook account, where she was in contact with ISIS recruiters in Paris. Three days after disappearing she telephoned her family from the Syrian–Turkish border, saying that she was OK and did not want to return to France. She then communicated with her brother via SMS, telling him that she had learned to use a firearm but would not be fighting with ISIS. Her brother managed to get into Syria and see Nora. She told him, 'I've made the biggest mistake of my life.' Her brother claims: 'She was thin and sick. She never sees any light. With other women she has to look after young children [and] orphans.'[19] The al-Bathy family is now taking legal action, claiming that their daughter was brainwashed by extremists and 'kidnapped'.

Though not all experiences of jihadi cheerleaders work out in accordance with their aspirations, most would seem to share the reactions and attitudes of Um Habiba. A French citizen married to Algerian fighter Abu Qays, Um Habiba was accepted to medical schools in two top European universities before joining ISIS. Joanna al-Samman, now married to an ISIS member in Aleppo, drove a small green Citroën during her previous life in Amsterdam. She went to a trendy gym and dined out with friends on weekends. These ISIS newcomers were certainly not poor. Um Habiba adds: 'Contrary to what you read in the European press, none of us are being kept here against our will. We are here by choice. We are not children. We know *exactly* what we are doing!' In March 2015, three British girls from Bethnal Green Academy in east London were declared missing and were believed to have crossed into al-Raqqa to join ISIS, via Turkey.[20] Since then, one of the girls has contacted her relatives back in the UK telling them that she is healthy, safe and well but has insisted that she and the others do not intend to return home soon.[21]

The free publicity that these ISIS women have generated, along with their online activism, certainly strengthens a narrative that says ISIS is not a terrorist group, but a state that all Muslims must join. It is just like any other state, with its family values, social norms, state institutions, flag, police and army. These women try to give a feminine 'normalcy' to the Islamic State and have received direct blessing for their activities from none other than the caliph himself, Abu Bakr al-Baghdadi. It is public knowledge in al-Raqqa, says the wife of one ISIS warrior, that the caliph wants to increase the ratio of women in the Islamic State. He reportedly once said: 'This state has no future if it has nothing but men. Never in my life have I heard of a state with no women. We *need* more women!' Not only that, al-Baghdadi wants them to be more than 'baby factories', and is calling for female engineers, doctors, nurses, teachers and fighters to come to al-Raqqa. The caliph wants to give those women with experience and a university degree who pledge full allegiance to ISIS a plot of land, a fully furnished residence and astronomically high salaries by the standards of the Islamic State. They have to be married to an ISIS commander or fighter, of course. Once the war stops, al-Baghdadi has promised, they can eventually make up to US$3,000 per month in al-Raqqa. 'Our women have the wives of the Prophet to follow for inspiration,' he told an informal gathering in the winter of 2014. 'They were the Mothers of Believers and we want our wives and daughters to become Mothers of Believers as well.' Al-Baghdadi hates the term 'jihadi brides' and insists that ISIS women are 'citizens of the Islamic State'.

THE FIRST WOMEN OF ISIS

Al-Baghdadi understands the monumental role that women played during the early days of Islam. They supported the Prophet's rise and were instrumental in building the Islamic nation. Muhammad's early career, for example, was bankrolled by his beloved first wife Khadijah, a wealthy Christian. Khadijah was a powerful woman, who is still held in high esteem by Sunnis and Shi'a alike (although during her time there were no Sunnis and Shi'a, just Muslims). She was 25 years his senior and bore him six children including his famous daughter Fatima al-Zahra, the wife of the fourth and last Righteous Caliph, Ali ibn Abi Talib (whom the Shi'a regard as the first caliph). Khadijah was the first woman in Islam, and is generally regarded as the 'mother of all Muslims'. After she died, Muhammad created a strong network of tribal alliances through front-line political marriages. In addition to marrying off his daughter to Ali ibn Abi Talib (the first/fourth caliph), he gave the hand of two other daughters consecutively to the third caliph and wealthy Mecca notable, Uthman ibn Affan. He himself married Hafsa, the 20-year-old daughter of the second caliph Umar ibn al-Khattab, and later married Aisha, the teenage daughter of his immediate successor and friend, Abu Bakr al-Siddiq. Khadijah was the first and oldest of the Prophet's wives; Aisha was the youngest (between 9 and 12 when she married the Prophet). In between, he married Safiyya Bint Huyayy, a Jew, and Maria al-Qibtiyya, a Christian, in addition to several war widows.

When the Prophet's wives went out to battle, they left their faces uncovered. Aisha was a redhead, for example, and everybody knew that in Mecca. The Prophet even once told his followers to 'take half of your religion from *that* redhead.' Very surprisingly, like the wives of the Prophet, Abu Bakr al-Baghdadi's own wives also all wear the hijab, with no niqab. Tracking information about al-Baghdadi's multiple marriages has been a difficult task, but apparently three are officially registered and a fourth is recent, after the establishment of the Islamic State. Since the laws of Muslim Shari'a are strict about marriage, al-Baghdadi cannot marry more than four women at the same time. His first wife is his cousin and the mother of his children. Her name is Asma Fawzi al-Qubeisi. Very little is known about her and nobody in ISIS territory has ever seen her in public or knows for sure if she lives with him in Mosul and al-Raqqa. She is the mother of his five eldest children: Hufaiza, Omayama, Yaman, Hasan and Fatima. The second wife is Israa Rajab Mahal al-Qaisi, the mother of his youngest son Ali. The most recent wife – until proven otherwise – remains the product of social gossip in al-Raqqa. She is reportedly a German woman who joined ISIS in early 2015. Nobody knows her name or age, but tongues are wagging in the Islamic State. The third and last confirmed wife – and the one we know the most about – is the young Saja al-Duleimi, an Iraqi like al-Baghdadi himself.

Saja was photographed once, and her picture quickly spread widely on social media. A snapshot showed her coming out of a Syrian prison in March 2014. She was released as part of a famed prisoner swap in exchange for nuns kidnapped in the ancient Christian village of Maaloula. Jabhat al-Nusra took the nuns hostage at their monastery in December 2013, when its fighters stormed the historic Christian town of Maaloula. The nuns were released by al-Nusra in exchange for the authorities in Damascus releasing the wives of Islamist leaders held in jail. As Saja was released, her light complexion was bare for all to see. She was not wearing black, like all other women from ISIS, but a long beige coat.[22] On her release, Arab and Western media actively syndicated a photograph saying that this was the 'first lady' of the Islamic State. That photo, easily locatable on Google, shows a thin young woman, probably in her early thirties, with black eyes. The real Saja is a brunette born into one of the most powerful Iraqi tribes, the Duleims, in 1978.

The Duleims stand at around seven million people, stretched across Iraq, Syria, Jordan and Kuwait. They were courted lavishly by the Iraqi monarch Faisal II in the 1950s, and were treated well by the subsequent state leaders who came to power, starting with Abdul Karim Qasim and continuing to Saddam Hussein. They were rich, well-connected and could be trusted if they gave a word of honour. Under Saddam Hussein, 10–12 per cent of the Iraqi army was drawn from the Duleim tribe. The entire clan fell from official grace with the US occupation of 2003. Like the Baathists of Iraq, they took up arms and headed for the underground, at first leading a secular resistance to the Anglo-American occupation. When al-Qaeda surfaced, Saja's father Ibrahim al-Duleimi joined Abu Musaab al-Zarqawi. This is where he befriended Abu Mohammad al-Golani, the young Syrian who was to introduce him to the man who was to become his future son-in-law, al-Baghdadi.

Al-Baghdadi saw plenty of reason to marry into the Duleim tribe, despite the fact that Saja was a widow, her first husband having been killed in 2010. As a political and social nobody, it would make al-Baghdadi more important, providing a tribal umbrella that he desperately needed. A tribal network is vital for any aspiring politician in Iraq. Saddam Hussein played tribal politics brilliantly, treating tribal leaders like kings in exchange for unlimited support from their community elders. Al-Baghdadi is trying to do the same with Iraqi tribes. The Duleims have all been incorporated into ISIS. Saja's older brother Omar is commander of an ISIS unit in Mosul, while her younger brother Khaled is part of al-Baghdadi's entourage. Her sister Du'aa is an al-Qaeda member who once worked with Abu Musaab al-Zarqawi where she tried – and failed – to blow herself up in a crowd in the all-Kurdish city of Irbil, back in 2008. She was more of an active fighter than an ISIS wife. Their father Hamid Ibrahim al-Duleimi was a founding commander of ISIS and a member of its Shura Council. The Syrian army killed him in September 2013.[23]

There is no official post for Saja al-Duleimi in the Islamic State. The wives of caliphs in Islamic history have generally lived in the shadows of their husbands. One notable exception was the Umayyad princess Atkeh Bint Yezid. She was granddaughter of the dynasty's founder Muawiya I, daughter of his son and successor Yezid Ibn Muawiya, and wife of the grand Umayyad caliph Abdul Malik Ibn Marwan. Some have called her a scholar because she studied Islam and excelled in recounting the Prophet's Hadith. She was also a philanthropist and strong-minded woman who influenced the decisions of her caliph relatives. Abu Bakr al-Baghdadi sees a major role for his wife in the future of the Islamic State. Although ISIS warriors have done great injustice to the women citizens of al-Raqqa, this contradicts Abu Bakr al-Baghdadi's vision for the future of his state, or at least that of his four wives. He wants the state's women to be like the Prophet's wives – Khadijah and Aisha – wealthy individuals, supportive wives and warriors when needed. Dress attire aside, he almost wants his wife to play an active political role similar to that of modern Arab queens and first ladies, like Rania of Jordan or Sheikha Mozah of Qatar. One of the manifestations of his vision is the Khansaa Brigade, as already discussed: the all-women unit created by the caliph to monitor female activity on the streets of al-Raqqa. Unmarried foreign women who come to al-Raqqa are treated well and lodged with other single female members of ISIS. They pay no rent and an ISIS officer is charged with running all of their errands from a distance until each of them is properly wed. Widows are given an ISIS pension of US$300 per month (S£60,000). Al-Baghdadi's wife, Saja, handles their affairs; taking care of ISIS widows is her purview, in addition to being the caliph's revered wife. Europeans communicating with ISIS from afar are encouraged to complete their university degree before making the lifetime decision of coming to al-Raqqa. Additionally, al-Baghdadi and his wife want to revamp university campuses in Mosul and al-Raqqa, and restrict one to a women-only institution. Not only would its classes be free of charge, but women would also get a state grant to complete their higher education. Al-Baghdadi is willing to pay ISIS women – and only ISIS women – in order for them to obtain a higher education.

Despite his efforts, however, female defection from ISIS had already started by the spring of 2015, although the figures are still very low when compared to recruitment. At least one European officially escaped from Syria in 2014. Her name was Aisha, and she returned to her hometown of Maastricht after marrying Omar Yilmaz, a Dutch-Turkish jihadi in al-Raqqa.[24] If we scratch beneath the surface of all of these stories, brushing away all the gossip, we will find something very serious – and enduring – about ISIS. It has to do with producing a new generation of both believers and fighters. ISIS commanders, headed by al-Baghdadi, realize that because they live in a war zone, their days are numbered. If they don't die today, then it will be tomorrow – if not tomorrow, then perhaps in a week's time or in a month. This is the crux of jihadi thought, after all. Ultimately, the role of these jihadi pioneers is to establish a sustainable state that will live longer than all of its founders. This is where women come into play – in their role as childbearers. As mothers, they will shoulder responsibility for indoctrinating ISIS babies. It is too early to tell how these children will grow up and in what environment. According to ISIS statistics, approximately 220 babies were born to residents of the Islamic State in 2014.

Only time will tell if these children will one day rebel against their parents, or grow up into fully fledged soldiers to serve as the vanguards of the first generation born under the cloak of ISIS, who will reach fighting age in little over a decade from now.

TEN

ISIS's Next Frontier

IN AUGUST 2014, JUST A FEW WEEKS AFTER THE DECLARATION
of the ISIS caliphate, a photo of the White House went viral on Twitter.
Carrying the signature of the Islamic State, with the black banner of
ISIS, the picture was seemingly taken on Pennsylvania Avenue on the
photographer's smartphone. The hashtag read: 'A message from ISIS
to US.' Chillingly, the picture was captioned: 'We are in your state. We
are in your cities. We are in your streets. You are our goal anywhere.'
Secret Service spokesman Ed Donovan dismissed the photograph,
saying that his team was well aware of it and would take 'appropriate
steps'. Perhaps Donovan and others thought it was a spoof.

Since then, ISIS's presence throughout the Western world has
become a reality, no longer restricted to online sympathizers or those
who leave home to fight in Iraq and Syria. In December 2014, Man
Haron Monis, an Australian of Iranian descent, took 17 hostages at
a Lindt chocolate café in the central business district of Sydney. He
forced them to wave a black Islamic banner and demanded that an ISIS
flag be delivered to the café. Monis was a self-proclaimed Shi'i cleric
who had recently converted to Sunni Islam and pledged allegiance to
ISIS. He had a criminal record and a history of erratic behaviour that
made him a fringe figure in Sydney's Islamic community.[1]

On 7 January 2015, two brothers of Algerian descent, Cherif and
Said Kouachi, stormed the offices of the French satirical magazine
Charlie Hebdo in Paris at approximately 11.30 a.m. The two men were

carrying assault rifles as they shot at the staff, killing 11 and wounding another 12. Among the dead were some of France's top cartoonists. *Charlie Hebdo* had repeatedly published cartoons poking fun at the Prophet Muhammad. As the two assailants hurried out of the building, they also shot – at close range – a French policeman rushing to the scene. That victim, the policeman Ahmed Merabet, was Muslim. Hours after the *Charlie Hebdo* attack, an associate of the Kouachi brothers of Malian-Muslim descent, Amedy Coulibaly, shot a 32-year-old man jogging next to his home in Paris. On 8 January, he shot and killed a municipal police officer at the junction of Avenue Pierre Brossolette and Avenue de la Paix in the Parisian suburb of Montrouge. He also shot and critically wounded a street sweeper. Then, on 9 January, Coulibaly broke into a Jewish kosher store in Porte de Vincennes in east Paris wielding a sub-machine gun. He killed four innocent civilians and held others hostage until French police raided the apartment and gunned him down.

According to witnesses at the scenes of the attacks, the Kouachi brothers claimed allegiance to al-Qaeda in Yemen. The organization posted a video afterwards hailing the Kouachi brothers and claiming responsibility for 'punishing' the *Charlie Hebdo* caricaturists. Coulibaly, however, claimed himself to be 'a soldier of ISIS'. In a video recorded before the attacks, he spoke in French and was carrying a gun with an ISIS flag on the wall behind him. He muttered his oath of allegiance to ISIS in broken Arabic and went on to deliver his manifesto in French. 'What we are doing is completely legitimate,' said Coulibaly. Hours after the attacks, it was reported that Coulibaly's wife, Hayat Boumeddiene, had crossed over to ISIS-held territory in Syria from Turkey. Boumeddiene left France a few days before the attacks, and according to Abu Mansur al-Libi, an al-Raqqa-based ISIS commander close to the caliph himself, she now does the translation for French-speaking women arriving in the Islamic State.[2] He claims that ISIS reached out to her after the saga unfolded in France and once she was already inside Syrian territory. What is certain is that she crossed into Syria via Turkish territory on

2 January, and stayed at a hotel in Istanbul. Pictures of Coulibaly and Boumeddiene emerged in which the couple appear holding a hand-gun while Boumeddiene is dressed in full black niqab (the Islamic dress mandatory in ISIS territory). In mid-February *Dar al-Islam*, an ISIS Arabic magazine, ran an interview with Boumeddiene, identify-ing her as 'Um Bassir al-Muhajira'. The magazine was published by ISIS's famed Hayat Media. When asked how she felt about being in ISIS territory, she replied, 'Praise be to Allah who made the road easy.'[3] She then commented on her husband's reaction when Abu Bakr al-Baghdadi announced the creation of the caliphate six months earlier: 'He rejoiced greatly. His heart burst with desire to join his brothers and fight enemies of Allah in the Caliph's land.' Coulibaly was unable to do so, she added, because of his commitments to jihad in France itself. She went on to say that his eyes 'gleamed' whenever he saw Islamic State videos, asking her to turn them off because they triggered an uncontrollable desire to join the *mujahideen* in Syria. Abu Mansour al-Libi, who never met Coulibaly but claims to know Um Bassir well, says that she offered her translation services free of charge to ISIS, and even offers consultation and advice to female newcomers who don't speak the language and are arriving in al-Raqqa.[4] Nobody refers to her by her former name any more, he adds, and 'if you come asking about Hayat, everybody will tell you no such person exists in our lands.'[5] He adds that she remains single, although she has received many offers of marriage. In Islam, a woman cannot marry until four months and ten days after her hus-band's death have passed, which Um Bassir has observed obediently. It is still not known whether Coulibaly and the Kouachi brothers had visited ISIS-held territory in Syria or Iraq prior to the *Charlie Hebdo* attacks in January 2015. The Kouachi brothers had previously been arrested and imprisoned for 18 months in 2008 after a French court found them guilty of recruiting fighters for al-Qaeda in Iraq, the biological father of ISIS. Abu Mansour al-Libi, who himself arrived in Syria in 2013, had no answer but replied, 'It seems that [Um Bassir] knows her way pretty well!'[6]

The *Charlie Hebdo* attack came less than four months after the United States and its allies began their military campaign against ISIS in Iraq and Syria in September 2014. By October, ISIS troops had managed to capture 350 Kurdish villages surrounding the strategic border town of Kobani in northern Syria – a clear indication that the US-led coalition was doing little to clip the wings of al-Baghdadi's army. ISIS troops were locked into a vicious street battle inside Kobani against Syrian-Kurdish militias, supported by coalition air strikes and reinforcements from Iraqi Kurdistan's armed forces the Peshmerga, passing through Turkey from Iraqi Kurdistan. The ISIS offensive was finally repelled in February 2015, when Kobani and many towns around it were recaptured by Syrian Kurds. At the time of writing in 2015, ISIS is still simultaneously fighting on many fronts: against the Iraqi army and Shi'i militias in several Iraqi provinces; the Kurdish Peshmerga forces in northern Iraq; several opposition groups; and the Syrian army in Deir ez-Zour, while American-led coalition fighter jets roam the skies over Syria and Iraq, striking at ISIS targets.

The Sydney and Paris attacks reminded the world that ISIS's fight was not restricted to the battlefields of Syria and Iraq and that the American-led campaign did not preclude ISIS's ability to fulfil its promise of striking at the heart of the West. In February 2015, an ISIS fighter thundered: We will conquer Rome!"[7] Less than a month later in March, the ISIS spokesman and Camp Bucca veteran Abu Muhammad al-Adnani addressed the 'West' in a voice booming with confidence: 'We will blow up your White House, Big Ben and the Eiffel Tower.' In a chilling 28-minute video, al-Adnani officially laid claim to Paris and Rome. In another recording released, al-Adnani called for worldwide 'lone wolf' attacks, mentioning Australia by name after it agreed to join the US-backed coalition. ISIS seems to be banking on the 'lone wolf' phenomenon, taking credit for attacks it did not help plan, finance or execute. However, the danger of ISIS terror cells abroad remains very real. Two weeks after the Paris attacks, dozens of suspected radical Islamists were arrested and questioned in France, Germany, Britain and Belgium. Many of the suspects were accused of recruiting fighters to join ISIS in Syria. It is not clear whether those apprehended were planning attacks on European soil. In late February 2015, two men were arrested in New York for pledging allegiance to ISIS and planning to travel to Syria. It is also not clear whether they planned to carry out attacks within the United States. The line between Syria-bound jihadis, ideological zealots, online sympathizers, lone wolves and organized terror cells is becoming ever more blurred, posing immense risks to societies and greater challenges to law-enforcement agencies across the world. This type of threat is a far cry from the post-9/11 war on terror, when the world feared an alleged organized al-Qaeda terror network plotting and preparing attacks on a large scale.

DISGUISED AS REFUGEES

At the time of writing in early 2015, ISIS has successfully penetrated pockets throughout Europe and North Africa. They have reportedly managed to slip into different cities disguised as Syrian refugees. Hundreds of Syrians arrive periodically in the Turkish port cities of Mersin and Izmir, almost on a daily basis, begging for a ride to the shores of Greece. The journey is a dangerous one, and many have died trying to escape the turmoil of war in their country – sunk in the waters of the Mediterranean. Some are willing to pay up to US$6,000 for a boat seat, with no guarantee of safe arrival or even survival. Once close to European shores, they disembark and are picked up by Greek police. All destroy their Syrian passports and are given temporary residency as refugees, claiming that although illegal, they cannot be deported back home, where certain death awaits them. After settling in Greece, smugglers provide them with fake European IDs, which are finally used to reach one of the many airports of central Europe. The second route to Europe runs through Libya. Tripoli, after all, is only 482 km from Ragusa, Sicily's southernmost city. Other migrant boats head to Lampedusa, a small Italian island near Sicily.

ISIS fighters have reportedly entered Europe to establish dormant cells, disguised as Syrian refugees. It is easier to travel by sea than by air, given the strict security at European airports. Making use of the massive numbers of people making the trip by boat, ISIS fighters have a higher chance of blending in with the crowd and avoiding being picked up by airport intelligence. Nobody knows exactly how many ISIS fighters have slipped into Europe in such a manner, and ISIS media has refused to comment on the matter. Russian and Iranian media have referred to the scheme as an ISIS Trojan horse that is marching deep into European territory. The other form of penetration, of course, is to recruit European Muslims already residing in the EU. Instead of calling on them to take up arms and come to Syria, ISIS is now shifting its strategy into keeping them in Europe, according to interviews with multiple ISIS advisers in al-Raqqa. They are to strike behind the lines of the infidel enemies, especially in those countries that join the war effort against ISIS. 'We have plenty of fighters coming from the Arab and Muslim worlds,' says Gamal Ibrahim al-Hasan (aka Abu Khaled al-Filastini), a Palestinian curriculum adviser to ISIS's Department of Education, speaking from al-Raqqa in early 2015. 'The foreigners are more useful sometimes if they stay in their own countries, awaiting a signal to march through Europe.' This view was shared by his colleague Salim, a schoolteacher in al-Raqqa, who says: 'In recent weeks, we have been hearing from our *mujahideen* brothers that sometimes, it's best for our European brothers to stay in Europe. They will become useful in the future.' Some of those ISIS members or affiliates are indeed staying behind in Europe. In July 2014, for example, Moroccans covering their face with the black-and-white chequered *kuffiyya* of the Palestinians staged a demonstration at The Hague in the Netherlands, carrying the black flag of ISIS. They were ostensibly protesting the detention of a young Dutch-Moroccan, accused of recruiting jihadis into ISIS inside Europe.

ANSAR BAYT AL-MAQDIS

The greatest manifestation of how powerful ISIS's influence has become is the number of 'branches' that it has opened, especially in

Africa. ISIS has been gaining plenty of ground in North Africa, namely in the Sinai Peninsula of Egypt, wedged between the Mediterranean Sea to the north and the Red Sea to the south. The peninsula, occupied for years by Israel, is famous for its biblical history, thanks to Mount Sinai, and for the famed resort of Sharm al-Sheikh, frequented by American and Israeli tourists. The ISIS-affiliated terror group to emerge in Sinai was first known as Ansar Bayt al-Maqdis (Supporters of Jerusalem). It reportedly came to life after living off dormant cells that were established in Egypt back in the 2000s, originally on the instructions of Osama bin Laden himself, says Abu Khaled al-Filastini. In a nine-minute video posted on Twitter, Ansar Bayt al-Maqdis swore allegiance to Abu Bakr al-Baghdadi on 10 November 2014. 'We have no alternative but to declare our pledge of allegiance to the Caliph – to listen and obey him.' The Egyptian group has since rebranded itself as Vilayet Sinai (Sinai Province). This is in line with the Islamic State's official terminology for ISIS-run territory, putting Sinai on a par with al-Raqqa and Mosul.

Ansar Bayt al-Maqdis was officially founded during the Egyptian Revolution against long-standing President Husni Mubarak in January 2011. Their original ideology was anti-Israeli, but they always spoke of their new goal to bring Islamic Shari'a to Egypt. An Islamic state was on their mind, governed by laws of the Holy Qur'an and ruled by a caliph. They fed off the chaos that engulfed Egypt after Mubarak's ousting and the rise of the Muslim Brotherhood, prompting many to claim that they were the military wing of the Egyptian Brothers. Both the Brotherhood and Ansar Bayt al-Maqdis deny this. In February 2012, they fired rockets from Sinai into the southern Israeli resort of Eilat, and five months later blew up a pipeline that exports gas to Israel. In September 2013, they tried to assassinate the Egyptian Interior Minister Mohammad Ibrahim, targeting his motorcade in Cairo with a bomb. In October, they attacked south Sinai's Security Directorate and military intelligence in Isma'ilia, in north-eastern Egypt.

Something changed in mid-2014. Ansar Bayt al-Maqdis mushroomed in size – and strength – transforming into more of a small army, rather than a militia. Later that same year, they had risen to between 750 and 1,000 fighters of different nationalities including Palestinian, Libyan, Sudanese and Yemeni. According to ISIS operative Huzaifa al-Omari (aka Abu Ubayda al-Shami), the bulk of Ansar Bayt al-Maqdis come from neighbouring Gaza City and are ex-members of Hamas. There are no Levantines in the group: no jihadis from Syria, Lebanon or Jordan. In fact, although branded an 'Egyptian group', Ansar Bayt al-Maqdis has very few Egyptians. The locals who have joined Ansar Bayt al-Maqdis hail from the Armilat and Sawarka Bedouin clans of Sinai, who have long complained of being neglected by Egyptian officialdom. Two of the organisation's co-founders are Egyptians: Mohammad Bakri Haroun (aka Tarek Ziad), a clothes merchant turned jihadi, and Mohammad Ali Afifi (aka Muhsen Osama), a lawyer turned restaurateur. Both of them had tried and failed to travel to Syria to join the jihad in 2012. Other jihadis were one-time members of Abu Musaab al-Zarqawi's Mujahideen Shura Council in Iraq. The ISIS influence manifested itself clearly in August 2014, when the group posted a 30-minute video showing four Egyptians blindfolded and beheaded, in the manner of ISIS. In October, the group killed 28 Egyptian soldiers with a car bomb – an attack carried out with clean precision. They began to become more active on social media, especially on Twitter, and issued thundering declarations calling for rebellion against President Abdul Fattah al-Sisi. According to the ISIS fighter Seifullah Shanshal (aka Abu Khaled al-Baghdadi), all of this was the doing of Islamic State. Abu Bakr al-Baghdadi had been watching developments in Egypt with extreme interest since mid-2012, but he had nothing to do with Ansar Bayt al-Maqdis in its early stages. He agreed to help, however, by sending advisers and know-how, but refused to send arms, money or fighters to Sinai.

One of the military advisers sent to help was Abu Talha al-Filastini, a Palestinian renegade from the camps of Lebanon. He was a sports instructor turned jihadi, born in 1986 to a family from Acre at the Naher al-Bared camp in northern Lebanon. He was despatched to Egypt at Abu Bakr al-Baghdadi's orders in autumn 2014, along with five other ISIS members. They all entered Egyptian territories ostensibly as drivers, labourers, cooks and car mechanics, carrying a variety of Yemeni, Sudanese and Libyan passports. Once in Sinai, they began training militants and helping them set up four- to five-man cells in different cities across Egypt. 'They didn't bring a single weapon with them to Egypt,' confirms an ISIS source in al-Raqqa, who adds: 'Their job is to tutor their brethren in Sinai, rather than to fight alongside them.' When the Ansar Bayt al-Maqdis' call for help was discussed at ISIS's Shura Council, al-Baghdadi initially refused to help, saying that it was wrong for ISIS to stretch out horizontally in such a manner. Al-Baghdadi prefers to allow others to do the fighting on behalf of the Islamic State. This was made clear by how he delegated authority to Ansar Bayt al-Maqdis, empowering them with words through his spokesman, Abu Muhammad al-Adnani, who commanded: 'Ring the roads with explosives [for them]. Attack their bases. Raid their homes. Cut off their heads.'[8] He wasn't calling on his fighters to do the job, but rather asking his Egyptian 'brothers' to carry out 'blessed operations against the guards of the Jews, the soldiers of Sisi, the new Pharaoh of Egypt.'[9] Since then, ISIS has constantly paid homage to the 'brave *mujahideen* of Sinai' in many of its communiqués.

ISIS's advice and support has paid off. Ansar Bayt al-Maqdis quickly changed their profile. Their operations became swifter and their precision higher. By early 2015, the group had expanded into Palestinian territories, setting up a branch in the Hamas-held Gaza Strip. On 13 February 2015, pamphlets signed by 'the Islamic State in Gaza' were distributed claiming responsibility for an explosion at the French Cultural Centre which set off a fire that devoured the building but failed to claim any human lives. The attack was in response to the French centre's 'moral corruption' and the 'alien vice' that it was introducing into Palestinian society – such as theatre, music and poetry. ISIS has also instructed its Sinai proxies to avoid speaking to the international press, which makes gathering information on the group a difficult task, unlike Jabhat al-Nusra or ISIS itself, both of which have opened up to the media since the summer of 2014.

Currently, Ansar Bayt al-Maqdis has a wide arsenal of weapons – all stolen from the Libyan battlefield. This includes Grad rockets, mortars, rocket-propelled grenades and air defence systems. They have no tanks or aeroplanes. Ansar Bayt al-Maqdis realize that they are no match for the US-funded and well-trained Egyptian army. Instead of taking them on in face-to-face battles, they are creating havoc by remote control, by planting bombs and explosives at different locations, realizing that the Egyptian army cannot monitor all the roads in Sinai. They use wireless communications and UHF radio, equipping themselves with electronic intensifiers to strengthen the signal of their detonation bombs from afar – from a distance of up to one kilometre. Over the course of one month, Ansar Bayt al-Maqdis has planned 21 bomb attacks throughout Egypt. Seven of them were dismantled by Egyptian authorities and 14 exploded, claiming innocent lives.[10] In October, they detonated a car bomb at a heavily guarded security checkpoint at Sheikh Zuwaid, a Bedouin town in north Sinai, and then ambushed the guards who came to rescue and reinforce their comrades. In total, 33 Egyptian soldiers were killed in the operation. In November, they assassinated a colonel in the Egyptian army and two soldiers in the heart of Cairo. They also killed an officer and a soldier in the Qalyubia Governorate, north of Cairo in the Nile Delta region. In December 2014, Ansar Bayt al-Maqdis killed the 58-year-old American oil worker William Henderson in the Karama Desert. On 29 January 2015, they carried out a series of coordinated attacks using suicide bombers and car bombs at military checkpoints, bases, a hotel and a police station. The massive operation, which had ISIS's fingerprints all over it, left 30 Egyptians dead.

The leader of Ansar Bayt al-Maqdis is a little-known Egyptian jihadi named Ahmad Salama al-Mabruk. He had never met Abu Bakr al-Baghdadi in person but was a fan of his predecessor, Abu Musaab al-Zarqawi in Iraq. Born in the al-Matania village in Giza in 1956, he grew up studying at state-run schools and was active in student politics. He enrolled at the Faculty of Computer Science at Cairo University and graduated in 1979, months before the Soviet invasion of Afghanistan. During his college years, he frequented the home of Mohammad Abdulsalam Faraj, a ranking jihadi ideologue inspired by the teachings of Ibn Taymiyya and a good friend of the Cairo-based surgeon Ayman al-Zawahiri. Faraj was one of the loudest adherents of the Egyptian Brotherhood, who strongly advocated the elimination of President Anwar al-Sadat after his 1978 Camp David accords with Israel. Mabruk joined the armed forces, serving for five months in military intelligence. His radical Islamist views led to his transfer to another unit, and he was discharged completely in 1981. That same year he was arrested after the assassination of President Sadat on 6 October 1981. Mabruk was charged with trying to seize control of television headquarters, and remained in jail until 1988. Upon his release, like so many Islamists of his generation, he fled to Afghanistan, joining the Arab Afghans at the behest of Ayman al-Zawahiri. The two men founded an Egyptian contingent for al-Qaeda, Jama'at al-Jihad al-Masriya (Egyptian Jihad Group). During a visit to Azerbaijan in 1988, Mabruk was abducted by US and local intelligence and deported to Egypt, where he spent over 20 years in jail. He was released after the 25 January Revolution of 2011. With vengeance in his eyes, he set up Ansar Bayt al-Maqdis a few months later, in mid-2011. Of all the ISIS-affiliated jihadis, he is the one receiving the least attention in the Western press, probably because his militia is significantly smaller than those in Iraq and Syria.

THE ISLAMIC STATE IN LIBYA

As of mid-2015, owing to a combination of opportunism and ideology, ISIS's next target is Libya. The country – once/if it falls to ISIS – is a gateway not only to Europe but also to its six neighbours: Egypt, Tunisia, Algeria, Chad, Niger and Sudan. ISIS already has an affiliate in sub-Saharan Africa, with the notorious Nigerian Islamist group Boko Haram pledging allegiance to the caliphate in March 2015. Without a doubt, it will become a magnet for African jihadis. Libya has disintegrated into chaos since 2011, making it perfect territory for the jihadis. The Libyan army is currently holding much of the country's east, while an assortment of Islamic militias occupies western Libya. The strongest of these groups is Majlis Shura Shabab al-Islam (MSSI), which translates as 'Shura Council of Muslim Youth'. Little is known about MSSI except that it was established in April 2014 and pledged its oath of allegiance to Abu Bakr al-Baghdadi in June of the same year. According to CNN, the ISIS affiliate has 800 fighters as of early 2015. Of that number, 300 are Libyan militants who fought with ISIS, first in Deir ez-Zour and then in Mosul.[11] In November 2014, MSSI fully occupied the Libyan city of Darna, 240 km east of Benghazi, officially annexing it to ISIS's Islamic State. Videos of Libyan jihadis made the rounds online, showing them carrying machine guns and wearing beige fatigues, taking down mannequins from shop windows and shutting down hairdressers, just as they did in al-Raqqa and Mosul. MSSI now controls schools, mosque pulpits and the city's local radio. A police force was created similar to that of ISIS, charged with monitoring public vice. Abu Bakr al-Baghdadi refused to send any weapons or money to his Libyan proxies, advising them to make money from trafficking, kidnapping and other illegal means, just as they did in Syria. Instead he sent them two of his top aides to advise on how to run the state: Abu Nabil al-Anbari (Iraqi) and Abu Baraa al-Azdi (Saudi). Both were long-time members of ISIS who had spent time with the caliph at his US jail in Camp Bucca.[12] In August 2014, they posted on their Facebook account that they had proudly confiscated alcohol and drugs in the 'Vilayet of Darna'. They passed down laws banning women from walking the streets unveiled and forced all residents to attend mosque prayer, or otherwise suffer lashes at the hands of ISIS militiamen.

Many of the jihadis operating in Libya today are Yemeni and Tunisian jihadi veterans of the Iraq and Syria wars. Foreign fighters in Libya currently stand at 400, although the number is disputed by ISIS itself, which claims that it is much higher.[13] Some are former Gaddafi supporters who went underground after their leader's death in October 2011, similar to how ex-officers in Saddam Hussein's army took up arms with the jihadis after their president's fall in 2003. Like in Syria and

Iraq, ISIS is feeding off the uncontrollable chaos and ruling by striking fear into the hearts of the locals. In August 2014, they executed an
Egyptian citzen at a Libyan football stadium, with one shot through the
head. The execution was carried out beneath the black flag of ISIS. In
January 2015, the ISIS-affiliated group attacked the luxury Corinthia
Hotel in Tripoli, killing four foreigners (including an American contractor) and four Libyans. In February 2015, they attacked an oilfield –
just as they did in Sinai – killing nine Libyan guards. In March 2015,
they laid claim to a car bomb in the capital Tripoli, which went off near
the Ministry of Foreign Affairs. The video was posted in ISIS style on
the Libyan jihadi forum, decorated with ISIS iconography – namely
the black flag that is now common in al-Raqqa and Mosul. They also
seized nine foreigners at the al-Ghani oilfield, from Austria, the Czech
Republic, Bangladesh and the Philippines.[14] On Twitter the jihadi
group wrote: 'We have prepared for you the most bitter of cups and
the worst of deaths!' In May 2015, ISIS achieved another astounding
victory by seizing control of Sirte International Airport, prompting
Western officials to sound alarm bells once more due to Sirte's proxim-
ity to Europe, across the Mediterranean.[15]

The epitome of ISIS atrocities in Libya was the abduction and
execution of 21 Egyptian Copts, all working as labourers in Sirte, the
birthplace of Libyan dictator Muammar al-Gaddafi. They were collectively beheaded on 15 February, kneeling in their orange jumpsuits
along the Sirte shoreline. The video shows them walking down the
beach with their masked captors. The scenery was no accident – ISIS
wanted the world to see that this wasn't the deserts of Iraq and Syria but
the shores of the Mediterranean facing Europe. ISIS was expanding
and inching closer to new territory. The victims, all from impoverished
Coptic Christian families, had come to Libya searching for a better life,
since salaries were four times higher than in Egypt. Their Muslim colleagues had been forced to identify them at the compound, threatened
with death by ISIS if they didn't.[16] The video of their mass execution
on the shores of Libya was posted on ISIS's media channels. In the
video, the jihadi leading the execution points to the ocean – to nearby

Italy – threatening with the famed, 'We will conquer Rome!' Modern-day jihadis also long for the days when the Umayyad caliphate conquered Spain and established Muslim rule on the European continent. This nostalgia for a 700-year rule of a part of Europe by Muslim troops who marched from the Levant fuels ISIS's European aspirations.

ISIS'S EXPANDING FRONTIERS

The rapid advancement of ISIS throughout Europe and North Africa will be a game-changer in the war on terror. As this book goes to print in late summer 2015, the world is just starting to grasp that ISIS is no longer simply a Levantine threat confined to the borders of war-torn Syria and Iraq. It has now reached the shores of the Mediterranean. Darna and Sinai are looking disturbingly like al-Raqqa and Mosul. If not combated immediately, nothing will prevent ISIS from striking at Cairo or Tripoli as well. The black flag of ISIS is seemingly everywhere. Fear is in the air, and nobody has answers as to why ISIS is advancing and how to bring it to a final end. This speaks of many realities. One, of course, is the failure of the US-led coalition that was set up in September 2014. Another is the desperate need of local communities for money and leadership, no matter how skewed. ISIS is providing both in al-Raqqa, Mosul, Darna and Sinai. Had Egypt and Libya produced strong leaders after the Arab Spring toppled their long-time dictators, then the likeliness of an ISIS takeover of entire cities would have been slim – or perhaps non-existent.

The third reality of ISIS's expansionism is that Abu Bakr al-Baghdadi is a good strategist who is not biting off more than he can chew. If the decision was not his, then it was probably made by his top Iraqi lieutenants, who realize from their Saddam Hussein days that it is military madness to try and tackle more than what is possible. To date al-Baghdadi and his generals have refused to offer more than lip service and technical advice to their proxies in North Africa. He hasn't been swept away by the pledges of support he received from Libya and Egypt. Otherwise, he might have committed the grave error – from

ISIS's viewpoint – of sending troops to these war-torn territories, thereby leaving his main base in Syria unchecked and prone to invasion by one of his many enemies. Some leaders have done that when their proxies seek their assistance, often treating it as a golden opportunity to grab new territory, bolster traditional allies or topple arch foes. President Gamal Abdul Nasser rushed his troops into Yemen in the 1960s, and so did different US administrations in the Vietnam War. The Red Army of the Soviet Union stretched itself thin by getting involved in so many military adventures during the height of the Cold War, all of which began eating away at the Soviet Union from within. The hot-headed caliph is not as erratic as many originally claimed him to be. He is creating affiliates and provinces without firing a bullet or spending a penny, which speaks plenty about how popular the man has become since self-appointing himself caliph. More importantly, the expansion into North Africa makes it certain that ISIS is going nowhere any time soon.

This expansion will make degrading and eventually destroying ISIS, as President Obama has promised, an almost impossible task. Even if a grand coalition or a group of coalitions were able to destroy ISIS in Syria and Iraq, another similar effort would have to be organised in Libya and other parts of Africa. The process could drag on for decades. As for Europe, ISIS is slowly but surely increasing its ability to strike at the heart of the continent. The *Charlie Hebdo* attack shocked the world and rattled the social peace in France. There was little the French air force could do in terms of retaliation, as air power alone has proved futile in defeating, much less severely wounding, ISIS. Sleeper cells and lone wolves would take the fight to the heart of Europe, striking behind enemy lines. Yet more critical is the impact of radicalization on the European integration process of generations of immigrants. As long as YouTube videos from Syria and Iraq make it online, ISIS will gain ground with the disaffected Muslim youth in Europe, thus endangering the social peace, which is a far greater threat than that of a random attack here or there.

Conclusion

IN TRYING TO BREAK DOWN THE ISIS PHENOMENON, WE OUGHT to first fully agree on the reasons behind its rise and where it might be heading. We need to accept the fact that it is not just an overnight phase that will soon disappear. Depending on whom one talks to in the complex web of Middle East politics, fingers are always pointed at Saudi Arabia, Turkey, Israel, or Syria itself. At one point or another, all of these states have been accused of funding ISIS or facilitating its dramatic rise to power. Accusations have varied since 2011. The Syrians were accused of releasing jihadis from prison in Damascus, the Turks of facilitating their cross-border activities, the Saudis of bankrolling and arming them. What people often ignore is the fertile territory within Syria and Iraq which gave the Islamic State an audience willing to listen, fight and pledge its *bay'a* (oath) to the caliph. Had there not been a population ready to embed ISIS, then the Islamic State would not have cemented its rule that swiftly. People were tired and fed up with the old way of doing things, and desperate for a break with the past. Something in ISIS, beneath the layers of terrorism, was seemingly attractive at least to some people in the Middle East. The societies in which ISIS has flourished were suffering from long-term plagues like military rule, sectarianism, lack of social mobility, joblessness, unequal distribution of wealth, and mediocre education. Those who joined ISIS did so not only because of the money and Abu Bakr al-Baghdadi's long swords. They did it because their former societies had fallen apart and failed them, leaving them to rot in poverty and ignorance. Ironically, 'citizenship' of the Islamic State is mainly composed of rural dwellers, often the children and grandchildren of the very same families that formed the crux of Baath Party rule after 1963. They were once the incubators of Baathism; now they are incubating ISIS. Islam is certainly a reason, but so is the failure of Baathism itself.

Power corrupts. It is that simple. Revisiting the Baath Party founding documents reveals a very promising vision for how society and the Arab world should have looked after 1963. Young men in al-Raqqa and Mosul once spent hours absorbing these flowery texts, memorizing them at school, university and work. The Baath promised what its very name means: an Arab 'renaissance', or 'rebirth'. Because of that, the Baath managed to attract the brightest and most capable of Syrian and Iraqi youth during the 1950s and 1960s. During those times, Baath Party veterans would tell aspiring young members that they had to be 'number one' in order to be considered for Baath Party membership. From the 1980s onwards, however, it became the opposite: Baath Party members were given 'number one' status in work, pay and professional development not because of their merit or achievement, but simply because they were members of the ruling party. This created three generations of mediocre and below-average party members who rose to positions of authority in the state not because they were good, but because they were Baathist. As the Baath dominated the state, it controlled the media and the judiciary, hindering the rule of law and the scrutiny of the public over the affairs of the state. The Baath turned into self-interested closed cliques, promoting a culture of favouritism and discrimination against non-Baathists. The direct product of this monopoly was corruption, an ever-hungry beast that consumed the financial and moral resources of the state and hijacked the potential of the Syrian and Iraqi people. This eventually completely destroyed the very same societies that the Baath Party had promised to develop.

For 50 years the Baath and the state melded together. As a result, the party became bulky, disorganized and very vulnerable from within. Because of the exclusivity, implicit political immunity, lack of competition and absence of scrutiny, the Baath became an active breeder of corruption on the political and corporate level. Joining the Baath Party meant one thing to a new class of opportunist Baathists: access to power. Cronyism, nepotism, influence peddling, collusion, extortion and bribery all prevailed under the Baathists, in many cases due to its unrivalled control of the state. The line between the symbols of the Baath and the State became thinner and thinner, destroying all principles of nationalism and statehood. The Baath flag was always flown alongside the Iraqi and Syrian flags, with their anthems played back to back, and they shared one figurehead as a leader. Schoolchildren and university students sang its anthem, chanted its slogans and celebrated Baath holidays because of coercion rather than conviction. Rather than respecting the Baath Party, people began making fun of its slogans and its programme, seeing that none of it was trickling down to the grassroots of society.

ISIS was born out of the failure of the Baath. The Baathists know that only too well, and are trying to return to society in al-Raqqa and Mosul through Islamic garb and doctrine. The major problem is that they did not learn from their mistakes the first time round. They are repeating the very same errors of 1963–2011: greed, authoritarianism, cult worship, nepotism and embezzlement.

By virtue of how far he has come, it is time that the world starts taking Abu Bakr al-Baghdadi – and his power base – more seriously. Perhaps they already are, but they need to accept the hard reality that ISIS is not going to disappear any time soon; far from it. They also have to understand that the US-led air strikes are not working. One year after military operations started, the Islamic State still holds al-Raqqa and Mosul. Al-Baghdadi himself currently has anywhere between 35,000 and 50,000 fighters at his command and controls a territory as large as Great Britain with a population of six million people. The caliph claims to be the successor to the Prophet Muhammad, and his subjects swear an oath of allegiance to him and to the institution he represents. He has all the trappings of statehood: a metropolitan capital, an army, a police force, an intelligence service, a school curriculum, a national anthem, a national flag – and coffers oozing with oil money. Soon ISIS will start minting its own money. The Boko Haram terrorists of Nigeria have sworn allegiance to him, and so has Ansar Bayt al-Maqdis in Egypt; terrorist operations have been carried out in their name in Paris, Tunisia and Yemen. The Islamic State's motto has been: '*Bakiya wa Tatamadad*' (staying and expanding). So far they have been loyal to it. There is something appealing about al-Baghdadi that people like and follow. It is his job title. He *really* thinks he is the caliph of Islam. Some people apparently *really* believe him.

There are many things in life that Abu Bakr al-Baghdadi doesn't like. For starters, he doesn't like to be called 'Abu Bakr al-Baghdadi' – this was his *nom de guerre*, used during his underground years in Iraq. His official name is 'Caliph Ibrahim'. Officially he is no longer an outlaw but the head of an unrecognised 'state' that encompasses all Muslims, attracting followers as far off as Nigeria, Egypt and Libya. Additionally, the caliph doesn't like the Arabic acronym for his state, Daesh. He insists on using 'The Islamic State'. He doesn't like his men to be called a militia – because technically they no longer are; they are a fully fledged army. And, of course, he doesn't like being called a terrorist. In short, he wants recognition as an official head of state – a de facto 'president' of all true Sunni Muslims.

So the problem is with Abu Bakr al-Baghdadi and the radicalization he inspires, and not with the Islamic State or the caliphate. If the conditions were ripe and the caliph were a capable and sane leader, many would not be complaining about him. Let us imagine what would happen if a coup rips through the Islamic State one day, toppling Abu Bakr al-Baghdadi. Coups are common in the Arab world and in no place have they been more frequent than in Syria and Iraq. Top Iraqi generals surround the caliph, after all, and all of them are well trained in coup politics. Perhaps the coup leaders would execute the caliph, on grounds of having strayed from the core principles of Islam, blaming everything on al-Baghdadi. If al-Baghdadi is replaced by a caliph who pledges non-intervention, wears a modern suit and trims his beard – one who doesn't order decapitation of prisoners or the destruction of statues – would more people be willing to come out expressing public support for the Islamic State? And if that happens, would the Westphalia-style Islamic State receive official recognition as a new country in the Middle East – perhaps with demarcated borders, embassies and a UN seat? History is riddled with states which have been founded by thugs with big swords and brutal tactics. To blend in with the international community and receive recognition, they eventually toned down their rhetoric and practice, but only after securing their borders. They then forced themselves upon everybody as a de facto reality. This is the potential future of ISIS today, in 2015.

Key Figures

EARLY MUSLIMS

Abu Bakr al-Siddiq (573–634): Mecca notable, father-in-law and prominent *Sahabi* of the Prophet Muhammad, who assumed the caliphate of Islam from 632–4. He is the first of the Rashidun (Righteously Guided) Caliphs.

Umar ibn al-Khattab (577–644): Mecca notable, father-in-law and prominent *Sahabi* of the Prophet Muhammad, who assumed the caliphate after Abu Bakr's death in 634 and ruled with famed justice for ten years, until he was assassinated at the hands of a Persian in 644, in response to the Muslim conquest of Persia. A ranking politician, jurist and philosopher, Muslims also call him 'Al-Farouk'. He is the second of the Rashidun Caliphs.

Uthman ibn Affan (577–656): Mecca notable and prominent *Sahabi* of the Prophet Muhammad, who was married to two of his daughters. He assumed the caliphate after Umar ibn al-Khattab's assassination in 644 and ruled for 12 years. Accused of nepotism and bad governance, he too was murdered by rebels while reading the Qur'an at his home. He is the third of the Rashidun Caliphs.

Ali ibn Abi Talib (600–61): Prominent *Sahabi*, cousin and son-in-law of the Prophet Muhammad, he was married to the Prophet's favourite daughter Fatima. Considered the first youth to convert to Islam, he was a fearless warrior who engaged in early Muslim conquests, and assumed the caliphate after Uthman ibn Affan's assassination in 656. A rival caliphate emerged to challenge his authority in Damascus, and he ruled from present-day Iraq until his own assassination in 661. His followers eventually established the Shi'i sect of Islam after Ali ibn Abi Talib's death, and still consider him the rightful heir to the Prophet Muhammad. He is the fourth and last of the Rashidun Caliphs, recognized by both Sunnis and Shi'a.

Khadijah (555–620): A wealthy Meccan businesswoman who was the first wife of the Prophet Muhammad and the first person to convert to Islam. Muslims revere her as the 'Mother of all Believers'. She is the mother of Fatima, the favourite daughter of Muhammad who was married to his cousin, Ali ibn Abi Talib.

Fatima (605–32): The beloved daughter of the Prophet Muhammad and wife of the fourth Righteously Guided Caliph, Ali ibn Abi Talib. She is the mother of his two sons Hasan and Hussein, two figures essential to the Shi'i faith. She took care of her father after her mother Khadijah's death, and died a few months after Muhammad in 632. Sunnis and Shi'a alike hold her in high esteem.

Aisha (613–78): The daughter of Islam's first caliph, Abu Bakr al-Siddiq; she married the Prophet Muhammad as a teenager, and became his favourite wife after the death of his first, Khadijah. A controversial figure during her husband's own lifetime, she worked in politics after his death, waging war against the fourth caliph, Ali ibn Abi Talib, by personally leading troops at the Battle of the Camel. She was defeated and spent the remainder of her years recounting Hadith, documenting 2,210 stories about the Prophet, all which are essential history to Sunni Muslims. Because of her feud with the Prophet's daughter Fatima, she is abhorred by the Shi'i faith to this day.

Muawiya ibn Abi Sufyan (602–80): A wealthy Mecca notable and early opponent of the Prophet, he converted to Islam and became a prominent *Sahabi* during the final years of Muhammad's life. He was appointed governor of Syria in 639, and in 661 laid claim to the caliphate of Islam. He went to war and managed to topple Ali, leading a separate branch of the Muslim Empire from Damascus. He created the first Muslim Empire in Damascus, with its first police, navy and public administration. He is detested by the Shi'a for challenging Ali ibn Abi Talib and bypassing his two sons from the caliphate of Islam. Muawiya is founder of the Umayyad dynasty and was the first caliph to bequeath power to his son Yezid, making the caliphate hereditary.

Hasan ibn Ali (625–70): The eldest son of the fourth Rashidun (Righteously Guided) Caliph Ali ibn Abi Talib and his wife Fatima, he was the grandson of the Prophet Muhammad. A ranking jurist and man of letters, he relinquished his right to the caliphate after his father's murder in 661 and spent the remainder of his years in seclusion in Medina. He was reportedly killed by poison at the hands of the Umayyads when still in his mid-forties.

Hussein ibn Ali (626–80): The second son of the fourth Rashidun Caliph Ali ibn Abi Talib and his wife Fatima, he was the grandson of the Prophet Muhammad and a pivotal character in the history of the Muslim faith. A brave soldier and an authority on Islam, he refused to pledge allegiance to the Umayyad caliph Yezid, claiming that being grandson of the Prophet he was the natural heir to his father Ali and grandfather Muhammad. Hussein left from Medina to Kufa in present-day Iraq, where he gathered an army of supporters and went out to challenge the Umayyads. Yezid's army confronted them at Karbala, laid siege to his men, starved them out, and then had Hussein killed and beheaded. His decapitated head was brought to Damascus and his death fuelled the Shi'a–Sunni divide. Hussein is revered by the Shi'a of today, and the date of his death is commemorated by an annual ceremony, the Mourning of Muharram, observed by wailing and mourning over the loss of Hussein.

Yezid ibn Muawiya (647–83): The first hereditary caliph of Islam, he assumed the caliphate in Damascus after the death of his father Muawiya I in 680 and ruled for three years, effectively becoming the second leader of the Umayyad dynasty. The Shi'a accuse him of corruption, greed, gluttony and murder. He was responsible for the killing and beheading of Hussein ibn Ali, the grandson of the Prophet, whose death sparked the Sunni–Shi'a divide.

Abdullah ibn al-Zubeir (624–92): A *Sahabi* of the Prophet Muhammad and grandson of the second caliph Abu Bakr al-Siddiq. He refused to recognise the Umayyad dynasty in Damascus and led a rebellion from Mecca, proclaiming himself caliph in the birthplace of Islam. He soon overtook Iraq, Taif, Medina and parts of Syria. The Umayyads enforced a six-month siege of Mecca, bombing the city with catapults. Ibn al-Zubeir, who some consider a rightful caliph, was killed at the hands of the Umayyads and his rebellion was crushed.

POST-MUHAMMAD FIGURES

Haroun al-Rashid (763–809): The fifth Abbasid caliph and war hero who ruled from Baghdad and briefly from al-Raqqa in present-day Syria, running the Muslim empire from the very same city that became ISIS's capital in 2014. His era was marked with military victories and both cultural and scientific prosperity, making him a legendary and yet controversial figure in the history of Islam.

al-Mutassim (833–42): The eighth Abbasid caliph and son of Haroun al-Rashid, he founded the city of Samarra in present-day Iraq, making it capital of the Muslim world. This is where Abu Bakr al-Baghdadi was raised as a child, drawing great inspiration from the history of Samarra in the founding of his Islamic State.

Ibn Taymiyya (1263–1328): A Damascus-based theologian and scholar who lived through troubled times of the Mongol invasion of Iraq. He called for a purified form of Islam, based on the early teachings of the Qur'an and the actions of the early Muslims. He sought to 'cleanse' Islam from all un-Islamic practice, and his views had a profound influence on later-day jihadism, Salafism and Wahhabism. He excommunicated the Shi'a and Alawites, seeing both sects as atheists and non-believers, and asked that they be put to the sword. His teachings form the crux of both al-Qaeda and ISIS, and are the guiding philosophy behind the Wahhabi thought of the House of Saud.

Muhammad ibn Abd al-Wahhab (1703–92): An ambitious preacher from Najd in central Arabia, his views had a great influence over the Najd warrior Muhammad Ibn Saud. He called for purification of the Muslim faith and return to the practice of early Muslims (*Salaf*), as dictated by his ideological mentor, Ibn Taymiyya. He is the founder of Wahhabism, a school of thought that had a profound effect both on al-Qaeda and its successor, ISIS.

Muhammad ibn Saud (d. 1765): Known as Ibn Saud, he came under the influence of Muhammad ibn Abd al-Wahhab and the two men helped found the first Saudi state, which was destroyed and overrun by the viceroy of Egypt, Mehmet Ali Pasha. His descendants vowed revenge, and managed to follow in his footsteps, founding the modern kingdom of Saudi Arabia. Ibn Saud is the military arm that gave Wahhabism its might and territory.

MUSLIM BROTHERHOOD

Hasan al-Banna (1906–49): A schoolteacher and mosque imam, he founded the Egyptian Muslim Brotherhood in March 1928. His teachings influenced an entire generation of Syrian Islamists, who set up their own branch of the Egyptian Brotherhood in Damascus in the mid-1940s. He was assassinated by a gunman, reportedly on the payroll of King Farouk of Egypt.

Mustapha al-Sibaii (1915–64): A Syrian cleric and early disciple of Hasan al-Banna, he founded the Syrian branch of the Muslim Brotherhood in the mid-1940s. He called for an Islamic state throughout the Arab world, but tried to achieve it through democratic means, through membership of the Syrian Parliament and the Constitutional Assembly. He was founder and Dean of the Faculty of Islamic Shari'a at the Syrian University, which taught an entire generation of Arab Islamists, notably Abdullah Azzam, the ideological founder of al-Qaeda. Al-Sibaii died before the Muslim Brothers took up arms to bring down the Syrian regime. He was a man of letters and an advocate of gentleman politics, playing by the rules of Syrian democracy in the 1950s.

Marwan Hadid (1934–76): A member of the Syrian Brotherhood, he established its military wing, called the Fighting Brigades, and waged war against the Baathists in his hometown of Hama in 1964. His rebellion was crushed and he was subsequently arrested and died in jail in 1976. He is credited with militarization of the Islamic quest in modern-day Syria and influencing the fighters who went to war against the Syrian government in 1982. An al-Qaeda-affiliated militia named after him was formed after 2011, and Syrians on the battlefield today call him the 'father of military jihad'.

Yusuf al-Qaradawi (b. 1926): A ranking Egyptian scholar and theologian, he is the intellectual mentor of the Muslim Brotherhood, currently based in Doha, Qatar. Al-Qaradawi had a strong influence on the thought and action of Syrian Islamists and was aggressively involved in the anti-government protests of 2011. He is critical of ISIS and of its self-proclaimed caliph, Abu Bakr al-Baghdadi, but supportive of other Islamic militias on the Syrian battlefield.

AL-QAEDA

Abdullah Azzam (1941–89): Hailed as the founder of global jihad, Abdullah Azzam is the Palestinian spiritual mentor of Osama bin Laden and ideological founder of al-Qaeda. After studying Islamic Shari'a in Damascus, he went to Saudi Arabia and then Afghanistan, recruiting Arab jihadis to fight the Soviet invasion that began in 1979. He raised funds, created training camps and influenced an entire generation of Arab *mujahideen*, but was killed in a car bomb in Peshawar, Pakistan, shortly before al-Qaeda was officially founded in November 1989.

Abu Musaab al-Souri (b. 1958): Born Mustapha al-Setmariam Nassar in Aleppo, he joined the Muslim Brotherhood and took up arms with the Fighting Brigades against the Baathists. He fled to Afghanistan to join al-Qaeda, becoming one of its chief jihadi ideologues. He trained Syrian and Arab Islamists at Afghan camps and created underground cells in Europe. He was arrested in Pakistan and extradited to Syria, where he remains in custody as of 2015. His students emerged to lead the jihadi struggle in Iraq after 2003 and are now plenty in number on the Syrian battlefield, fighting with Jabhat al-Nusra. He has pledged total allegiance to Osama bin Laden.

Abu Khaled al-Souri (1966–2014): A Syrian Islamist from Aleppo, he and Abu Musaab al-Souri joined the Syrian Muslim Brotherhood and then the Fighting Vanguards, taking up arms against Hafez al-Assad. When defeated, both fled to Afghanistan, where they joined al-Qaeda and worked closely with Osama bin Laden. Abu Khaled returned to Syria after 2011, joining the Ahrar al-Sham group. Bin Laden's successor Ayman al-Zawahiri delegated him to settle a feud between al-Qaeda's envoy to Syria, Abu Mohammad al-Golani, and his former friend Abu Bakr al-Baghdadi, the self-proclaimed caliph of ISIS.

Abu Musaab al-Zarqawi (1966–2006): A Jordanian outlaw and ex-convict, he joined al-Qaeda in the 1980s, working with Osama bin Laden at training Arab jihadis in the use of explosives. He travelled to Iraq after the 2003 invasion and established a branch for al-Qaeda in the Iraqi underground, known as the Islamic State of Iraq (ISI). Al-Zarqawi led vicious battles against the US troops and was responsible for the slaughter of many Shi'a, whom he considered agents of the US occupation and religious heretics who ought to be killed. He was killed by the Americans in 2006 but his disciples survived, travelling to Syria to set up a Syrian branch of al-Qaeda known as Jabhat al-Nusra. He is one of the most influential Islamists in modern times, compared in influence to Osama bin Laden himself.

JABHAT AL-NUSRA

Abu Mohammad al-Golani (b. 1981): Born Usama al-Hadawi in the eastern province of Deir ez-Zour, he studied medicine at Damascus University and dropped out in 2005, travelling to Iraq to join al-Qaeda. After pledging loyalty to its leader Ayman al-Zawahiri, he was arrested at Camp Bucca in 2007, and came to Syria to set up Jabhat al-Nusra in January 2012. During his prison term he met his friend and future rival, Abu Bakr al-Baghdadi. The al-Qaeda-affiliated militia is the second strongest in Syria after ISIS, once controlling strategic cities like al-Raqqa and now in full control of Idlib and its fertile countryside. Abu Mohammad al-Golani, also known as 'al-Fateh', is a murky and controversial figure, whose appearance remains in doubt despite the existence of online photographs. He has given several interviews to the Doha-based Al Jazeera TV, and his troops are currently engaged in battles both with the Syrian army and the Free Syrian Army, in addition, of course, to taking on ISIS.

Abdulmuhsen Abdullah Ibrahim al-Sarikh (b. 1978): Third cousin of Osama bin Laden and ranking co-founder of Jabhat al-Nusra, he is a Saudi citizen whose entire family is affiliated with al-Qaeda. Also known as Sanafi al-Nasr, al-Sarikh has six brothers in al-Qaeda, and two of them were held at Guantanamo Bay. He lived briefly in Pakistan and then headed al-Qaeda's underground operations in Iran before moving to northern Syria in 2013. He works closely with Abu Mohammad al-Golani and has pledged allegiance to al-Qaeda chief Ayman al-Zawahiri.

Hamid Hamad Ali (b. 1960): Kuwaiti co-founder of Jabhat al-Nusra, he studied in London and Riyadh, returning to his native Kuwait City to work at the Ministry of Religious Endowments. He soon got in trouble with the Gulf authorities and fled to Syria in 2013, where he joined Abu Mohammad al-Golani, becoming his secret-keeper, fundraiser and a certified accountant. He has pledged loyalty to al-Qaeda leader Ayman al-Zawahiri.

Abu Yusuf al-Turki (1967–2014): Master sniper and Jabhat al-Nusra co-founder, he was a close associate of its founder Abu Mohammad al-Golani. Al-Turki came to Syria from Turkey in 2013, where he started to train Nusra snipers and pledged loyalty to al-Qaeda chief Ayman al-Zawahiri. He was killed by air strikes in September 2014.

ISLAMIC STATE

Abu Bakr al-Baghdadi (b. 1971): Born Ibrahim Awwad Ibrahim al-Badri in Samarra, Iraq, he is the world's most wanted terrorist, following the death of Osama bin Laden in 2011. Abu Bakr al-Baghdadi studied Islamic Studies in Baghdad and joined the Islamic State of Abu Musaab al-Zarqawi, becoming a member of al-Zarqawi's Mujahideen Council. He began his underground work after the US occupation of 2003 and was arrested at Camp Bucca by the Americans in 2006, where he first met Abu Mohammad al-Golani, the future chief of Jabhat al-Nusra. Abu Bakr al-Baghdadi created the Islamic State for Iraq and the Levant (ISIS), recruiting a high number of ex-Baathists from Saddam Hussein's entourage. In the summer of 2014, he swept into Mosul and declared his Islamic State in the Syrian city of al-Raqqa, self-proclaiming himself Caliph of Islam and going by the name Caliph Ibrahim.

Abdul Mehdi al-Harati (b. 1974): Second-in-command of the Tripoli Military Council that was formed after the fall of Libyan leader Muammar al-Gaddafi, he came to Syria in 2013, setting up his own militia with funds stolen from his native Libya. Liwaa al-Umma soon blended into the Free Syrian Army (FSA) and al-Harati became leader of the 650–700 Libyan jihadis in the Syrian battlefield, mostly working with ISIS.

Abu Muhammad al-Adnani (b. 1977): Born in the town of Binnish in northwestern Syria, he went to Iraq to join the resistance to the US occupation of 2003. The Americans arrested him in 2005 and he spent time at Camp Bucca, where he met both Abu Mohammad al-Golani and Abu Bakr al-Baghdadi. He joined al-Qaeda and then shifted to ISIS, becoming its official spokesman after pledging loyalty to its caliph, Abu Bakr al-Baghdadi. He is one of the few senior Syrians in ISIS, and announced the creation of the Islamic State in al-Raqqa in the summer of 2014.

Abu Huraira al-Amriki (1992–2014): Moner Mohammad Abusalha, a US citizen who joined the Islamists in Syria and carried out a suicide attack in 2014, becoming the first American to die in the Syrian conflict.

Ahmad Salama al-Mabruk (b. 1956): Commander of the ISIS-affiliated Ansar Bayt al-Maqdis in the Sinai Peninsula, he is a computer scientist turned jihadi and an ex-officer in the Egyptian army. He was discharged for Islamic activities in 1981 and fled to Afghanistan, where he joined al-Qaeda and pledged loyalty to Osama bin Laden. In 1988, he was arrested in Azerbaijan and deported to Egypt where he remained in jail until the outbreak of the Egyptian Revolution in 2011. He later formed Ansar Bayt al-Maqdis and pledged loyalty to Abu Bakr al-Baghdadi in 2015.

Aqsa Mahmood (Umm Layth): Travelling from Glasgow to Syria in 2013, she married into ISIS and blogs regularly with her immensely popular *Diary of a Muhajirah*, offering advice and tips to foreign women joining ISIS, especially from Europe.

Asma Fawzi al-Qubeisi: The Iraqi first wife of Abu Bakr al-Baghdadi and the mother of his first five children.

Isra Rajab Mhal al-Qaisi: The second wife of Abu Bakr al-Baghdadi and the mother of his youngest son, Ali.

Saja al-Duleimi (b. 1978): The current wife of Abu Bakr al-Baghdadi, who was arrested and then released by the Syrians in early 2014. She hails from a prominent Sunni Iraqi tribe and all her family are members of ISIS. Her younger brother is her husband's bodyguard while another is commander of ISIS in Mosul. Her sister worked with al-Qaeda in Iraq and her father, who was a founder of ISIS, was killed by the Syrians in 2013.

Walid Jassem Alwani (d. 2014): An ex-captain in the Iraqi army and a member of the Baath Party, he went underground after the US occupation of Iraq and joined al-Qaeda. He pledged allegiance to the Islamic State and then to Abu Bakr al-Baghdadi, becoming chairman of ISIS's Military Council.

Samir Khlifawi (d. 2014): Born in the al-Anbar province, he joined the Baath Party and enlisted in Saddam Hussein's army, serving as an officer in the air force's intelligence division. He was charged briefly with weapons procurement for Saddam Hussein and went underground in 2003, joining Abu Musaab al-Zarqawi. The Americans arrested him at Camp Bucca, where he met his future boss Abu Bakr al-Baghdadi. Given the code name Hajj Bakri, he became a ranking member of ISIS, charged first with al-Qaeda operations in Aleppo and then joining ISIS's Military Council. He became al-Baghdadi's top man in Syria in 2013, and was killed on the Syrian battlefield in 2014.

Abu Mohammad al-Suwaidawi: An ex-officer in the Iraqi army, he joined al-Qaeda after the US occupation of 2003 and emerged as a ranking member of ISIS after 2013. During his years with the Iraqi army he was a protégé of Saddam Hussein's deputy, Izzat al-Douri. He is now a member of ISIS's Military Council and one of the top Iraqis working with Abu Bakr al-Baghdadi.

Awwad Makhlaf: A Syrian jihadi from Deir ez-Zour, he pledged allegiance to Abu Bakr al-Baghdadi and joined ISIS in 2013. He was appointed emir of al-Raqqa and currently resides in Mosul. He is among the few senior Syrians in Abu Bakr al-Baghdadi's orbit.

Abu Hureita al-Jazrawi: A Saudi citizen in ISIS's top command, he swore allegiance to Abu Bakr al-Baghdadi, who in turn appointed him commander of western al-Raqqa after US air strikes killed its emir Abu Sara in 2014.

Ghaleb Ahmad Bak'ati (b. 1985): A Yemeni high school drop-out, he joined al-Qaeda in Iraq after the US occupation of 2003. The Americans arrested him and deported him to Yemen. He escaped, returned to Iraq and joined the Syrian battlefield in 2013, pledging allegiance to ISIS. He is the official singer of ISIS's national anthem and other war-inspiring songs used by ISIS fighters on the battlefield. He now goes by the code name Abu Hayar al-Hadrami.

Jihadi John (b. 1989): The internationally famous jihadi who appeared in the ISIS videos beheading prisoners, speaking with a perfect British accent, Mohammad Emwazi grew up in London, where his Iraqi family had moved after the Gulf War of 1991. Educated at Westminster University in London, he graduated in 2009 and moved first to Tanzania, then to Kuwait and then Saudi Arabia, before landing in Syria to join the jihadis. He was first tasked with guarding Western hostages in Idlib and pledged loyalty to Abu Bakr al-Baghdadi, achieving international infamy thanks to the beheading videos of 2014–15.

Notes

1. ALL RISE FOR THE CALIPH

1   *Al-Ahram*, 4 March 1924.
2   Ibid., 28 October 1928.
3   Reza Pankhurst, *The Inevitable Caliphate?: A History of the Struggle for Global Islamic Union, 1924 to the Present* (London: Hurst & Co., 2013), p. 17.
4   Muhammad Rashid Rida, *Al-Khalifa* (Cairo: Dar al-Zahraa, 1922), p. 73.
5   Ibn Taymiyya, 'The obligation of adherence to the leadership', *Al-Kitab al-Siyasah al-Shariyah*.
6   Gabriel Said Reynolds, *The Emergence of Islam: Classical Traditions in Contemporary Perspective* (Minneapolis, MN: Fortress Press, 2012), p. 174.
7   Ibid., p. 124.
8   Ibid.
9   Abdel Bari Atwan, *Al-Dawla al-Islamiyya* (London: Dar al-Saqi, 2014), p. 135.
10 Ibid.
11 Brian Ross, 'U.S.: Saudis Still Filling Al Qaeda's Coffers', *ABC News*, 11 September 2007.
12 Declan Walsh, 'WikiLeaks Cables Portray Saudi Arabia As a Cash Machine for Terrorists', *Guardian*, 5 December 2010.
13 Ibid.
14 Atwan, *Al-Dawla al-Islamiyya*.
15 Hoda Gamal Abdel Nasser, *Britain and the Egyptian Nationalist Movement 1936–1952* (Reading: Ithaca Press, 1994), p. 57.
16 Sean Oliver-Dee, *The Caliphate Question: The British Government and Islamic Governance* (Lanham, MD: Lexington Books, 2009), p. 146.
17 FO 684/111/98, Smart (Damascus) to FO (15 March 1923) and FO 371/4141 vol. 10164 (Damascus Consul to FO on 28 April 1924), National Archives, Richmond, Surrey.
18 Hasan al-Banna, *Majmu'at al-Rasa'ael lil Imam al-Shahid Hasan al-Banna* (Dar al-Da'wa, 1999), p. 110.

19   Hasan al-Banna, *Fi al-Da'wa*, p. 107.

20   Ibid., p. 80.

21   Pankhurst, *The Inevitable Caliphate?*, p. 161.

22   Lucy Williamson, 'Stadium Crowd Pushes for Islamist Dream', *BBC News*, 12 August 2007.

23   Pankhurst, *The Inevitable Caliphate?*, p. 2.

24   Pankhurst, *The Inevitable Caliphate?*, p. 138.

25   Ibid.

26   Matthew Philips, 'Bush's New Word: "Caliphate"', *Newsweek*, 11 October 2006.

27   *Voice of America*, 11 December 2006, cited in Pankhurst, *The Inevitable Caliphate*, p. 2.

28   Andrew Anthony, 'Richard Dannatt: "If the Tories Win, I Will Not Be a Defence Minister"', *Guardian*, 20 December 2009.

29   Pankhurst, *The Inevitable Caliphate?*, p. 3.

30   Ibid., pp. 2 and 4.

31   Ibid., p. 93.

32   Ibid., p. 4.

33   *Al Jazeera*, 29 June 2014.

34   Ibid.

35   *Al-Arabiya*, 1 August 2014.

36   Ibid.

37   Suhaib Anjarini, 'Al-Nusra Front Not Yet Dead As Its Emir Devises "Islamic Emirate of the Levant"', *Al-Akhbar*, 12 July 2014.

38   Michael Weiss and Hassan Hassan, *ISIS: Inside the Army of Terror* (New York: Regan Arts, 2015), p. 184.

39   Pankhurst, *The Inevitable Caliphate?*, p. 62.

40   Tom Heneghan, 'Muslim Scholars Present Religious Rebuttal to Islamic State', *Reuters*, 25 September 2014.

41   'Qaradawi Slams ISIL's Caliphate: Void Under Sharia', *Al-Manar*, 6 July 2014.

2. GENTLEMEN TO JIHADIS

1   *Al-Qudsi al-Arabi*, 9 March 2015.

2   *Al-Ayyam*, 16 October 1953.

3   Patrick Seale, *Asad: The Struggle for the Middle East* (Berkeley, CA: University of California Press, 1990), p. 323.

4   Hanna Batatu, *Syria's Peasantry, The Descendants of its Lesser Rural Notables, and Their Politics* (Princeton, NJ: Princeton University Press, 1999), p. 262.

5   Thomas Pierret, *Religion and State in Syria: The Sunni Ulama from Coup to Revolution* (Cambridge: Cambridge University Press, 2013), p. 64.

6   Stephen Longrigg, *Syria and Lebanon under French Mandate* (Oxford: Oxford University Press, 1958), p. 8.

7 Seale, *Asad: The Struggle for the Middle East*, p. 93.

8 President Amin al-Hafez speaks to programme host Ahmad Mansour on *Shahed Ala al-Asr* (Eyewitness to History), Episode 12, *Al Jazeera*, April 2001.

9 Ibid.

10 Ibid.

11 Ibid.

12 *Al-Thawra*, 2 February 1972. *Al-Thawra* and *Tishreen* are two newspapers which were allowed to publish in Damascus after the Baathist Party took power in 1963.

13 Batatu, *Syria's Peasantry*, p. 260.

14 Seale, *Asad: The Struggle for the Middle East*, p. 324.

15 *Jerusalem Post*, 10 April 2011.

16 R. Hrair Dekmejian, *Islam in Revolution: Fundamentalism in the Arab World* (Syracuse, NY: Syracuse University Press, 1995), p. 115.

17 Seale, *Asad: The Struggle for the Middle East*, p. 325.

18 Batatu, *Syria's Peasantry*, p. 266.

19 Author interview with Defense Minister Mustapha Tlass (Damascus, 6 November 2010).

20 Ibid.

21 Author interview with Grand Mufti Ahmad Hassoun (Damascus, 16 July 2014).

22 Ibid.

23 *Al-Thawra*, 3 February 1980.

24 Batatu, *Syria's Peasantry*, pp. 271–2.

25 Ibid.

26 *Tishreen*, 1 July 1980. See Chapter 2, n. 12.

27 Seale, *Asad: The Struggle for the Middle East*, p. 327.

28 Ibid., p. 328.

29 *Tishreen*, 7 July 1980.

30 Tlass interview, 6 November 2010.

31 Seale, *Asad: The Struggle for the Middle East*, p. 322.

32 Ibid.

33 *The Times*, 19 February 1982.

34 Amin al-Hafez, *Al Jazeera* (2001).

35 Author interview with the Parliamentary Speaker Abdul Qader Qaddura (Damascus, 9 August 2011).

36 For the Brotherhood/Fighting Vanguard version of the Hama events of 1982, see *al-Nadhir*, issue No. 40 (27 February 1982) and issue No. 46 (8 May 1982).

37 Author interview with Patrick Seale (London, 11 November 2010).

38 Batutu, *Syria's Peasantry*, p. 273.

39 *Damascus Radio*, 7 March 1982.

3. THE ISLAMIC REBOUND IN SYRIA: 1982–2011

1 Michael Weiss and Hassan Hassan, *ISIS: Inside the Army of Terror* (New York: Regan Arts, 2015), p. 4.

2 *CNN*, 9 May 2011.

3 Author interview with with Taj al-Din al-Mawazini (Damascus, March 2014).

4 Author interview with Farouk Abdul Rahman (Damascus, March 2014).

5 Ibid.

6 Ibid.

7 Mohammad Basil, *Al-Ansaru l'Arab fi Afghanistan* [The Arab Helpers in Afghanistan] (Jeddah: Matabe' Sharikat Dar al-Ilm, 1991), pp. 100–13, 123, 227.

8 Brynjar Lia, *Architect of Global Jihad: The Life of Al-Qaeda Strategist Abu Mus'ab al-Suri* (New York: Columbia University Press, 2008), p. 32.

9 Ibid., pp. 88–91.

10 Ibid., p. 233.

11 Ibid., p. 272.

12 Ibid., p. 39.

13 Peter L. Bergen, *Holy War, Inc.: Inside The Secret World Of Osama Bin Laden* (New York: Touchstone, 2002).

14 Brynjar Lia, *Architect of Global Jihad*, p. 170.

15 Ibid.

16 Ibid.

17 Lawrence Wright, 'The Master Plan', *The New Yorker*, 11 September 2006.

18 Ibid.

19 Thomas Pierret, *Religion and State in Syria: The Sunni Ulama from Coup to Revolution* (Cambridge: Cambridge University Press, 2013), p. 198.

20 Author interview with Qutaiba al-Omari (January 2015).

21 Ibid.

22 Ibid.

23 Ibid.

24 Ibid.

25 'Syria Says Isolated Islamist Group Staged Damascus Attack', *Reuters*, 16 May 2004.

26 Sami Moubayed, 'Syria, US Shrouded in the Fog of War', *Asia Times Online*, 15 September 2006.

27 Line Khatib, *Islamic Revivalism in Syria: The Rise and Fall of Ba'thist Secularism* (Abingdon: Routledge, 2011), p. 140.

28 BBC, 12 September 2006.

29 *Al-Arabiya*, 4 June 2006.

30 Sami Moubayed, 'Syria's Abu al-Qaqa: Authentic Jihadist or Imposter?' *Terrorism Focus,* Jamestown Foundation Vol. 3, Issue 25, 27 June 2006.

31 *Al-Rai al-Aam*, 14 June 2006.

4. THE RISE OF JABHAT AL-NUSRA

1   Thomas Joscelyn, 'Head of al-Qaeda "Victory Committee" in Syria', *Long War Journal*, 6 March 2014.

2   'Profile: Syria's al-Nusra Front', *BBC News*, 10 April 2013.

3   Michael Weiss and Hassan Hassan, *ISIS: Inside the Army of Terror* (New York: Regan Arts, 2015), p. 144.

4   'Nusra leader: Our mission is to defeat Syrian regime', Abu Mohammad al-Golani in exclusive interview, *Al Jazeera*, 27 May 2015.

5   David Ignatius, 'Al-Qaeda Affiliate Playing Larger Role in Syria Rebellion', *Washington Post*, 30 November 2012.

6   'Competition Among Islamists', *The Economist*, 20 July 2013.

7   The Facebook page of Public Management for Services is at: www.facebook.com/general.management.of.services (accessed 15 July 2015).

8   'Profile: Syria's al-Nusra Front', *BBC News*, 10 April 2013.

9   'Al-Qaeda Leader in Syria Speaks to Al Jazeera', *Al Jazeera*, 19 December 2013.

10   Ibid.

11   Ibid.

12   'Syrian Protesters Slam U.S. Blacklisting of Jihadist Group', *Daily Star*, 14 December 2012.

13   Ruth Sherlock, 'Syrian Rebels Defy US and Pledge Allegiance to Jihadi Group', *Telegraph*, 10 December 2012.

14   Abdel Bari Atwan, *Al-Dawla al-Islamiyya* (London: Dar al-Saqi, 2014), p. 75.

15   *Syrian Arab News Agency* (SANA), 6 January 2012.

16   'Syrian TV Presenter Executed', Doha Centre for Media Freedom, 5 August 2012.

17   Bill Roggio, 'Suicide Bombers Kill 14 in Damascus', *Long War Journal*, 11 June 2013.

18   Anne Barnard and Hwaida Saad, 'Nuns Released by Syrians After Three-Month Ordeal', *New York Times*, 9 March 2014.

19   Baz Ratner, 'Syria's Nusra Front Releases U.N. Peacekeepers in Golan', *Reuters*, 11 September 2014.

20   ISI refers to the Islamic State of Iraq of al-Zarqawi et al.; it was the predecessor of ISIS.

21   *Al Jazeera*, 30 July 2013.

22   Ruth Sherlock, 'Inside Jabhat al Nusra – The Most Extreme Wing of Syria's Struggle', *Telegraph*, 2 December 2012.

23   Mohammed al-Khatieb, 'Jabhat al-Nusra, IS Compete for Foreign Fighters', *Al-Monitor*, 18 July 2014.

24   *Al-Akhbar*, 14 July 2014.

25   Ibid.

26   *Al-Hayat*, 31 March 2015.

5. THE JIHADIS OF IRAQ

1   Michael Weiss and Hassan Hassan, *ISIS: Inside the Army of Terror* (New York: Regan Arts, 2015), p. 180.
2   Abdel Bari Atwan, *Al-Dawla al-Islamiyya* (London: Dar al-Saqi, 2014), p. 21.
3   'Profile: Abu Musab al-Zarqawi', *BBC News*, 10 November 2005.
4   Weiss and Hassan. *ISIS: Inside the Army of Terror*, p. xiv.
5   Ibid., p. 11.
6   *CNN*, 9 June 2006.
7   Ibid.
8   Jim Miklaszewski, 'Avoiding Attacking Suspected Terrorist Mastermind', NBC, 2 March 2004.
9   Charles Lister, 'Profiling the Islamic State', Brookings Doha Center Analysis Paper, No. 13, November 2014, p. 7.
10 Nile Gardiner, 'The Death of Zarqawi: A Major Victory in the War on Terrorism', The Heritage Foundation, 8 June 2006.
11 Atwan, *Al-Dawla al-Islamiyya*, p. 75.
12 Adrian Blomfield, 'How US Fuelled Myth of Zarqawi the Mastermind', *Telegraph*, 4 October 2004.
13 *Al Jazeera*, 23 June 2006.
14 Ibid., 30 June 2006.
15 Lister, 'Profiling the Islamic State', p. 7.
16 Iraq Coalition Casualty Count, 14 November 2006, icasualties.org (accessed 15 July 2015).
17 *Asharq Al-Awsat*, 13 June 2006.
18 Sami Moubayed, 'Abu al-Ghadia to Build on al-Zarqawi's Legacy in Iraq', *Terrorism Focus*, Jamestown Foundation, Vol. 3, No. 26, 9 July 2006.
19 'US says 80% of al-Qaeda leaders in Iraq removed', *BBC News*, 4 June 2010.

6. THE BIRTH OF ISIS

1   Abdel Bari Atwan, *Al-Dawla al-Islamiyya* (London: Dar al-Saqi, 2014), p. 23.
2   *Assafir*, 14 October 2014.
3   Michael Weiss and Hassan Hassan, *ISIS: Inside the Army of Terror* (New York: Regan Arts, 2015), p. 117.
4   James M. Dorsey, 'Football Fields: A Way Station En Route to the Islamic State', *Daily News Egypt*, 4 March 2015.
5   Tim Arango and Eric Schmitt, 'US Actions in Iraq Fueled Rise of a Rebel', *New York Times*, 10 August 2014.
6   Weiss and Hassan, *ISIS: Inside the Army of Terror*, p. 21.
7   Bill Roggio, 'ISIS Confirms Death of Senior Leader in Syria', *Long War Journal*, 5 February 2014.

8   Christoph Reuter, 'The Terror Strategist: Secret Files Reveal the Structure of Islamic State', *Der Spiegel*, 18 April 2015.

9   Ibid.

10 Ibid.

11 *Al Jazeera*, 9 July 2014.

12 Atwan, *Al-Dawla al-Islamiyya*, pp. 26–7.

13 Ruth Sherlock, 'Inside the Leadership of Islamic State: How the New "Caliphate" is Run', *Telegraph*, 9 July 2014.

14 Charles Lister, 'Profiling the Islamic State', Brookings Doha Center Analysis Paper, No. 13, November 2014, p. 17.

15 Adam Schrek and Qassim Abdul-Zahra, 'Abu Ghraib Prison Break: Hundreds of Detainees, Including Senior Al Qaeda Members, Escape Facility', *Huffington Post*, 22 July 2013.

16 Lister, 'Profiling the Islamic State', p. 16.

17 Michael R. Gordon and General Bernard E. Trainor, *Cobra II: The Inside Story of the Invasion and Occupation of Iraq* (New York: Vintage Books, 2007) and *The Endgame: The Inside Story of the Struggle for Iraq, From George W. Bush to Barack Obama* (New York: Vintage Books, 2013).

18 Gordon and Trainor, *The Endgame*, p. 21.

19 'More than 1,000 Killed in Iraq in January: Officials', *Al-Arabiya*, 1 February 2014.

20 Basma Atassi, 'Qaeda Chief Annuls Syrian–Iraqi Jihad Merger', *Al Jazeera*, 9 June 2013.

21 Weiss and Hassan, *ISIS: Inside the Army of Terror*, p. 185.

22 Atwan, *Al-Dawla al-Islamiyya*, p. 62.

23 'Nusra Leader: Our Mission is to Defeat Syrian Regime', Abu Mohammad al-Golani in exclusive interview, *Al Jazeera*, 28 May 2015.

7. THE HOUSE OF BLOOD

1   Patrick Cockburn, *The Rise of Islamic State: ISIS and the New Sunni Revolution* (London: Verso, 2015), p. xii.

2   Ibid., p. 18.

3   Ceylan Yeginsu, 'ISIS Draws a Steady Stream of Recruits From Turkey', *New York Times*, 15 September 2014.

4   'Two Arab Countries Fall Apart', *The Economist*, 14 June 2014.

5   Charles Lister, 'Profiling the Islamic State', Brookings Doha Center Analysis Paper, No. 13, November 2014, p. 3.

6   Ibid., p. 38.

7   'UN Security Council Adds Libya Islamists to Terror List', *Telegraph*, 19 November 2014.

8   Katharine Lackey, 'Boko Haram Pledges Allegiance to the Islamic State', *USA Today*, 8 March 2015.

9   *Al Jazeera*, 31 August 2014.

10 Michael Weiss and Hassan Hassan, *ISIS: Inside the Army of Terror* (New York: Regan Arts, 2015), p. 230.

11 Lister, 'Profiling the Islamic State', p. 32.

12 Weiss and Hassan, *ISIS: Inside the Army of Terror*, p. 230.

13 Liz Sly, 'Islamic State Appears to be Fraying from Within', *Washington Post*, 8 March 2015.

14 'Beheading in the Name of Islam', *Middle East Quarterly*, Spring 2005, pp. 51–7.

15 Ibid.

16 Ishaan Tharoor, 'Israeli Foreign Minister says Disloyal Arabs Should Be Beheaded', *Washington Post*, 10 March 2015.

17 *Al-Hayat*, 14 September 2014.

18 *Al Jazeera*, 28 June 2014.

19 SANA, Syrian News Agency, 30 August 2014.

20 *Tishreen*, 20 November 2014.

21 'Iraq Crisis: Islamic State Accused of Ethnic Cleansing', *BBC News*, 2 September 2014.

22 Chris Pleasance, 'Hundreds of Yazidi Women Held in Islamic State Prison', *Daily Mail*, 28 August 2014.

23 *Al Jazeera*, 28 October 2014.

24 Steve Hopkins, 'Full horror of the Yazidis who didn't escape Mount Sinjar', *Daily Mail*, 14 October 2014.

25 Stephanie Nebehay, 'Islamic State Committing "Staggering" Crimes in Iraq: U.N. Report', *Reuters*, 2 October 2014.

26 'ISIS Claims Beheading 18 Syrians, An American in New Video', *Al-Akhbar*, 16 November 2014.

27 James Nye, Michael Zennie and David Martosko, 'I'm Back, Obama', *Daily Mail*, 2 September 2014.

28 Souad Mekhennet and Adam Goldman, '"Jihadi John": Islamic State Killer is Identified as Londoner Mohammed Emwazi', *Washington Post*, 26 February 2015.

29 Ibid.

30 '"Jihadi John": Extremists "Not Radicalised by MI5"', *BBC News*, 26 February 2015.

31 Mekhennet and Goldman, 'Jihadi John'.

32 Ibid.

33 Monica Sarkar and Catherine E. Shoichet, '"Jihadi John's" Emails Revealed', *CNN*, 9 March 2015.

34 Mekhennet and Goldman, 'Jihadi John'.

35 Paul Wood, '"Jihadi John": Mohammed Emwazi was a Cold Loner, Ex-IS Fighter Says', *BBC News*, 1 March 2015.

36 Mekhennet and Goldman, 'Jihadi John'.

37 'ISIS Video Appears to Show Beheadings of Egyptian Coptic Christians in Libya', *CNN*, 16 February 2015.

38 Adam Taylor, 'The Islamic State Threatens to Come to Rome: Italians Respond with Travel Advice', *Washington Post*, 20 February 2015.

39 Ministry of Education Records – Damascus (Academic Year 2014–15: al-Raqqa Governorate).

40 Scott Bronstein and Drew Griffin, 'Self-Funded and Deep-Rooted: How ISIS Makes its Millions', *CNN*, 7 October 2014.

41 Abdel Bari Atwan, *Al-Dawla al-Islamiyya* (London: Dar al-Saqi, 2014), p. 32.

42 Ibid.

43 Ibid.

44 Lister, 'Profiling the Islamic State', p. 28.

45 Author interview with anonymous government source in Damascus (26 October 2014).

46 Lister, 'Profiling the Islamic State', p. 28.

47 Louise Loveluck, 'Islamic State Sets Up "Ministry of Antiquities" to Reap the Profits of Pillaging', *Telegraph*, 30 May 2015.

48 Patrick Cockburn, *Rise of Islamic State: ISIS and the New Sunni Revolution* (London: Verso, 2015), p. 12.

49 'Isis to Introduce its Own Currency, the Islamic Dinar', *Guardian*, 14 November 2014.

50 *USA Today*, 15 September 2014.

51 Robert Mendick, 'Banker who Financed 9/11 Mastermind Now Funding Terrorists in Syria and Iraq', *Telegraph*, 4 October 2014.

52 Ian Black, Rania Abouzeid, Mark Tran, Shiraz Maher, Roger Tooth and Martin Chulov, 'The Terrifying Rise of ISIS: $2bn in Loot, Online Killings and an Army on the Run', *Guardian*, 16 June 2014.

53 Terrence McCoy, "ISIS Just Stole $425 Million, Iraqi Governor Says, and Became the "World's Richest Terrorist Group"', *Washington Post*, 12 June 2014.

54 Edith M. Lederer, 'UN: ISIS Got Up to $45m in Ransoms', *Daily Star*, 25 November 2014.

55 Keith Johnson, 'The Islamic State is the Newest Petrostate', *Foreign Policy*, 28 July 2014.

56 Joseph Cotterill, 'Insurgent Finance', *Financial Times*, 16 June 2014.

57 Martin Chulov, 'How an Arrest in Iraq Revealed Isis's $2bn Jihadist Network', *Guardian*, 15 June 2014.

58 Catherine Taibi, '11 Rules for Journalists Covering ISIS, Issued by ISIS', *Huffington Post*, 10 July 2014.

59 Josh Kovensky, 'ISIS's New Mag Looks Like a New York Glossy – With Pictures of Mutilated Bodies', *The New Republic*, 25 August 2014.

60 *Dabiq*, October 2014.

61 Author interview with Abu al-Nada al-Faraj (al-Raqqa, 16 November 2014).

62 Lister, 'Profiling the Islamic State', p. 30.

63 Ibid., p. 24.

64 Rick Gladstone, 'Twitter Says It Suspended 10,000 ISIS-Linked Accounts in One Day', *New York Times*, 9 April 2015.

65 Walbert Castillo, 'Air Force Intel Uses ISIS "Moron" Post to Track Fighters', *CNN*, 5 June 2015.

8. FOREIGN JIHADIS

1 Ulrike Putz, 'Foreign Fighters Join Syrian Rebels: Jihadists Declare Holy War Against Assad Regime', *Der Spiegel*, 30 March 2012.

2 *Tishreen*, 28 July 2013.

3 *Fox News*, 20 September 2013.

4 Adam Goldman, Greg Miller and Nicole Rodriguez, 'American Who Killed Himself in Syria Suicide Attack Was from South Florida', *Washington Post*, 31 May 2014.

5 Bill Gertz, 'Syria is Jihad Central: 6,000 Terrorists Flood New Al Qaeda Training Ground', *Washington Times*, 2 July 2013.

6 Spencer Ackerman, 'Foreign Jihadists Flocking to Iraq and Syria on "unprecedented scale" – UN', *Guardian*, 30 October 2014.

7 *Al-Arabiya*, 14 August 2014.

8 Saleyha Ahsan, 'Operation Mum Won't Stop British Muslims Going to Syria. But Peace Will', *Guardian*, 25 April 2014.

9 'The Belgian Fathers Who Lost Their Sons in Syria', *BBC News*, 18 July 2014.

10 Ian Traynor, 'Major Terrorist Attack is "Inevitable" as Isis Fighters Return, Say EU Officials', *Guardian*, 25 September 2014.

11 'Move to Curb Foreign Fighters in Syria', *Al Jazeera*, 24 April 2014.

12 'Foreign Fighters Flow to Syria', *Washington Post*, 11 October 2014.

13 *Al-Hayat*, 14 July 2014.

14 *Al-Akhbar*, 1 July 2014.

15 Ibid.

16 *An-Nahar*, 11 September 2011.

17 Chris Harris, 'Which Country in Europe has the Most Jihadists in Syria and Iraq?', *Euronews*, 4 November 2014.

18 Harriet Alexander, 'French 13-Year-Old Youngest Jihadi to Die Fighting for ISIL', *Telegraph*, 19 March 2015.

19 Tom McTague, 'British Women Fighting in Syria', *Daily Mail*, 24 June 2014.

20 *Al Jazeera*, 12 January 2014.

21 'Five Britons A Week Joining IS, Top Cop Warns', *Sky News*, 21 October 2014.

22 'Pakistan Taliban Set Up Camps in Syria, Join Anti-Assad War', *Reuters*, 14 July 2013.

23 'PM: Incidents in China "Almost Genocide"', *Hurriyet Daily News*, 10 July 2009.

24 *Asia Times*, 1 July 2014.

25 Qiu Yongzheng and Liu Chang, Xinjiang Jihad Hits Syria', *Global Times*, 29 October 2012.

26 Jamestown Foundation, 12 July 2014.

27 *Al Jazeera*, 29 October 2012.

28 Radio Free Asia, 12 October 2012.

29 'The Truth Has Supporters as the Tyrant Has Soldiers', *Islamic Turkistan*, Vol. 13, March 2013.

30 *The Hindu*, 1 July 2013.

31 *Guardian*, 30 July 2013.

32 'Kyrgyz Youths Recruited to Join Syrian Opposition', *Voice of Russia*, 20 April 2013.

33 Mairbek Vatchagaev, 'Chechens Among the Syrian Rebels: Small in Number, But Influential', *Eurasia Daily Monitor*, Vol. 10, Issue 223, Jamestown Foundation, 12 December 2013.

34 Murad Batal al-Shishani, 'Islamist North Caucasus Rebels Training a New Generation of Fighters in Syria', *Terrorism Monitor*, Vol. 12, Issue 3, Jamestown Foundation, 7 February 2014.

35 Bill Roggio, 'Chechen Commander Forms "Army of Emigrants", Integrates Syrian Groups', *Long War Journal*, 28 March 2013.

9. WOMEN IN ISIS

1 Brenda Stoter, 'European Women Convert, Join IS', *Al-Monitor*, 29 October 2014.

2 Mehdi Hasan, 'What the Jihadists Who Bought "Islam for Dummies" on Amazon Tell Us About Radicalisation', *Huffington Post*, 21 August 2014.

3 'ISIS Fighters Open "Marriage Bureau"', *Al-Arabiya*, 28 July 2014.

4 Harriet Sherwood, Sandra Laville, Kim Willsher, Ben Knight, Maddy French and Lauren Gambino, 'Schoolgirl Jihadis: The Female Islamists Leaving Home to Join Isis Fighters', *Guardian*, 29 September 2014.

5 Michael Weiss and Hassan Hassan, *ISIS: Inside the Army of Terror* (New York: Regan Arts, 2015), p. 170.

6 Umm Layth, *Diary of a Muhajirah*, 3 June 2014.

7 Ibid., 9 April 2014.

8 Ibid., 11 September 2014 and 9 April 2014.

9 Ibid., 11 September 2014

10 'Blocked Online, Islamic State Supporters Launch CaliphateBook', *Reuters*, 10 March 2015.

11 Damien McElroy, 'Austria Teenage Girl Jihadis "Want to Come Home" from Isil', *Telegraph*, 10 October 2014.

12 Tony Paterson, 'Austrian "Jihad Poster Girls" Tell Friends: We Want to Come Home', *Independent*, 13 October 2014.

13 Sam Webb, 'Mother of British "Terror Twins" Who Went to Syria to Become

Jihadi Brides is Snatched by ISIS While on Rescue Mission to Find Them', *Daily Mail*, 2 November 2014.

14 Harriet Sherwood, Sandra Laville, Kim Willsher, Ben Knight, Maddy French and Lauren Gambino, 'Schoolgirl Jihadis: The Female Islamists Leaving Home to Join Isis Fighters', *Guardian*, 29 September 2014.

15 Ray Sanchez and Ana Cabrera, 'Colorado Teen Pleads Guilty in Plan to Join ISIS', *CNN*, 10 September 2014.

16 Sherwood, Laville, Willsher, Knight, French and Gambino, 'Schoolgirl Jihadis'.

17 '15-year-old girl Would-Be Jihadist May Have Been with Others', *Dutch News*, 3 July 2014.

18 Jim Bittermann and Bryony Jones, 'Why are So Many Young French People Turning to Jihad?', *CNN*, 2 October 2014.

19 Sherwood, Laville, Willsher, Knight, French and Gambino, 'Schoolgirl Jihadis'.

20 David Barrett and Martin Evans, 'Three "Jihadi Brides" from London Who Travelled to Syria Will Not Face Terrorism Charges if They Return', *Telegraph*, 9 March 2015.

21 Ben Quinn, 'UK Schoolgirls Lured to Syria by Isis "Have Made Contact With Their Families"', *Guardian*, 28 May 2015.

22 'Photos Surface of ISIS Leader Baghdadi's Wife', *Al-Arabiya*, 17 July 2014.

23 Abdel Bari Atwan, *Al-Dawla al-Islamiyya* (London: Dar al-Saqi, 2014), p. 48.

24 'Dutch Teenager in Court After Syria "Rescue"', *Al Jazeera*, 22 November 2014.

10. ISIS'S NEXT FRONTIER

1 Helen Davidson, Peter Walker and Michael Safi, 'Sydney Siege Ends as Police Storm Lindt Cafe and Hostages Run Out', *Guardian*, 15 December 2014.

2 Author interview with Abu Mansour al-Libi (al-Raqqa, 2 June 2015).

3 *Dar al-Islam Magazine*, 15 February 2015.

4 Author interview with Abu Mansour al-Libi (2 June 2015).

5 Ibid.

6 Ibid.

7 Charlotte McDonald Gibson, 'How ISIS Threatens Europe', *TIME*, 26 February 2015.

8 Michael Wilner, 'Middle East Must Fight for Itself, Says Kerry', *Jerusalem Post*, 22 September 2014.

9 Stephen Kalin, 'Islamic State urges more attacks on Egyptian security forces', *Reuters*, 22 September 2014.

10 'After Joining IS, Ansar Bayt al-Maqdis Expands in Egypt', *Al-Monitor*, 1 December 2014.

11 *CNN*, 15 February 2015.

12 Ibid., 16 February 2015.

13 Laura Dean, 'How Strong is The Islamic State in Libya?', *USA Today*, 20 February 2015.
14 'Foreigners Seized by Islamic State in Libya – Austria', Reuters, 9 March 2015.
15 Suliman Ali Sway and David D. Kirkpatrick, 'Western Officials Alarmed as ISIS Expands Territory in Libya', *New York Times*, 31 May 2015.
16 Sophia Jones, 'For Egyptian Survivors of Islamic State Raid, The Nightmare Continues', *Huffington Post*, 23 February 2015.

Index